RIVERSIDE TEXTBOOKS
IN EDUCATION

EDITED BY ELLWOOD P. CUBBERLEY

PROFESSOR OF EDUCATION AND
DEAN OF THE SCHOOL OF EDUCATION
STANFORD UNIVERSITY

Greeting his pupils, the master asked:
  What would you learn of me?
And the reply came:
  How shall we care for our bodies?
  How shall we rear our children?
  How shall we work together?
  How shall we live with our fellowmen?
  How shall we play?
  For what ends shall we live? ...

*And the teacher pondered these words,
and sorrow was in his heart, for his own
learning touched not these things.*

PRINCIPLES OF EDUCATION

J. CROSBY CHAPMAN
B.A. (Cantab.), D.Sc. (London), Ph.D. (Columbia)
Late Professor of Educational Psychology
Yale University

GEORGE S. COUNTS
Ph.D. (Chicago)
Professor of Education, Teachers College, Columbia University, and
Associate Director of the International Institute

HOUGHTON MIFFLIN COMPANY
BOSTON · NEW YORK · CHICAGO · DALLAS · SAN FRANCISCO
The Riverside Press Cambridge

COPYRIGHT, 1924

BY J. CROSBY CHAPMAN AND GEORGE S. COUNTS

The Riverside Press
CAMBRIDGE · MASSACHUSETTS
PRINTED IN THE U.S.A.

TO

CHARLES H. JUDD
EDWARD L. THORNDIKE

EDITOR'S INTRODUCTION

WITHIN recent years, the demand of students in education in colleges and universities has seemed, more than ever before, to be for practical rather than for theoretical courses. This tendency is in keeping with the new demands in other fields of study, and indicates a healthy interest in concrete materials and in training that gives the ability to do. While this is very good and very encouraging, and indicates a desirable change in education itself from a philosophy about instruction to professional preparation for an important phase of social engineering, there is danger that those in training to-day may grow up and pass out of our training institutions without gaining that sound grounding in the philosophy of the educative process which has been the great strength of the older generation of professional educators. Say all we may in favor of the newer engineering-type courses of instruction in education, and there is much to be said for them, the fact remains that one of the most important duties of the young teacher or student is gradually to formulate, for himself, a sound working philosophy of the educative process. Such a philosophy will guide him in his future work and vitalize all his later procedure.

While the importance of practical courses in his training cannot be gainsaid, he must still somewhere be led to see how education itself has slowly evolved, until it stands to-day as the most important creative institution of the State; the institution whereby its citizens anticipate and solve the problems of national welfare. To meet this specific need in his training there is nothing that can take the place of a good course in the history of our educational evolution. He must also be led to seize intelligent hold on the conception that education stands for the higher evolution of both the individual and the race, and that, after all, the details of organization and administration and supervision must be relegated to their proper places in the scheme of human training. For this second need there is no substitute for a good course in the principles or philosophy of education. Without a unified view of the whole educative process, and such a guiding conception as to purpose and plan, administrative work soon becomes dull and fruitless routine and the worker fails to reach the higher levels of professional service.

To meet this second need for a course on the philosophy of the educative process the present volume in this series of textbooks has been prepared. As the quotation opposite the Title-Page indicates, its viewpoint is thoroughly modern. Discarding the old philosophical conceptions and terminology, the two authors have based their work firmly on the conceptions of modern biology and psychology and the changing needs of an economic and industrial civilization. They have thus built up for us a philosophy of the educative process centered about the desirability of knowledge under conditions of modern civilization concerning the six fundamental life-needs — health, family life, economic adjustment, civic life, recreation, and religion — and then have applied the results of the study to the organization and work of the different divisions of the school.

For the writing of such a book the authors have had an especially good preparation. Their education and training — one brought up in the best schools of England, and one in the public schools and colleges of the Middle West in the United States; one finishing his training in the atmosphere of Columbia, and the other in the atmosphere of Chicago — have given each quite a different background for an educational philosophy, and have served to make their joint production much more than a reflection of a local point of view or of a single school of thought. Still more, the book, from beginning to end, is a thoroughly joint product, and as such free from the usual demerits of joint work. The book was outlined together and each section roughly sketched; it was used for a time in classes at Yale, and then so written and criticized and combined by both men that practically every page reflects the point of view of the two authors. That the work has been well done the arrangement and style of the book reveals, for the text is interesting throughout, and at times the style rises to unusual levels in clearness and charm and force of expression.

The methodology of the book, from the instructor's point of view, is especially good. Having been written in and around a series of fundamental educational problems, the arrangement of the text is such as to give material aid to the teacher. The additional problems for discussion, which close each chapter, have been carefully thought out and organized to enable the teacher to carry forward the discussion of principles laid down in the chapter. Often the questions are those raised by the authors' own students, and as an outgrowth of group thinking on the problems under consideration. In consequence these supplemental problems have been more carefully selected and formulated than would be the case with questions which the instructor ordinarily would raise. In a way they are questions which the authors themselves would like to have dealt with in the text, had there been time and space for their consideration.

In the form as presented it is believed that this book on the Principles of Education offers a thoroughly modern philosophy of the educative process, and that this, coupled with its readable style and good teaching organization, serves to make it an important textbook for use in colleges and universities giving courses in the Principles of Education.

ELLWOOD P. CUBBERLEY

AUTHORS' PREFACE

BECAUSE of the growing number of specialized professional courses given within our colleges and schools of education, as the Editor of this series in his introduction suggests, there is grave danger lest those who are preparing for teaching to-day "grow up and pass out of our training institutions without gaining that sound grounding in the philosophy of education which has been the great strength of the older generation of professional educators." Contrary to the assumption underlying current practice, the growth of our specialized knowledge has made it more rather than less imperative that the student be given a systematic view of the larger rôle played by education. Such a view is obviously essential for the general student, and it is equally important for the research student. Even though the specialized investigator may scorn philosophy, every investigation reflects some fundamental philosophical bias, and without the correct sense of values which principles of education should furnish, valuable energy may easily be dissipated in fruitless and meaningless research.

There is always occasion for a restatement of educational philosophy. On account of the rapidity of social change, the advance of human thought, and the changing conception of the worth of personality, there can be no final formulation. Educational aims and values must evolve from generation to generation. Though certain human trends are abiding, objectives, emphases, and methods must change with changing times. As knowledge grows, as ideals expand, and as the direction of social evolution veers, a re-synthesis of educational experience and knowledge is essential. There is particular need to-day for varied formulations of a philosophy of education — formulations which, in the light of educational and psychological research, take into account the development of science, the revolution in industry, the rise of democracy, and the integration of the peoples of the world.

Amidst the numerous subjects of the curriculum, its countless disciplines and varied procedures, amidst the conflicting demands made upon the school by rival social forces, amidst the ever-shifting winds of educational doctrine, the student of education can only lose his way unless the large objective of education is clearly revealed to him and kept as a lodestar constantly before his eyes. This objective is that of inducting the child into the life of society and of training him in the use of the instrumentalities of civilization. To give to each individual, consistent with his capacity, a maximum share in the enterprise of furthering health, of promoting family membership, of ordering and humanizing industry, of advancing the civic interest, of enriching the recreational life, and of fostering the religious aspiration — these, we believe, are the objectives and touchstones of educational practice.

Only as a theory of education is guided by such a conception of human values and needs can it hope to fulfill its function in a democratic society. If those who control thought in education and determine its objectives have a sound philosophy, we may confidently assume that an increasing scientific control of the methods of education will help the school toward its true goal; but, if, owing to a false philosophy of education, wrong objectives are set up, scientific procedures can only confirm and make us more effective in error.

Quite apart from the contribution of a philosophy of education to professional training, education as a social study must come to occupy a place in the general field of the humanities. Viewed as a mode of social control and as the most powerful force for good or evil in the Great Society, it becomes the most significant, and at the same time the most humanistic, of all the social sciences. In its education we see Society attempting to liberate itself from its own folkways, we see it seeking to become conscious of its own aims, we see it essaying to control the course of its own evolution, we see its genuine philosophy brought into the arena of action.

In such a work as this there is aways danger lest the patient and detailed studies which have resulted from the scientific investigation of educational problems will not be given due recognition. The more dignified position which education has so recently come to occupy in the academic family is largely traceable to the spirit which animates these studies. The vast majority of the problems discussed in this volume have already been submitted to careful quantitative investigation. To these numerous studies we should have liked to make constant reference. But we were compelled to recognize that, even though the patience of the reader and our own abilities had permitted, such a detailed treatment of these experiments would have defeated the purpose of the book. We trust, however, that the general undercurrent of our thinking reflects both the spirit and the findings of the ever-enlarging mass of scientific data which is so rapidly accumulating. Since it is impossible to present the experimental evidence, and even to consider in any detail the many-sided aspects of each problem, we have often been forced to simplify the discussion. As a consequence the text often savors of dogmatism; but this is the price to be paid for conciseness and clearness of presentation.

Our indebtedness to the total stream of thought in social and educational philosophy is apparent. In such a wide domain no claim to originality can be made. If at any point the web is taken to pieces, threads from various fabrics will be found woven into it. The reader familiar with educational writings will recognize the more general influences of

Plato, Rousseau, Herbart, Spencer, Hall, James, and
Dewey; and within the psychological field he will note the
more technical contributions of McDougall, Thorndike,
Watson, Binet, and Freud. Within the stricter educational
field we acknowledge the special guidance of Adams, Adamson, Angell, Ayres, Bobbitt, Bode, Bolton, Cattell, Charters,
Colvin, Cubberley, Garnett, Gesell, Henderson, Holmes,
Inglis, Judd, Kilpatrick, McMurry, Monroe, Nunn, Parker,
Snedden, Spaulding, Strayer, Terman, Welton, Whipple, and
Withers; and within the more general field of social philosophy we have been influenced by Bryce, Chesterton, Croly,
Ferrero, Grundtvig, Hobhouse, Lippmann, Robinson, Russell, Santayana, Sumner, Tawney, Wallas, Ward, Webb, and
Wells.

Many passages are the development of germs whose origin
we have forgotten, but the more direct and definite obligations we have been careful to acknowledge. Where the quotations are of considerable length and there has been danger
of trespassing on copyrighted material, formal permission
for their use has been granted by the author or his publisher.
For their generosity in allowing us to incorporate their ideas
clothed in their own language, we tender our thanks, and, we
feel sure, the thanks of our readers. In spite of our heavy
obligations to the labors of others, the volume leaves us with
a keen sense of its imperfections. May we venture the hope
that the largeness of the aim may in some degree excuse the
poverty of the performance?

J. C. C.

G. S. C.

ACKNOWLEDGMENTS

WE are glad to make specific acknowledgment and to express our obligation for the use of quotations from the books and journals listed below. In each case permission for their use has been granted either by the author or by the publisher.

Andreae, Johann Valentin, *Christianapolis*. Tr. by F. E. Held. Oxford University Press.

Bryce, J., *Modern Democracies*. The Macmillan Company.

Bryce, J., *The American Commonwealth*. The Macmillan Company.

Chapman, J. C., *Educational Review*. Doubleday, Page & Company.

Chapman, J. C., *School and Society*. The Science Press.

Coffman, L. D., *The Social Composition of the Teaching Population*. Teachers College.

Counts, G. S., *The School Review*. University of Chicago Press.

Dewey, J., *Human Nature and Conduct*. Henry Holt & Co.

Dewey, J., *Democracy and Education*. The Macmillan Company.

Drake, D., *Problems of Religion*. Houghton Mifflin Company.

Ferrero, G., *Ancient Rome and Modern America*. G . P. Putnam's Sons.

Ferrero, G., *Between the Old World and the New*. G. P. Putnam's Sons.

Garnett, J. C. M., *Education and World Citizenship*. Cambridge University Press.

Harrison, F., *Autobiographic Memoirs*. The Macmillan Company.

James, W., *Principles of Psychology*. Henry Holt & Co.

James, W., *Varieties of Religious Experience*. Longmans, Green & Co.

Lippmann, W., *Public Opinion*. Harcourt, Brace & Co.

McDougall, W., *Social Psychology*. John W. Luce & Co.

Martineau, James, *Hours of Thought*. Longmans, Green & Co.

Parker, Carleton, *The Casual Laborer and Other Essays*. Harcourt, Brace & Co.

Pruett, L., *Psycho-Analytic Review*. Nervous and Mental Disease Publication Co.

Reisner, E. H. *Nationalism and Education since 1789*. The Macmillan Company.

Robinson, J. H., and Beard, C. A., *Development of Modern Europe*. Ginn & Co.

Robinson, J. H., *The Mind in the Making*. Harper & Brothers.

Robinson, J. H., *The New History*. The Macmillan Company.

Russell, B., *Free Thought and Official Propaganda*. B. W. Huebsch & Co.

Russell, B., *Proposed Roads to Freedom*. Henry Holt & Co.

Spencer, H., *Education*. D. Appleton & Co.

Welton, J., *Psychology of Education*. The Macmillan Company.

In shaping the thought of the book, as well as in preparing the manuscript for publication, both Daisy Rogers Chapman and Lois Bailey Counts have liberally contributed. For this service, as for countless others, we owe them a debt of gratitude.   J. C. C.
                                          G. S. C.

CONTENTS

PART I. WHAT IS THE PLACE OF EDUCATION IN INDIVIDUAL AND SOCIAL LIFE?

PART II. WHAT ARE THE PSYCHOLOGICAL FOUNDATIONS OF EDUCATION?

PART III. WHAT ARE THE SOCIOLOGICAL FOUNDATIONS OF EDUCATION?

PART IV. WHAT PRINCIPLES GOVERN THE CONDUCT OF THE SCHOOL?

PRINCIPLES OF EDUCATION

∴

PART ONE

WHAT IS THE PLACE OF EDUCATION IN INDIVIDUAL AND SOCIAL LIFE?

ALL living things possess some capacity for adjusting themselves to the conditions of existence: through the modification of response, adaptation occurs throughout the whole range of life. This process of adaptation is education in its widest sense. The scope of education is dependent in part on the complexity of the environment, but much more on the capacities for learning possessed by the organism. In man the inner desires and learning capacities are so great that he has not only adjusted himself most intimately to his surroundings, but also has remoulded the world nearer to his heart's desires. So extensive has been the shaping of this environment that in the course of ages he has created a most complex material and social world: a world which is constantly making increasing demands on his adaptability. So far-reaching is this demand that, in recent generations, man, finding incidental and unorganized learning inadequate and uneconomical, has brought into existence the special agency of the school. This institution, born in obscurity, but occupying a strategic position in the life of society, must be guided and criticized by the most intelligent and high-minded counsel.

An understanding of the place of education in individual and social life requires the discussion of the following problems:

PROBLEM 1. HOW IS EDUCATION RELATED TO ADJUSTMENT?

PROBLEM 2. WHAT PROPERTIES OF THE HUMAN ORGANISM MAKE EDUCATION POSSIBLE?

PROBLEM 3. WHAT PROPERTIES OF SOCIETY MAKE EDUCATION NECESSARY?

PROBLEM 4. WHY HAS SOCIETY ESTABLISHED THE SCHOOL TO PROMOTE EDUCATION?

PRINCIPLES OF EDUCATION

PROBLEM 1

HOW IS EDUCATION RELATED TO ADJUSTMENT?

How universal is adjustment in life? — Why is adjustment not merely adaptation to the environment? — How does biological differ from educational adjustment? — What is the scope of education? — How is adjustment a function of an organism seeking its own ends? — What is the range of educational adjustment? — How do biological and educational adjustment give continuity to life? — What factors necessitate adjustment? — What is education?

How universal is adjustment in life? In the thought of to-day education is regarded as a method of adjustment. Education is such an essential part of the fabric of life that we should expect it to be interwoven with that process of adaptation which characterizes every level of life at every moment of existence. Man, in common with all living organisms, is compelled to bring himself into harmony with his surroundings. The penalty of extreme and long-continued failure to make the larger adjustments is death; the penalty of failure to make the smaller adjustments is arrest of growth. Man is goaded into the eternal vigilance which characterizes living by the punishments and rewards which attend his action.

Why is adjustment not merely adaptation to the environment? The term "adjustment" as commonly employed may easily carry too narrow a meaning. While in the case of the animal the process may be regarded as consisting essentially of a "fitting into" the environment, in the case of man, especially in his more advanced types of activity, such a simple statement is apt to be misleading. Adjustment is something more than the forcing of a plastic and passive individual into agreement with a fixed and unchangeable environment. The animal, owing to its small capacity for altering the external conditions of life, is forced into the simple type of adjustment and accepts nature as it is. But in man adaptation involves much more, including not only the changing of the individual to fit the environment, but also the most thoroughgoing attempts on his part to change the conditions under which he lives.

As man removes political tyrants who would require his complete submission to their purposes, so in the realm of physical nature he may banish from the earth scourges, such as bubonic plague and typhus, which threaten his existence. By harnessing the forces of his environment and converting its materials into tools, he is enabled to overcome its more formidable and dangerous aspects. Thus he alters the conditions of life. The artificial environment found in any advanced civilization is illustrative of the manner in which aggressive action can modify and even determine the conditions under which life is led. Any adequate conception of adjustment as a life process must therefore include its twofold aspect, involving, on the one hand, the modification of the organism to meet the external environment, and, on the other, the modification of the environment to further the ends of life.

How does biological differ from educational adjustment? In preparing man to meet the conditions of life, Nature may be said to have endowed him with two methods of response which in their extreme form may be contrasted. Both of these modes of response find their basis in biological inheritance. The first shows itself in the development of a definitely specialized organic structure or in certain fixed modes of response to particular stimulations of the environment, while the second involves a system of response which is generalized in its character and not immediately serviceable to meet any specific condition. Under the process of living these generalized tendencies make possible all those adjustments which are necessary to meet the different aspects of an environment which is constantly changing.

As illustrations of the first type of direct and fixed biological adaptations we may cite the circulatory, digestive, excretory, and reproductive systems. These mechanisms provided by heredity adapt the organism to meet certain aspects of the life-condition which are relatively unchanging from age to age. As an illustration of the second method of adaptation we may cite any of the processes of learning found in man. He is able to learn to use the hand and fingers for many and varied purposes, ranging from carrying food to the mouth to painting an elaborate canvas. He is enabled to make this wide range of adjustment because in his biological structure the mechanisms which control the movements of the arm, hand, and fingers are so flexible at birth as to permit a diversity of useful movements. Instead of the specialization and fixity of response to which reference has just been made, there is a flexibility in action and modifiability of response which facilitate adaptation. Because man inherits a nervous system that is exceptionally plastic, he is the adaptable animal *par excellence*. Were man to inherit a very much richer repertoire of fixed responses, he might, without experience, be in a better position to meet the more immediate demands of his environment. But, since he would for that very reason lack the modifiability which is the foundation of all learning and progress, he would purchase this initial facility at a heavy price.

The fixed and abiding methods of reaction, which are the free gift of heredity, can only serve, therefore, to adjust the individual to certain elemental and immutable aspects of his existence. To the rapidly changing conditions of the ordinary environment this type of biological inheritance is totally incapable of providing the individual with adequate modes of response. If we are to understand the manner in which the human organism meets the complex and fleeting demands of life, attention must be focussed on that flexible part of the biological inheritance which is chiefly resident in the nervous system.

The biological inheritance, exhibiting these two different aspects, may with obvious limitations be likened to a legacy received by a son from his father. A certain part of the inheritance is invested in fixed directions and, by the terms of the will, must always be devoted to these purposes, while the remainder of the property is in an unsettled form. This convertible portion of the inheritance, after it has been worked over, may then be applied in many and diverse ways. If we assume that the fixed portion provides merely the irreducible minimum for existence, obviously any growth or any entrance into new fields is dependent on the development of the remainder of the legacy which comes down in flexible form. The greater the amount of this adaptable inheritance, the greater is the chance for growth, and the larger is the opportunity to take advantage of any changes which conditions create.

To the type of adaptation secured through these fixed modes of response the term " biological adjustment " has been applied; and to the other type, made possible by the flexibility of other portions of the biological inheritance, the term "educational adjustment" has been given. While all adjustment is clearly conditioned by the biological inheritance, it is convenient to make this distinction between the universal biological accommodations and the other forms of adaptation which are individual in their nature and are dependent on the experience and education to which each member of the race is subjected. If we are to understand the complex process of adaptation in its entirety, we must take into account the gradual enrichment over long periods of time of the biological inheritance, particularly as this enrichment proceeds in the direction of increased plasticity and the accumulation of those resources which facilitate educational adjustment.

What is the scope of education?   At this point the relation which exists between adjustment and education should be made more explicit.   While many have restricted the connotation of the term "education" to those changes which are consciously made in the immature individual by society through the special institution of the school, such a restriction of the term is unwarrantable and indefensible.   Under education, used in its widest sense, must be included all those changes which from birth to death are wrought in the individual by the process of learning.   Whether these changes take place in extreme infancy or old age, whether they occur in the home, in the school, or in the market-place, is a matter of no consequence — they are all essentially alike in form and must be included under the term "education."   It is only through the writings of a special group of individuals known as schoolmasters, possessing a false sense of values with reference to their own particular occupation, that the term "education" has been restricted to certain processes that take place in the limited environment of the school. In so far as any individual holds rigidly to this idea of education, he is in fact, as in name, a master of a school and not an educator.

How is adjustment a function of an organism seeking its own ends? As we have already noted, man is not merely a passive organism which adapts itself to certain external conditions; adaptation is more properly described as a process whereby the organism takes advantage of certain elements of its environment to further its own ends. The individual endowed with certain native urges and drives, finding himself in an environment which is partly friendly and partly hostile, seeks to direct its forces towards the satisfaction of these cravings within himself. Group life, with its infinite ramifications and subtle relationships, has evolved unconsciously and consciously a mode of existence whereby man can gratify his impulses in increasing measure. A progressive society seeks only within certain limits to make the individual member conform, but rather strives to make the nature of its organization such that scope will be given to the social and inventive powers of the individual. Considered from the more comprehensive point of view, the total process of adjustment and education may properly be regarded as a reaction between man and the environment which results in furnishing the conditions for his physical, intellectual, and moral growth. While common parlance speaks of the environment producing certain changes in the individual, interpreted too strictly this form of speech is in error. The environment can never produce an adjustment; adaptation is always the act of the organism in response to a certain stimulation. While it is conditioned by the environment, the initiative is always with the organism. Failure to make the adequate adjustment may always be traced to one of two causes: either the individual does not possess the necessary contributing mechanisms to consummate the adaptation, or else, given the necessary contributing mechanisms, the wrong combination of actions is elicited.

What is the range of educational adjustment? Adaptations may be of all degrees of complexity, ranging from the simplest form of physiological adjustment, typified by improvement in the sucking reactions of the infant, to intellectual adaptations which demand the highest form of consciousness. While many writers have sought to draw a sharp line of demarcation between the lower types of adjustment, which they have termed physical, and the higher types termed mental, it is extremely difficult to make such a distinction. We must merely note, at this time, that there are great differences in the degree of complexity required for adjustments of various kinds. The highest form of mental adaptation must be regarded as having elements in common with the more simple types of adjustment at a purely physiological level. The scientist, attempting to solve an intricate intellectual problem, is engaging in an activity which, in many respects, is not essentially different from that occurring in some of the very elementary adaptive processes of childhood.

How do biological and educational adjustment give continuity to life? Having shown the relationship between biological inheritance and the educational process, we must now view, as from a distance, the wide sweep of the vast process of adaptation taking place during the progress of the ages. With feverish haste each generation attempts to make those adjustments which are essential to its continuous life and growth. Each generation, starting with the plasticity characteristic of infancy, when subjected to the processes of a formal and informal education, undergoes certain changes which bring it into harmony with the more pressing aspects of its environment. Useful at the time of inception, these adaptations are rendered obsolete by continuous variation in the environment; moreover, they inhibit the formation of new habits and result in an old age which, on account

of its fixity of response, is incapable of meeting the changing
scenes of life.   At this time death draws the curtain and
the veteran actors leave the stage.

If this were all, the tale would have been told.   But the
process of reproduction enables the play to continue, for at
the time when the previous generation is losing its capacity
for further growth a new generation arises, buoyant and
impressionable, which, while capable of acquiring the advantageous adaptations of the preceding generation, has
still before it, owing to the non-transmission of acquired
physiological characteristics, the possibilities of growth
which its forebears have lost.   Birth, education, reproduction, death form the four acts of this life-drama.   The
infant, through a process of training, becomes the responsible adult, who having reproduced himself in his offspring
tarries sufficiently long to coach the new generation in its
initial parts.   When the stage is becoming full and the
older actors are losing the mental and physical energy
necessary to the later scenes, they are called away by the
great prompter Death, and the play is carried forward by
their erstwhile pupils.   Unhampered by the weakness and
conservatism of those who have been called, the younger
performers carry on the drama until such time as they
in their turn, losing their flexibility and resiliency, must
make room on the stage for their children.   This overlapping of the successive generations, during which the
process of education may take place, supplies to mankind
a continuity of growth which is denied to each single generation.

What factors necessitate adjustment?   Mention must
still be made of the various factors which make adjustment
necessary.   Whenever the environment makes demands
upon the individual which cannot be met by instinctive
or habitual responses, the process of adjustment is condi-

tioned.   A consideration of the simple types of reaction
of which the new-born infant is capable, and the complexity of the environment into which he is born, reveals
the range of the adjustment which would be necessary
even if the environment were static.   But a static environment is impossible; its very complexity works for changes
which augment the demand for adaptation.   In addition,
certain changes within the individual which are partly
the result of the environment, but largely due to internal
processes, bring about the necessity for further adjustments.   The development of the instincts and inborn
capacities bring with them their imperative urges to new
types of activity and new modes of response.   Adjustment is a state that is never completely attained; it is a
continuous process, made necessary by: (1) the complexity of the environment; (2) changes in the environment;
(3) inner changes in the organism.   While often defined in
terms of adjustment, education should for scientific purposes be considered as a series of adjustments.   The complexity of the environment and other factors that we have
discussed make complete adaptation out of the question;
only certain limited adjustments may be made.   It is the
obligation of society to ascertain the peculiar adjustments
which are desirable for each particular individual, and,
then, to discover the most economical methods of aiding
this individual to bring these changes into effect.

What is education?   Looked at from this point of view,
education, as a social process, is nothing more than an
economical method of assisting an initially ill-adapted
individual, during the short period of a single life, to cope
with the ever-increasing complexities of the world.   One
thing is certain, either we must contrive to make education
more effective, or else we must be satisfied with a simpler
civilization.   The biological equipment of the individual

cannot be altered; the life-period of man cannot be extended beyond threescore years and ten; the conditions of our natural and social life do not lend themselves to simplification. These limitations create the necessity for more clearly conceived ideals of conscious effort in the service of education. To creative thought in this field the best minds of each age must be dedicated, for education is the parent and guardian of civilization.

ADDITIONAL PROBLEMS FOR DISCUSSION

1. How is adjustment exhibited in the realm of inanimate nature? How does this type of adjustment differ from that shown by living things?
2. What bearing has the evolutionary concept of adjustment on the attempt to formulate a final and fixed aim for the process of education?
3. What are the main distinctions between the process of adaptation as found in the animal and as found in man?
4. Why is the genius impelled to make so many more adjustments than the feeble-minded individual? How does the method of adjustment differ in these two extremes?
5. How would the process of adjustment be modified if the life-span of each member of the race were four times its present length?
6. What strong evidence is there for the statement that the adjustment process in the social and moral realm has not kept pace with the advance in the adjustment in the material and scientific realm?
7. Show in detail how: (1) internal bodily changes, and (2) mental changes, bring about a condition of maladjustment.
8. Is the environment a stronger factor in controlling the nature of the adaptive forms in the case of the animal than in the case of man?
9. List all the environmental influences which work for the education of man in the savage state. Compare these with those now brought to bear on civilized man.
10. In the case of man, how is education made necessary by the fact of reproduction?

PROBLEM 2

WHAT PROPERTIES OF THE HUMAN ORGANISM MAKE EDUCATION POSSIBLE?

How does reproduction necessitate educational adjustment? — How is education dependent on infancy? — What is man's equipment for educational adjustment? — How do individuals differ in this equipment? — How is behavior modified by experience? — What is the mechanism underlying habit formation? — How is memory related to habit formation? — How do social impulses motivate adaptation? — How does the integration of habits complicate behavior? — What rôle does reflection play in adjustment? — How does integration culminate in personality?

How does reproduction necessitate educational adjustment? In the discussion of the previous problem, mankind was shown to make its long-range adjustment, involving countless ages, through a process of reproduction which in each generation rejuvenates the race. On the other hand, the short-range adjustment made necessary through reproduction, takes place during the limited life-period of the individual; consequently the properties of the organism conditioning this process must now receive our attention.

How is education dependent on infancy? We have seen how the immaturity of the new-born infant, involving a total incompetence in its unchanged form to meet even the simple requirements of its existence, makes necessary a lifetime process of adjustment. Stressing, as it does, the inadequacy of the initial equipment of the child, this is a negative way in which to regard infancy. Looked at from the standpoint of plasticity, it must be noted that the physiological factors which characterize infancy carry within themselves positive forces and powers which more than compensate for the inadequacy of the initial responses. The young chick, hastening from its prison shell, is far better adapted to meet its limited environment than is the human infant. The former, inheriting certain fixed modes of useful response, becomes at once capable of a relatively independent existence; the latter, muling and puking in its nurse's arms, is helpless and must be tended for many years.

Nevertheless, hidden in the nervous system of the child are the possibilities of a far-reaching development denied the chick. In fact, the capacity for development seems to vary directly with the length of infancy; the longer this period and the greater the initial helplessness, the more the final achievement. This helplessness, while not good in itself, serves to call forth a solicitude and tender care on the part of the parent and society, a care which in an advanced civilization may extend over twenty or more years, covering a third of the span of a well-rounded life. How is it that the child can derive benefit from such prolonged dependence? What properties of the human organism make possible such diverse and intricate adjustments?

What is man's equipment for educational adjustment? The answer to this question must be found in the human body, including the grosser structures of head, neck, arms, legs, and trunk, the tissues of bone, cartilage, blood, and flesh, and the functioning systems for respiration, circulation, digestion, excretion, secretion, reproduction, together with that marvelously intricate and delicate mechanism for coördination and control to which the term "nervous system" is given. It is the unification in this intricate physiological structure, made possible through the continuous functioning of the higher mental processes, that permits the process of growth to be so far-reaching and prolonged.

Regarded from the widest viewpoint the human body is

an exquisite mechanism which is adapted, on the one hand, to receive impressions and, on the other, to make certain internal and external reactions as a result of these impressions. To liken this human connection system to any invention of man, such as a vast telephone exchange, while possibly helpful to the student, is totally inadequate to convey a conception of its complexity, its precision, and its vitality.

For the most part, the grosser physical equipment is not markedly different from that of the higher animals; but a superficial examination of the nervous system of man shows an unusual degree of complexity resident in the higher nerve centers of the brain. Confining our attention chiefly to man, we may note four possessions of the human organism: (1) certain reflexes, instincts and original capacities with their corresponding wants, cravings and drives, many present at birth, and the others maturing more or less independently of external conditions; (2) an action system through the functioning and modification of which the equilibrium is maintained; (3) a sensitivity to a lack of adjustment, causing the individual to attempt to reëstablish equilibrium; (4) a power to retain impressions as a result of a physiological structure which registers the responses of the past and thereby changes the organism. Although this classification is somewhat arbitrary and forced, it is helpful in educational analysis. The sensitivity and the action system cannot, of course, be divorced from the instincts themselves; nor can the retentivity be considered apart from the action system. In the last analysis the only properties which the individual brings into the world are found in his reflexes, his instincts, and his inborn capacities. These, constituting his total action system, make him sensitive to lack of adjustment, and cause him to initiate a wide variety of responses from which permanent modifications of the action system result. With this word of caution in mind no misconception need arise from the use of this classification.

How do individuals differ in this equipment? In the adaptive system of every child, by virtue of inheritance, these four possessions are found; but the qualitative and quantitative differences in each one of these properties varies greatly from individual to individual. At the one extreme is the master mind dominated by powerful drives and sensitive to the smallest maladjustment, possessing a nervous system which is capable of a rich variety of responses and able to retain in a marked degree the impressions left by previous successful reactions; while, at the other, is the idiot, who, deficient in both instinctive drives and sensitivity, is equipped with an inadequate action system from which the effects of past experience are quickly erased.

How is behavior modified by experience? Starting with the four elementary properties of the organism just outlined, we may now trace that gradual process of development whereby the infant progresses from the stage of diffuse and ineffective response to that ordered and unified behavior which characterizes what is commonly called adult personality. In this brief statement we can only point out the more important stages which mark the long journey from a helpless infancy to an adult competency. Whenever the child, driven by its inner urges and feelings, or disturbed by some change in the environment, finds itself in a state of maladjustment, certain reactions are made in an effort to reëstablish a condition of equilibrium. If these reactions are successful, the adjustment takes place and the path along which the discharge of nervous energy occurs suffers change. As a result there is facilitation of the same response to the same situation in the future. If, however, the initial reactions are unsuccessful, other types of response are tried until the organism either makes the adequate response or becomes exhausted through fatigue. Even in the case of the unsuccessful reaction, as is indicated by the reduced probability of the repetition of this response in the future, some trace is left in nervous tissue.

But, confining ourselves to the successful reaction which eventuates from the process of trial and error, we must assume certain changes taking place in the nervous system which increase the likelihood that the successful response will recur on the return of the same or a similar situation. This whole process is illustrated by the infant which, lying in its crib and impelled by the urge of hunger, makes a host of random movements, eventuating sooner or later in a lusty cry that attracts the nurse and brings relief. Day by day, thereafter, as the infant faces the ever-recurring problem of hunger, these random and unnecessary movements gradually fall away; there finally remains only that element which attracts attention — the cry. The process illustrated by the formation of this simple reaction is found in all higher types of human response.

What is the mechanism underlying habit formation? To this alteration of the path of discharge, to this formation within the organism of certain preferential associations, to this memory trace of past experience, the name habit formation is given. Through habit all previous acquisitions of the system tend to be preserved to form a basis for the later acquisition of more complex forms of behavior. The phenomena of habit formation are dependent on the inherent property of the physiological structure to suffer change by experience and, at the same time, to preserve the new set that has been given. In other words, plasticity and retentivity are the essential factors in this fundamental process. Thus each new

method of response, growing out of the original responses
and contributing to the total reaction system of the individual, is made available for yet higher forms of adjustment. The simpler habit systems are combined to form
higher systems until the organism acquires a vast repertoire
of habits which, by selection and coördination, enable the
individual to adjust himself to the more complex aspects of
the environment. An example of the existence and co-
ordinate functioning of such a repertoire may be observed
in the debater who, while pursuing a line of rigorous thought,
brings into service the extraordinarily intricate mechanisms of speech, the habits of bodily posture and equilibrium,
and the acquisitions of appropriate gesture and delicate
facial expression. To put it briefly, in making a most difficult and complicated adjustment the trained speaker is
able, through the use of countless habits and habit systems,
to marshal forces that represent the results of years of
practice and effort.

How is memory related to habit formation? Habit formation clearly bears an intimate relation to memory; for
the latter is merely a name for the phenomenon which reveals itself when an acquired group of connections, which
has been idle, manifests itself at a later time. In spite of
many attempts to differentiate between these two types of
activity, no useful purpose will be served at this time by
stressing the distinction. Emphasis should rather be laid
on the close similarity, if not the identity, of the two processes. This is recognized even in common speech, since,
in referring to the formation of the motor habits involved
in some game, such as billiards, we speak of *forgetting* a
certain shot; and since, after years of absence from the
skating rink, we wonder to what degree the various movements involved in skating will be *remembered*. In just the
same fashion with reference to language habits, ten years

after learning a piece of poetry, we are interested in the degree that the *skill* acquired at the initial learning has been retained.

How do social impulses motivate adaptation? Before going further the reader must note that adaptations to the material environment, though fundamental, consume but a small part of the energy of man. The social instincts and tendencies which man inherits make him peculiarly sensitive to the actions and the thought of others, with the result that the more numerous adjustments which he is called upon to make are to the social aspects of his environment. To the powers which grow out of this inherent desire to pay attention to others, to seek the approval and avoid the disapproval of his fellows, man's biological success must be ascribed. His sensitiveness to the social part of his environment, his consciousness of kind, his capacity for working in co-operation with others like himself, his adaptability to the thought, feeling, and action of his associates, his willingness to submit, his desire to exploit — these social traits give man his elevated and unique status. In so far as these powers are highly developed, the organism becomes distinctively human; in so far as they are lacking, it degenerates to the animal level. On this capacity of the human organism to form social habits, a capacity conspicuously absent in any high degree in the lower animals, we must focus, if we are to understand man as an adaptive mechanism.

How does the integration of habits complicate behavior? The alterations which are made in the action system by experience and which constitute our habits and memories, together with inborn differences, serve to differentiate one individual from another. As these alterations or changes in the individual become increasingly numerous, as higher and higher integrations of lower mechanisms take place, the process of training and education proceeds. The skills, the information, and the character of the individual, however intricate these may seem in the adult, must be traced, on the physiological side, to the growth of these preferential paths of energy discharge. Taking into account the initial complexity of the nervous system, combined with the almost infinite capacity for registering changes resulting from the material and social contacts incident to living, it is not difficult to realize how intricate may become the final reactions of the individual. If we assume at birth a highly endowed nature to whose physical wants the closest attention is given, and if we assume that this nature is submitted to a wise and rich home training, followed by a balanced and economical formal education in the school and university, rounded by a life of travel full of diverse experiences, how subtle may be the final product! How different are the reactions of such an individual from those found in the ordinary man! How totally different from those found in the highest animal!

What rôle does reflection play in adjustment? To understand the process of integration and unification which produces this difference, attention must be concentrated on the higher mental processes of reflection. To these processes must be ascribed the leading rôle in the production of those types of behavior which are exclusively human. While it is a mistake to attribute the most complex forms of conduct to the working of some mysterious " self " or " selective force " divorced from the rest of the reaction system, it seems equally fallacious to attempt to explain behavior, which is commonly attributed to thinking, choice, and purpose, wholly in terms of physiological mechanisms. We are not prepared to believe that thinking, the biological climax of a long period of selection, is nothing more than an unnecessary accompaniment of an elaborate interplay of physiological forces. While recognizing the manner in which thinking is dependent on these physiological mechanisms, we do not believe that the unification of behavior which it brings can be wholly explained in terms of physiological changes. While we may be forever in ignorance as to the relation that exists between mental and nervous processes, and as to the exact manner in which thought can affect action, this enigma must not cause us to overlook the fundamental part played by the higher thought processes in the determination of conduct. But this theoretical point we shall consider later; meanwhile it will be sufficient to regard the processes of thought and will, with their obvious selective functions, as being the highest means yet evolved of making adjustments to the more intricate aspects of the environment.

How does integration culminate in personality? From this discussion, even though the more delicate lines and tints are still lost in shadow, the bold outline of the integrated individual emerges. This outline reveals a reaction system in which there is greater and greater complexity of nervous structure, in which the lower mechanisms are combined to form higher mechanisms, and in which these higher mechanisms form the basis of still higher adjustments until, in reflective conduct, the highest form of coördination of behavior is achieved. To the individual exhibiting this last form of integration, with its vast range of possibilities, we have every right to ascribe personality

ADDITIONAL PROBLEMS FOR DISCUSSION

1. What instinctive tendencies have you observed in children? Illustrate. How do you know these tendencies are instinctive?
2. How does the instinctive equipment of man resemble and differ from that of the dog?
3. How would you justify the statement that "all education is dependent on the instinctive equipment"?

4. What is the distinction between an instinctive action and an action which is the result of habit formation?

5. What habits are formed by man and domestic animals alike? What are the habits which distinguish man most completely from the animal?

6. What is the relationship between habit and what is commonly called memory? Why is memory so essential to adjustment?

7. Can man conduct elaborate trains of thought without language? What is the relationship in the child between language habits and motor habits?

8. Why is there often a conflict between the "dictates of reason" and the "dictates of instinct?"

9. When does the child begin to think?

10. How does the phenomenon of the total eclipse of the sun differ in its meaning for the astronomer and his dog? Show further that every experience we undergo is relatively meaningless unless accompanied by the thought process.

11. How do the emotions help or hinder clear thinking?

12. What economy does thinking introduce into the process of adaptation?

13. In what sense are all men created equal? What is the distinction between equality in the sight of the law and equality in native equipment? Can education "destroy" physical, mental, and moral differences?

PROBLEM 3

WHAT PROPERTIES OF SOCIETY MAKE EDUCATION NECESSARY?

How universal is group life? — Why do men live in groups? — What is the survival value of group life? — What rôle has the family played in the development of group life? — How does the growth of folkways make education necessary? — How may education at this level bar the way to progress? — How has the primitive group expanded? — What are the advantages of life in the Great Society? — Can man prosper in the Great Society? — Is man's versatility adequate to the task? — Can education make man equal to the task?

How universal is group life? Group life is a universal characteristic of mankind. Into the group man is born, through it he acquires skills and knowledges, at its behest he learns the use of tools and processes, in its ranks he earns his daily bread, under its banners he marches forth to battle, with its members he learns to sing and dance and play, from it he receives religions and philosophies, and by it the last rites are said over his inanimate form. Mythology, it is true, tells us of a Romulus nursed and cared for through infancy by a she-wolf, fiction has created for us a Robinson Crusoe cast up on an uninhabited island, and an occasional individual voluntarily withdraws from human companionship to live a life of solitude; but such cases are either the product of imagination or so rare as to be quite unrepresentative of normal human behavior. Throughout the long ages of man's career upon the earth, and probably during many preceding ages, as the slowly evolving primate was assuming the human form, man and his progenitors have experienced more or less constant membership in the family, if not in some larger group. To-day there is no race known to the anthropologist whose members avoid social contacts and pursue a life of complete isolation.

Why do men live in groups? Although the philosophers of earlier centuries speculated much upon the problem, the question as to why men live in groups is not difficult to answer to-day. If we confine ourselves to the situation as it presents itself in the modern age, the obvious reply to our query is that men live in social groups because they are born into them, and cannot very well get out of them. Another and more fundamental answer directs attention to that native equipment of the individual which was the subject of analysis in the preceding discussion. Men live in groups because they are constituted as they are; for the same reason in fact that geese fly in flocks, and cattle run in herds. They participate in social life because they like it; and they like it because every member of the race possesses, as part of his original equipment, certain social tendencies which can only find their satisfaction in the contacts afforded by a social environment. If it is denied him for a season, man actually hungers for human companionship. He continually derives satisfaction from securing the approval and avoiding the disapproval of others, from assuming the leadership of others in group undertakings, and from following some dominating personality in the achievement of a desired social end. In and through the group the nature of the individual finds expression and develops into what is commonly called human personality.

What is the survival value of group life? This tendency of man to be interested in his fellows and to seek their companionship has great utility. The advantages of group life in adjusting the individual and the race to the conditions of life are many and obvious. Any organism that develops a compact group life in which individuals work together for common ends has greater chances for survival than the organism that clings to modes of isolated living. The poet, the moralist, and the philosopher have all described and marveled at the truly extraordinary achievements of ants, wasps, and bees; achievements which may be traced directly to their remarkable powers of coöperative endeavor. Many simple though heavy tasks, capable of being performed easily through the coöperation of a few individuals, are utterly beyond the powers of a single member. When the task is one that requires various types of special talents, skills, and knowledges, there is an added advantage. Then individuals, following the line of aptitude and specializing in training and experience, may raise the general level of achievement far above the possibilities of that isolated individual effort which permits no specialization. When an organism possesses the property of learning from the experience of others, group life becomes yet more significant and advantageous. Association then makes possible not only the pooling of native abilities for collective effort, but also the pooling and transferring of experiences from one individual to other members of the group. Furthermore, this pooling and transference of experiences through the instrument called language makes the effective group include the dead as well as the living, and the dead in increasing measure as generations come and go. In a word, social life makes possible the discovery, accumulation, and utilization of an unlimited number of tools, skills, procedures, and appreciations through which the welfare of the race may be promoted.

What rôle has the family played in the development of group life? There is one part of man's life that is so essential to an understanding of the origin of the group, and so central to the growth of human society, as to deserve explicit attention. We may say without exaggeration that the group has grown up around the infant and the phenomena of reproduction. Wherever an animal species is perpetuated through sexual reproduction, forces are in operation which require in the process of mating at least the fleeting contacts of the sexes, even though the more extended process of courtship is absent. Likewise, among all those organisms which bring forth their young in a fully formed condition, or incubate their eggs during the period of embryonic development, an intimate relationship of shorter or longer duration is established between the mother and the offspring. If, at the time of birth, the organism is relatively helpless, this period of contact between mother and offspring is lengthened beyond the time consumed in the actual process of birth to cover the entire period of helplessness. With an occasional visit from the unhampered male, this group of two constitutes the beginning of genuine social life. As soon as this period of dependence exceeds the period of gestation a third member is automatically added to the group, and the ties which bind the father are drawn a trifle closer. In the case of man, this period of infancy is greatly lengthened, and there grows up about the mother and father a family of children. Here is the opportunity for the development and elaboration of social tendencies.

How does the growth of folkways make education necessary? As this family group persists, as it becomes more permanent, and eventually expands into the larger kinship groups of primitive times; and, as this group adjusts itself more fully to life situations, there is a gradual and constant accumulation of practices, customs, laws, and traditions. This accumulation widens the gulf which separates the infant from the adult. Through the efforts of the older members of the group these past achievements are conserved and transmitted to each succeeding generation. In considerable measure this is apparently a by-product of the endeavor of the elders to secure stability within the group and to maintain their own supremacy. It must not be supposed that there is any large conscious recognition of the wider functions which stability serves, but rather, a natural resistance on their part to the modification of their own customs. They occupy a position of privilege in the group and their habits and dispositions constitute a vested interest. Thus, these ways of doing and thinking, these folkways, as they have been styled, gradually take on great authority and come to be regarded as wholly good, true, and final.

Viewed from this standpoint, group life may be likened to an intricate game; those who are playing it are jealous of its rules; their habits and supremacy, as well as the immediate success of the game, depend on a careful adherence to the code; and all beginners are required to learn and follow it. In this great social game of life the children are the beginners. In fact every individual is a complete stranger in the group into which he is born. He is ignorant of every rule; he knows neither its language nor its customs; and he possesses none of those skills on which the very existence of the group depends. He must become a full-fledged member of the group; he must come to act and feel and think as its older members do; he must become a robust trustee into whose care all its possessions may be confidently committed. Since the renewal of social life is possible only through the induction of new members, unless he is able to sustain this difficult rôle, the group perishes. As nothing is more certain than the eventual death of each member, the education of the young in the customs of the group — in the ways of the folk — is absolutely essential to the stability and perpetuity of society.

How may education at this level bar the way to progress? This demand for the acquisition of and conformity to the folkways is not however an unmixed blessing, for many of the practices of the group are based on error and others are vicious. This dominant interest of the primitive group in conserving the achievements of the past is a powerful obstacle to the promotion of more comprehensive and delicate adjustments in the interests of future security. Returning to the analogy of the preceding paragraph, we may note that some of the rules of the game are not worthy of observation, and that others need radical alteration. Conservatism must therefore be balanced by some creative principle, if social stagnation is to be avoided.

This principle of change is found in that non-conforming, restless and adventurous element which exists at least potentially in every group. This element is always on the look-out for inadequacies in the old methods of adjustment. Moreover, while man possesses certain inborn social tendencies that require group life for their expression, he is at the same time only imperfectly equipped by nature for participation in such life. He brings with him powerful egoistic impulses that keep him in more or less constant conflict with the group. From the earliest times, therefore, by taking advantage of crises precipitated by external changes, certain of the bolder individuals, chafing at the restraints put upon them by the vested interests, have occasionally challenged group customs and, gathering to their standard the like-minded and the dissatisfied, have effected substantial alterations in the social order.

How has the primitive group expanded? These two forces, the one conservative and the other creative, constitute the basis of all orderly social change. In primitive society the former played the dominant part, while in recent generations the latter has become increasingly active. As we look over the world to-day, we realize that the character and conditions of social life have undergone striking changes since the days when the first men, in search of food and shelter, wandered in loosely formed bands over the face of the earth. For countless ages man lived in small and isolated groups, composed of individuals brought together by the accidents of kinship and united by the bonds of frequent association. Through the primitive and direct occupations of hunting and fishing these groups wrested a meager subsistence from the earth. By invention and discovery, the achievement of the daring and gifted individual, man was gradually able to supplement his own limited-action system by means of fire, tools, weapons, and machines, and such immaterial instruments as language, number, and moral codes. Through these achievements the power and range of human operations were greatly extended in both space and time. Because of this ability to invent and to utilize the results of invention man, a being of but moderate physical powers, is now able to move more rapidly than the swiftest of animals, to destroy with ease those savage and powerful beasts which struck terror into the hearts of his primitive ancestors, to live in relative comfort in arctic snows and under the tropic sun, to create new forms of animals and plants for either use or fancy, to move mountains and turn the course of rivers, to see further than the eagle and more minutely than the fly, to make his voice carry around the world and even to future generations.

Accumulating at a constantly accelerating rate, this long series of inventions has given birth to a new world, a world unlike anything that has existed in the past. Measured in terms of travel and communication the earth has been greatly reduced in size, while, through more effective control of the forces governing the food supply, its population has been vastly augmented. Since ancient times the small kinship group, as the unit for human association, has given place to larger and larger societies. First, as an expansion of the family there came the large tribal organization, then the city-state of the ancient world, followed in more recent times by the nation. But to-day human association refuses to recognize the boundaries of nations, with the result that a war arising from the immediate rivalries of two minor States becomes of world moment. Thus the smaller societies in which man has lived in the past are being integrated into a great industrial and cultural society which knits the whole of mankind together in intimate association; a society which is now seeking in halting fashion to give itself political expression through a League of Nations. It is in this Great Society that modern man lives and moves and has his being, and it is to this Great Society that his nature must be attuned.

What are the advantages of life in the Great Society? The benefits that accrue to the individual from this expansion of social life are many. Adjustment has been facilitated and the satisfactions of life have been increased. Most of the advantages afforded by the small group are found in greater measure in the larger group. The extraordinary advance in the control of the forces of nature has markedly improved the material basis of life. Greater specialization of function has been made possible. So far has this process of differentiation been carried that in some instances a whole people or region, because of its possession of certain natural advantages or gifts, specializes in the production of some useful commodity or cultural service. Other peoples or regions, specializing in other directions, make necessary the development of a complicated system of exchange and communication whereby the material and spiritual products of all are made generally accessible. A gigantic undertaking, like the construction of a Panama Canal, which would have been regarded as an extravagant and fantastic dream in a more primitive age, can now, in the course of a few years, be carried through to a successful end.

Released from the necessity of bending their energies to the making of the more immediate and direct adjustments to life, individuals and peoples of special and superior talent can apply themselves to the study of those natural and social forces upon which man's existence depends. Through an understanding of these forces a yet more complete adjustment to the environment is furthered. Man has already banished from the great society one of the three great scourges that in ancient times periodically decimated the race, namely, famine; he has greatly reduced the ravages of a second, disease; and he is seriously considering the early abolition of the third, war. If space permitted, this list of advantages could be indefinitely prolonged.

Can man prosper in the Great Society? There is another side to the picture, however. Many thoughtful men to-day are wondering if these great societies of the present are not too large and complicated for the promotion of the genuine interests of mankind. Is man able to control the forces which he has unloosed on a primitive world? Has he not through his inventions opened a second Pandora's box, more real than the first, out of which has come ills that will eventually work his own destruction? In our economic life there looms a bitter struggle between the different interests engaged in the production and the distribution of the fruits of coöperative endeavor; and the conflict is further embittered by that differentiation and mechanization of the productive process which, by fostering the development of a highly unnatural life, creates a situation so artificial as to thwart the expression of powerful inborn tendencies. Because of the impracticability and even impossibility of sustaining close contacts in the wide associations of the larger groups the relationships of individual to individual, of group to group, and of individual to group, have of necessity become largely impersonal. Man's original social nature was evolved under conditions of most intimate personal relations, and it responds to situations arising in such a setting.   We are disturbed again and again in our political life because the level of achievement of even a group of intelligent, sincere, and public spirited legislators is too low to meet the needs of society.

This situation recalls the dictum of the Greek philosopher, who claimed that the extension of efficient democratic government was definitely limited by the number of persons who are able at one and the same time to come within the range of a single human voice.   While the miraculous development of the means of communication in the form of newspapers, telegraph, telephone, amplifiers, and radio makes necessary the revision of this early political notion, it serves to direct attention to the type of group life for which man is naturally fitted.   This equipment seems yet more inadequate to meet the difficulties arising out of the relations of nations, races, and religious sects.   Here, especially, the process of adjustment halts.   These relations seem to generate conflicts that in recent years have destroyed a goodly portion of civilization, and in the future may destroy it beyond redemption.   The man of thought to-day holds up his hands in intellectual despair at the sight of two peoples engaging in deadly conflict, each thoroughly convinced that it fights in a righteous cause and for the ultimate welfare of mankind.   Many of these difficulties may be traced to the fact that man's biological inheritance was evolved to make adjustments to a much simpler environment than that in which he finds himself at present. Equipped by nature to settle family squabbles, man now finds himself compelled to adjust the conflicts of nations.

Is man's versatility adequate to the task?   While it is impossible to avoid such disquieting thoughts, one cannot help feeling that the general tone of pessimism current to-day comes from an undue emphasis upon what man is by original nature, rather than on what he may become through education. It may also be traced to the tendency to assume that this inborn equipment is relatively fixed in its expression, and that in general there is but one type of environment to which it can be made to respond. Do not those who insist on the hopeless nature of the maladjustment which we see in the world to-day make the mistake of placing the emphasis on that part of the native endowment which insures stereotyped and unmodifiable responses, rather than on that portion composed of highly adjustable mechanisms which not only adapt the organism to changes in the environment but also enable the organism to modify the environment in its own interests?

Through his own thought and labor the mighty inventions and the great societies have come into existence. By yet greater thought and more arduous labor man will find the means of controlling these children of his brain. Such is a legitimate educational faith. Those who would sound the note of despair must admit that they know next to nothing regarding the absolute potentialities of this nature of man. If we turn from man's primitive nature and with Hamlet exclaim, " What a piece of work is a man! How noble in reason! How infinite in faculty! " — the more hopeful and equally human side of the picture is exhibited. If only man can be brought to use those higher powers, which he possesses and which are as real as the more primitive ones, for the solution of the very problems which his efforts have created, he can put his house in order. But to do this he must be prepared to turn his back on the folkways; he must rid himself of ways of thinking, feeling, and behaving which are not adapted to the present conditions of his life.

Can education make man equal to the task? The complex and intricate problems of a scientific, intellectual, and social world cannot be met by an education which is not equally scientific, intellectual and social in its conception. The marvelous expansion of the material culture has not been accompanied by a corresponding expansion of the moral culture. Only through the latter may the former be made to serve the purposes of mankind. In our mastery of the forces of physical nature, thanks to the genius and devotion of a relatively small number of men, we have made extraordinary advances during the last few centuries, and have developed skills and knowledges of endless variety, complexity, and usefulness; but advances and improvements of equal significance in the world of social relations have been notably lacking. To use a figure, the chariot of human destiny, which at one time rumbled slowly along its path, now, driven by vastly more powerful forces, is rushing along a road at such a pace as to invite disaster. In the slowly moving vehicle of primitive times man was quite at home, and a very mediocre level of horsemanship was sufficient to keep it on its course; but, as the power of its steeds has increased and as its pace has accelerated, the driver has been forced to carry heavier and heavier responsibilities. This he has been compelled to do with a native equipment but little changed and with a cultural equipment adapted to the simple tasks of the less strenuous past. To a carefully-planned and rigorous system of education, consciously conceived in the light of the need, society must turn, if man is to come into the possession of the skill, knowledge, and character commensurate with his great social responsibility.

Is not the impasse in which the race finds itself to-day to be explained partly by the fact that an unanalyzed process of education is still imparting old habits which had their origin and justification in an environment of an earlier and simpler age? Owing to a social and intellectual inertia, are we not still insisting that our children acquire adjustments which articulate with conditions that have passed from the earth? Under these circumstances is it any wonder that men are overwhelmed by the demands of the present social life? Moreover, universal formal education has been contemplated only in most recent times, and has never been thoroughly analyzed or adequately enforced. We must not fatalistically lament the limitations of human nature, as in ages past our ancestors bowed resignedly before the forces of physical nature. It is our bounden duty to set ourselves definitely to the task of utilizing more effectively the potentialities for good resident in our own capacities. Whatever may be the view as to the possibility of man's controlling and guiding the vast social mechanisms which he has brought into existence, he is, perforce, driven to accept the challenge and engage in the heroic struggle. And this heroic struggle can only be carried to a successful issue by equipping him with an education which in its scope and thoroughness matches the forces which must be controlled.

ADDITIONAL PROBLEMS FOR DISCUSSION

1. Why do men live in groups? What are the advantages of group life?
2. Why is solitary confinement regarded as one of the most severe forms of punishment?
3. What truth is there in the statement that the child is anti-social? What human traits cause friction in society?
4. Why has the family been called the mother of society and of all social institutions?
5. How do you explain the increased power of successive generations in the light of our definite knowledge that man's native equipment has changed but little since the days of savagery?
6. What is the relation of progress to social change?
7. How has society been transformed by great inventions in the realms of transportation, communication, and economic production?
8. In what respects has the growth of the Great Society increased both the demands and the possibilities for systematic education in the fields of: (a) health; (b) family life; (c) industry; (d) citizenship; (e) recreation; and (f) religion?

9. Show how the impersonality and complexity of the Great Society have raised all but insoluble problems in the realms of industry, politics, and religion.

10. How do folkways come into existence? Are they good or evil? How are they changed?

11. What are the advantages and disadvantages of imposing the folkways of one generation on the succeeding generation?

12. It has been remarked that the folkways are the product of intelligence and at the same time the negation of intelligence. Explain this paradox.

PROBLEM 4

WHY HAS SOCIETY ESTABLISHED THE SCHOOL TO PROMOTE EDUCATION?

How universal is the process of education? — Why is informal education adequate in primitive society? — When did informal education become inadequate? — Why did formal education precede the school? — For what ends were the first formal educational agencies established? — How did the initiation ceremony foreshadow universal education? — How did the development of language affect education? — How has the growth of the Great Society made necessary a new and wider conception of education?— How has the formal educational agency become differentiated? — What advantages may the school environment possess over a chance environment? — What dangers commonly accompany the formal institution? — How may these dangers be mitigated? — What must be the foundations of a sound educational program?

How universal is the process of education? As an individual process, education in its wider sense has existed since the appearance of the first organism possessing the property of learning. As a social process, education has existed since organisms possessing this property first associated in groups. Man has therefore experienced the process of education throughout his long career upon the earth. Wherever man reacts to some inadequacy in his environment, wherever man is subject to the influence of his fellows, the process of education advances. In a word, all living men are being educated. Depending on the operation of factors internal or external to the organism, here the process moves forward rapidly and there slowly.

Why is informal education adequate in primitive society? During the early history of mankind, education was directed by no conscious purpose. As a by-product of living, each individual born into the world gradually acquired those forms of adjustment necessary in the relatively simple en-

vironment of his age. The young accompanied the parent
as the latter moved about in search of edible roots or succu-
lent berries, a wounded animal or a stranded fish. There
were no highly specialized skills associated with the securing
of food, nor were there complex processes involved in its
preparation. Likewise, as with food, no specialized skills
were demanded to satisfy the needs for shelter and clothing.
Life was raw, simple, and direct. The acquisitions of the
race were not many, and the action-system was not greatly
extended beyond that of the higher animals. The adults
were not conscious of the process of teaching, and the young
acquired the little there was to be learned as they at an
early age sought food, shelter, and clothing to satisfy their
own organic cravings. Unaware of the process, they learned
from the older members of the group and from the harder
school of individual experience.

When did informal education become inadequate? As
social life became more complex, as successive generations
added to the stock of skills and ideas: as man learned to
control fire and apply it to the satisfaction of his wants; to
fabricate robes, coats, and shoes to shield himself from the
winds and frosts of winter; to construct traps, knives, and
spears to increase and stabilize the food-supply; to fashion
pots, kettles, and baskets to be used in cooking and transportation; to use the rudiments of speech as the basic instrument of thought and social coöperation, — as all these
precious secrets were wrested one by one from nature, it
became increasingly necessary for the adult members of the
group to give explicit attention to the process of tuition lest
some of the group-acquisitions be lost. When the first
parent, with conscious intent, slowed up the productive
process in order to facilitate and perfect the learning of the
child, the beginnings of formal education were made. Education then became an end to which the more immediate

demands of existence were subordinated. Under these conditions there was no clear line of cleavage between incidental
and formal education. As the boy accompanied his father
on a hunting expedition, or as the girl took part with her
mother in the dressing and curing of game, these two forms
of education went on side by side or in alternation.

Why did formal education precede the school? For
ages the entire education of the young was gained through
this participation in the life of the group. But during this
period, without the assistance of any formal or specialized
educational agency, the maturer members gave an ever increasing amount of attention and effort to the process of
instruction. The conscious direction of learning greatly
antedated the rise of the formal institution. There is a law
of social evolution that the worth of a function must be
demonstrated through the services of an unspecialized
agency before a specialized agency is brought into existence
in the social order.

Moreover, the beginnings of education may be traced
back to that generalized and undifferentiated source of all
institutions, the primitive family, which performed all the
functions necessary to the maintenance of social life. With
its limited membership this small group could not establish
a special agency for the performance of any special function,
since the only possible division of labor was that which followed the line of sex. Any further differentiation waited
upon the expansion of the group; and expansion, in turn,
was dependent on the development of a technique to increase the food supply. So long as the social group remained small, however necessary the education of the
immature may have appeared, it was quite impossible to
devote the entire services of one of its few members to this
special task. Such a differentiation of function would have
involved the direction to this purpose of more of the energy

of the group than could well be spared. The force of this argument is apparent when we consider that, even in our own extraordinarily wealthy society, we find it a burden to dedicate the talents of but one in a hundred of our number exclusively to the enterprise of education.

For what ends were the first formal educational agencies established? Probably the earliest manifestation of a formal educational agency with a conscious educational purpose centered around those individuals, of superior skill and knowledge, to whom the group had become accustomed to turn in times of crisis for its defense and perpetuation. A warrior or hunter of uncommon courage and skill was expected to give instruction not only to his own sons, but also to the sons of his kinsmen; and the matron of exceptional proficiency in the arts of the home and peace was called upon to serve the group by giving its daughters tuition in the deft performance of those duties allotted to her sex.

But it seems probable that the most systematic and thorough efforts at transmitting the acquisitions of the group to the younger generation grew up around religious belief and practice. Through this division of the social inheritance, surprisingly elaborate and intricate even among the most primitive of peoples, man sought to determine the course of events in the world of sense by influencing through prayer, sacrifice, threat, or cajolery, the spirits and powers of an unseen world — a world which his primitive mind postulated as lying back of and controlling all the phenomena of nature. Here was a body of tradition that was looked upon as immeasurably precious, for it was thought to give control over those happenings, which though vital to group welfare, were not directly amenable to human influence. Through these practices they fondly thought to become masters of their own fate: to control the forces of life and death, to increase the number of their children and defer the approach of age, to check the ravages of disease and promote the blessings of health, to forestall the visits of famine and insure an abundance of food, to soften the rigors of winter and bring the warmth of spring, to determine the issue of battle and shape the ends of peace, and to give their souls safe convoy to a land of eternal bliss.

Little wonder that this heritage, so freighted with power over good and evil, was guarded with the most jealous care. Little wonder that there gradually evolved an order of specialists whose sole business was to preserve this lore and, through its use, to promote the welfare of the group. In the hands of the specialist, whether priest, shaman, medicine-man, or magician, this body of tradition was gradually elaborated and consequently became, in yet greater measure, the unique possession of a class. This made necessary the formal organization of instruction about certain callings intimately associated with the life of the group. In one way or another, provision was made for the selection of promising youth who, under the direct tuition of the elders, were trained to discharge this important and esoteric social function. Out of this situation emerge the beginnings of professional training.

How did the initiation ceremony foreshadow universal education? The earliest formal educational agencies affecting directly the entire membership of the group were in a sense complementary to those agencies which were provided for the training of its leaders. Side by side with the development of the latter there appeared a considerable variety of ceremonies to which all the members of the group were submitted. Whether designed for the younger or older members, the great object of these ceremonies was social control. Certain of them, serving to initiate the youth into the fuller and wider life of the adult, were models of solemnity and were calculated to convey to the initiate the impression that the authority of the group, the authority of its customs, and the authority of its leaders, were absolute and binding on all its members. The entire proceedings bore a sanction that transcended the limits set by a single generation. Through feasting, fasting, fatigue, and elaborate ceremonial, and through appeal to supernatural sanction, the whole initiation was enveloped in an emotional mist that inhibited the process of thinking. Involving but little intellectual content and no thorough mastery of any tools of knowledge, this special form of exoteric education was directed to moral and social ends. Transmitting unchanged the inheritance of the group, this form of tuition stressed the great passive virtues of undivided loyalty and unswerving obedience. While a powerful conservative force in society, and necessary for group survival under the hard conditions of the time, it was undoubtedly a serious obstacle to change and progress.

How did the development of language affect education? With the refinement of the mechanisms of speech, by means of which increasingly delicate shades of meaning could be conveyed from one individual to another, and with the extension of the powers of speech through space and time by the invention of writing, the development of formal educational agencies was greatly stimulated. No longer dependent for their transmission on oral speech, the traditions, laws, and customs of the group were worked into clay, stone, or papyrus, and thereby given a permanence and an inflexibility which were previously lacking. The variable elements of individual experience and the imperfection of transmission, so long as dependence on oral speech is complete, are certain to change both the form and the meaning, the letter and the spirit, of that which is handed down. But with the invention of writing, the dead hand of the past takes a firmer grip on the present and the written word becomes sacred. The natural conservatism of a primitive race drives it to find refuge in the thoughts, struggles, and achievements of past generations whose leaders become gods and humblest members demigods. Under these conditions education tends to become a worship of scripture, both error and truth are dressed in identical garb, and the folkways are hardened into a Mediæval Europe or an Historic China. In such a world may be observed the perfect and final expression of the spirit of the initiation ceremony of the savage tribe.

The development of speech and writing, however, influenced education in other ways. The integration of mankind into those larger groups, in which great differentiation of structure and function is possible, was dependent on improved methods of recording and transmitting thought. The size of a group is definitely limited by the stage reached in the development of the means of communication. In a very real sense the modern world is built upon writing and reading. Thus, while the invention of writing was superficially conservative, seeming but to perpetuate the established order, it was fundamentally radical. Writing is the *sine qua non* for an enlarged social life, and ultimately the solvent of its own conservatism. This invention did much more than make possible the rigorous teaching and learning of the content of scripture; in time it made necessary the teaching of reading and writing. And, since these arts are not easily acquired, society was compelled to establish special agencies for the purpose of ensuring their acquisition.

At first the social need was met by training a few specialists to do all the reading and writing required by the group — to keep the records, to send and interpret messages, to make, transcribe, and decipher important documents. But even this limited use of written language promoted that widening of the group and that complex organization of the political and economic life which in turn created an increased need for both reading and writing. This was a potent factor fostering the growth of the formal educational agency. With the passage of time, civilization becomes so dependent on written language that every fully functioning member of society is forced to master the rudiments of the literary arts. The ordinary tasks of life come to require the acquisition of the elementary phases of reading, writing, and arithmetic. Thus the school for the masses has naturally placed its great emphasis on the mastery of the tools of knowledge. And these arts have so placed their stamp on the school, and even on the idea of education, that to the uncritical mind to-day education is identified with literacy and book learning.

How has the growth of the Great Society made necessary a new and wider conception of education? This narrow conception of education and of the function of the school is undergoing rapid modification in the modern world. It no longer meets the educational needs of social life. On an ever-increasing scale those very forces, which in primitive times created the initiation ceremony and in a later age the reading and writing school, continue in operation. The life of the group is renewed from generation to generation, but always on a more complicated pattern, always with an enlarged experience. Consequently the generation that required only to be taught to read and write and figure has given place to one that must be introduced to the life of society in many of its aspects through the medium of a carefully prepared environment. Society has become a vast and intricate mechanism. At many points, its proper functioning requires the long and careful training of its members.

The world of to-day is based not only on reading and writing and arithmetic, but also on a great body of tested and refined experience regarding the working of the various forces which condition human existence. Man has evolved a method of studying this world which has created the ever-growing sciences of physics, chemistry, biology, psychology, and sociology. From this body of refined and organized knowledge there flows to the race a constantly increasing number of benefits. In recent centuries man has learned that the world in which he lives is but a tiny speck in an un-measured universe, and not the major and central part of creation; he has discovered that the history of the world can be measured only in geologic ages, and not in generations of men; he has found that he lives in a world of law, and not in a world of caprice. To this new world, this large world, this complex world, the child, without expert guidance and merely as an incident to the satisfaction of his own wants, can no longer make his adjustments.

Moreover, because of the development of the factory, the city, and the State, certain non-specialized educational agencies, such as the home, the community, and the church, which in the past have borne large educational burdens, are losing much of their vitality. And with the growth of our knowledge of psychology and with the clearer formulation of social ideals, attention has gradually come to focus on education as a means to the reconstruction of individual and social life. The school is thus gradually becoming a spe-cialized environment through which every individual must pass, if he is to render the largest service to his fellows and enjoy to the full the advantages of life in the Great Society.

How has the formal educational agency become differ-entiated? We have now passed in brief review those forces working in human society which make necessary the estab-lishment of this specialized institution known as the school. We have seen how the perpetuation of the group has always required that the new generation be educated by the old, and how, as society has grown more complex and increased its acquisitions, the educational function has been gradually given over in increasing measure to this special agency. To the two-fold task of guarding the interests of the group and assisting the individual in his efforts to adjust himself to the environment this agency has been dedicated. So far has this development proceeded that to-day a school is associated with almost every complex activity found in the life of society. There are the common schools, emphasizing the universal needs of men, to which all are admitted; there are differentiated schools for those following specialized occupations — schools for cooks and clergymen, for farmers and teachers, for salesmen and nurses, and, according to a recent press dispatch, a school for burglars in one of our large cities. It has even been thought necessary in our colleges to give hours of theoretical instruction in some classroom far removed from the gridiron to the athletes who compose the football squad. In view of the rapid rise of these specialized educational agencies we may well consider the merits and demerits of formal education.

What advantages may the school environment possess over a chance environment? The school is a specialized environment in which the child is placed. It cannot in the original sense create powers. At most the school serves as an instrument for the selective stimulation of the powers already inherent in the child. There are three primary advantages of this environment of design over an environment of chance which have been suggested by Dewey. In the first place, at least for the earlier years of childhood, it is a simplified environment from which the more difficult and complex aspects of the adult world have been removed. The child, if introduced directly into the larger life of the Great Society, would be overwhelmed. This is true in some measure in even the simplest and most primitive societies.

In the second place, it is a purified environment, from which the harsh and corrupt practices of social life have been banished.   There is much in any society, which certainly does not merit perpetuation.   In the third place, it is a broadened environment through which the individual may derive perspective for evaluating and passing judgment on the affairs of his group.   Into the school may be concentrated all the experiences of the race which history records, as well as the customs, knowledges, and ideals of the various peoples inhabiting the earth to-day.   A fourth advantage, although a corollary of Dewey's first principle, should be mentioned. The school is a graduated environment, which is consciously organized in such a way as to facilitate the process of adjustment.   Since these activities are arranged in a graded series the individual is led, step by step, from the simple experiences of childhood to the complexities of adult life.   Each of these features of the school has played an important part in securing the support of society.

What dangers commonly accompany the formal institution?   But these advantages are apt to be accompanied by two dangers which always attend the development of a specialized institution, and which manifest themselves in full strength in the educational agency.   In the first place, the school may become isolated from the rest of life, and lose touch with the world of men and things.   Particularly, among social institutions, has the school tended to become highly artificial, so artificial indeed that at times it has not only failed to promote adjustment to the actual conditions of life but has even increased the difficulties attending the process.   Taking place in a natural medium, incidental and informal education always manifests a genuineness and exhibits a directness that formal education so frequently lacks. While the latter may give the impression of an adventitious and external acquisition, the former is made an integral part of one's personality and tends to become second nature.

In the second place, because of the resistance to change on the part of the vested interests within itself, the school may block the way of progress. The teacher, always taught in a school of an earlier generation, tends to perpetuate the knowledges and skills that he was taught; he opposes quite naturally any important change in either method of presentation or materials of instruction. Such a change is pernicious because it interferes with his routine, and even destroys a part of his working capital! Whenever society establishes an institution, it creates a structure that resists change, it gives a hostage to things as they are; and, while this institution at the time of its inception may represent an advance over the past, it may also be an obstacle to further achievement. If its functioning requires a class of specialists whose security in the social order is contingent on its perpetuation, this reactionary tendency becomes especially pronounced. As Todd has remarked, throughout the history of education the school has never wholly on its own initiative introduced a single subject into the curriculum.

How may these dangers be mitigated? For these ills to which the formal educational agency is subject, no simple remedy has been discovered. Although their virulence and frequency of attack may be greatly reduced, they probably can never be wholly banished. The great desideratum, and all for which we may legitimately hope, is the maximum advantage and the minimum disadvantage attainable in a special agency. Artificiality, the basic evil of formal education, is amenable to treatment. Those features of incidental and informal education, that are not indissolubly linked with the unspecialized environment, must be introduced into the school. Unless the child feels the genuineness of the activity in which he engages, unless that activity is charged with meaning to him, unless it comes within the range of his life and interests, it is difficult to make the process truly educative. In so far as this vital element fails to be introduced into the work of the school the final outcome of its ministrations, however glibly its victims may repeat the formulæ of the classroom, can be nothing more than sounding brass and tinkling cymbal. Only to the degree that the pupil enters wholeheartedly into the life of the school and reacts vigorously to its curriculum, will the aims of education be fulfilled.

The second great evil towards which the school is inclined, is that of making adjustments to the world of the dead rather than to the world of the living. Since the days of the initiation ceremony formal education has perpetuated the folkways. In them the group has always had supreme confidence, and through them the group has always exerted its authority. Two great attributes of the folkways are fixity and finality. In them therefore we see the negation of progress — a deep-seated mistrust of that process of continuous change upon which the advance of mankind depends. These practices of course, have always contained much of worldly wisdom, but they are very imperfect and in constant need of revision. They are foreign to the genius of education; they are far too rigid to render the highest service in the world of to-day. Our attitude towards them must undergo radical alteration. We need a new type of education — an education that recognizes frankly the temporary nature of all that is. Whatever may have been the conditions of primitive life, or of the life of the day before yesterday, we are certain that the world of the present is moving. We know of a surety that in another generation the conditions of human life on the earth will be greatly changed through an application of the logic of inventions already made and of others certain to follow; but what the aspect of this new world will be in detail nobody knows, the guess of the stupid being only less trustworthy than that of the wise.

The educator of to-day, as he faces this situation, could learn much from the ways of nature. She, having wrought into the organism certain fixed modes of response to life's conditions and discovering the limitations of such a form of adaptation, may be said to have turned her attention to the much more difficult but fruitful task of creating an adjustable mechanism capable of gradually working out adaptations to varied and changing situations. The same methodology must be exhibited by that serviceable education which would adapt man to the world of to-morrow. Instead of being perfectly adjusted to any particular environment, his educational equipment should be made as flexible as possible. Rather than stress perfect adjustment, we should emphasize perfect adjustability. In the world of the future the individual will require many habits, but habits that serve rather than habits that govern. Thus, by placing trust in his extraordinary gift of intelligence, man will reverse the process of education in its beginnings, and, by bending his energies to the removal of obstacles blocking his progress, move forward to a happier world.

What must be the foundations of a sound educational program? In the past the development of education has proceeded in response to the more immediate and pressing demands of the environment. As a rule the shaping of educational policy and institutions has not rested on a thorough consideration of educational needs. Society has usually provided for no more education than was required by the dictates of convention and the demands of powerful interests. In actual practice its possibilities as a great positive social force have seldom been recognized. Our own educational system, with its varied forms and activities, has grown up without design; in very large measure it is a product of the blind give and take of circumstance. Institutions which originated for one purpose have been turned to the achievement of others. At no time have we exhibited a strong educational consciousness; never have we vigorously and wholemindedly set ourselves to the task of bringing education into relation with modern life. But, if the school is to render that very exceptional service to society which lies latent within it to-day, this task must be undertaken. Without delay we should seek the formulation of an educational program bold in its conception and humane in its outlook.

This program must be based on patient study of the nature of the individual and of society. It should be so shaped as to take into strict account the forces which condition the growth of the human organism from birth to maturity. Taking its departure from the inborn equipment of man, it must seek, in accordance with the laws of his development, to bring into being an individual educated to participate effectively and sympathetically in the social life of his time. This program must consequently reflect the social situation in which man is placed to-day. We may advantageously think of human activities as centering about six great interests — health, family, industry, citizenship, recreation, and religion. Through a balanced participation in all of these six fields of activity the nature of the individual finds fulfillment; and, through the gradual perfecting of these interests, the race moves onward. Hence an education that is related to life, an education that is life, must introduce man to these activities, for *they* are life. In the three remaining divisions of this volume we shall attempt a somewhat elaborate analysis of man and society, and then draw in broad outline the educational program suggested by this analysis.

ADDITIONAL PROBLEMS FOR DISCUSSION

1. Illustrate from your own experience powers socially acquired: (1) without any conscious attempt at teaching on the part of others; (2) through the efforts of others outside any formal educational agency; (3) through the instrumentality of the school.

2. Why is there an intimate relation between the growth of culture and the duration of education? Why would a twelve-year period of formal education have been an absurdity under primitive social conditions?

3. How has the steady growth of culture made increasingly necessary the education of specialists?

4. Why in modern society has education for leadership been supplemented by some form of education for all?

5. Justify the statement that the process of formal education is the "initiation ceremony of the Great Society."

6. How has the growth of culture been dependent on the development of oral and written speech? Show how this development has rendered inadequate the methods of incidental education.

7. Explain in detail the meaning of Dewey's statement that the school is a simplified, a purified, and a broadened environment.

8. What in your own educational experience justifies the statement that the school is artificial in its methods and motivation, and conservative in its administration and influence?

9. On what grounds would you defend the introduction of any particular subject into the curriculum of the elementary school?

10. Why are the more advanced countries moving towards the goal of extending secondary education to all children?

11. What are the educational functions which the college, as a selective and formal agency, should perform?

12. Why from the earliest times has professional education made exacting demands on the formal agencies? Why has the number of professional occupations been greatly increased during the last century?

13. How are the methods of education employed in the school superior to those used in incidental education?

14. Comment on the statement made by Bernard Shaw that "He who can, does; he who cannot, teaches."

15. Justify the statement of H. G. Wells that the teacher is the most important person in society.

16. What may be said for and against the proposition that the State should support education by public taxation and control it through its representatives?

PART TWO

WHAT ARE THE PSYCHOLOGICAL FOUNDA-
TIONS OF EDUCATION?

MAN owes the favored position which he occupies in the animal kingdom and in the world to his inheritance of a peculiar array of reflexes, instincts and capacities. These inborn tendencies, by making him extremely sensitive to small differences in environmental stimulation, cause him to lead a restless, inquisitive and creative existence. Due to the interplay of these inborn tendencies with environmental forces, habits eventuate which modify later behavior. This modifiability conditions versatility. As behavior becomes dependent on the higher forms of habit integration involving the symbolism of language, the adaptive process termed thought or reflection is predominant. Adequate adjustment demands reaction to the more remote social implications of the situation, implications which can only be manifest to the thinker. As a result of habit formation and reflection in the countless experiences of life, man's behavior becomes modified almost beyond the limits of recognition. Particularly the approval and disapproval of his fellows mould his conduct to a social form. The results of these experiences are reflected in personality or character. Naturally so complicated an experience is liable to show abnormalities which manifest themselves in unbalanced or anti-social conduct. Effective guidance of the learning process requires a prolonged period of guardianship, in which the child is freed from the more pressing economic demands. Physiological infancy covers ten to fifteen years, but social infancy may in modern society cover a third of the span of life. The nature of the guidance and education given during this period is the outstanding problem of society, because upon education hangs the fate of civilization. This problem is much complicated by the diverse activities and occupations of modern life, and by the great differences in original capacities possessed by men. To adjust the multiform varieties of human talent to the multiform activities and opportunities of life, and by so doing to satisfy each individual and advance the common good, is the highest service each succeeding generation can render to the generation which it begets.

An understanding of the psychological foundations of education requires the discussion of the following problems:

PROBLEM 5. HOW IS EDUCATION CONDITIONED BY ORIGINAL NATURE?

PROBLEM 6. HOW IS EDUCATION CONDITIONED BY HABIT FORMATION?

PROBLEM 7. HOW IS EDUCATION CONDITIONED BY LANGUAGE?

PROBLEM 8. HOW IS EDUCATION CONDITIONED BY REFLECTION?

PROBLEM 9. HOW DOES PERSONALITY EMERGE THROUGH EDUCATION?

PROBLEM 10. HOW IS EDUCATION CONDITIONED BY PROLONGED GUARDIANSHIP?

PROBLEM 11. HOW IS EDUCATION CONDITIONED BY INDIVIDUAL DIFFERENCES?

PROBLEM 5

HOW IS EDUCATION CONDITIONED BY ORIGINAL NATURE?

How does man's behavior reflect his inner drives? — How do these inborn tendencies differ in complexity? — Why is it so difficult to catalogue these inborn tendencies? — What common errors vitiate the ordinary classification? — What rôle do the emotions play? — What is the relation of instinct to consciousness? — How may an instinct be described? — Why is it difficult to isolate the instinctive element in behavior? — What is the simplest picture of human motivation? — What factors complicate final behavior? — How is education conditioned by original nature? — How may the rôle of instinct be overemphasized?

How does man's behavior reflect his inner drives? Man spends all his days in a valiant struggle to satisfy his imperious wants. On entering the world the first inner tension is relieved by crying; he eats, drinks, fights, loves, mates, and thinks, to relieve other tensions; and on his death bed, in the act of blessing his family, he relieves a last tension. The play is meaningless unless interpreted in terms of desire, appetite, yearning, and passion. To explain human action as an environmental moulding of a sluggish, inert, and passive individual is to misread the whole process. Only because man is so helpless at birth, and because so many of his powers are latent, has this strange idea found a foothold in the popular mind. Man's nature is not to be compared with a mass of putty in the hands of the moulder. It has dynamic properties whereby it repairs itself; it is not like the elements of the inorganic world, " kicked around " by external forces. Rather is it to be likened to an explosive compound which, unless carefully handled and studied, is liable at any moment to dissipate itself and damage its surroundings. What are these inborn dynamic properties which, under the stimulation of the material and social environment, quicken, agitate, and make effervescent the process of living?

What are the inborn dynamic properties of man? Were it possible to answer this question by saying that man inherits eight or ten perfectly distinct tendencies to react, just as he inherits two separate kidneys, our problem would be simple. We should then be able to catalogue these tendencies and, allowing for the effect of experience upon them, interpret all behavior in terms of their action and reaction upon one another. While such a simple presentation works for clarity, it conveys such an erroneous conception of the original equipment that the student must be guarded against it. Unfortunately the picture of the human mechanism that we shall be compelled to draw will lack both the brevity and simplicity of this false teaching.

Man is born into the world with a definite physiological structure. This structure contains mechanisms which cause him to make certain responses when he is submitted to various situations. To these sets of structure, with their corresponding functional possibilities, the terms reflex and instinct have been applied. The colorless phrase — a set of the structure — gives a much truer account of the nature of the instinct than do the statements of many authors who write almost as though the instincts were disembodied forces which, by some miracle, control the behavior. Instincts only exist when some one is attending, feeling, or acting in a specific situation. The instinct is the behavior. The animistic terms we are bound to apply must not lead the reader away from this important point — the behavior is not in scientific literalness caused by the instinct; to postulate an instinct is only a convenient way of saying that here is a certain set of structure, which, when stimulated, produces a certain type of behavior. On account of these mechanisms man will become hungry and cry for food, he will spit out any acid substance that is put into the mouth, he will register fear when suddenly dropped, anger when tightly held, he will utter strange sounds, he will seek the company of others, he will at a certain stage of his growth exhibit characteristic sex behavior, and so we might continue the list of typical activities.

How do these inborn tendencies further adjustment? There can be no question that these responses to stimulation of the environment and to stimulation from inside the organism itself, by relieving tensions which arise in the body, serve in general to further the life process. Only because man is endowed with these countless mechanisms, which are capable of being modified by training, is he able to adjust himself to his environment. To a consideration of these fundamental mechanisms attention must now be directed.

How do these inborn tendencies differ in complexity? A cursory examination of the behavior of a young child reveals the fact that there are great differences in the number and complexity of the mechanisms which contribute to various characteristic types of action. Starting with a very simple type, such as that found in the closing of the eye on the near approach of an object, we may note that the minor mechanisms which contribute to such a response are relatively few in number and fixed in manner of operation. Such a combination of mechanisms is called a reflex. In a less simple type of behavior, such as that shown by a young child when made thoroughly angry, many more minor mechanisms are required to bring about the response, and this response is not so fixed as that found in reflex action. To such a grouping of mechanisms which, when adequately stimulated, produce without training a fairly definite group of responses, the term instinct is applied.

Instinct, rigorously defined, is a complex response determined wholly by inherited structure. As such a description of the reflex and instinct clearly shows, there is no sharp line of demarcation which divides the two. The reflex involves but comparatively few mechanisms, while the instinct requires the functioning and integrating of a large number of smaller reaction units. These response integrations are dependent on an inherited pattern in the reaction system which serves as the physiological basis of the instinct. Under appropriate stimulation the instinct reveals itself in a series of activities which, in their manifestation, follow a definite order. The nature and order of these activities are independent of experience. In the language of McDougall, the presence of the instinct causes the individual, without training, to attend to certain objects of the environment, to feel in a certain way towards these objects, and to react to them in a characteristic manner. It is the presence of the instinct that lowers the threshold of stimulation. To attempt to explain why the child becomes angry when tightly held is as stupid as it is futile to wonder why the dog is so violent in his reactions to the rat and so apathetic to the frog. The answer to both of these questions must be found in certain hereditary pattern reactions.

Why is it so difficult to catalogue these inborn tendencies? That man inherits a repertoire of reflexes and instincts, and that all his future powers evolve from modifications and elaborations of this repertoire, every one in practice agrees. But as to the exact cataloguing of this repertoire there is the greatest difference of opinion. To see how inevitable is this disagreement as to what constitutes the instinctive equipment of man is not difficult. As we have already stated, the body is the seat of a host of reaction mechanisms. An infinite mind studying human behavior would clearly recognize and definitely label each one of these behavior-patterns. Such a mind, because of its ability to grasp each of these mechanisms separately and in its relations, would not have to resort, as the finite mind must, to the expedient of grouping certain of these reaction units together and attaching definite names to these somewhat arbitrary arrangements. There would be no need, except in the interests of economy, to speak of the instinct of flight, the instinct of fighting, the instinct of curiosity, etc., for these tendencies would be thought of in terms of the behavior-units from which they are built.

What common errors vitiate the ordinary classification? If this were possible, the two following errors would be avoided which at the present moment are made by many educational and social psychologists:

(1) The error of regarding the instinct as a definite isolated entity, and not as an arbitrary grouping of certain forms of reaction; and

(2) The error of supposing that many forms of behavior are manifestations of the instinct in its unmodified form, while, in reality the behavior is partly the result of habit formation.

The first error is exhibited by the psychologists who, disregarding the fact that only to arbitrary groupings of mechanisms, resulting in certain general forms of behavior, may the terms flight, repulsion, curiosity, etc., be assigned, furnish a perfectly definite and final list of supposedly easily isolated instincts. Thus each writer furnishes a very different list of what he is pleased to term the fundamental instincts of man.

This simple and obvious fact accounts for the wide discrepancies in the lists furnished by various authors. One will explain behavior on the basis of three wide instincts, such as sex, herd, and self, while another will furnish a list covering a number of pages. Both are viewing the same mechanism, and their analyses are both made in the attempt to classify human conduct; one has made a very general analysis of the behavior machine, while the other has embarked on a description of the smaller contributing mechanisms.

How detailed, then, should the analysis be? Convenience and the specific purpose for which the analysis is being made must determine the answer. The analysis must not be so general as to furnish an inadequate basis for an understanding of the complexity of original behavior; on the other hand, it must not be so detailed as to hamper the explanatory process. It is as absurd to describe man's original behavior in terms of a single instinct of sex as to explain it in terms of the interaction of a thousand tendencies. There is a happy mean and, for convenience of thought, this mean should veer in the direction of a list of tendencies sufficiently few in number to make each one fairly inclusive in its scope.

The second error is so universal that it has made the term instinct one of the loosest in psychological literature. In the study of all save the youngest children it is impossible to say just what is original and what is acquired in any response. Instinct is, when used strictly, a most definite concept. Rigidly defined, it is a tendency, apart from all training, to attend to certain objects, to feel in a certain way towards these objects, and to act in a characteristic manner towards them. The difficulty resides in the statement " apart from all training." A child cannot be brought up *in vacuo*, and so there is room for endless and fruitless discussion as to whether a particular reaction observed at any time is original, or a slight modification of original tendencies.

How may these tendencies be conveniently classified? We shall avoid both errors by the following statement. With the minimum of stimulation afforded by the simplest environment, every individual will exhibit, in varying degrees, behavior-phenomena indicative of tendencies [1] which may roughly and arbitrarily be classified as follows:

TENDENCIES	ACCOMPANYING EMOTIONAL STATES
To fight	Anger
To flee, or be paralyzed	Fear
To mate	Lust
To be self-assertive	Arrogance
To be submissive	Humility
To be curious	Wonder
To be repulsed	Disgust
To cherish	Tenderness
To seek the company of others	Sociability

Because this classification is designed to form the basis of an understanding of complex conduct, it does not include excretion, such tendencies as those accompanying the simpler organic processes of breathing, seeking food, drink, warmth, etc.; nor is mention made of the tendencies to vocalize which manifest themselves as part of so many of the other tendencies, and from which evolve the delicate language mechanisms upon which communication of thought and thought itself become so intimately dependent.

No one is in a position to state, with reference to any of these forms of behavior, what precisely is the contribution of original nature and what has been superimposed by the experience of the individual. Nor can this debatable point be settled here; it is sufficient to call attention to the fact that there are groups of mechanisms corresponding to each one of these tendencies which are called forth by the appropriate internal or external stimulus. These tendencies, when each is interpreted widely, furnish a list which is reasonably useful in classifying human behavior.

What rôle do the emotions play? So far, merely a passing

[1] The descriptive terms covering these tendencies, and particularly the emotional states, are extremely vague and misleading unless the reader realizes that they are taken ready-made from a language which has read into each a wealth of meaning and intellectual significance which is necessarily absent in the term as used of an original or "near-original" tendency.

mention has been made of the emotional state which accompanies the stimulation of these tendencies. We have
called attention to the fact that a particular tendency not
only causes the individual to pay attention to a particular
type of stimulation, and to make certain observable reactions as a result of this stimulation, but we have also stated
that a characteristic feeling accompanies the process.
These emotions are to be traced to sensations aroused by
the bodily changes which follow directly upon the stimulation. Thus, when an individual is aroused to a state of anger, within the organism certain visceral tensions are set up
and particular glandular secretions are called forth. These
changes serve to brace the organism for the conflict. To
the sensations which accompany these bodily changes the
strong and characteristic feelings of anger must be traced.
Furthermore these tensions, with their corresponding elements in consciousness, serve to carry on the activity and to
impart to it its specific drive. Were it not for these peculiar
emotional disturbances life, if possible at all, would be lived
or rather endured on a vegetative level. Man might derive
benefit from the absence of certain harmful feelings attending the arousal of fear and anger, but he would lose the joys
and thrills which accompany the satisfaction of other tendencies. These emotional disturbances furnish the drive and
serve as the motivation of the elaborate life-long process of
habit formation upon which learning depends. In fact the
chief function served by these tendencies in promoting adjustment to a complex environment is to initiate activities
which, through conflict, lead to new forms of behavior.

How differentiated is emotional reaction? Whether the
majority of these tendencies carry with them their own
unique emotional state is a matter of dispute. We realize
that when fighting we are angry, when fleeing we are afraid,
when caressing and fondling we are experiencing tender

feelings, when mating we are moved by lust, etc. While certain of these emotional states have been carefully studied, our knowledge is very fragmentary and does not permit us to assume that each one of these tendencies has its own peculiar and separate emotional accompaniment. The work of Cannon and Watson would suggest that there are but few fundamental emotional reactions, prominent among which are love, rage, and fear. These, presumably, are compounded together in various proportions to form the particular emotional state which the individual experiences when stimulated.

What is the relation of instinct to consciousness? Having considered the emotional accompaniment of the excitation of an instinct, we should mention in passing the dispute that has arisen concerning the relation of consciousness to the instinctive process. This dispute is due to the twofold manner in which the term consciousness has been interpreted. The instinctive process is certainly not conscious, if by this term we mean that the individual clearly anticipates, when the behavior-pattern is first stimulated, the nature of the end or outcome of the act. On the other hand, it is distinctly conscious in the sense that there is a keen awareness of certain stimulation, and of the movements involved in the course of the instinctive action. In fact it may be said that consciousness is at its height at those times when certain of the more intense instincts are aroused.

How may an instinct be described? To return to the main issue, each one of these tendencies that we have listed impels its possessor to make certain characteristic responses to certain fairly definite types of internal and external stimulation, and it also impels him to make aggressive search for stimulation. In illustration of the former a few of the typical situations and the characteristic responses which are connected with the manifestation of fear may be cited.

That the infant reacts to the situation created by "being suddenly dropped," or subjected to a "loud noise," with many of the usual signs of fear is a well-established fact. Such a careful writer as Thorndike claims that "on the whole it seems likely that an unlearned tendency exists to respond by the physical and mental condition known as fear to the situation, thunder-storm, reptiles, large animal approaching one, certain vermin, darkness, and strange persons of unfriendly mien." The more observable responses in the case of this instinct are numerous, including running to cover, clutching, clinging, nestling, remaining stock still, being semi-paralyzed, falling down, raising the eyebrows, sweating, manifesting diminished action of the salivary glands, exhibiting erection of the hair, etc. Similarly each one of the other tendencies could be analyzed in terms of situations and responses. For such an account the student is referred to one of the standard text-books of psychology.

Why is it difficult to isolate the instinctive element in behavior? Careful study of the situations and the responses which are listed by most authors as characteristic of any particular instinct raises the question to which reference has already been made. Is not the potency of a large number of these situations to be ascribed to the effects of experience? Is their potency not to be traced to acquired reaction-patterns rather than to truly original tendencies? Watson's recent work on very young children seems to suggest that but few original situations are liable to cause fear, and that we must attribute the long list of supposedly original excitants of fear to the effects of learning and not to original nature. Just as the adult learns to be afraid of the dentist's chair, so the child, under an environment which cannot fail to provide the adequate situations, learns to be afraid of animals, darkness, and crawling insects. In fact, owing to the ready manner in which the individual learns, it is almost impossible to decide what is truly instinctive behavior. Unless the particular reaction is observed on its first appearance and under conditions controlled with extreme care, when seen at a later time, it is already changed by experience and has ceased to be truly instinctive in its nature. Most of the instincts about which the social and educational psychologists write, and to which they trace the motivation of human conduct, are not unalloyed instincts at all, but rather behavior-patterns created out of the original patterns by the effects of a simple environment — an environment so necessary to life that it may be regarded as being approximately uniform for all individuals. To such combinations, which grow out of the original instinct even in the simplest environments, the term "instinct-habit consolidation" has been aptly given. From many points of view it is of little practical concern whether a particular phase of behavior can be traced to the purely instinctive fear-mechanism or to the instinct-habit-fear consolidation. Certain it is that, at the age of five or six, most children will be afraid of other than original excitants of fear. These instinct-habit consolidations, which appear to grow with the minimum stimulation out of the original instinct may, when they are once formed, be regarded as the raw material of education and be treated almost as if they were inborn.

What is the simplest picture of human motivation? Bearing in mind the facts that we have just stated, we may now focus attention on the simple picture of the original equipment to which reference was made at the opening of the discussion. We may now, without fear of great error, conceive of man as possessing, and being driven through the stimulation of, the tendencies which we have listed as well as through other tendencies which escape the broad classification supplied by our list. Given the adequate situation, these tendencies not only carry the mechanism for their arousal, but also the necessary energy or drive to keep them in operation.

What factors complicate final behavior?   The complexity of man's final behavior must be traced to three causes:

(1) The large number of tendencies to action;

(2) The modification through habit formation of these separate tendencies from the standpoint of the situation calling them forth, as well as from the standpoint of the overt responses accompanying their excitation;

(3) The interaction of these tendencies, due to an environmental stimulation which is usually so complex as to call forth, at any particular time, many of these tendencies.

At all times, in considering human behavior, it should be remembered that even under a narrow stimulation the whole organism reacts.   Convenience necessitates isolation for purposes of thought, but the unity of the organism must never be forgotten.

How does the process of modification take place?   On account of certain instinctive tendencies man will, wholly without training, be made violently afraid by sudden and loud noises; he will exhibit curiosity in a brightly colored object that is dangled before him; he will when roused fight in random fashion with his arms and legs.   With a minimum of training he will show his fear of darkness and animals; he will direct his curiosity to all kinds of pictures; and he will readily learn to defend himself and attack others with an orderly system of arm-and-fist movements.   If he is educated carefully, he may be taught to be afraid of attractive and sparkling waters the purity of which is unknown; his attention may be directed to a tedious and laborious research; and he may learn to fight his deadly enemy with the refined instruments of rhetoric and the slow process of the law.   Only as initially we can use the drive attaching to these original tendencies, and later as we can use the drive attached to acquired tendencies which have evolved from the original ones, can we train and educate the individual.

How is education conditioned by original nature? Though the instinctive basis of his conduct becomes increasingly less and less obvious as habit formation and intelligence modify and direct its original modes of expression, human life is permeated through and through with instinctive action.   This instinctive equipment, regarded by certain stern moralists as essentially bad, viewed by certain irresponsible lovers of liberty as essentially good, furnishes the only groundwork for the process of training and education.   To eradicate these innate tendencies is no more possible than to allow them an uncharted liberty.   Any system of education or morals is certain to fail unless it recognizes these inextinguishable forces.   By adapting its methods it must exercise, curb, modify, and harness them for the achievement of its purposes.

> "The common problem, yours, mine, everyone's,
> Is not to fancy what were fair in life,
> Provided it could be — but, finding first
> What may be, then find how to make it fair
> Up to our means — a very different thing."

To spend time evaluating the equipment is futile; whether we like it or not, this equipment is the raw material of the educative process.   Because of the similarity among all men of this original equipment, the behavior of diverse races and peoples remains much the same.   As Bryce, in his *Modern Democracies*, has said: [1]

There is in the phenomena of human society one "Constant," one element or factor which is practically always the same, and

---

[1] Bryce, James: *Modern Democracies*, vol. I, p. 94.

therefore the basis of all the so-called "Social Sciences." This is Human Nature itself. All fairly normal men have like passions and desires. They are stirred by like motives, they think upon similar lines. When they have reached the stage of civilization in which arts and letters have developed, and political institutions have grown up, reason has become so far the guide of conduct, that sequences in their action can be established and their behavior under given conditions can to some extent be foretold. Human nature is that basic and ever-present element in the endless flux of social and political phenomena which enables general principles to be determined. And though the action of individual men may often be doubtful, the action of a hundred or a thousand men all subjected to the same influences at the same time may be much more predictable, because in a large number the idiosyncrasies of individuals are likely to be eliminated or evened out.

The great institutions, such as the family, the church, the school, and the theater exist to give economical and social expression to the instincts of man. While the more primitive of these must be rigorously curbed, repression as a method of social control is only tolerable in so far as it is the necessary accompaniment of a more adequate and satisfying type of expression. Re-direction of native impulses rather than repression is, as a rule, the wiser policy.

Allowing for this process of modification we may say with McDougall: [1]

that directly or indirectly the instincts are the prime movers of all human activity; by the impulsive force of some instinct, or of some habit derived (either directly or remotely) from an instinct, every bodily activity is both initiated and carried along towards its end. The instinctive impulses determine the ends of all activity and supply the driving power by which these ends are attained.

Education can build only on the original equipment. Using the inherited tendencies, it must teach the individual to react to many situations to which nature provides no

[1] McDougall, William: *Social Psychology*, p. 44.

adequate response; it must teach him to make many complicated responses which in combined form are not present in the original repertoire of reactions; it must teach him to find satisfaction in a multitude of activities which make no direct emotional appeal to primitive man. It is because the individual inherits such a marvelous modifiability as an essential property of his instinctive system that the behavior of civilized man is so different in different environments and always so far removed from that of the savage.

How may the rôle of instinct be overemphasized? Dewey, considering the relative social significance of instinct and habit, while admitting the importance of the former, emphasizes the opposite point of view from Bryce when he calls attention to the fact that the modes through which original nature expresses itself may follow the most diverse patterns. He says: [1]

At some place on the globe, at some time, every kind of practice seems to have been tolerated or even praised. How is the tremendous diversity of institutions, including moral codes, to be accounted for? The native stock of instincts is practically the same everywhere. Exaggerate as much as we like the native differences of Patagonians and Greeks, Sioux Indians and Hindoos, Bushmen and Chinese, their original differences will bear no comparison to the amount of difference found in custom and culture. Since such a diversity cannot be attributed to an original identity, the development of native impulse must be stated in terms of acquired habits, not the growth of customs in terms of instincts.

Such considerations as these are often overlooked in naïve attempts to reduce social behavior to the direct manifestation of instincts. At the risk of being misunderstood, we may say, original nature determines the animal, but habit formation creates man. To this question of the modification of original nature by habit we must now turn.

[1] Dewey, John: *Human Nature and Conduct*, p. 91.

ADDITIONAL PROBLEMS FOR DISCUSSION

1. Why is it impossible to draw a sharp line of distinction between reflex action and instinctive action?

2. What is the physiological basis of instinct? How can an instinct be regarded as a mechanism?

3. Why have students of human nature abandoned the old practice of explaining conduct in terms of "an instinct of self preservation?" What type of instinctive behavior could not be classified under this broad category?

4. Why is it more consistent with the mechanistic conception of behavior to speak of "tendencies to fight," rather than a single "tendency to fight"?

5. What original tendencies in modified form are obviously expressed or repressed in the following occupations? (1) Physician; (2) the parent; (3) the capitalist; (4) the common laborer; (5) the labor agitator; (6) the miser; (7) the philanthropist; (8) the sister of mercy; (9) the scientist; (10) the gambler; (11) the politician; (12) the private soldier; (13) the general; (14) the explorer; (15) the statesman; (16) the stamp collector; (17) the professional pugilist; (18) the amateur sportsman; (19) the executioner; (20) the priest; (21) the ascetic; (22) the libertine; (23) the teacher; (24) the grade pupil; (25) the research student.

6. What justification is there for the statement that modern civilization demands the eradication of many of the instinctive tendencies? In the absence of war, what outlet would be provided for those tendencies which war calls forth?

7. What happens when an instinctive tendency is thwarted?

8. Why, under the old-fashioned type of rigorous education, was it easy to gain the idea that the child was "sluggish, inert, and passive? How does modern education recognize the inner properties of the child?

9. In a high school, what instinctive tendencies in modified form are involved in the following situations? (1) The giving and receiving of marks and grades; (2) the promotion of students; (3) co-education; (4) the disciplining of students; (5) the study of civics; (6) secret societies; (7) participation in athletics; (8) dancing parties; (9) truancy.

10. Why is it extremely difficult to distinguish between action which is purely instinctive, and action which is a combination of instinct and habit?

11. How do you reconcile the position of Bryce and Dewey as stated in the text?

12. How can modern society, in the interests of human happiness encourage the expression of the creative rather than the acquisitive tendencies?

PROBLEM 6

HOW IS EDUCATION CONDITIONED BY HABIT FORMATION?

How does the behavior of civilized man differ from that of the savage? — What is the widest conception of habit? — How do original tendencies function in habit formation? — How does trial and error function in habit formation? — How do old habits function in the formation of new habit systems? — What forces resist the formation of new habits? — How do habit systems integrate? — How does the external situation function in habit formation? — What general rules should control habit formation? — What are the ethical implications of habit formation? — How do language habits refine behavior?

How does the behavior of civilized man differ from that of the savage? Each generation witnesses the transformation of a potential savage into a responsible citizen. Only the frequency of this process blinds us to the miracle. The problem with which we are now concerned is, What is the nature of this process which modifies, almost beyond the limits of recognition, the original behavior of man? Answering this question in the broadest fashion we may say that:

(1) The responses of the cultured to any particular situation vary markedly from those of the untrained individual.

(2) The cultured man reacts to and finds significant many situations which to the untrained are virtually nonexistent.

The untutored is as incapable of understanding the studied restraint of the cultivated man when angry, as he is mystified by the absorbed attention which a few hieroglyphics on a piece of parchment can command in the person of literary habits. In the words of Plato: " Man, if he

enjoys a right education and a happy endowment, becomes
the most divine and civilized of all living beings; but he is
the most savage of all the products of the earth if he is
inadequately and improperly trained." And Santayana
makes the same point: " the intelligent man known to history flourishes within a dullard and holds a lunatic at leash."

What is the widest conception of habit? Through a process of training a situation derives a significance, it acquires
a meaning, it calls forth a response which is not linked with
it by original nature. On the physiological side, all habit,
memory, and association phenomena may be reduced to the
simple concept of the organism acquiring certain connections
— connections which cause it to meet a situation with a
response that is not native, or cause it to react to a situation
which has only become significant because of training.
The connections may be the precipitate of:

(1) A process akin to animal learning.

(2) A process involving what are commonly called ideas.

(3) A process of reasoning (reflection).

In these pages the term habit will be made to include all
effects on behavior of the physiological traces left in the
nervous system as a result of these three processes working
alone or in combination. Habit is the modification of behavior — executive, emotional and intellectual — consequent
upon experience.

**How does this wide conception differ from the popular
notion of habit?** To the extent that the so-called popular
instincts are not original modes of response, but rather
habit-consolidations built up by a simple and uniform experience, the subject of habit formation gains in importance.
It is to the slow but continuous changes made in the original
equipment, to the series of habits developing from the native
impulses, to the acquired behavior-patterns built up neu-
rone-mosaic-fashion out of the original behavior-patterns

that the complexity of the adult's conduct must be ascribed. A habit in this wide psychological sense is nothing more than a disposition left by previous experience. Even though the effect of later experience may wipe away all apparent trace of the ephemeral change, every response that is made forms a habit. To restrict habit formation, as is popularly done, to certain sensori-motor connections which by repetition become relatively automatic and fixed in their nature, is to miss the psychological significance of habit formation. Even though a particular reaction — executive, emotional or intellectual — is made but once, however fleeting may be its nature, some trace is left. In this process is the essential mechanism of habit formation. The number of times the connection may be made is merely a quantitative matter; as we employ the term, whether the connection is used once or a million times, the process of habit formation appears.

Convenience suggests that separate words be employed to distinguish popular from scientific usage, but it is too late to make such a distinction. What has just been said must serve to warn the reader against the narrow conception of this term. To repeat, any change made in the nervous system through learning, however slight this may be, constitutes a habit; whether it be a transitory and fugitive change or one that is deeply rooted, it is a habit nevertheless. Throughout the discussion of education the use of habit in this double sense will be necessary, but in every case the context will make clear whether reference is to the mere fact of making, at a particular time, a connection but once, or to the fact of so firmly establishing this connection as to form a habit in the ordinary sense. If the term habit be used to cover all the connections made in the nervous system as the result of experience, it will readily be seen that the phenomena of memory and association must receive their explanation on the physiological side from the study of habit formation.

How do original tendencies function in habit formation? While the large fact is patent that all acquired tendencies can be nothing more than the outgrowth of the original tendencies, the manner in which habits evolve from simple native unit-reactions tends to be fogged by the presence, at any particular time, in the older child or adult of a vast number of habits previously formed. That the process, shorn of all complications, may be seen, a few illustrations of the acquisition of very simple habits — habits so simple indeed as to bring out the obvious instinctive nature of the contributing mechanisms — will be given.

Pavlow's famous experiment on salivary flow in the dog will provide a point of departure. In this experiment, by taking a healthy dog in which the taste of food produced a plentiful flow of saliva, Pavlow devised a technique whereby the actual quantity of the secretion could be measured. The original or adequate stimulus of such a flow is, of course, the taste of meat. Now suppose, over a number of trials, the animal is stimulated by a light and immediately afterwards fed. Experiment shows that after a short period of training the meat is not necessary to start the secretion. The light, by itself, is sufficient stimulus. In this experiment the process of learning is reduced to its simplest terms. A situation — stimulation by light — having by native endowment not the slightest effect on the response — flow of saliva — becomes connected with it, and, after a period of training, causes the animal to react in a definite way to a previously neutral and indifferent stimulus.

Such a substitution of stimulus cannot be effected unless at the beginning the experimenter can provide the original stimulus to call forth the response. A homely illustration will make this clear. Consider the difficulty which would be experienced by the reader in associating the movement of the ears with a verbal command. This difficulty is to be traced to the relative impossibility of finding an original stimulus which will cause the ears to move. The relative impossibility in this case should be compared with the ease with which the eyelid can be trained to close in response to a verbal suggestion. The process of habit formation is limited by the modes of response which are native to the individual; only as certain responses are physiologically possible and only, then, as they are capable of being called forth, can habit systems be constructed.

Another simple case of habit formation will further the discussion. Suppose a child of two years is, for the first time, brought into a room where a steam radiator is in use. The child, stimulated by the sight of the unfamiliar object, will in the process of exploration approach and touch it; in the most general way it is permissible to say that certain of the responses loosely associated with curiosity have been called forth. On touching the object the child, experiencing the painful sensations of burning, exhibits an avoidance response. The sight of the radiator, after one or two experiences of this kind, will immediately call forth an avoidance reaction. There is a change in the internal structure of the nervous system so that a situation which originally prompted to exploration and manipulation now calls forth a definite response of an opposite character. To add a slight complication to the illustration, we may further suppose that, just as the child is about to touch the radiator, his action attracts the attention of the nurse. Uttering the word " hot," she thereby initiates a process which may result in the association of the mere sound " Hot " with an avoidance response.

How does trial and error function in habit formation? So far only the simplest types of learning have received con-

sideration. A slightly more complex illustration will focus
attention on the manner in which all habit formation is dependent on a trial-and-error process. A child is shown a
metal puzzle box in which he is told a bon-bon has been
placed. On being given the box he at once proceeds, in a
trial-and-error fashion, to use his repertoire of manipula-
tory responses. After some time spent in fruitless effort, anger ensues, and the guarded exploration and manipulation
give place to coarser random movements. Eventually in
despair the box is thrown to the ground and stamped upon
in rage. None of these actions avails to open the box and
the child, attracted by some other interest, abandons the
problem. In a few minutes, however, he hears the remark,
" You surely aren't such a baby as to give up." Nettled
into action by this additional stimulation he takes up the
box again, and, after further careful manipulation, discovers
the exact spot which, when pressed, causes the lid to fly
open and the candy to be released. After two or three
further trials the puzzle box will elicit, without delay, the
appropriate response. The long process of trial and error,
the reader will observe, was motivated in this case by a desire for the candy, a certain curiosity, anger, and a desire
for approval. All these drives were necessary to bring the
activity to a successful conclusion.

**How do old habits function in the formation of new habit
systems?** At the hazard of being tedious we must give one
further illustration, which is designed to bring out the manner in which previously acquired habits function in the
formation of more elaborate hierarchies. Imagine a man,
who has played baseball, basketball, and tennis, taking up
the game of football. His first attempts to meet the novel
situations induced by the new game show how the old
habits of judging the flight of the ball, of throwing, of catching, of running and dodging etc. etc., are being used with but

little modification as they were built up in the other games. Initial skill is due to these factors contributed by previous experience.   The individual, however, if he is to become a superior player, will have to modify a large number of these responses in order to meet the conditions peculiar to the game; his action after catching the ball cannot be the same as in basketball, and the hand-and-arm movement must be different from that in baseball.   Furthermore, he will be compelled to break himself of certain habits acquired with great pains in the other games — modes of behavior which positively interfere with the acquirement of skill in the novel sport.   The acquisition of the added skills demands that some of the old skills be used unchanged, that other skills be modified, and that still others be completely eradicated. Legion is the number of adult golfers who find their progress barred by the extreme difficulty which is experienced in " dropping " the baseball or the cricket " swing."

Why is trial and error evident even in the higher forms of habit formation?   In general, when facing some new aspect of the environment, the individual tries a repertoire of inherited and acquired responses until an adequate response relieves the internal tension created by the situation.   Later when the habit is established, it causes the individual to initiate a series of activities which follows a certain well-defined order.   This system of reactions, built up from more elementary reactions, is termed an acquired-reaction pattern.   Often, through the disintegration of a complex habit, certain elements which compose it are released and are made available for further habit formation.   The new habit is nothing more than the integration of a series of separate responses which finally function as a unit.   As the repertoire of habits possessed by the individual increases, and this repertoire becomes available for future habits, the trial-and-error nature of the process becomes obscured.

Nevertheless, as an essential accompaniment of any new adaptation, this method of learning is always present.

What is the physiological basis of habit formation? Perhaps, at the risk of being sketchy, we may make some brief mention of the physiological basis of habit formation by revealing the mechanical process which conditions the acquirement of new modes of response. This may serve to make the phenomenon more intelligible. The nervous system may be regarded as a vast telephone exchange, of which the smallest communicating unit is the *neurone*. Any habit involves a coöperative functioning or a unified action of a large number of these neurones. Each neurone connects with neighboring neurones through a junction of varying resistance, called the " synapse." The fact that a discharge, which originally passed from neurone A to neurone B, now passes from A to C must be ascribed to some alteration, through fatigue, drainage, or other means, in the synapse between A and B. In some way or another a resistance is set up in the latter synapse, which makes the path of least resistance no longer A to B, but A to C. This passage of energy in the new direction alters the synapse more or less permanently, making the path A to C more readily traversable on future occasions. The acquirement of new behavior-patterns must in the last analysis be traced to certain bio-chemical changes which take place at the synapses.

What forces resist the formation of new habits? Habit formation of any kind is dependent on the modifiability of the nervous system. Inability to form new habits must be ascribed to two allied causes. In the first place, the lack may be traced to certain general physiological changes which, occurring with age, prevent the formation of new methods of response. The aged scholar who in spite of strong desire is unable to acquire a new language or a new terminology is a case in point. One can only have compassion on such an individual. But the less kind and more common explanation for most of the lack of modifiability is found in a certain physiological set which, on the psychological side, can only be described as a certain stubbornness or loyalty to old and established habits. The presence of preferential associations formed by past experience gives a sense of adjustment which is illusory, and the individual refuses to overcome the inertia of the old and satisfying " habit ways." The man who is always justifying his conduct by saying that what was good enough for his father is good enough for him, is a sad example of this blocking of new activity by old habits. The scientists in the late eighties and nineties who refused to reorganize their thought in the light of the evolutionary theory cannot be said to have lost their inherent physiological elasticity, but their previous habits of thought bound them to their old moorings and prevented their sailing on new and uncharted seas.

How do habit systems integrate? From hour to hour, day to day, month to month, these countless trial-and-error experiments take place, each one of them making through the synapses certain changes in the inner organization, each one leaving its trace in an acquired behavior-pattern wrought in the physiological structure. From original modes of response, there first develop the very simple habits; with these habits formed the child then proceeds, through the combination and recombination of these more simple patterns, to form further and more complex habits. On the basis of these habit systems the higher forms of habit can then be built up, until, in the most complex form of behavior which man is called upon to initiate, before the responses necessary for successful adjustment are forthcoming, vast numbers or hierarchies of lower habits have to become integrated together. On this account a particular habit system may have but slight terminal value; its desirability resides in its transitional value. It must be judged by its usefulness in facilitating further adaptation. Most habit systems must be progressive, they must lead on to something better. This is the basis of Dewey's statement that the aim of education is to produce capacity for further education.

How does the external situation function in habit formation? From what has been said, two important aspects of habit formation should be apparent. In the first place, habits are not changes which can be thrust upon the individual. The external situations by themselves do not determine what shall be learned; they merely " upset " the organism so that certain responses are initiated. This " commotional state " but serves to rouse the organism to initiate certain more or less random reactions designed to relieve the existing tension. If one type of reaction is not successful, the internal state of tension, though modified, persists, and further reactions are tried, until, eventually, the successful reaction is made. The individual feels the want and registers the sensitivity to the situation; the individual, through the reaction system, initiates the process of trial-and-error learning. An internal tension starts the activity and the final relief from strain, accompanying the successful reaction, closes the activity. Situations can never in the strict sense cause reactions; reactions are expressions of the individual organism.

Why is the individual enslaved by his habit systems? In the second place, habits are not mere additional trappings to be donned or removed at will; habits — motor, emotional, or intellectual — are nothing more than dispositions to react to certain aspects of the environment. The formation of a habit implies the giving of an hostage to the environment; for as long as this habit endures the individual will react, or at least tend to react, in the manner determined by this habit. Just as an instinct is defined as an inborn tendency which compels us to attend to certain objects, and to feel and act in certain ways towards these objects, so a habit, which is not perfectly automatic may well be regarded as an acquired tendency which makes us pay attention to certain objects, to feel in a certain way towards these objects, and to act in a certain way with respect to them.

The similarity between habit and instinct in their effect on behavior is obvious. The peculiar habit, or group of habits, which rides us at any particular moment may seem to be rather arbitrary, but the apparent arbitrariness is to be explained in terms of the internal set of the individual. The internal states produced by previous experience, especially the relatively immediate experiences, are all present to determine which aspect of the situation will claim our attention, and what series of responses will be forthcoming. Unless we consider, at any moment, the state of tension prior to every action, man's conduct, far from being determined by previous experience, appears as free and as variable as the wind. When this factor is taken into account there is every reason to suppose that man, except in earliest infancy, is habit-ridden at every moment of his existence.

The manner in which habits control us is not particularly apparent when we consider such groupings of habits as skating, typewriting, and piano-playing, which are commonly isolated from the main trends of life. Because we can avoid the situations that evoke these responses the idea is easily gained that habits are mere servants to be called upon when they happen to further our purpose, and equally to be held in check when they are not serviceable. To the so-called bad habits we may turn for peculiarly apt illustrations of this point. Smoking, drinking, idling, and backbiting all illustrate the hold which habits can take upon us and the manner in which, perforce, they mould our conduct. Having once formed a thorough dislike for a person, however much we may wish or however much it may be to our advantage to be well disposed towards him, to control our conduct and more particularly our feelings is all but impossible. Having formed a habit of idling, how a host of situations lures us to our wasted hours! On the other hand, our good habits function in the same way; for an industrious man almost any situation arouses the desire to control and direct the sequence of events. So tightly held is man by his habits that, in case they are bad, he is only able to rationalize their fatal effect on his conduct by claiming himself possessed and ridden by the devil; but when good habits are in the saddle, with pardonable partiality, he ascribes his actions to his " better self " and not to the guiding hand of the angels!

What general rules should control habit formation? Interpreting situation and response in the comprehensive manner indicated, we can see that the problem of education and of human engineering consists in building up certain connections within the individual. We choose our schools, we choose our teachers, we choose our subjects, and we frame our institutions in order that this connection-forming may proceed economically and socially. The rules of such a complex process can no more be covered by a few simple statements than the difficult game of diplomacy can be guided by a few wise canons. The art of making and breaking connections is too continuous with the whole process of living to be reduced to a few rubrics. In spite of this obvious fact, attention may be directed to certain helpful rules which serve as guideposts on the road to learning.

The first is the *Rule of Repetition*. In establishing any connection, cause the connection to be made a sufficient number of times to make the bond as strong as is demanded. The second is the *Rule of Distribution of Practice*. In the case of those connections that have to be made relatively permanent, so control the learning as to allow longer and longer intervals of time to elapse between the successive periods of practice, which should become increasingly shorter in duration.

The third is the *Rule of Direct Action.* As far as possible form every connection in the exact form and in the exact setting in which later it is to be employed.

The fourth is the *Rule of General Motivation.* Whenever it is desired to establish connections, so arrange the conditions that satisfaction will accompany or follow the adequate response; and, conversely, that dissatisfaction will accompany or follow the inadequate response.

As a further guide there follows a fifth rule, the *Rule of Self-Motivation.* Whenever possible, so arrange the conditions of learning that the connections established shall be the outcome of self-initiated and self-driven activity, rather than the result of externally-imposed and artificially-motivated labor.

Professor James, in his famous chapter or rather sermon on habit formation, says that the great desideratum is to make our nervous system our ally instead of our enemy. With great effect he points out that habit formation not only simplifies the movements necessary to the achievement of a certain result, but, also, by diminishing the attention necessary to attain this end, enables the individual to give his attention to more complicated features of the situation. Writing with reference to the formation of habits, using habit in the popular sense, he cites the following three maxims:

1. Launch any new habit with as strong and decided initiative as possible.

2. Never suffer an exception to occur until the new habit is securely rooted.

3. Seize every possible opportunity to air the habit until it is securely formed.

What are the ethical implications of habit formation? To show the fundamental rôle played by habit formation in the conduct of the individual, we cannot do better than quote verbatim the passage with which James closes his exhortation. He says: [1]

The physiological study of mental conditions is thus the most powerful ally of hortatory ethics. The hell to be endured here-after, of which theology tells, is no worse than the hell we make for ourselves in this world by habitually fashioning our characters in the wrong way. Could the young but realize how soon they will become mere walking bundles of habits, they would give more heed to their conduct while in the plastic state. We are spinning our own fates, good or evil, and never to be undone. Every smallest stroke of virtue or of vice leaves its never so little scar. The drunken Rip Van Winkle, in Jefferson's play, excuses himself for every fresh dereliction by saying, "I won't count this time!" Well! he may not count it, and a kind Heaven may not count it; but it is being counted none the less. Down among his nerve-cells and fibres the molecules are counting it, registering and storing it up to be used against him when the next temptation comes. Nothing we ever do is, in strict scientific literalness, wiped out. Of course this has its good side as well as its bad one. As we become permanent drunkards by so many separate drinks, so we become saints in the moral, and authorities and experts in the practical and scientific spheres, by so many separate acts and hours of work.

How do language habits refine behavior? As this life-long interplay of restless organism and a changing environment takes place, the process of habit formation continues. Thousands and hundreds of thousands of situations become linked or bound through the acquired structure of the individual with thousands and hundreds of thousands of responses. The situations, at first original in their nature,

[1] James, William: *Psychology*, vol. i, p. 127.

become more and more refined and symbolic until a word heard, read, or spoken, becomes potent in its effect on behavior, and a motto such as *noblesse oblige* may drive the man, attuned to its stirring message, to the most heroic acts of devotion.   In the same manner the responses which are at first crude and gross become increasingly refined and implicit, until a major part of the response of the highly trained adult will, on the physiological side, be found to center in the explicit or implicit language mechanisms.   In the case of a political prisoner, whose death sentence is conveyed to him by means of a few black symbols on a piece of official paper, and whose only overt action to the news is contained in the spoken phrase, " I am ready and glad to die for my cause," we see the extreme manner in which both the situation and the response can be refined.

ADDITIONAL PROBLEMS FOR DISCUSSION

1. What is the distinction between the popular and the scientific usage of the term habit?   In what respects is the latter usage the wider?   Illustrate your answers.
2. Why in the case of the acquirement of a habit on the part of an adult is it so difficult to trace the process back to instinctive origins?
3. What are the physiological mechanisms upon which plasticity depends?   In what way do these mechanisms set bounds to the plasticity of the child?   How was Locke wrong when he spoke of the human mind as a sheet of blank paper on which experience writes?
4. What prompts the individual to form a habit?   Under what conditions does he continue to use the habit?
5. Why, in the case of the formation of new modes of reaction by the adult, is the process of trial-and-error so short-circuited as to be barely noticeable, even when meeting apparently new situations?   Why is it so difficult to get a novel situation for an adult?
6. How can you reconcile the statement of Rousseau that Emile should form but one habit, namely, the habit of forming no habits, with that of James who urges the individual to make automatic as early as possible a large number of habits?
7. Why does the objective situation alone never determine the response?   Show how the same person, at different times depending on his set, will react to the same objective situation in radically different ways.

8. From the standpoint of habit, what justification is there for the statement that the genius, on facing a familiar situation, does not react in the customary manner?

9. How is (a) the learning of French pronunciation: (b) the following of scientific procedure; (c) the learning of algebra; (d) the formation of health habits; and (e) learning to read in the first grade, hindered and helped by habits previously formed?

10. Taking the five arbitrary rules of learning, show in detail how they are followed and violated in the learning process of the classroom. What devices might be employed in recognition of these laws in teaching the multiplication table, a poem, handwriting, or honesty?

PROBLEM 7

HOW IS EDUCATION CONDITIONED BY LANGUAGE?

What is the objective physiological theory of behavior? — What rôle does language play in behavior? — What is thinking? — How does the behaviorist justify his position? — Does his theory cover the facts? — Is behaviorism a helpful methodology? — How may our position be summarized?

What is the objective physiological theory of behavior? The reader may feel that, in the previous treatment, we have beguiled him into a false position in that we have reduced all behavior to the interaction of the physiological mechanisms. Such a position is the logical outcome of the foregoing discussion, and is championed by an influential school of students of human behavior. With the physiological evidence before them which so clearly shows that there can be no psychical process, or consciousness, which is not accompanied by the corresponding neural process — a fact which is usually referred to as the law of psycho-neural parallelism — a large number of psychologists feel themselves forced to go even further and deny the least influence on behavior of the conscious processes. This school contends that if we could get a complete picture, at any time, of the structure of the nervous system, and had a perfect knowledge of the laws of the physical and chemical processes that occur therein, we should be able to account completely for all the conduct of the individual. Put more bluntly, the popular notion that the conscious process of thought in some way presides over behavior and determines its nature is in error.

In view of the fact that so many writers on education, in

laying the foundations of their psychology assume a rigid mechanical physiological theory, and later, without any attempt to pave the way for a complete change in their position or terminology, assume in their subsequent treatment that consciousness affects conduct, the authors have deemed it essential to give this aspect of the behavior problem some slight attention before passing on to the question of the modification of conduct by reflection.

To introduce ourselves to the cogent and attractive arguments of the physiological school, to which reference has been made, we may put an extreme question: Does the conscious process of thought influence behavior, or is such behavior completely explicable in physiological terms? To put the question in a slightly different form: Is the behavior which accompanies thinking explicable wholly in terms of an elaborate interplay of the inherited and acquired habits registered in physiological mechanisms? The first tendency is to conclude that behavior accompanied by thinking and behavior controlled by habits are poles asunder. But, on the other hand, the conscious process called thinking is itself dependent on past habits, especially language habits, and may, it is urged, be conceivably nothing more than an accompaniment of the functioning of a large number of these mechanisms. To help us to see this point, we may note that when a habit or particular group of habits can run itself off in straightforward fashion, thinking and deliberation are at a minimum. But when a situation becomes so intricate as to call forth not one group of habits, but many groups of conflicting habits, then the so-called process of deliberation supervenes. This would at least suggest that thinking may be merely the psychological accompaniment of a clash of habit forces, no one of which is for the time capable of overcoming its opponents and leading to overt action.

To continue the argument and to make this position clearer, we will direct attention to an aspect of habit formation which has already been illustrated. Just as, in the case of the dog and the salivary flow, an indifferent stimulus is substituted for an adequate one, so in the case of the child and the radiator, the word " hot," uttered by the nurse, is made to evoke an avoidance response. May we not suppose that due to this experience the word " hot," when repeated by the child himself, can in the same way call forth this response? Here is the clue to the understanding of the manner in which a language mechanism (saying the word " hot ") may control the behavior (the avoidance response). This is a very simple illustration of the way in which the physiological mechanisms of language begin to take their place with other mechanisms and through the process of integration begin to exert a powerful effect on conduct. If the reader grasps, once and for all, the general principle that a word may serve as a substitute stimulus for the individual who speaks it, many of the difficulties which attend the understanding of the position here considered will disappear.

What rôle does language play in behavior? Aristotle suggests that man is a political animal; it might perhaps be more profound to say that man is a talking animal. In a world in which language is such a constant source of communication, and therefore of stimulation, experience cannot fail to introduce many language mechanisms which interact with each other and with the remaining mechanisms controlling behavior. As the individual develops in this language-controlled world, the situations to which he reacts and the responses which he makes become more and more symbolic through the aid of language. Owing to the extreme flexibility of speech, the situations which can be compounded out of a vocabulary of even one thousand words are almost infinite in number. Similarly with such a vocabulary the verbal responses to situations are innumerable.

When once the mechanisms of language have been built up the range of stimulation is increased, and, at the same time, an enormous complexity is introduced into human behavior. An external stimulus arouses a large number of these conflicting language mechanisms; an intense conflict of a trial-and-error order arises among these various mechanisms; finally, after a prolonged process of interference and facilitation, the conflict resolves itself and eventuates in a definite line of conduct. Needless to say there is no clear consciousness of the manifold language mechanisms; but delicate instruments attached to certain parts of the throat reveal implicit movements of the vocal organs. Even our most private thinking is dependent upon a subvocal use of those habits which, expressed in overt form, result in speech. Thought without traces of laryngeal movements, it is claimed, is in the normal person extremely rare, and in these cases can only occur through the use of other substitute stimulus mechanisms, such as the hands in the deaf or other gestural forms.

What is thinking? What is thinking in these terms? On the physiological side it is a type of behavior in which language mechanisms play an important rôle. On the psychical side it is the necessary concomitant of the functioning of these language mechanisms. The popular conception of the " thought behind " the final action as the cause of the action is, from this extreme point of view, a myth, like the nature myths of a savage people. The conscious process termed thinking exists; it is, so to speak, the shadow — the ever-present shadow — of the reality, language mechanism; but it is merely an idle accompaniment and, because of its immaterial nature, can never affect the physiological mechanisms that condition behavior.

Such is a fair statement of one theory of behavior. Unless we step out of the narrow confines, many think wide confines of objective science, we are compelled to accept this view. We are bound to assume, if we are loyal to our scientific method, that a scholar, when brought face to face with an abstruse problem, and driven by certain internal physiological tensions, goes through his repertoire of physiological reactions. The only difference between the scholar in his intellectual maze and the dog in his physical maze is in the nature of the mechanisms used; the latter goes through a form of trial and error in his overt reactions, while the former follows a similar process of trial and error in which a vast host of implicit language mechanisms occupies the central position.

Will our loyalty to the canons of objective science carry us so far? Is this position tenable? The reader may feel inclined to laugh this principle of explanation out of court. What would be the reply of the thorough-going physiological psychologist? He would urge the argument already put forward that, as more and more habit mechanisms are built up, including the vast number in the realm of language, a simple line of discharge of energy is often not available. To the peculiar conscious accompaniment of the conflict that arises between the various mechanisms, the terms reflection and deliberation have been applied. The indecision and temporal duration of this process gives merely an appearance of control which, could we realize the mechanical nature of each element in the activity, would be seen to be illusory.

How does the behaviorist justify his position? Holt has presented the arguments in favor of this theory in their most appealing form. He shows that, as the process of habit formation progresses, the individual exhibits a greater and greater independence of the immediate situation and a correspondingly greater power to react to the wider aspect of the environment. This is made possible through the integrative properties of the nervous system. In the higher forms of behavior, the importance of the immediate stimulus diminishes.

The belief in conscious control of the activity, which is popularly assumed, is in error. The appearance of deliberate control is to be ascribed to these complex mechanisms of facilitation and inhibition which delay the reaction and prevent it from culminating in overt conduct before it has become compounded with responses to earlier and later and different aspects of the situation. When finally the process of resolution has been carried to the point where overt action takes place, the behavior shows an adaptation to the more remote aspects of the situation. To this process may be traced the appearance of conscious control which characterizes the whole activity. If at all times the immediate reaction were to an obvious environmental stimulus, conscious interference would never have been postulated; but, when through the integration of the nervous system, the reaction is more and more to a wider aspect of the situation, the sense of control is felt. To the enormous complexity of mechanism, especially to the large number of language mechanisms, and to the manner in which, owing to the physiological properties and structure of the nervous system, these mechanisms are integrated, the final complexity of conduct must be ascribed.

Does this theory cover the facts? Such is, perhaps, the most satisfying statement of the rigid parallelist or physiological view of the life process. But does this statement take into account all the facts? The interactionists who claim that psychical and physical processes interact or react upon one another, and that psychical processes (consciousness) play an important part in determining conduct, reply emphatically in the negative. But this philosophical question cannot be settled; for the benefit of the reader interested in this theoretical problem, the position of the interactionist is briefly stated in the following sub-section.

Is behaviorism a helpful methodology? Meanwhile, solely for the purpose of methodology, we shall assume the objective physiological theory to hold. An exact natural scientist studying the phenomena of behavior is forced into this as the only tenable position. As we consider the topics of reflection and the growth of character we shall, therefore, continue to suppose that the same mechanical principles of explanation operate as in the simpler processes of reaction. We shall, in the interests of methodology, regard thinking as a product of hosts of language habits; we shall regard character as a convenient term for expressing the mechanistic possibilities of the individual.

In the interests of straightforward expression, and with a freedom of approach and a lack of verbal restraint which is wanting to the whole subject, when treated in these strictly scientific terms, we shall feel perfectly free to use the popular terminology. To avoid a great deal of circumlocution we shall speak of thought controlling action, etc., without feeling the necessity of translating such phrases into the more recondite terms of habit mechanisms, and saying — "my action was controlled by a series of past language habits." To the meticulous scientific reader it will be comforting to observe that the same license is taken by the astronomer when he refers to the " rising " and " setting " of the sun; but such popular usage must be sanctioned if we are to avoid such an absurdly pedantic statement as " the earth revolved to a position where the rays of the sun were beginning to strike the observer."

How may our position be summarized? Before proceeding to a consideration of the reflective process, a digression into the realm of philosophy must be pardoned; the more practical reader is at liberty to omit this excursion. But for the benefit of the reader who wisely exercises this prerogative we may point out that it is only as a methodology that we embrace behaviorism. As psychologists, writing an exact psychology, we champion it for its usefulness, but as philosophers, writing a theory of education, we reject it for its arrogance. A philosophy of education bound by a rigid behaviorism, disregarding by definition the core of human experience, would be fatuous and futile.

SUB–PROBLEM 7

Do conscious processes affect behavior? — What determines the choice between behaviorism and interactionism? — What are the limitations of behaviorism for an educational philosophy?

Do conscious processes affect behavior? In interpreting the facts of behavior in the text, we have followed strictly the line of argument used by the extreme physiological psychologist. We have done this because behaviorism provides, as far as one can now see, the only possible hypothesis on which to build an exact science of conduct. That this behaviorist explanation, however, is but hypothetical must be clearly realized; it is resorted to only because the scientist, concerned with objective phenomena, is totally unable to fit into his scheme of thought any theory which assumes the interaction of conscious processes with those neural processes which form the legitimate object of scientific study. Within the narrow limits of the natural scientist who would reduce everything to an objective situation, there is no room for consciousness as a causative factor. Every phenomenon must be explicable in terms of the usual physical entities. It is significant to note that physicists, such as Einstein and Bohr, and philosophers, such as Russell and Whitehead, seem to be much more open-minded as to the nature of these entities than do the physiologists and psychologists. Therefore, the scientist adopts the necessary hypothesis; he disregards consciousness and builds up his system of explanation without its introduction. Loyal to the rules of his game, he has formulated his theory.   And the extremists [1] have even persuaded themselves that the conscious states of the individual, except as they are the necessary companions of certain scientifically respectable neural processes, are so superfluous as not to merit even a nod in passing!

What is the reply of the interactionist?   Before leaving this matter, however, the question may fairly be asked, Does this physiological theory of behavior cover adequately all the facts, and, on this account, satisfy all competent students of human conduct?   Not to the objective scientist, trammelled by his physical concepts, but to the philosopher with his wider range of interest, we shall have to address this question.   To it, the interactionist, who claims that psychical and physical processes interact or react upon one another, and that psychical processes play an important part in determining conduct, returns, as we have already said, an unequivocal " No."   He claims that, however attractive may be the behaviorist explanation of conduct, unless it is able to give a more gripping explanation of those peculiar and intimate processes called memory, choice, deliberation, reasoning, persistence, imagery, its claim to be the whole explanation must be rigorously rejected. The interactionist is perfectly willing to accept, as we have done, the mechanistic idea as a scientific hypothesis, and work with it as far as it will carry him; but, if some important aspect of human experience still defies explanation in these terms, he claims that a wider hypothesis must be sought — an hypothesis that will include all the valuable elements of the behaviorist explanation, and, at the same time, leave room for the entrance of conscious processes as determiners of conduct.   The behaviorist conception certainly serves the valuable purpose of providing a psychological methodology by directing attention to the intimate manner in which the higher mental processes are related to physiological dispositions, but when it says that they are completely subsumed under an elaborate conflict of physiological mechanisms it passes outside the realm of possible proof into a realm of speculation.   In the

---

[1] Weiss goes to the logical extreme: "The formulation of the behavioristic position is then expressed in the statement that all human conduct and achievement is nothing but (a) different kinds of electron-proton groupings characterized according to geometrical structure: (b) the motions that occur when one structural or dynamic form changes into another."   *Psychol. Rev.*. Jan. 1924.

first realm decision is forced by the weight of evidence, but in the second varied interpretations are permitted by the facts, even when there is no disagreement as to what shall be accepted as a fact. The interactionist refuses to believe, as the behaviorist theory implies, that consciousness is a mere epi-phenomenon, that "thinking" while a necessary concomitant of complex neural processes, does not and can not produce an effect on action. He refuses to regard the psychical part of the activity as having no influence on conduct, and on this account a biological superfluity. He refuses to make man a mere puppet whose behavior is controlled wholly by physiological mechanisms. Above all he refuses to believe a recent behaviorist writer[1] when he says that "the statement, 'I am conscious' does not mean anything more than the statement that such and such physiological processes are going on within me."

What determines the choice between behaviorism and interactionism? The choice between a rigid behaviorism and the common-sense interactionism is at best hard. The choice cannot be made in the interests of convenience, nor can it be made by the appeal to our present knowledge of the facts. The behaviorist and the interactionist are both studying the same total process, and they come to diametrically opposite conclusions. The behaviorist rightly claims that there are great difficulties in the assumption of the interactionists, in so far as we cannot conceive the "how" of the process. To conceive of psychical energy as interacting with physical energy is indeed most difficult. But we have just the same difficulty in conceiving in the physical realm the "how" of gravitation. Furthermore, the behaviorist points out that the law of conservation of energy — the most fruitful generalization in the natural sciences — would forbid our assuming that thought (immaterial) can control behavior (material). To this argument the reply of the interactionist is that the law of conservation of energy is at best an hypothesis, and that there is no justification for supposing that physical energy is the only type of energy, and therefore that the physical universe is a closed system which excludes any possibility of psychical and physical energy being measured in some common units.

The common-sense position of interactionism is supported by as distinguished names as is the theory of parallelism. James con-

---

[1] Lashley, K. S.: *Psychol. Rev.*, July, 1923.

cluded, when considering this question: "There result two conceptions of possibility, face to face, with no facts definitely known to stand as arbiter between them." As Garnett points out:[1]

If the theory (of parallelism) that the psychic side of human nature is not free to influence the stream of thought and to direct the accompanying neural activity so as to produce desired movements be correct, then we need make (or, rather, pretend to make) no further effort, whether to formulate laws of thought or to accomplish any other thing: all will happen as is foreordained. And, if we were to make the mistake of assuming that the psychic side of human nature — our souls and their agents, our wills — were free, no harm would be done by our (imaginary) decision to accept the wrong theory; for our mistake (like everything else) would be inevitable. But if the second theory is right, if psycho-physical interaction is a reality and human souls are really free to influence neural activities by the exercise of will and so to modify behaviour, the consequences of assuming and acting upon the opposite theory would be terrible in the extreme. Being born to freedom, we should live as slaves. There is therefore everything to lose, and nothing to gain, by deciding against the hypothesis of interaction, unless and until we are forced to do so by the facts.

What are the limitations of behaviorism for an educational philosophy? The reader is free to choose between these two interpretations. In the interests of presenting a coherent account of the development of personality, it is possible, as an exact natural scientist, to assume, as we have done in the text, the behavioristic position, and yet, with the wider sweep of the philosopher, to suppose that in some way or another the psychical and the physical do interact, or possibly that the two sets of data are but different aspects of a single process.[2] Even if the reader champions the doctrine of interactionism, the behaviorist hypothesis we have tentatively adopted as our psychological groundwork will be serviceable as far as it goes. It has at least the merit of being a consistent and most fascinating theory, though, in our opinion, in spite of the cogent arguments of Perry, it can never form the sole psychological foundation for a philosophy of education which is concerned with the choice of human purposes and the weighing of human values.

The point cannot be overstressed that human purposes and

---

[1] Garnett, J. C. M.: *Education and World Citizenship*, p. 97.

[2] No dogmatic position can be taken as to the final nature of physiological process. Perchance, this process, as Royce, Russell, and Whitehead have hinted, may, in the last analysis, be inherently conscious.

values, and even attitudes and appreciations — the central concern of education — cannot be described in mechanistic terms without losing their meaning and significance. Behaviorism as a methodology for the scientific investigation of the habit processes in education is invaluable, and as a methodology we embrace it willingly. But, as a theory covering all aspects of human experience, especially the more intimate facts of consciousness, it must be vigorously rejected. Unless it is made to play the subsidiary rôle of an instrumentality for the achievement of educational purposes its influence on educational thinking will be pernicious. A philosophy of education must not be held in bondage by its servant, behaviorism.

After this short excursion into the realm of philosophical speculation, the reader will be gratified to turn to the study of reflection.

ADDITIONAL PROBLEMS FOR DISCUSSION

1. Why is language always symbolic? Why is language, whether gestural, spoken, or written, of such essential significance to man?
2. Why is man unable to conduct elaborate trains of thought without language?
3. Why is a wealth of language mechanisms so important for economical and accurate thinking?
4. Why, in times of emotional and intellectual tension, is there a constant tendency to allow the implicit language mechanisms to become explicit?
5. What are the main objections to the common-sense view that "thought" can affect "conduct"?
6. What is the objection to the theory which assumes that consciousness is a biological superfluity?
7. Why is the theory of behaviorism so useful from the standpoint of methodology in education?
8. What rôle does imagery play in the adaptive process?
9. How would the establishment on firm scientific ground of the fact of telepathy upset the general theories of causation in psychology?

PROBLEM 8

HOW IS EDUCATION CONDITIONED BY REFLECTION?

What is reflection? — What is the adaptive significance of reflection? — What is the occasion of thought? — What is the process of thought? — What constitutes the solution of a problem? — How do errors in inference arise? — Why must society cultivate the reflective attitude in its members? — What are the uses and abuses of reflection? — What is the attitude of society towards creative thinking? — Can reflection be fostered? — How is reflection dependent upon intellectual fertility? — How is reflection dependent on effectual auto-criticism? — Does the school encourage reflection? — What must the school do to encourage reflection?

What is reflection? Reflective conduct, on its physiological side, must be regarded as a manifestation of a complex interaction of internal drives working through mechanisms in which those related to language largely predominate. Nevertheless, the difference in complexity between habitual sensori-motor action, as popularly known, and reflective behavior is so great that for purposes of exposition it is permissible to stress the distinction. We may rightly contrast unreflective behavior, controlled by simple habits, with reflective behavior, the product of the action of the more intricate and symbolic language mechanisms. Whereas conduct of the first type may be readily predicted, the complexity and symbolic nature of the interacting mechanisms in reflection make prediction a most hazardous undertaking.

In common parlance, reflection has a narrower connotation than thought. Through ordinary usage the latter has come to mean any form of mental activity from day dreaming and idle imagining to the most profound speculation of which man is capable. According to the custom of psychologists, thinking is restricted to those cases in which there is a conscious attempt to control activity by tracing out implications, deductions, and inferences. Binet, in his study of intelligence, calls attention to three characteristics of the reflective process: (1) its tendency to take and maintain a definite direction; (2) the capacity to make adaptations for the purpose of attaining a desired end; (3) the power of auto-criticism. Thinking occurs when the process of trial-and-error learning is transferred from the sensori-motor to the so-called ideational realm. Under these conditions, the behavior in question is adapted not to the immediate situation, but to a situation spatially, temporally, and socially enlarged. Whatever makes the past, the distant, or the future predominate over the present, advances us in the dignity of thinking beings. This expansion of the adjustment process is made possible through the dispositions built up by past experience. Only to such processes, included under thinking, may the term reflection be strictly applied; but in the rest of this discussion the terms thinking and reflection will be used interchangeably.

What is the adaptive significance of reflection? Biologically considered, reflection is the most highly evolved device for coping with the problems arising from the interaction of the individual with his natural and social environment. This is apparent, but that the degree of the complexity of the environment of the cultivated man is due largely to this power of reflection is not always so obvious. The idiot and the genius may both be submitted to the same external environment, but the complexity of these surroundings to the latter will only be equalled by their simplicity to the former. The degree of complication which any environment is capable of assuming is a function of the reflective powers. The philosopher not only attacks the obvious practical problems which are forced upon him by circumstances, but he, also, creates problems which to an unreflecting mind are non-existent.

How does reflection operate in a concrete situation? Perhaps the most helpful way in which to gain a useful conception of the nature and significance of the process of reflection is by a concrete illustration. The other day one of the writers walked into his lecture room expecting to find his class, when to his great astonishment he discovered an empty room. This was a situation that had never arisen before; it put him in a state of hesitation, for the event conflicted with routine. Any ready-made response to this peculiar situation was not immediately available; the novelty of the circumstance was arresting. How was this astonishing state of affairs to be harmonized with the rest of experience? What missing link could possibly be introduced into the chain of events to give order and sequence to an otherwise perplexing world?

At once, various possible explanations or solutions of this disquieting problem came to mind. Certain tentative and likely guesses were followed up. Was this the usual hour? The watch said so. Was the watch right? Yes, it agreed with the university clock system. Had some mistake been made in the day or room? The previous occurrences of the day confirmed the fact that such was not the case. This was the only lecture room used on that day. Had classes been sacrificed to some other event by university authority? On telephoning to the office he had to abandon this hypothesis. Perchance there had been a strike? As an instructor he had never been a taskmaster; his teaching was probably no worse than the usual efforts in this direction; furthermore, he had seen no signs of a bellicose disposition in any members of the class. Was there some practical joke? Perhaps, but no known reason for it. So, hypothesis after hypothesis, guess after guess was tried, each one increasing the tension. He was about to give up the matter, and, with the problem unsolved, turn to some other work, when it suddenly occurred to him that two weeks previously he had made tentative arrangements for the class, instead of attending the usual morning period, to engage in experimental work in the laboratory during the afternoon. He was not aware that this tentative arrangement had been given any finality; but here was a promising lead. To test it he walked over to the library, and discovered several of his students quietly reading. All thought of a strike was dissipated! But was his guess correct? Yes, on questioning the students, he was glad to hear that they were of the belief that the tentative suggestion was a final arrangement; they were coming to the laboratory in the afternoon. The knowledge of this fact brought order into the sequence of events and relieved the state of tension.

What is the occasion of thought? In the light of this illustration the act of thought can be considered from the standpoint of: (1) its occasion; and (2) its process. Put briefly, the occasion of all thought is some problem or perplexity which necessitates adaptation on the part of the individual through a process of trial and error in the mental rather than the motor realm. To the vast majority of situations, at least in their more superficial aspects, previous habits and experience furnish adequate responses. Only as a situation arises to which previous experience provides no ready-made adequate mode of behavior is the reflective process made necessary. Thinking takes place only when automatic responses fail. Whatever may be the minor or accidental elements of the situation which provokes thought, the one common element is some perplexity or obscurity, some event which does not harmonize with other events, some end which can be attained only by a conscious adaptation and use of the means at disposal. As long as it is possible to follow the beaten track and run in the easy groove of habit, the higher mental processes are inactive. Only when some practical or intellectual difficulty arises, when some unexpected hindrance appears, is the mind quickened into activity; and even when the obstacle is present the thinker must be intent on surmounting it. The obstacle, in other words, does not of itself cause the individual to think, it provides merely the occasion for thought. In summary, reflection occurs and proceeds: (1) when there is a definite problem which calls for an ideational trial-and-error process; (2) when the problem is of sufficient interest to rouse the energy necessary for the attack; and (3) when the difficulty of the problem is within the capacity of the thinker. Most thinking is done for the purpose of solving relatively simple practical problems. In cases of this type, owing to the limited use of abstraction, relatively little demand is made on the more intricate language mechanisms. But in the degree that the problem becomes complex all the resources of a highly abstract symbolism are employed.

How do problems originate? The straightforward statement that thinking is occasioned by some problem arising in the course of experience, is misleading, if it conveys the impression that all problems force themselves upon attention. This simple notion must be combated. Problems of the higher order do not challenge attention as does the rising sun, or as a fence blocking the path of the pedestrian. The problem does not spring Minerva-like out of the surroundings, but is, at all times, the product of the interaction of the environment and an individual, whose past experience has left a certain behavior-set. In the absence of these considerations the common fact may not be explained that a situation, to which habit has furnished a satisfying response a thousand times or more, suddenly takes on a new meaning and manifests a new problem. What has caused the change? Obviously nothing in the external world. Why then, failing to react in the habitual manner, does the individual hesitate and ponder the circumstance? What causes this familiar situation to become so unexpectedly pregnant with further significance? The answer to this question must be found in the state of the individual at the time the familiar situation is encountered. Due to past experience, remote or immediate, a certain behavior-set must be functioning which is so different from the previous sets as to make the old reactions inadequate. To these subtle changes of set, that vary from moment to moment, the great intellectual and social inventions must be ascribed.

Education, by changing the behavior-set, fills the environment with problems; not only is the student made to realize the presence of new perplexities, but he is also stimulated to be extremely critical of, and in many cases dissatisfied with, customary and commonly accepted explanations. So far is this carried in modern society that in our research departments specialists devote their time exclusively to the search for problems which, in the ordinary course of living, would never thrust themselves on the unreflective. Only as society frees certain of its members from the necessity of devoting their attention to the more pressing and primitive problems growing out of the need for clothing, shelter, and food, can it expect to have its more subtle problems perceived and solved. In a democratic society, relative freedom from the more immediate and petty demands of life should be a free gift only to those individuals who can make this respite socially profitable by attacking the more recondite problems of our civilization.

What is the process of thought? Having considered the occasion of thought, the process itself remains to be examined. When, as in the illustration given, habitual responses no longer suffice to remove the perplexity, suggestions or leads from previous experience are followed. From the standpoint of its bearing on the question, each one of these leads or suggestions is carefully examined.   Adoption or rejection of the tentative hypothesis takes place according as it appears to satisfy or to fail to satisfy the conditions of the problem.   Dewey, in his analysis of the complete act of thought, directs attention to the following "five logically distinct steps":

   (1) Occurrence of the vague problem — a felt difficulty;
   (2) Localization and limitation of the problem, analysis of its precise nature;
   (3) Exploration for possible suggestions, hypotheses, generalizations, and explanations;
   (4) Rational and experimental elaboration of the proposed hypothesis; and
   (5) Adoption or rejection of the hypothesis in the light of its implications and consequences.

If not interpreted too rigidly, such an analysis is helpful and illuminating.   It presents different forms which the thought-process is capable of assuming, rather than five stages which must be passed through in a serial order.   Each one of the steps, instead of involving an isolated and different mental process, requires the act of thought itself.   To realize, for example, that the situation is problematical, that it presents some factor which does not harmonize with the rest of the experience, involves the processes of inference and deduction.   That the realization of the problem demands inference is apparent when the problem is complex, but this point is equally true when the problem is comparatively straightforward.   A stalled engine on a hill is only a problematical situation as one realizes that the present state of affairs means lateness and inconvenience and responsibility for an inert piece of machinery.   To the small child the halting of the car means nothing more than a glorious opportunity to gather flowers by the roadside.   Similarly, in the second stage of localization of the precise nature of the problem, to see that the wider question reduces itself to the narrower issue requires a process of deduction, inference, and guessing. If we bear this fact in mind, and, on this account, refuse to force the most subtle mental process into a stereotyped sequence of events, the analysis is valuable because it calls attention to the different aspects which a complete act of thought assumes.

What constitutes the solution of a problem? In order to decide what constitutes the solution of a problem, attention must be directed to the fact that logically all reasoning, which does not, as in mathematics, follow axiomatically from certain definitions, takes place on a balance of probabilities. When the inference is made from a broken window that a missile of some kind has been thrown, the process of thought is guided by a balance of probability. On finding a foreign object in the room, the inference is commonly regarded as established. This can only mean that the balance of probability in favor of the inference has been greatly increased, but the proof is not absolute and rests merely on a more favorable balance of probability. Conceivably the window might have been broken with a hammer and the missile thrown through the broken pane. Naturally, when the balance of probability becomes sufficiently great, it is feasible to speak of an inference as being established. Not, however, until every conceivable hypothesis but one has been tested and rejected, can the correctness of the solution be assumed. This shows that probability can only become certainty for an infinite mind.

This brings us to the question: What constitutes for a finite mind the solution of any difficulty or perplexity? It has already been pointed out that the problem arises because it sets up within the thinker an internal tension; we must suppose therefore that psychologically the solution is reached when this internal tension is relieved. But does this mean that a satisfactory solution has been reached? For the particular individual and for the moment, " Yes." But may not the solution be erroneous? For the individual, solution only means that the particular fact has been made to harmonize with his own limited experience. What then constitutes an adequate solution? Such a solution must bring the particular occurrence into relation with all the relevant facts, and not merely with those facts which are known to an isolated and unenlightened person.

Two illustrations will make this point clear. The native Australian, on discovering himself afflicted with some illness, will reconcile this fact with the rest of his experience by attributing it to a spell thrown by the witch doctor in the service of his enemy. This solution of the problem is so adequate to the sufferer, and is so in accord with his usual modes of thought that, in the event of his death, his friends, bound by the same system of explanation, will feel themselves in honor bound to exact the life of his enemy. Superstitions are nothing more than inadequate explanations. The second illustration will show, at a more sophisticated level, the manner in which incorrect solutions are readily accepted. The political partisan, compelled to reconcile the overwhelming defeat of his party at the polls with his own unbounded faith in its sterling integrity and consummate wisdom, easily does so by ascribing the debacle to the nefarious practices of the opposing group.

How do errors in inference arise? Wrong inferences of this kind are all too readily made. The field of reasoning is such a fertile soil for fallacy that the formal statement of a few commonly accepted principles may be useful. If we follow the analysis of Karl Pearson, four caveats may be issued: *[caution / warning]*

1. Superfluous or more remote causes must never be sought until the more obvious methods of explanation have proved inadequate.

2. In the minor affairs of life where rapidity of decision is essential, inference must inevitably take place on slender evidence, and belief, on a small balance of probability, but this necessity must not blind the individual to the dangerous consequences of this practice when applied to the more important affairs of life.

3. The truth of any statement may be safely inferred only when its contents are consistent and continuous with the rest of experience, and when there is reasonable ground for supposing that the source of the statement is an individual knowing and reporting the facts.

4. Inference from the known to the unknown is possible only in so far as the unknown is of the same nature as the known, and in similar surroundings.

Space will not permit more than a brief comment on each of these points. When the first principle is not recognized, the way is open for all kinds of magical explanation, such as that found in the superstition associated with the falling of a picture. The second statement calls attention to the ever-present tendency to justify thoughtless behavior on the grounds that life is short and time is fleeting. In the third principle, where the importance of examining the reliability and source of any statement or doctrine is stressed, the credibility of evidence is given consideration. Unless care is taken to observe this rule, thought is spent in explaining events that were falsely reported, and mere tradition or hearsay is regarded as furnishing adequate material on which to rear the superstructure of explanation. Often it is the " will to doubt " that needs encouragement. The fourth principle emphasizes the point that, while thinking must proceed from the known to the unknown, only in so far as the unknown has the properties of the known is sound inference possible. To assume that an administrative device which has worked well in one country will, when translated to another, function with equal success, is legitimate only as the relevant conditions of the two countries are identical.

Why must society cultivate the reflective attitude in its members? Urgent need exists for the cultivation of the reflective attitude of mind. For the sake of economy of action, ideational adjustment must be substituted for the time-consuming and dangerous trial-and-error process characteristic of animal behavior. In the interests of attaining a richness and breadth of action, the powers of reflection must be cultivated by each individual to the limit of his capacity. Only in so far as we are capable, through the process of reflection, of passing from the present event to its past and future meaning are we able to sense those persistent and ideal harmonies which impart worth to life.

The person, whose inability to reflect renders him incapable of taking heed to his ways, is so dangerous to society that special institutions have been created, at public expense, to guard him and others from the consequences of his action. In these institutions the life of the inmates is reduced to the simplest elements, and routine takes the place of decision. Their problems are solved for them; their life-plans are imposed by others. In such an institution a gracious paternalism fittingly rules, but such a system of control, when applied to individuals capable of reflection, is rightly regarded as immoral. If the process of living is to exert its maximum educative effect, the normal members of society must be carefully guarded from any form of government which interferes unduly with their liberties of action and thought. Without clear thinking in all departments of life, man easily, and one might also say willingly, degenerates into a creature of circumstance, a slave of superstition, and a vassal of prejudice. Only as man understands the activities and processes of life can he guide them, or receive from them their intellectual and moral teaching. In the day of crisis reflection is the only resort; and at all times it is the one activity which is essential " if a steadfast art of living is to supervene upon instinct and dream." Without it life becomes flat, stale, and unprofitable, for living then loses its most precious element — its educative value.

What are the uses and abuses of reflection? James Harvey Robinson, who may be accused of overstressing the power of reflection in solving the problems of mankind, has brought out in an interesting, if provoking, manner the way in which thought is employed for three different purposes. Its most familiar occasion is found in the minor practical problems which arise from hour to hour in the ordinary course of living. Thought of this kind demands no elaborate cultivation, and is used by savage and civilized man alike. This indispensable use of thinking is contrasted with the second and illegitimate use of such a high function, known as rationalization. In this process the individual justifies lines of conduct which are not pursued for the purpose of achieving reasonable and social ends, but because they have that imperative urge which accompanies a primitive desire or the almost equally imperative urge of custom, habit, or tradition. How often do we catch ourselves in the act of using a laborious process of reasoning to justify a line of conduct, the true motive of which we know to be irrational, or even anti-social! The mental energy which should be devoted to evaluating behavior is prostituted to the task of justifying, to ourselves and our fellows, the selfish pursuits of individual ends.

Presumably the reader is not so completely dominated by humane and intellectualistic considerations that his own experience will not provide all too many illustrations of this deplorable practice. How rare is the man who can say with Anatole France, " I have sought truth strenuously: I have met her boldly — I have never turned from her, even when she wore an unexpected aspect." Could the energy which is used in rationalization be applied to the third use of reflection, and employed in the solution of the problems of our civilization, nothing short of a new world would arise — the dreams of young men would come to pass, and the visions of old men would be realized. The problems of mankind, the problems of health, of family life, of economic existence, of national and international relations, of leisure, of religion and morals — these can only be met by creative thinking, and then only by thinking guided and enriched by deep feeling. Rationalization holds man in the grip of the folkways; creative thought guides him out of the folkways into the path of progress. False rationalization tends to reconcile man to the fetters which creative thought bursts asunder.

What is the attitude of society towards creative thinking? To the fact that the enthusiasm for creative thought is comparatively rare must be added the fact that it is extremely modern. Its conscious cultivation is exhibited by but a small part of mankind, and by that part for but a short period during a history of incalculable length. Sir Henry Maine has attributed the stagnation of the Chinese civilization to the fact that, over long periods, attention was given exclusively to the copying and the memorization of relatively useless classics. This learning contained neither mathematics nor science, and involved an emphasis on rules of thumb rather than on principles. Similarly, to the long delay in the coming of scientific invention in the western world must be attributed the way in which a narrow religion, stressing other-worldliness, occupied the attention of the most acute and devout minds of the middle ages. By directing attention to the solution of arid problems, accepted intellectual prejudices can stifle creative thought. This is well illustrated by the following resolution,[1] which was passed in solemn conclave at the Congregation of Prelates and Cardinals on June 22, 1633:

The doctrine that the earth is neither the centre of the universe nor immoveable, but moves even with a daily rotation, is absurd, and both philosophically and theologically false, and at the least an error of faith.

One may smile at such an edict as this, but Darwin, two hundred and fifty years later, faced the same conservatism. In our own day experimentation in the field of medicine and eugenics, and bold speculation in the region of economic and political, social and religious theory, is given the same hostile reception. And even in modern education there are still relics of the medieval finalism which sought to give finished explanations to all problems of existence; in many departments that interrogative attitude, that straightforwardness, that open-mindedness which is essential to thought, is repressed so that some sacred dogma or established social privilege shall remain uncriticized. As Bertrand Russell says:

Men fear thought as they fear nothing else on earth — more than ruin, more even than death. Thought is subversive and revolutionary, destructive and terrible; thought is merciless to privilege, established institutions and comfortable habits: thought is anarchic and lawless, indifferent to authority, careless of the well-tried wisdom of the ages.

The conservative, and, therefore, the larger element of society, while it gives lip service to great thinkers and reformers, is too prone to curb them whenever the results of their thought begin to disturb the more intimate folkways and break the cherished cake of custom. For this reason, education, with its evolutionary concept stressing the neces-

[1] Cited by Karl Pearson, in his *The Grammar of Science.*

sity for continuous change and greater adaptability, must direct its energy and order its ways so that thinking in every member of society, with reference to every phase of life, may be not merely tolerated but whole-heartedly and studiously encouraged.

Can reflection be fostered? In enlightened circles, whatever differences there may be with regard to the objectives of education, there is unanimity respecting the fundamental importance of inculcating sound habits of thinking. Unfortunately the agreement with reference to the objective does not extend to agreement on the methods which can be most profitably used in its attainment. While all are prepared to regard this function as one of the main goals, the methods by which various schools propose to reach this end have been astoundingly diverse. The reasons for this diversity are to be traced to the extreme complexity of the thought process; fruitful reflection is dependent upon a multiplicity of factors. It is not surprising, therefore, that the various schools of educational thought have, in their attempt to train this process, given very different weights to these contributing factors.

The dream of the educator is to formulate so clearly the steps of the complete act of thought, to issue such clear warnings as to possible places of stumbling, that, in spite of the difficulty of the journey, all the faithful may be guided safely along the road which leads to effective and critical behavior. But it will always remain a dream, for the path of thinking can never be made so straight that the wayfaring man though a fool shall not err therein. Such a direct statement of the various aspects of the thought process as that made by Dewey tends to convey the impression that, for its successful operation, a clear recognition of these various steps will suffice. Many have felt that if only sufficient ingenuity could be used, if only the requirements of the process could be completely laid bare and rigidly enough defined, somehow or other, this most important adaptive process could be brought within the reach of all. With the best of motives people have even gone so far as to suggest that special courses in the art of thinking should be included in the curriculum of the schools. Three considerations will be sufficient to show the absurdity of trying to reduce thinking to a mechanical procedure, a procedure which will be available to all in much the same way that a mechanical invention can be made available to the whole population.

How is reflection dependent upon factual information? In the first place, thinking does not proceed *in vacuo*. Thinking takes place only with reference to a particular body of facts; defactualized thinking is as absurd as a de-mechanized automobile engine. So important are facts for this process that the school, forgetting that knowledge only serves its function as it may be used in reflection, has gone to the extreme of imparting facts for their own sake. To attempt to train a person to think in a certain realm of knowledge, without providing him with information in the field, is veritably to attempt to make bricks without straw. This, then, is the first difficulty in any project for training thought in general.

How is reflection dependent upon intellectual fertility? The second difficulty lies in the fact that every problem is dependent for its solution upon a fertility of thought which will provide the necessary suggestions, inferences, and hypotheses. After the hypothesis is advanced the process of testing is often relatively simple. It is at this crucial stage in the complete act of thought, the point at which brilliant guessing must take place, that any reduction of the thought process to straightforward pattern halts. There is no method of forcing the suggestion; the mind may be tense with expectation; desire for solution may be at a maximum; but still the happy thought may not come to mind.

If the reader will try to solve the following problem, noting very carefully what happens when the guess or hypothesis stage is reached, he will see the utter impossibility of forcing this part of the process: A certain word contains seven letters, the second letter is *v* and the last is *e*. It is a human trait and facilitates the accumulation of wealth. It is also the cause of much suffering. In his *Inquiries into the Human Faculty*, Galton illustrates the same point.[1]

When I am engaged in trying to think anything out, the process of doing so appears to me to be this: The ideas that lie at any moment within my full consciousness seem to attract of their own accord the most appropriate out of a number of other ideas that are lying close at hand, but imperfectly within the range of my consciousness. There seems to be a presence-chamber in my mind where full consciousness holds court, and where two or three ideas are at the same time in audience, and an antechamber full of more or less allied ideas, which is situated just beyond the full ken of consciousness. Out of this ante-chamber the ideas most nearly allied to those in the presence-chamber appear to be summoned in a mechanically logical way, and to have their turn of audience. . . . The successful progress of thought appears to depend — first, on a large attendance in the ante-chamber; secondly, on the presence there of no ideas except such as are strictly germane to the topic under consideration; thirdly, on the justness of the logical mechanism that issues the summons. The thronging of the ante-chamber is, I am convinced, altogether beyond my control; if the ideas do not appear, I cannot create them, nor compel them to come.

" The wind bloweth where it listeth " seems to be, as far as self-analysis reveals, a fair description of the subtlety of the processes which lie back of this elaborate act of guessing. If the reader had difficulty in guessing the word " avarice "

[1] Cited by Thorndike, in his *Principles of Psychology.*

in the riddle cited, the significance of this statement will be apparent.

If tentative solutions come to the mind, well and good; if not, neither prayers, entreaties, nor sweat of the brow can force them to appear. All that can be said is that a person, well equipped with the necessary factual information and endowed with high native intelligence, is more apt to be fertile in suggestion than one possessing less information and endowed with inferior intelligence. Certainly the process itself can never be coerced; one can merely urge the thinker to keep his attention focussed on the main problem by repeatedly putting subsidiary questions to himself, in the hope that the desired solution will eventually be reached.

How is reflection dependent on effectual auto-criticism? The third obstacle which has to be encountered, when attempting to reduce thought to a simple process, is the pitfall which ensnares the mind into accepting superficial and inadequate solutions. This matter has already been discussed, but it is well to mention it again. Unfortunately there is no magic bell which announces the correct solution of the problem. Thought arises because of internal tension, and ceases when this internal tension is relieved. Only in an extremely acute mind, which is already capable of strenuous and rigorous thinking, is the disappearance of the tension any adequate guarantee that the correct solution has been reached. While this difficulty is not met in dealing with simple practical problems, where failure is attended by an obviously unsatisfactory result, it forces itself on attention in all abstract fields. If a man fails to solve the problem of a stalled engine, his failure is patent — the machine refuses to budge; but the same individual, when pondering the cause of a particular war, may accept an erroneous answer and, at the same time, feel satisfied with the explanation. All of us " solve " hundreds of problems

in this unsatisfactory way without being brought to book
for our sins. Into a vicious circle is the immature thinker
thrown when given no guidance in the more abstract fields
of learning; for the purpose of being trained in reflection he
engages in the activity, and yet only as his mind is already
disciplined is he capable of evaluating the solution. These
considerations, showing how utterly futile is the endeavor to
reduce correct thinking to any mechanical process, reveal
the extent to which the learner, if he is to receive the maximum benefit from the activity, is dependent on skilful
guidance.

Does the school encourage reflection? Enough has been
said to indicate how Herculean, or rather Socratic, is the
task which the school undertakes when seeking to foster in
its pupils the power of thought. Later a more detailed analysis will be made of this problem, but to give point to the
present discussion at this juncture, methods, curriculum,
and personnel of the teaching force should be briefly evaluated from the standpoint of this objective.

To aid the reader in making this evaluation the following
questions may be asked. Does the teaching of the school
center around problems? Are such problems as arise of
sufficient intellectual or social interest to warrant the effort
expended in solution? Is the curriculum selected and organized from the standpoint of furthering growth in reflection? Are the textbooks written in a manner calculated to
foster the problem-solving attitude of mind? Is the teaching personnel itself highly endowed with the mentality that
seeks and aggressively attacks problems? Question after
question of this disquieting nature might be asked, to each
of which the answer would have to be largely in the negative. Why has the school fallen so far short of its high
calling? Our duty is not merely to point out the failure of
the institution; we must push the inquiry further and show

reasons for the error. It is a safe canon to assume that no widespread evil exists without good reason. In order to institute remedial measures, and at the risk of appearing to condone the faults of the school, we may well examine here some of the more obvious extenuating circumstances.

How does the memoriter tradition of the school discourage reflection? In the first place, all thinking is dependent for its content on a body of information; only as the pupil is informed will problems be visible or soluble. The schoolmaster has been so impressed with the need of imparting information, of filling the void of immaturity, that he has studied and reduced to a fine art the process of cramming uninteresting material into passively resisting or passively assisting minds! In his lust for facts he has forgotten too often that these are only significant as they contribute to the solution of problems. But the schoolmaster, knowing that thinking is a slow and laborious process, contents himself with presenting to memory the material for thought and, losing heart, fails to give exercise in the thought process itself. For many teachers information has ceased to be a means and has become an end in itself. But in defence of the classroom teacher it must be remembered that he is called upon to present material which in its nature and amount makes the problem-method of instruction extremely difficult.

This evil in present practice can only be laid at the feet of the teacher to the extent that he is responsible for the construction of the course of study. It must be traced rather to the detached administrative official who has either never known, or has completely forgotten, the limitations of the human mind. This office-bound individual insists that year after year the sterile procedure of imparting information be repeated, in the hope that after a certain period of latency the pupil will begin spontaneously to think for himself.

How does the dulling of curiosity in the teacher discourage reflection?   A second difficulty facing the teacher must also be mentioned.   A considerable period of time elapses between greeting material as a learner and imparting it as an instructor.   Any sense of mystery, therefore, which at one time enshrouded a study has long since vanished.   The subject-matter, if it has not been repeated a hundred times, has all the staleness of a twice-told tale.   Only interest in the constantly varying psychological processes of the learner will avail to counteract the necessary but unfortunate circumstance that prevents the teacher from being a co-discoverer with the child.

How do individual differences in the group discourage reflection?   The third and most widespread obstacle which the teacher meets remains to be discussed.   Thinking is the most intricate and exhausting mode of adjustment; it is the most highly evolved integrative device for meeting crises. Much as children differ in the gross physical traits of height and weight, much as they differ in such simple capacities as tapping, steadiness, or throwing a dart, they differ far more, at any particular age, in their powers of critical analysis and in their fertility of mental response.   Over these subtle forms of human behavior the teacher can at best have little control.   Yet he is confronted, in every large class, with the widest range of talent from the borderline case of feeble-mindedness up to the level of very superior intelligence.   To force an individual of low capacity to think with reference to a relatively abstract problem is an utter impossibility. Make the problem sufficiently easy and even the lowest will reflect in an elementary way, but this is the one thing that cannot be done in the school as now organized.   The curriculum is relatively fixed — the same for all pupils of the same chronological age.   Under these conditions it is little wonder that memory drills are substituted for thinking exercises.

What must the school do to encourage reflection? Here is not the place to take up the manner in which these difficulties may be met; it must suffice at this juncture, to point them out and call attention to the necessity for their careful study if the school is to change its ways. Different text-books, different courses of study, more homogeneous groupings, a different mental level of teachers, different training of teachers — these are some of the changes that must be made before any radical alteration can be made in the effectiveness of the school.

How does the task of encouraging reflection influence the curriculum? To avoid misunderstanding one must add that thinking, like appreciation, cannot be so cultivated as to function with equal effectiveness in all fields. The act of thought involves both method and content; while the former varies in different realms, the latter changes completely from field to field. A bitter war is now waging as to whether certain subjects such as Latin and mathematics, subjects rich in procedure values but meager in social values, shall be taught in preference to the more socially meaningful studies such as civics, sociology, and psychology, which, from their very nature, are less exacting in their intellectual demands. As far as one can judge the present trend is away from the more rigorous disciplines to the less exacting studies. To what extent shall procedure values be sacrificed to content values? For what individuals shall such sacrifice be made? These and many other questions of the curriculum will be dealt with later; their adequate solution awaits a vast amount of experimental work on interest and on the problem of the degree to which facility gained in thinking in one field transfers, in individuals of various levels of intelligence, to other fields of activity. These problems are the concern of the formal educational agencies, but the question of encouraging and stimulating thought has much larger implications. Our whole society must be so ordered and integrated that in the process of living each of its members will be called upon to exercise, to the limit of his capacity, those critical and creative powers upon which human betterment depends.

ADDITIONAL PROBLEMS FOR DISCUSSION

1. Why does the process of reflection necessarily involve delayed action? How does this delayed action bring a speedier solution?
2. Show how, in the case of reflection, the trial-and-error process persists, but in the ideational rather than in the realm of action? How are the life processes of the organism guarded thereby?
3. Are facility in the discovery of problems, fertility of thought, critical acumen, and effective action necessarily associated in the same individual? In a coöperative enterprise may these functions be specialized in different individuals?
4. Show how past experience works in the twofold direction of reducing the necessity for thought, and of furnishing the material for thought?
5. Why is reflection so fatiguing and annoying to individuals and society?
6. What justification is there for the statement that the so-called "practical man" is the man who meets situations as his grandfather did? Contrast the reflective type with the practical type? Why in the novel and complicated situation does the "practical man" fail?
7. What are the dangers to which the reflective type of mind is subject?
8. Why have earthquakes, floods, droughts, wars, and plagues played such an important part in the growth of thought and the advance of civilization?
9. Why is society so ready to allow the application of the scientific method to the study of the natural world, and so cautious in applying it to the world of men?
10. What limits are set to the free play of thought in the fields of health, family, industry, citizenship, recreation, religion? Illustrate your answers.
11. What factors in the ordinary large school system discourage, in the teaching force, the free play of thought on professional problems?
12. Why is it so easy for the school to concern itself with the imparting of information rather than with the encouragement of thought? How can this danger be avoided?
13. Why is the small group favorable to reflection? List the physical and psychological conditions favorable to effective discussion. What bearing do these conditions have on classroom procedure?

14. In what way could textbooks be improved in order that they might more effectively stimulate the problem-solving attitude of mind?

15. Arrange the following subjects in the order in which, as ordinarily taught, they make exacting demands on the thinking process: manual training, physical exercise, Latin, algebra, geometry, sociology, physics, history, geology, logic, chemistry, English composition, music, German, French, domestic science.

16. How does the skillful teacher give exercise to his class in each aspect of the complete thought process?

17. At what stage in the process of reasoning is rationalization defective? How do students rationalize the following: low academic standing, the use of ponies or keys, absence and tardiness, success of others, the defeat of school teams, the popularity of others? Why is there resort to rationalization?

18. How does the teacher rationalize the following: failure of the student, dislike of the supervisor, friction with parents and pupils, popularity of other teachers, failure to secure increase of salary, resistance to change in the curriculum or procedure of the school?

19. How can the pathetic credulity of the ordinary citizen be reduced? What specific methods would you use to attain this end in the (a) elementary school; (b) secondary school; (c) college?

PROBLEM 9

HOW DOES PERSONALITY EMERGE THROUGH EDUCATION?

What is personality? — What is the origin of the social self? — Is the growth of the self explicable in terms of habit formation? — What material and social forces modify behavior? — What are the limitations of these methods of control? — How may the school control the nature of the ideal gallery? — How do abstract principles derive force to modify behavior? — To what extent is conduct rational? — Why is personality so complex? — What is abnormal behavior? — What is Freud's central hypothesis? — What is the complex? — How does conflict arise? — How is it resolved? — How does projection operate? — What is the place of phantasy in mental life? — How does the inferiority-complex operate? — What is the educational responsibility?

What is personality? The personality of a man is revealed by the sum total of his specific responses to particular situations. When out of the sum total of these responses, those which have relation to the accepted conventions and codes of morals are specially considered, the term character rather than personality is commonly used. On account of our concern in education with those aspects of personality which are related to character, the two terms will be used interchangeably. A man's effective personality at any time is shown by the manner in which he thinks, feels, and acts in the manifold situations of life; his potential personality could only be revealed by the manner in which he thought, felt, and acted in a host of situations sufficiently wide to embrace all phases of the social and material environment. Interpreting reactions broadly we may say, with Watson, that the term personality covers "an individual's total assets on the reaction side." The problem under discussion may therefore be stated as follows: What is the general nature of that interaction between the environment and original nature from which personality emerges?

What is the origin of the social self? The answer to this problem is simplified by our previous analysis of habit formation and reflection. Through habits of action, feeling, and thought is character formed and expressed: in the last analysis the mechanisms which determine character are habit mechanisms. To those forces which control habit formation we must turn, if we are to gain any clear understanding of the manner in which personality develops.

We need not concern ourselves with the process whereby the child comes to recognize the objects of the external world as being distinct from himself. Through the sensation produced in his own body when he strikes or pinches any part of it, a sensation which is lacking when he encounters an external object, he comes to distinguish his own body from other objects. In a similar way, because of their movements and peculiar reactions to his stimulation, persons and animals in the external world become differentiated from the inanimate objects. This stage is usually marked by a crude type of animism in which the child ascribes human properties to some of the more important inanimate objects. The child who, laughingly, rubs the corner of a chair which he has accidentally struck is giving expression to an old animistic notion. With the passage of time, to the behavior of other individuals like himself, the attention of the child is mainly directed. While he still finds it necessary in steering his course in the physical world to have regard for the inanimate objects of the environment, their very fixity and limited power to stimulate prevent their occupying the place which is accorded to living things, and more particularly to the members of his group. These individuals, especially the adults, are fraught with such potentialities for good and evil, with such powers of satisfying and annoying, that the child finds them of absorbing interest. As we shall see later, the whole development of personality reflects the manner in which the rewards and punishments, the approvals and disapprovals, of society modify behavior. Due to his instinctive and acquired sensitiveness to the censure and commendation of others, a sensitiveness which leaps all rational bounds, man is continually moulded by the herd. " Nature has made man man's constant study. His thought from infancy to the drawing up of his last will and testament is busy about his neighbor." The desire to be not only in the herd, but of it, is to most individuals overmastering. As Whiting Williams, after studying closely the motivation of the working man, has said: " It is unnecessary, in organized society, to say that the ' wheels ' of each of us are turned, for better or for worse, by our mainspring desire to enjoy the feeling of our worth as a person among other persons, that individual feeling requiring always for its fullest satisfaction the surest possible substantiation at the hands of some particular group whose approval happens, at the moment, to appear especially pertinent and desirable." So important is this process of change that the idea of the bodily self becomes dwarfed into insignificance by the side of that social self which is created by the interaction of the individual with his fellows.

Is the growth of the self explicable in terms of habit formation? The reader has already studied the manner in which, at the beginning of life, all behavior follows instinctive lines; how gradually this instinctive behavior becomes modified by habit formation; how, as the habits become increasingly complex and symbolic, especially with the entrance of language mechanisms, the behavior tends to lose the marks of its instinctive origin; how, as a result of memory and reflection, the individual comes to react less and

less to the immediate situation and more and more to a
situation which is temporally, spatially, and socially enlarged.   Eventually, as a result of these processes, the
original instinctive behavior becomes so " sicklied o'er with
the pale cast of thought " that only the closest analysis can
detect the continuity which exists between the simple original behavior of the young child and the complex acquired
behavior of the highly intellectualized and socialized adult.
So great is the gulf that separates the final behavior of the
cultivated man from its origins that many have felt impelled to introduce some new principle to explain the transformation.   Not considering the process of habit formation
and reflection as adequate to the task, they have postulated
a special " moral faculty," " conscience," or " moral instinct "; through the efficacy of this new force, so it is
argued, the modification can only be explained.

By taking an extreme illustration we may easily see how
sweeping are those changes in original nature which force
some moralists to reject the somewhat prosaic explanation
of a slow change of disposition through habit formation and
compel them to resort to the more drastic, if more mystical,
position that some new force, some higher moral faculty,
is directing behavior.   Imagine an individual, schooled to
reflective conduct, wandering by an unfrequented stream
on a bitterly cold night.   Ahead of him he sees his life-long
enemy lose his footing, at a dangerous turn of the path, and
fall into the dark and icy stream below.   He watches him
struggle for a moment, thinks how his death will simplify
his own life, realizes that nobody will be aware of his presence at the scene of the tragedy, etc., etc.   Yet, in spite of
these reflections, in spite of the strong tendencies to avoid
the cold, in spite of the horror of gambling with death, something drives him into the icy waters, and, at great peril and
intense pain to himself, after an exhausting struggle, he

rescues the man from drowning and thus saves his enemy's life.

Is it any wonder that the moralist, when facing an heroic deed of this kind, so far removed from the instinctive level of behavior, feels impelled to introduce some higher principle of explanation?   Unless the psychologist can bring such an extreme illustration into accord with the theory of modification of instinctive behavior by habit and reflection he also must assume the operation of other forces.   No theory of character formation or of growth of personality is acceptable if it proves inadequate at the very point where character and personality manifest themselves in their most refined and elevated form.   Profound must have been the transformation in the original equipment of an individual who is capable of performing such an act of self-sacrifice.   Can alterations which convert animal reactions into conduct of this heroic mould be explained in terms of habit and reflective mechanisms?   The psychologist is compelled to assume this possibility.

What material and social forces modify behavior?   In order to justify this statement, we shall have to trace the changes wrought in the individual through his contact with the material and social environment.   Whether the habit changes produced by the interaction of the individual with his surroundings are sufficient to explain these altruistic modes of behavior which each man identifies with " his better self " is the problem now to be considered.

To this problem all students of ethics have offered solutions, but McDougall has presented in especially clear-cut form the various levels of conduct which must be reached before the highest form of moral conduct is possible.   We cannot do better than give his own description of each level: [1]

[1] McDougall, William: *Social Psychology,* p. 181.

1. The stage of instinctive behavior is modified only by the influence of the pains and pleasures that are incidentally experienced in the course of instinctive activity.

2. The stage in which the operation of the instinctive impulses is modified by the influence of rewards and punishments, administered more or less systematically by the social environment.

3. The stage in which conduct is controlled, in the main, by the anticipation of social praise and blame.[1]

4. The highest stage, in which conduct is regulated by an ideal of conduct that enables a man to act in the way that seems to him right, regardless of the praise or blame of his immediate social environment.

How do the experienced consequences operate? An illustration of modifications produced at each one of these levels will make the process of education clear. The child who overeats and is sick, or the boy who climbs to a height and falls, modifies his subsequent behavior in the light of the consequences. The punishments and rewards of nature, which Spencer lauds in his essay on *Moral Education* are here operative. In the second stage the actual rewards and punishments of nature are replaced by those of his fellowmen. As we have seen, man reacts to the approval and disapproval of his fellows; he alters his behavior when he experiences their individual and more particularly their collective censure. The child, when he ceases to manifest temper because of the actual disapproval that followed its appearance, is at this level of conduct.

How does the anticipation of the approval of the actual society operate? The important point to notice is that in the first two stages behavior is only changed because of the rebuff or encouragement experienced; there is no modification through anticipation of the consequences. But the third stage, for which the two earlier stages pave the way,

---

[1] This must, of course, include the anticipation of the rewards and punishments of nature.

marks a higher development; no longer is the individual constrained to change his behavior because he experiences actual approval or blame at the hands of his fellows; at this stage he anticipates the effects of natural forces and the rendering of the social judgment.   Long before engaging in the overt action he sees the consequences implicit in his conduct; he discerns the handwriting on the wall.   When the normal social force of approval and disapproval is augmented by great material and social rewards, on the one hand, and by formal ostracism and legal punishment on the other, the controlling effects of the anticipation of these rewards and punishments are vastly increased.   The cashier who refrains from an act of forgery in the belief that sooner or later his act will come to light; the manufacturer who sacrifices present advantages in order that later he may amass wealth; the scientist who narrows his interests and concentrates his research that he may gain the Nobel Prize — all are actuated by motives at this level of development. In an advanced social environment, conduct at this plane may be of a very high order, but if these are the highest considerations which motivate behavior, conduct of any grandeur or sublimity will never be achieved.   A narrow interpretation of the word " best " in the proverb, " Honesty is the best policy " always marks behavior at this plane.

How does the anticipation of the approval of an ideal society operate?   In the highest stage, conduct is no longer modified in the light of actual consequences — in the interests of securing the approval or avoiding the disapproval of members of the immediate group.   At this stage the drama is performed not before the limited spectators which crowd the house, but before an imaginary gallery peopled by the prophets, priests, and seers in whose ideal presence the individual has chosen to live.   Not by arbitrary etiquette, by convention, and herd morality of " his set," but rather by those great precepts, admonitions and ideals — the distillate of the wisdom and heroism of the ages — is his conduct shaped. Browning, in Bishop Blougram's Apology, gives us some idea of the manner in which this gallery becomes more refined.

> Like Verdi when, at his worst opera's end
> While the mad houseful's plaudits near outbang
> His orchestra of salt box, tongs and bones
> He looks through all the roaring and the wreaths
> Where sits Rossini silent in his stall . . .
>
> One wise man's verdict outweighs all the fools'.

From Rossini in his stall to Rossini absent or dead is but a step, and the translation is but slight to the imaginary gallery to which reference has been made. That such an interpretation of the control of conduct is not exceptional is illustrated by an incident which came within the experience of the authors. A scholar of international reputation, when engaged upon some abstruse investigation in an old Irish text, remarked that there was only one person whose opinion he really valued and, alas, this critic was dead. At certain stages of the work, he consciously strove to guide his researches by the imagined reaction of his former master. In his *Life of Queen Victoria*, Strachey, quoting from her diary, shows the Queen constantly framing her policies, not so much in accordance with her own judgments, as in the light of the imagined approval and disapproval of the dead Consort Prince. Such may be the influence of a single figure in the ideal gallery. On a larger scale, literature and history mould the thought and conduct of men. As Jean Paul says, " men elevated above all states, are now the educators of state — dead men, for instance, like Plato."

How is the anticipation of approval a present satisfaction? In so far as the approval or disapproval of the actual or ideal society is immediately felt there is little difficulty in this theory of conduct, but when the approval or disapproval is delayed the problem is more intricate. The idea must not be gained that the anticipation of approval and disapproval means that man is always sacrificing present activity to some future advantage or freedom from inconvenience; this would make life one long and bitter renunciation. The future approval and disapproval only exert an influence on my present state because an anticipation of such consequences, or the realization of the outcome in imagination, is an essential part of the present mental attitude. The individual does not give up some present good for a future good; the future good is only effective in so far as, through thinking and imagination, it assumes the rôle of a present good. One may, in spite of distraction, continue in an enterprise because it will lead to a reputation in ten years; but only as its imaginative realization is sweet, and only as it becomes an effective part of the self at the time, will it effectively guide conduct. The contemplation of future approval is more pleasing in the present state of the self than is satisfaction of the passing moment.

What are the limitations of these methods of control? An examination of the limitations which mark the control of conduct at each of these levels will be instructive. At the first stage, conduct can be modified only as a result of actually incurring natural penalties or receiving natural rewards. If, due to a lack of economy in nature, reward or punishment does not accompany or follow behavior, modification fails to take place. This calls attention to a further injustice of nature; she is neither systematic and diligent as a school mistress, nor is there any attempt to make the punishment fit the crime. Nature punishes years of undue physical indulgence, such as overeating, but slightly, whereas from a child allowed through a momentary inadvertence to play with a sharp razor, the death penalty is exacted. This failure to make the punishment fit the crime is the great weakness inherent in Herbert Spencer's theory of natural punishment. Such punishment may have the advantage of being impersonal, but it lacks the touch of personality, namely, intelligence.

At the second stage of control the same weaknesses are manifest; the individual is still only affected by the immediate experience of approval or disapproval. Anticipation of consequences does not occur. Moreover, as in the case of nature, society, lacking both diligence and insight, fails to proportion the social sanctions and social prohibitions in strict accordance with the worth of a service or the gravity of an offense.

At the third stage, the actual adjustment in the natural and social world with its accompanying danger is replaced by an ideational or symbolic adjustment which anticipates the more remote results of conduct. This marks a distinct advance, and introduces great economies into behavior. But conduct which is controlled wholly by such motives can never induce those courageous acts which, though essentially unselfish in their nature, require the defiance of group judgment. Conduct of this order can never rise to any great heights; its motivation is fundamentally egoistic, and absolutely dependent upon the moral standards which happen to be in vogue at the time in the group. The vast differences that exist in the nature of social sanctions, from nation to nation and from group to group, prevent any stable and universal mode of conduct from being conditioned by such arbitrary forces. Under such control man's actions take on the color of his surroundings, and when he moves " east of Suez, where there ain't no ten commandments," he becomes a veritable moral chameleon. Furthermore, there is always the added difficulty that many deeds are hidden; in spite of the proverb to the contrary, crime will

not always out. Consequently, if the individual is merely
reacting to the anticipation of the approval and disapproval
of his circle, no restraining force of wider authority enters,
and the motivation for those good deeds, which march far
in advance of the group or age, is totally lacking.

**How has the belief in supernatural sanctions motivated
behavior?** This invites the consideration of one of the
most interesting problems in the control of conduct. Where
the individual is, for one reason or another, insensitive to the
praise and blame of society, either because his deeds are
hidden or because his position is so superior that social
censure fails to touch him, the door is opened to unbridled
license. This difficulty has faced all those who have relied
on a strictly profit-or-loss theory of action. What possible
force, what punishment, can restrain a man who escapes the
influence of these ordinary forces for social control?

The method of negotiating this *impasse* is ingenious.
The punishments are no longer regarded as necessarily immediate and man-inflicted, but as delayed and sent by the
all-powerful and all-knowing gods. The tyrant may wade
through blood to achieve his ambition and shut the gates of
mercy on mankind; the villain may plot in secret and the
secret may never be revealed; through their power and guile
scoundrels may escape the punishment of men, but the gods,
from whom no secrets are hid, will in due season mete out
the punishment. True, the punishment is delayed in many
cases until after death, but to compensate for this delay the
punishments are made correspondingly severe. In similar
manner noble actions which receive not the approval of men
are recorded in the books of the gods, and, in the fullness
of time, receive their reward.

**How may the school control the nature of the ideal gal-
lery?** The nature of the ideal gallery, which is the peculiar
characteristic of the fourth stage and the quality of the

ideals which flow therefrom, is largely determined by education. Within certain limits, youth will people this gallery with those idealized figures, real or imaginary, living or dead, which command the respect and glory of their group and time. If in schools the great financial magnates are set up for emulation, personal success in pecuniary accumulation as the ideal, this conception of worthy conduct. except in a small number of the spiritually minded, will translate itself into the action and motives of the pupils.

For this reason the school must do all in its power to elevate its own sense of values; it must not merely reflect the practice of a falsely guided community. Whether many who are held up for popular admiration by our newspapers and our magazines should be permitted to crowd the ideal galleries of youth is a most disconcerting question. Schools in which pupils are encouraged to glorify great teachers, such as Horace Mann of Massachusetts, Henry Barnard of Connecticut, Thomas Arnold of Rugby, and Mark Hopkins of Williams, are difficult to imagine in industrial America; and yet we feign surprise when the more gifted young men and women never dream of entering the teaching profession. In this respect the school is reaping to-day what it has sown. Commercial enterprise draws more than its quota of talented men because success in business colors, not only the life outside the school, but even the ideal of the school itself. How hateful is the idea of a pamphlet entitled " The Money Value of a College Education "! If our schools and universities bow down to false gods, then the children of the nation will bend the knee before the same idols.

More hero-worship is not the need of our society; among the people of our nation this type of compensatory self-adulation is all too common. Our need is for the worship of different heroes, heroes who are rich in the things of the spirit. The heroes of politics, the heroes of finance, must give way to the less spectacular heroes of the creative life, whose deeds, in our present society, receive neither the plaudits of the multitude nor the more tangible awards of an aristocratic order.   Fortunately, these superior men can be indifferent to the opinions of their contemporaries, because they have the highest reward life can afford — a love for their own work.

How do abstract principles derive force to modify behavior? This statement that conduct is guided by the imaginary approval and disapproval of an ideal spectator or a moral connoisseur is, of course, little more than an expression of the fact in picturesque language. The dictates of such a gallery, consciously and unconsciously, become resolved into ideals of conduct which lose all contact with the particular individuals or the particular writings with which they were at one time associated.   In the process of character formation such ideals as those of good sportsmanship, the Golden Rule, and the principle of self-sacrifice, all derive their original warmth from direct connection with some actual or imaginary hero.   With the passage of time, however, these ideals or precepts, being given expression through hosts of particular acts, eventually become guiding principles which have lost their original personal connections.

From the standpoint of moral education this process of motivation, generalization, and application is most significant. The rules and principles of high ethical teaching will not sway action unless they are imparted in the beginning, around the acts of individuals who catch the imagination and move the feelings. The mere statement, " he that shall lose his life shall save it," unless it is linked with the action of some concrete person who for the learner assumes the rôle of hero, leaves the hearer as cold as do most of the sayings of Marcus Aurelius. Abstract principles do not make men valiant for truth. Herein lies one of the great problems of all moral education. Carlyle is unquestionably right in claiming that our highest ideals can in the first instance be kindled only through a refined form of hero-worship. The heart must be touched as with a live coal from the altar. The philosopher may reduce the golden deeds of the saviors of mankind to a few great principles of action, but these principles will remain frozen abstractions and will fail to fire saints and martyrs unless they have first been exemplified in the deeds of those that have gone before. The mythology of a race which lacks historical heroes may serve the useful function of quickening and giving life only to a body of abstract principles.

Is the higher self a product of habit formation? To see whether the process of modification that we have described is sufficient to explain an extreme act of self-sacrifice, we are now in a position to return to our test case of the man who rescued his enemy from drowning. This illustration will also be examined from the standpoint of the light it throws on the energy of will required for such an act. Careful scrutiny of these processes of modification has shown that the same psychological principle operates throughout; this principle exhibits itself in changes in habits of action, thought, and feeling through the effect of actual and anticipated rewards and punishments, approval and disapproval. These forces, as time advances, become more and more refined, until, in the last stage, the sanctions and prohibitions become those of an ideal gallery, a higher tribunal, or of an ideal self which has been built up through contact with the great of all time. This desire to realize the highest self, which is essentially the same in mechanism as the desire to realize any of the lower selves, accounts for the case in question.

The man risked his own life to save that of his enemy because of certain habits and sentiments which had become grouped around the ideal self. If these associations had not been embedded in the nervous system, nothing would have availed to prompt the action. Neglecting style, we may say that he did what he did because he was what he was; he was what he was because a long-continued and laborious discipline had wrought profound changes in his original nature. Consequently, he no longer pursued primitive lines of behavior, but rather exhibited modes of conduct which received their inspiration from a long procession of heroes and martyrs. Each larger act of self-sacrifice had left its impression, and in the moment of supreme trial his habits and dispositions decided the issue. This explanation of an heroic deed seems to be so adequate that resort to any magical or supernatural force, or any special moral faculty, is unnecessary. Those dispositions which were the product of a disciplined life exerted their influence, and in the moment of crisis the individual ran true to form — the form to which he had been trained and educated.

How is " will power " a product of habit formation? As no postulation of the existence of a special moral faculty has been made at any stage of this modification process, there is no necessity for assuming some reservoir of energy called will power upon which, in times of stress, the individual can call for assistance. The more refined impulses do not triumph over the more primitive because they are reinforced by some influx of will-energy drawn from a reserve, concerning which we know nothing. The refined impulses triumph because through education they have become the stronger; to follow the nobler course, has become the path of least resistance; paradoxical as it may seem, the harder has become the easier deed. Just as the expert golfer habitually drives a long and straight ball, so the expert in the art of living, the true humanitarian, through a more subtle process of habit and reflection, follows the straight and narrow path.

He draws on no reservoir of will energy for the simple reason that no such reservoir exists; the habits of self-sacrifice, through the instincts from which they develop, carry their own drive.

To what extent is conduct rational? Such a statement of the various levels of behavior is apt to give the impression that all conduct follows a careful rational weighing of profit and loss, satisfaction and dissatisfaction. No view could be more erroneous. As a later part of this discussion will emphasize, man conducts but a small fraction of his life on a rational profit-and-loss theory. He is more apt to consult his feelings than he is to obey the dictates of reason. It is therefore necessary, when interpreting such a classification as has been presented, to bear in mind that the dispositions which are created by past experiences are to a large degree emotional dispositions, and not directed mainly by the more rational habits which we have termed reflection. Most people are saints or sinners, not because they count the cost but because they have acquired, through inheritance and education, an emotional predisposition to one or other of the two behavior-sets. We cannot too often remind ourselves that, in spite of our best efforts, the checks and encouragements which reason can afford are but transitory and superficial. They often do little more than play upon the surface of an organism which is essentially primitive in its emotional stirrings. Even the few who attempt to steer by intellect allow their emotions to make generous alterations in the reckoning. Any system of morality, any system of justice, any system of education that overlooks this obvious fact is guilty of the intellectualistic fallacy. By so doing it neglects the sentiments and emotions that lie back of action, and treats man as a rational being who weighs disinterestedly his conduct from the standpoint of ultimate satisfaction.

This limited dependence on the process of reflection does not mean that educators should throw up their hands in a spirit of helplessness. Rather it implies that they should study the process of motivation from its emotional, as well as its intellectual side. This they must do, if they would attach to the higher form of social conduct those powerful sentiments, emotions, and compulsions which under present conditions become so easily linked with anti-social or narrowly social reactions. Because of their intellectual traditions educators as a group tend to disparage the emotional side of man's nature, and to value only rational controls. Such a rationalistic bias leads to profound and lamentable error. Logic can never raise the moral temperature of the world. For one individual who is stirred to right action by a Marcus Aurelius, millions follow the Christ.

What is the function of conscience? The reader will probably feel that no account of the development of personality is adequate unless the part which conscience plays in the determination of conduct is given explicit attention. In the terms in which we are speaking, what is conscience? Can we assume that conscience is some guiding entity which presides over our thoughts, feelings, and acts? This question may be more readily answered if the occasions when " conscience " is most imperious are examined. Every instance of this kind is marked by a conflict between a lower and a higher impulse. Conscience is usually regarded as " the active principle " which drives a man to choose what he believes to be the right way. On the physiological side it is a name given to a group of facilitating and restraining mechanisms, while its psychological counterpart actively predisposes the individual to right action.

Conscience, picturesquely regarded as an internal monitor which controls behavior, has psychologically been a powerful agent in reconciling man to the stern environmental and social conditions under which he has been compelled to lead his life. To more robust minds, especially, does externally imposed authority tend to be irksome. It is just at this point that "conscience" eases the rub, and removes some of the friction. As long as the individual bows to an external authority the yoke chafes, but when this external authority is reinforced and to a large extent replaced by inner sanction and direction, the individual, feeling that he is no longer a mere subject but rather a directive agent, accepts, without murmur, the restraining influences. The check of a conscience which has been built up from habits imposed by the approval and disapproval of our fellows, is often willingly accepted when the direct restrictions of society seem arbitrary and unjust. In this sense the internal monitor serves a most valuable function in reconciling the individual to the rules imposed by the community. Only as these mechanisms subsumed under conscience are acquired can moral character be developed.

Why is personality so complex? These processes whereby socialized behavior is achieved are exceedingly complex. The individual does not mould his conduct in accordance with the group as a whole; rather he builds up a number of personalities, each of which is adapted to the different rôles he plays. This is the point which James makes when he claims that a man has as many social selves as there are individuals and groups with which he sustains relations. Of course, there is a great deal of overlapping of the various selves, but the differences of these groups, and therefore the differences in the corresponding selves, are so great that at times a discordant splitting of the total personality results. This rivalry and conflict of the different selves is playfully represented by this author when he writes: [1]

[1] James, William: *Psychology*, vol. i, p. 309.

I am often confronted by the necessity of standing by one of my empirical selves and relinquishing the rest. Not that I would not, if I could, be both handsome and fat and well-dressed, and a great athlete, and make a million a year, be a wit, a bon vivant, and a lady-killer, as well as a philosopher; a philanthropist, a statesman, a warrior, an African explorer, as well as a "tone-poet" and saint. But the thing is simply impossible. The millionaire's work would run counter to the saint's; the bon vivant and the philanthropist would trip each other up; the philosopher and the lady-killer could not well keep house in the same tenement of clay.

What is meant by a personality? From the standpoint of these various selves the development of orderly personality only proceeds in so far as each is assigned its proper sphere. The main task is that of bringing harmony into a household which contains such diverse and often incompatible members. The opposing attitudes, habits and impulses must gradually be brought into accord and manifest an internal consistency. Variety of reaction is only good in so far as a unity can still embrace the variety. This process of integration of the minor personalities into a single harmonious self constitutes the essence of character formation and the emergence of personality. Of all the various selves the potential or ideal social self is the most interesting and, from the standpoint of moral education, the most important. This is the self with which the individual identifies himself in his highest and most enlightened moments. In order that this harmonization of the various selves may be achieved, each act performed in the interests of one of the lesser selves must pass the " censorship " of the higher social self. In a perfectly integrated and completely harmonized personality the habits of thought, action, and feeling called forth by a particular grouping of situations would be in perfect accord with the larger habits of thought, feeling, and action with which the individual identifies himself when he is, as we say, most himself. These reactions within different spheres must produce no lasting conflicts and set up no disturbing emotional and intellectual tensions.

What is abnormal behavior? Because of its extreme complexity such a long-continued and thorough-going modification of original nature as results from the varied and chequered experiences of life is often attended by grave disturbances. A process of integration which is so subtle can hardly be expected to run smoothly and, in its final state, to reveal no exaggerations. While that abnormal behavior which accompanies lesions and faulty anatomical structure presents the most striking cases of dissociation, this type of disturbance can hardly be considered in an educational treatise. Omitting all reference to such cases, then, we shall confine ourselves to certain eccentric forms of behavior produced not by any gross deterioration of the brain, but rather by a peculiar and unfortunate attitude which the individual has assumed towards certain aspects of his experience.

To present the most elementary facts from this field, certain terms, which have come into literature through the study of insanity, must be introduced. To the reader such an excursion out of the beaten track may seem not only unnecessary but hazardous. Its justification, however, will be found in the additional insight that a study of abnormal behavior throws on everyday conduct. That abnormality is a matter of degree, cannot be too often stressed. Abnormal conduct is conduct which has deviated from the norm to such an extent that it attracts attention. The most economical manner in which to study the slight deviations found in the conduct of each of us is to study them as they appear in greatly magnified form in other persons. This method of approach will show that " all the world is a little queer "; and the logical reader will be driven to forego the comforting exclusion of " thee and me."

What is Freud's central hypothesis? An adequate introduction to this field would involve a description of the main tenets of the psycho-analytic school. Here it must suffice to note that Freud has rendered a unique service in calling attention to certain tendencies of human behavior which exist at a low level and rarely, if ever, enter consciousness. These submerged tendencies, these ego-centric impulses, color both normal and abnormal behavior. He supposes that the powerful primitive urges of " the unconscious " [1] are continually in conflict with the desires of men in civilized society. As a result of the wholesale and artificial restraints of modern life, vast tracts of this primitive self are repressed and never reach the level of consciousness except in distorted form. The degree of distortion must be sufficient to pass the " censorship," which Freud conceives as a force guarding the confines of consciousness. That such phenomena as Freud describes manifest themselves in the life of each individual, that sex restraint is a fruitful cause of conduct distortion, no one doubts, but that Freud has been unfortunate in his terminology and mystical in his concepts is equally obvious. Unfortunately, an adequate consideration of the position of Freud is impossible here.

What is the complex? Abandoning, because of the limitation of space, any attempt to present in exhaustive form the phenomena of abnormal behavior, we may introduce our partial account by considering the concept of the complex. According to Hart's definition, a complex "is a system of connected ideas [2] with a strong emotional tone, and a tendency to produce actions of a certain definite character."

[1] The precise meaning of this term has never been made clear.

[2] The term "idea" and its corresponding adjective "ideational" is used as a convenience to signify the acquired dispositions which condition reflection. The reader is warned against the danger of regarding "ideas" as isolated and unchanging entities, or as "atoms" from the combination of which thinking arises.

As used in this way, it includes any group of associated ideas and actions, provided the consolidation is produced by a strong emotional tone. This emotional accompaniment functions whenever the complex is aroused. On account of its powerful affective quality, and the large number of elements that it may contain, a complex is extremely liable to be stimulated. When this happens, the accompanying behavior is characteristic. The point which differentiates a complex from any other group of habits, or group of connected ideas, is that its cementing principle is the strong feeling tone. It causes the individual to be peculiarly attentive to certain types of stimulation, to be extremely sensitive when so stimulated, and as a result of the strong emotional excitement to behave in a way which is more or less irrational. A man who has an overmastering hobby finds this complex so strong that very remote objects and ideas will arouse it. Moreover, his behavior, when once the complex is stimulated, will reveal a characteristic lack of balance. For example, a man with a golf complex will be unable to see a green sward without dreaming of golf, he will justify to himself the spending of long afternoons on the course, and he will bore his friends for hours after the game with a recital of his successes and failures on the various holes.[1]

A more extreme manifestation of such a grouping or integration of behavior responses is shown in the lover's complex. To the individual suffering from this well-nigh universal malady, almost every element and act of his life will call to mind the adored one. Her most trivial remark will be weighed as though of profound importance; ecstasy and dejection will alternate in rapid succession; and the behavior

---

[1] From the choice of illustrations in this portion of the text, the astute reader will already have noticed that the writers are suffering from a golf complex of a most violent nature!

within the complex may be so irrational that sonnets are written to the eyebrows of the beloved! The whole world may scoff, the uninspired may rack his brains to discover the imponderable and sterling virtues crystallized in the chosen individual, but to no avail!

We may smile at the folly of others, but, if we are sincere with ourselves, we shall be compelled to recognize that our own behavior is only explicable in terms of the many complexes resident within us. Complexes involving our health, our home, our children, our friends, our business, our country, our sports, our religion, and a host of our other interests, are responsible for many of the peculiarities of our actions. We may justify our eccentric conduct in each one of these realms by resorting to the most ingenious and laborious process of rationalization, but the fact still remains that there is an irreducible minimum which defies reasonable explanation. This residue can only be accounted for by the presence of the peculiar emotional dispositions that happen to have been built up around these interests.

How universal are these complexes? An ideally integrated personality would not manifest such strange behavior; against our will the evidence forces us to the view that, in but few matters, are we wholly or largely swayed by the dictates of reason — *quantula sapientia mundus regitur*. Only in the dreams of mental philosophers is the human mind a smoothly running, cold, logical engine. The feelings and actions of even the most disciplined disprove this conception at every turn. As Trotter says, " When therefore, we find ourselves entertaining an opinion about the basis of which there is a *quality of feeling* which tells us that to inquire into it would be absurd, obviously unnecessary, unprofitable, undesirable, bad form, or wicked, we may know that the opinion is a non-rational one."

Only when the presence of these disturbing complexes is

taken into consideration are the prediction, control, and interpretation of behavior possible. The old intellectualistic explanation of conduct has only had its long reign because the scientific study of behavior has been confined to a few thinkers who have themselves been schooled, at great pains, in rational methods. Those who have viewed life, not from the cloister but from the market place, have never been duped by this simple fallacy. Only as the educational process takes full account of these irrational tendencies of men, and studiously strives to prevent anti-social and other serious complexes from dominating thought and action, can it hope to build up an harmonious personality.

How does conflict arise? How is it resolved? These complexes vary in their scope from those covering insignificant fragments of behavior to the large complexes which embrace very wide aspects of life. The various social selves, described by James, are representative of the wider complexes. After a considerable number of such complexes has been formed, a single situation serves to arouse several of the comprehensive groupings of mechanisms. Under these conditions the stage is set for what is called a " conflict." The mother who is fired by a rabid puritanical complex which impels her to a scathing denunciation of drinking and cards, may discover that her own son, at college, has been attending late poker parties. The puritanical complex leading to denunciation here conflicts with the child or parent complex which causes the mother always to shield and excuse her offspring. How is she to reconcile this conflict without the displacement of one of the complexes? There are four possibilities:

(1) She may keep her puritanism and her parent reactions in logic-tight and emotion-tight compartments, and by this method of segregation prevent conflict;

(2) She may rationalize the situation by persuading her-

self that her son, being led into wicked paths by evil companions, was innocent of guilt;

(3) She may, repressing the knowledge that her son has fallen into what she regards as disgrace, refuse to recognize the unwelcome fact;

(4) She may be willing to face the facts, stand by her notions of right and wrong, recognize that her son has greatly disappointed her, and in the light of both events proceed to direct her conduct.

The fourth method of settling the conflict involves no compact with delusion; such facing of reality is the mark of a superior mind. Where segregation takes place there is an incompatibility in the behavior, a lack of harmony in the personality, which is accompanied by grave dangers. The integrity of the mind is lost; single-mindedness disappears. The dangers of rationalization have already received attention; reason is prostituted in this service. Repression of deep-seated and wide complexes with their correspondingly powerful feelings, if it reaches a certain point, may bring about a breakdown of the self. When this occurs usually the explanation may be found in the utter incompatibility of two or more conflicting foci of behavior. This incompatibility may eventually become so great that any harmonization is rendered impossible. In this event the attempt may be made to repress, to banish from the mind the offending complex. This process is fraught with serious consequences. The repressed elements, if they ever come to dominate behavior, since they are divorced from the main stream of life, may give rise to the phenomena of multiple or double personality. When this acute stage is reached, all appearance of harmony in the self disappears. Each self is unaware of the thoughts, feelings, and actions of the other. Cases of this kind are, of course, so extreme as to be pathological, but mental hygiene is revealing to-day that many nervous disturbances may be traced to the repression, especially in early youth, of certain behavior trends. A wiser system of education would force these tendencies into the open, and attempt to harmonize them with the rest of the mental life.

How does projection operate? In considering the rôle played by rationalization, another interesting mental process must be considered. Passing reference has already been made to certain behavior-processes so radically opposed to the main trend of the individual that he finds it extremely difficult to reconcile himself to their presence. While repression may ensue, another path of escape is possible. Instead of refusing attention, as in repression, the individual ascribes the evil thoughts and actions to some outside agency.

In its most exaggerated form, this is seen in the insane, who explain away all their derelictions by attributing them to external influence. In a neighboring asylum is an inmate who from time to time attacks his fellows. After each assault the explanation is the same: " I am controlled by some wireless, which a Yale professor who has stolen my patent, is operating to keep me locked up here! " Since this process involves the projecting outside the self of certain painful mental contents, it goes by the name of " projection "; it is an attempt to find an excuse for a departure from normal behavior. This phenomenon is exhibited in a wider form in the crude conception of the devil, which works mischief in human hearts and lives. Instead of boldly and openly confessing our sins and assuming the blame for them, by ascribing them to an external agency the feeling of responsibility, if not removed, is much diminished. To-day " environment and heredity " are apparently taking the place of the former ubiquitous " devil."

This same principle operates at the other extreme of con-

duct. When some ecstatic state is experienced, when some
sublime and heroic deed of sacrifice is performed, an external beneficent force is postulated. " It is not I that do it,
but the spirit that worketh in me." While both these forms
of rationalization are magical in their origin, the first is, of
course, much more dangerous than the second. Any mental
process which takes away from the individual the feeling of
personal responsibility, and thereby causes him to condone
his own acts of indiscretion, is dangerous both individually
and socially. Education must not allow reality to be distorted by mirages of this kind. The individual must recognize his own responsibility, and take gracefully the blows
which cannot be inflicted upon an imaginary and external
" whipping boy."

What is the place of phantasy in mental life? Closely
allied to the phenomenon of projection, with its imaginary
accompaniments, is the mental process known as " phantasy." A complex finds its normal outcome in action.
When, however, through obstacles in the environment or
through the impotence of the individual, the activity of the
complex is blocked, there yet remains one channel through
which it may find partial expression. Let us suppose that
an individual is very desirous of amassing a fortune, and
that defects in his personality or the limitations of his surroundings prevent the consummation of this desire. Realizing that his craving can never be satisfied in the world
of reality, he may fly to the land of dreams where obstacles
melt away, and his own pusillanimous and submissive will
becomes inflexible and sovereign. In this realm of phantasy
he may build up business organizations of which Rockefeller
never dreamed, and amass fortunes for which Crœsus never
sighed. All of us, especially in adolescence, indulge in daydreams of this kind. We rescue fair damsels from burning
buildings amid the plaudits of the crowd; we perform

Herculean labors with easy grace; amidst countless retainers we dwell in marble halls; we attain social and intellectual prominence within a day; we scatter plenty on a smiling land, and read our glory in a nation's eyes.

This playful mental activity, affording in the realm of fancy a compensation for the sternness of reality, cannot, in its entirety, be condemned.   The discouraged prisoner rallies his spirit and gathers strength to burst his bonds and slay his captors.   Used in this way, phantasy has great possibilities as a motivating force.   Such is the legitimate use of this mechanism; it may function illegitimately, however, by becoming the perpetual resort of a vacillating and timid mind.   Instead of refreshing the warrior for new conflict, it may sap the energy which should be used in destroying his antagonist.   If such day-dreaming is allowed unbridled license, the individual becomes, at length, divorced from reality, and incapable of undergoing those sterner disciplines demanded by the problems and exigencies of life. Education, by encouraging the individual to undertake suitable tasks which, through continuous effort, yield a product in the world of reality, must prevent him from falling a prey to the dangerous habit of substituting " castles in Spain " for substantial achievement.   Too much thwarting, the natural outcome of impossible goals, is liable to induce this compensating tendency to live in the domain of phantasy.

How does the inferiority-complex operate?   Perhaps, in closing, it is well to call attention to another concept much used in the study of human behavior. This is the " inferiority-complex." Adler noted that, under certain conditions, when the body exhibited some marked defect, the attempt on the part of the bodily mechanism at physical compensation was followed by an over-compensation.   This is the inferiority-complex of physical origin, but the same term may also be applied to the complex of psychical origin. Complexes of this type are apt, likewise, to manifest themselves in over-compensation. The shy and nervous individual may often mask his inner feeling under a brazen exterior, and the pessimist may often present an overjoyous countenance. Particularly are phantasy and day-dreaming the channels through which the individual suffering from an inferiority-complex attempts to establish a behavior equilibrium. While certain students of human behavior have overworked this concept as an explanation of conduct, there is no question that it is of service in classifying some manifestations of human conduct. Whenever there is extreme sensitiveness in certain social situations, combined with great eagerness for social recognition and an aggressive type of reaction, the possibility of the behavior being explicable in terms of a persistent effort to overcome the sense of inferiority should be considered.

Under these conditions we find the possessor of such a complex not merely trying to overcome his deficiency by continued striving to attain the ends which are direct, but in many cases he chooses other ends which may serve as a compensation for failure to attain the direct objectives. Towards these other compensatory activities he directs his attention and the attention of his associates. The boy of weak body may turn from sport and make heroic efforts to excel in his studies. At the same time he is careful to make clear, to himself and to others, the superiority of intellectual attainment, and, in extreme cases, he may manifest a complete contempt for physical prowess. Pruett elaborates this point in the following words: [1]

The woman without brains uses every device to be beautiful and charming, the woman who cannot be beautiful goes to college and takes an interest in "higher" things, the menial compensates

---

[1] *Psychoanalytic Rev.*, Jan., 1922, p. 29.

by insolence to superiors.   The Southerner clings to his belief in
his aristocratic descent and the tradition of *noblesse oblige*, seeking
to forget the relative inferiority of his section in economic and
intellectual development.   The New-Englander makes a virtue of
necessity and cherishes the faults as well as the excellences of the
middle class.   The Westerner boasts the material greatness of his
country because he has not yet taken time to acquire cultural
greatness.   Compensation for inferiority may be found in many
ways, perhaps chiefly through attracting attention away from the
very defect.

How fruitful are these concepts in studying behavior?
Before leaving the subject it is necessary to warn the reader
that such concepts as we have described, the unconscious,
the complex, the inferiority-complex, phantasy, compensation, projection, etc., etc., may easily be abused.   As
methods of explanation or, more accurately, of classification, it is easy to bandy these words around and, in the
face of the complex problems of human behavior, to feel a
false security.   In the hands of popular writers, and, at
times, in the hands of those who claim to be psychologists,
these terms have been employed as explanations to such a
degree that the standards of proof in psychology seem to
be even lower than those found in theology.   These concepts have a proper place; they may aid clear thinking,
but, unless used with great discrimination, they may " lay
the intellect to rest on a pillow of obscure ideas."

What is the educational responsibility?   In the short
space at our disposal we have been able to do little more
than sketch the larger psychological and sociological implications of that vast and intricate process of habit-formation
and reflection out of which character emerges.   In the brief-
est possible manner, certain modes of behavior which are
detrimental to the development of an ordered and unified
personality have been discussed.   The total process of character formation is too interwoven with the whole fabric of

life to make feasible a systematic formulation of definite regulations for its guidance.   Education is only successful in so far as it furnishes a purified and simplified environment which is calculated to favor the growth of sound habits of action, thought, and feeling.   For this reason the school must reproduce in miniature a socialized community; its rules and regulations, its conventions and its ideals, must be planned not only for the attainment of intellectual growth, but still more for the attainment of moral stature.   Within this ideal community each member, by subordinating his lower self, by realizing his better self, should unconsciously and consciously form those mental dispositions from which moral conduct flows.

An individual does not become a personality all at once; he becomes so only gradually, and even then he cannot be regarded as existing for himself alone, but only as a member of an organism.   To accomplish this end, the questions of freedom, constraint, competition, socialized and group activity, individual responsibility, formulation of aims, differences in personality, must all be given the closest study. Only individuals who have once enjoyed such a community in the school can confidently be expected to work for the socialization of the greater society — a society in which it will be recognized that one of the important functions of every department of life is that of making more humane the individual coming within its sphere of influence.

ADDITIONAL PROBLEMS FOR DISCUSSION

1. To what factors would you trace man's irrational desire for approval and recognition of others?
2. From the standpoint of the individual, what are the advantages and disadvantages which accompany extreme sensitiveness to the approval and disapproval of the immediate group?   What are the corresponding advantages and disadvantages to the group itself?
3. How do problems of discipline arise out of the fact that pupils fre-

quently prefer the approval of their classmates to the approval of the teacher?

4. What are the merits and demerits of the impersonal form of natural punishment, advocated by Spencer in his essay on *Moral Education?*

5. When is day-dreaming, as a compensatory mechanism, detrimental to the growth of personality? How can the school minimize the danger?

6. Why is the complex such a dangerous factor in conduct? Analyze the complexes which the ordinary individual builds up about: himself, his college, his country, his political party, his religious sect, his occupation, his family.

7. List the characteristics which your social self exhibits in each of the following rôles: teacher, pupil, son or daughter, brother or sister, parent, lover, member of fraternity, patriot, worshipper, employer, employee. What conflicts between these various selves do you experience? How are these conflicts resolved?

8. What types of personality are set up for approval by each of the following: the sport column of the newspaper, the moving picture, the pulpit, the stage, the market place, the dance hall, the college campus, the public school, the university.

9. How does the membership of the ideal gallery change at the various age levels? What systematic attempt does the school make to modify and refine the membership of this ideal gallery?

10. Why are moral precepts in themselves such ineffective instruments for the motivation of conduct? How may these precepts be given vitality?

11. Show, in terms of habit mechanisms, how "will power," as popularly known, is built up.

12. What is the effect on the growth of personality in children of the practically complete dominance of women in the teaching profession?

13. Illustrate, from your own experience as an adult, the modification of conduct at each of the four levels, according to the analysis of McDougall.

14. What danger does the teacher run, in the development of personality, through constant association with immature minds? How can these dangers in some measure be avoided?

15. Illustrate from your own experience, the phenomena of the complex, projection, phantasy, inferiority complex, the force of the primitive urges of the unconscious.

PROBLEM 10

HOW IS EDUCATION CONDITIONED BY PROLONGED GUARDIANSHIP?

Why is plasticity marked by initial helplessness? — What is the significance of infancy? — Why has prolonged infancy a survival value? — Why is the period of social infancy being extended? — What aspects of growth have been studied? — When does intellectual growth cease? — Why is it so difficult to measure the growth of social and moral traits? — What determines the value of an activity in infancy? — What qualities should characterize the school environment? — Does the school explore and recognize the capacities of the individual? — How may society exploit the docility of the young? — How may the school lose touch with life? — How may the school unduly sacrifice the present to the future?

Why is plasticity marked by initial helplessness? Nothing in the study of human behavior is more striking than the complete helplessness of the infant at birth. As compared with the lower animals its equipment with those adaptive mechanisms which are essential to the immediate demands of life is most inadequate. Were not the human infant carefully tended it would die within a very few hours of its birth; and this, in spite of close proximity to food, shelter, and clothing, and other necessities of life. We have already contrasted the independence of the recently hatched chick, capable of seeking its food, with the helplessness of the newborn infant, incapable of even crawling to its mother's breast. So striking is this utter helplessness that a hypothetical observer, unacquainted with the developmental history of the infant and the chick, would certainly predict a fuller life for the latter than the former. In the light of subsequent events, he who judged future possibilities from present effectiveness would be completely deceived.

Incapacity to meet present conditions can never of itself be advantageous to an organism. Unless the infantile helplessness is the necessary concomitant of a structural formation that has great potentialities for growth, it is wholly negative and disadvantageous. When we pass from the patent fact of the physical incapacity to its physiological basis, our attitude towards this helplessness is changed. A certain incompleteness at birth is the necessary condition of growth. Only as the final forms of response are absent can the organism form those habits through which future adjustment is secured. The lower one goes in the animal kingdom, the more one finds this fact to be true. Independence of the care of the parent is characteristic of the lower forms of animal life; the chick is better equipped to meet the conditions of its life than the kitten, and the kitten than the young elephant or the monkey. The chick possesses at birth, in a relatively fixed form, most of the responses which are necessary for life. These responses, being sufficiently adapted to the extremely simple environment to which the chick reacts, may be employed in approximately their original form. These hereditary preferential connections are so clearly and finally canalized in the physiological structure that, in the event of a considerable environmental change, the organism perishes.

Initial adaptation of this final order is purchased at the price of modifiability. The young of the primates inherit many more modes of response than do the offspring of any other animal species. Furthermore, these modes of response are less fixed and, under environmental stimulus, are more easily modified; or, to state the case more accurately, the inherited behavior-patterns are so numerous and conflicting that they facilitate and inhibit each other. In this manner the behavior of the organism suffers gradual though radical modification. To this possibility of compounding new forms of behavior, from the facilitation and interference of simpler modes of response, the term plasticity is given; and to the period during which this modification takes place in a marked degree, the term infancy has been technically applied.

What is plasticity? On its physiological side, the helplessness of the human offspring and the prolonged period of infancy must be traced to an absence at birth of many of the mechanisms which only develop with age and environmental stimulus. It is probably a mistake of emphasis to assume that the simple inherited modes of response which develop as the organism matures, and out of which complex behavior is built, are less fixed in man than in the lower animals. The point to stress is not that the simple reactions are indefinite and vague, but rather that they are capable of being integrated or compounded together to form new types of behavior. As a complex machine derives its versatility, not from a lack of rigidity in its various parts, but from the manner in which these various rigid parts work together to produce a complex series of movements; so, in man, plasticity and adaptability are due not to the absence of definite and fixed simple modes of reaction, but rather to the manner in which simple responses are coördinated and integrated. This coördination results in modes of behavior which have no appearance of fixity, but exhibit a degree of versatility found only in the human mechanism.

What is the significance of infancy? Using the term infancy to cover that period during which the offspring is markedly dependent upon the care of others, we may now observe that prolonged infancy seems to accompany capacity for future development. The lower animals which are virtually independent of the parent at the time of birth are incapable of modifying their behavior to any considerable degree, while man, who has a prolonged period of infancy, shows a great capacity for growth. This connection between the period of infancy and capacity for change is not a mere coincidence, but rather a causal relationship.

To view this fact in its most significant form, the student must go back of the time of birth and follow the gradual development of the organism in the pre-natal period. From the physiological standpoint there is continuity between pre-natal and post-natal existence. The separation of the offspring from the parental body, however dramatic in its nature and its social significance, marks no sudden break in the process of development. We may suppose, therefore, that in the lower animals the major part of that final integration, which sets definite bounds to the process of learning, takes place before birth, while, in the case of man, birth occurs before this process of final integration is consummated.

Owing to the lack of differentiation at birth, the process of integration, which has been discussed under habit formation, can occupy a long period of time, and can proceed under the influences of those forces which condition the social life of the child. Expressed in picturesque language, it may be said that the lower animals are adapted by heredity, whereas man is given by heredity merely the raw materials of adaptation. In the case of the lower animals, nature completes her task before the birth of the organism, while, in the case of man, she seems to lack the necessary time during the pre-natal period to fashion a finished product. The child is consequently born with an adaptable mechanism which can be made effective only by the educating influence of the environment. What nature does for man in shaping the more primitive mechanisms governing the action of the heart, kidney, stomach, liver, and other vital organs, she does for the animal throughout almost the whole of its reaction system.

Why has prolonged infancy a survival value? Were all the reactions of the child as isolated from the higher mental control, and therefore as unmodifiable, as are the simple physiological processes, education would be powerless to produce change. Any adaptation to a complex and changing environment would be impossible. Man, of course, is not endowed with this plasticity, which is the mark of a prolonged period of infancy, in order that he may adapt himself to the complexities of his material and social environment; instead these complexities have only arisen because of the learning capacity which is characteristic of the human infant. But from the standpoint of the individual, infancy, with all it implies, may be legitimately regarded as the period during which the process of habit formation is peculiarly active, and therefore as the period during which are formed the major number of adjustments to the world.

So essential is this plasticity to the formation of habits that we may assume the steady operation of certain selective influences throughout the course of evolution. These influences have favored those organisms that, through lack of differentiation at birth, are capable of adjusting themselves to the changing aspects of the environment. In the beginning of the struggle variations in gross size, in strength of muscle, in physical endurance, and in resistance to cold, hunger, and thirst, may well have been the determining influences in survival; but, as competition became more acute and as the environment was refined, the selective forces became increasingly operative upon variations in the plasticity of the nervous system. Consequently, with the passage of successive generations of men, a gradual increase in the degree of helplessness and in the duration of the period of dependence might be expected.

Why is the period of social infancy being extended? Under the conditions of our own complex civilization, even an approximate estimate of the period of time during which parental care is essential to the survival of the offspring cannot be conjectured. The specialization of occupation in our present society makes all of us dependent throughout our lives upon the labor of others; and the present " paternalistic " trend of government, with the social assumption of responsibility for the individual, makes dependence coterminous with life. However, that the period of dependence is over when the individual is capable of earning his own living may reasonably be assumed. According to the common judgment of society, as expressed in legislation and educational procedure, the child should not carry the responsibilities of earning a livelihood before sixteen, and the full membership in society is not granted until eighteen or twenty-one years. Furthermore, among the more favored classes, the period of dependence is extended even beyond the age at which legal status is conferred. In modern life, entrance to the higher professions, such as medicine, law, and university teaching, is hardly possible, if the individual is to be adequately equipped, before the age of twenty-five to twenty-eight. The increase in theoretical training demanded by many of the professions involves a financial dependence upon the parents or society for approximately one third of the life span.

The advance of civilization, too, encourages the extension of the period of dependence upon the parents or upon society for as long a time as benefit can be derived from deferred entrance to the profession or occupation. Where the financial resources of the family render the practice unnecessary, many parents and children make the mistake of assuming that, on the completion of the college course, the individual should be independent and, therefore, responsible for self-maintenance during the years of postgraduate study. This constitutes an unwarranted sacrifice of educational values to immediate productive efficiency. The same argument applies even more forcibly to those foolish parents who, in spite of financial competence, distract their children

during the secondary school or college period by requiring
them to engage in remunerative employment during hours
which might well be devoted to the prosecution of their
studies or recreations.   An understanding of the significance of infancy would correct this short-sighted practice.
In view of the extensive and prolonged training necessary
for those who later will be called upon to meet the more important crises of our social life, society must recognize that
these chosen individuals must be relieved from the necessity
of entering a gainful occupation before the early thirties.

What aspects of growth have been studied?   Having
shown the general significance of infancy and prolonged
guardianship, we now turn to a phase of our problem which
is of great interest to the educator.   This problem is concerned with the developmental history from birth to maturity.   By students of anthropometry, medicine, and education, the physical growth of the child has been carefully
studied.   By using groups of children of both sexes at the
various age levels, growth in stature, weight, and other
physical traits has been measured.   At the present time
several ambitious investigations are in progress in which
the same children are measured periodically in the various
physical traits.   The onset and manifestations of adolescence have also received considerable attention.

Paralleling this interest in physical and anatomical traits
the question of growth of intelligence has in more recent
years occupied the attention of psychologists.   The movement for the measurement of mental capacity is greatly
handicapped not only by the lack of objective units, but also
by the causal relationship that exists between growth in intellectual capacity and environmental stimulation.   Thus,
while an inch is always perfectly objective, an increase of a
certain number of units in performance in an intelligence
test has always to be interpreted in the light of the elements

comprising the particular test. In the Binet examination, since the tests are standardized on an age-level basis, the extent of the growth from year to year in absolute units can never be known. Again, all the tests which have so far been devised to measure mental growth are exceedingly dependent upon educational factors. Consequently, in the attempt to measure mental growth, any results obtained from such tests have always to be interpreted with reference to an environmental factor which changes from individual to individual.

When does intellectual growth cease? In spite of these difficulties it is probably safe to assume that somewhere between fourteen and a half and sixteen years the majority of individuals reach the limits set by nature to mental growth. From this time on they cease to show increased capacity to meet those novel situations which, for their solution, make demands on native ability rather than on mere experience. To suppose that the majority of individuals do not grow in intellectual effectiveness after sixteen is, of course, absurd; the experience of mankind is to the contrary. But there is considerable evidence to show that this effectiveness is to be ascribed to wider experience and more information, rather than to an increase in general mental capacity.

In view of the inadequacy of our instruments, and the unmeasured influence of the environmental factor, dogmatism is out of place, but it is interesting to note that cumulative evidence from the employment of a wide selection of the present so-called intelligence tests reveals the fact that the decline of mental growth coincides roughly with slackening of physiological development. The one disconcerting fact, however, is that the intelligence tests indicate a cessation in mental growth at the very age when the majority of children leave school. This at least gives rise to the suspicion that our intelligence tests are measuring a mental dexterity which is very dependent upon school environment. Were universal education extended to twenty years of age, we venture to predict that the present measures of intelligence would reveal the approach of mental maturity at a somewhat later age than fourteen years. The precise effect which this extension of education would have on the ratings by our current tests, can, in our present state of knowledge, only be surmised.

Why is it so difficult to measure the growth of social and moral traits?   While intellectual growth has occupied the center of the stage, during the past twenty years, serious attempts have also been made, at the various age levels, to measure such allied phases of growth as range of interest, choice of heroes, development of moral judgment, growth of moral behavior, etc.   But these measurements of social and moral traits are so dependent upon the social milieu in which the child is placed that they, much less than the gauges of intellectual growth, can be interpreted as reflecting an inner development of the child.

Is growth continuous?   In a general treatise of this character, even a brief summary of the vast amount of evidence that has been collected with reference to physical, mental, social, and moral growth is out of place.   The point especially worthy of emphasis is that growth in the individual, whether physical or mental, is on the whole uniform and continuous until maturity.   While in extreme cases individuals show periods of quiescence, followed by periods of extremely rapid development, and while in the vast majority of cases slight manifestations of the same phenomenon are found, yet, in the large, the old dictum — *Natura non saltum facit* — is unquestionably substantiated.   If data were to be presented to combat this sweeping generalization, we should turn to the early years of adolescence. The little existing evidence which supports the theory of well-marked periods of negative and positive acceleration in growth is drawn from this source.

Has measurement supported the theory of recapitulation? The collection of experimental evidence on rate of growth has undermined the influence of those theories of education which have been based on the attractive notion that all individuals more or less uniformly pass through temporally well-defined stages of development. The theory of recapitulation, which assumed that in the development of the individual, the instincts followed the order in which they were evolved by the race, and assumed that their time of appearance in the maturing of the child might be readily catalogued, is moribund. Upon this attractive theory the culture epoch system of education was based; but such easy solutions to the problems of educational procedure are not available. Any guidance which educators may obtain from the studies of growth will come from patient investigations similar to those which are now being made on groups of children in experimental schools and classes. Here the behavior of children from the earliest years, and under various types of environmental stimulation and psychological experimentation, may be subjected to continuous and close scrutiny. Already these investigations have progressed so far that one conclusion is almost certain: any sudden changes which take place in the behavior-growth of the child, must be explained in terms of social forces playing upon the child, rather than in terms of abrupt physiological or psychological changes within the organism.

How has infancy fostered the growth of the family? Sociologists have repeatedly pointed out that the prolongation of infancy has led to the stabilization of the family. In the process of organic evolution, selection must have worked in favor of those families in which the inborn social and other tendencies of both parent and offspring were conducive to prolonged infancy. From these parental and filial tendencies, original or readily acquired, the altruistic inclinations of mankind are usually assumed to have developed. To attempt to trace the rise of morality and religion without constant reference to the family relation, and its consequent effects upon group life, is futile.

What determines the value of an activity in infancy? Here, however, our concern is not with the evolutionary significance of prolonged infancy, but rather with the advantages which accrue to the individual from the protracted period of dependence characteristic of present civilization. Freedom from economic pressure and relief from the necessity of seeking food, shelter, and clothing enables the child to devote the major part of his time to the acquisition of those skills and knowledges, and to the formation of those moral and emotional dispositions which, in the judgment of his elders, are essential to successful participation in group life. Not that the child who is forced to surrender to economic pressure does not receive a valuable education through gaining a livelihood; but under these stern conditions the educative process is, perforce, sacrificed to economic production. In the case of the protected child, on the other hand, modifications of behavior constitute the aim of the activity and receive, on this account, the whole emphasis. The touchstone of the process is not a product in the external world, but a change in the conduct of the individual participating in the activity.

What qualities should characterize the school environment? This freedom from external aim gives opportunity to the educator to select from the total environment those aspects which are more calculated, than is a chance environment, to produce the desired changes. In place of a world that is too severe, too puzzling, too difficult for the child, an economical, ordered, simplified, tolerant, and balanced environment may be provided. When the word school is written on the portals of our educational institutions there is, alas, no mystical force which calls into existence this type of environment; the creation and ordering of such a special environment remains, and will always remain, an outstanding problem of society. Its solution should challenge the best minds of each generation.

In an enlightened society the personnel, the curriculum, the organization, the methods, and the physical equipment of the schools must be subject to continuous critical revision. The principles which control this peculiar environment must not be so doctrinaire as to cause the school to lose touch with the community. To make this agency foster a cloistered existence, and thereby to separate it from the prevailing conditions of life, is pernicious educational policy. The school should be the leavening force; only as its purified environment is closely articulated with the general life of the community can those who come within its range of influence be expected to give effective expression to the aims and ideals which are to purify our present social, industrial, and political order. There is reason for possessing a deep faith in education; through no other force can society be purged; but in the light of the present condition of our educational agencies this is little more than a pathetic faith. Can we expect a system of traditional education, which is unanalyzed and unsocialized, which is administered by a relatively inferior personnel, and which is guided by a limited vision, to equip our people for the creation of a democratic society?

Is the school environment healthful? Attention must also be directed to the admirable opportunities for an extensive program of health cultivation and instruction which prolonged guardianship affords. Freedom from economic pressure should enable, and indeed compel, the individual to give attention to this important phase of life. Up to the present the ascetic and scholastic traditions of education have fostered a criminal neglect of the physical life of the child; in fact many would say that the influence of the school has, on the whole, been detrimental to health. In view of the enforced artificiality of the indoor school life, it is particularly incumbent on education to work for the promotion of physical well-being. For the vast majority of pupils, a slightly superior scholastic achievement gained at the expense of the cultivation of sound health and recreational habits and dispositions, carries no adequate compensation. No longer can we assume that the home automatically provides the health and recreational facilities formerly found in an open-air life; on this account, the school must take upon itself the task which its own procedures and the crowded conditions of our city life have created.

Does the school explore and recognize the capacities of the individual? The extension of the period of social infancy and of economic dependence also furnishes a period of exploration and experimentation, during which, with a view to present educational and eventual vocational guidance, the development of the pupil's mechanical, social, and intellectual capacities can be closely studied by the educator. Decisions made in the experimental environment of the school can be regarded as tentative; they are not irrevocable, as are many similar decisions in the outside world. Within the school itself care must be taken lest avenues of study and work be closed to the pupil before his interests and capacities have fully revealed themselves. But, at the same time, the desire to avoid this evil must not lead to the even greater evil of submitting all pupils to the same curriculum.

In the light of the great individual differences in those traits which a broadened school should cultivate, early differentiation is absolutely essential; in many cases important decisions will have to be made early in the school history of the child. A few serious mistakes of classification must be expected; to sacrifice the improvement of educational practice which will follow from greater differentiation is not only short-sighted but cowardly. The evils flowing from such action will be negligible in comparison with the evils resulting from the patent blunders caused by our present policy of inaction. The two warnings that must be issued are: firstly, that the school, through objective tests, exploratory courses, and teachers' reports, must study more diligently than heretofore the capabilities of the child; and, secondly, that classifications must be as tentative as the general policy of differentiation will permit.

In spite of the advantages which have been discussed, protracted guardianship is attended by many dangers which are the necessary concomitants of the very advantages mentioned. To the extent that society fails to create the advantageous environment which has been described, the period of dependence fails to yield its maximum benefit. Some of these disadvantages, for which the prolonged period of dependence of the individual is partly responsible, may now be profitably reviewed.

How does prolonged guardianship foster social parasitism? Before considering the more direct educational implications, we must direct attention to two large social evils which may flow from prolonged guardianship. In the first place, the lengthy period during which the individual may rightly expect support from parent or community may breed the notion that society has the same obligation, even when the adult stage is reached. From this delusion the social parasite, whether exemplified by the idle rich at one extreme, or by the irresponsible hobo at the other, never emancipates himself. Reared in a system which satisfies their wants, without requiring service in return, the two extreme groups never free themselves from the habits formed during this period. Just as society provides them shelter, clothing, and food for the first fourteen to thirty years of life, so it must continue to support them for the rest of their days — such is their erroneous belief.

How does prolonged guardianship affect the birth rate? The second evil which is commanding the attention of sociologists is the increased postponement or even renunciation of marriage in those occupations which require not only a long course of professional training, but also a considerable further period of relatively unremunerative employment. Lest the racial stock be impaired, in these classes should be found the maximum birth rate; but, under present conditions, their relative contribution to the increase of population is disproportionately low. This reduction in the birth rate of the favored class is the product not only of deferred marriage, but also the long dependence which the more intelligent parents desire and know to be essential to the welfare of their offspring. To redress both these evils, the state may have to intervene with more stringent laws in the case of the idle and a subsidization of advanced study for individuals of superior gifts.

How may society exploit the docility of the young? We may now return to consider certain of the more direct educational evils which are apt to be the accompaniments of the prolonged period of guardianship. These, in spite of the fact that they have received general attention in Problem 4, are so important as to merit consideration in the setting of our present discussion of guardianship.

In the first place, the docility of the child and his desire for the approval of his elders permits and even encourages an undue domination of the rising generation by the older members of society; this domination becomes increasingly galling when, in spite of the obvious fact that it is the manifestation of a selfish conservatism on the part of the older generation, it is rationalized as the expression of a wise and benign parental solicitude. Few teachers can forego the opportunity to patronize rather than educate the young. Many individuals, who could never exact respect from their adult fellows, find a compensation for a feeling of inferiority in the slavish and sycophantic obedience of their pupils. We cannot too often remind ourselves that eventually the pupil is to pass out of the hands of the educator; if, during the period of schooling, he does not become increasingly independent of external regulation, no sudden moral or intellectual conversion can be expected to follow the release from the restraints of the school. In order that the pupils may increase, the teacher must decrease. Morley, quoting Plutarch, " warns young men that it is well to go for a light to another man's fire, but by no means to tarry by it, instead of kindling a torch of their own." In its more refined form this domination is expressed in a method of teaching which presents every subject of instruction, however debatable and uncertain, as a body of finished and established truth. The minds of the pupils are closed, their views are formed. This prestige-suggestion of the teacher working in the intellectual realm is especially dangerous, for it seeks to mould thought into a fixed and final form. Before the individual has had the opportunity of making those contacts with life which would equip him with the materials for criticism, his mind is closed, his judgment is systematically and purposively warped.

How may the school lose touch with life? In the second place, the purification and simplification of the environment which constitute the essence of sound education are necessarily accompanied by an artificiality of atmosphere and procedures. Within this environment there is an absence of those powerful drives which accompany activities engaged in to satisfy the primitive wants of hunger, shelter, and clothing. Furthermore, by parental or community authority, the child is compelled to enter the school environment; he cannot, as on the playground, disengage himself when the activities become meaningless, exacting, or irksome. Were this compulsion removed, educators would show more industry and ingenuity than at present in the construction of curricula and in the adaptation of instructional methods. Instead of trusting so entirely to the efficacy of the birch, the scourge of public opinion, or the stronger rod of the law, they would court the interest of their pupils, and would devise more effective means of securing pupil effort. Monopoly always creates abuse. Evidences of such abuse are not lacking in our own system of compulsory education. This point is well illustrated by the following comment, often heard in our colleges: "Why alter our entrance requirements or modernize our course of study, when the prestige of the college is already more than filling our halls "? The vanes of our educational institutions are directed by the winds of tradition; our courses of study are too often divorced from the main interests and concerns of life. Those who shape the policies of the school are too occupied by the narrow activities of passing, failing, and graduating to articulate its activities with the changing conditions of the world. School procedure, sanctioned by centuries of practice, has come to have a value in and for itself. The true function of the school, and indeed its *raison d'être*, is forgotten. The pupil enters the school, and soon uncritically accepts its archaic procedures and its medieval standards. Only in his extra-curricular life, and in the knowledge that his schooling must sooner or later come to an end, does he find an outlet and a safety valve which prevents him from being emotionally deranged by the artificiality of the environment.

How may the school unduly sacrifice the present to the future?   Closely allied to this danger is that of regarding the school solely as a place of preparation for an after school life.   Under this conception of the educational function, the object of instruction is not that of making the present social life of the pupils more meaningful, but rather that of turning out, at the end of a prolonged school period, an educated product.

As we shall see later, the nature of adult activities must exert a powerful influence on school procedures: to overlook this fact is disastrous.   But the present life and social contacts of the pupil must be capitalized.   This complete sacrifice of the present to the future is often referred to as the vestibule idea of education.   Instruction under this conception lacks the drive and purpose which accompany activity possessing present significance.   The necessary sacrifice of interest to future effectiveness which accompanies the beginnings of writing, reading, and arithmetic has much to answer for in creating this attitude toward all education.   This is a devastating idea, not only because of its failure to give any immediate incentive to the pupil, but because the remoteness of the goal makes any critical evaluation of school procedure almost impossible.   Just as the church has derived benefit by stressing the importance of present life as opposed to the life after death, so the school can derive a similar benefit by turning its attention to immediate rather than to remote values.   We cannot be too critical of any school procedure which lacks present significance and is justified solely on the grounds of remote future utility.   Life during the period of guardianship is not suspended or postponed.   It has its own problems and its own values; problems and values which a wise system of education can never neglect.

ADDITIONAL PROBLEMS FOR DISCUSSION

1. How does the length of the period of dependence differ among different races, and among different classes of the same race?
2. What experimental evidence is there to indicate that children can memorize more economically than adults? In what respects has the program of the elementary school been influenced by the notion that childhood is the age of rapid and easy memorization?
3. When do children begin to reason? Show the continuity that exists between the reasoning of a young child and the reasoning of an adult?
4. What intimate bearing does the theory of gradual growth have on educational practices — method, school organization, and curriculum?
5. Upon what evidence is the popular theory based that in his development the child passes through the stages through which the race passed in the course of its evolution? Answer this question both from the biological and cultural standpoint.
6. What beneficial effects would follow from making attendance at the elementary school optional?
7. How is it that the school, presumably dedicated to the revolutionary process of thinking, is so frequently decidedly reactionary in its influence?
8. Give illustrations from the schools of the past and the present of the passing on to children of prejudices, half-truths, and falsehoods about the world.
9. Is the prolongation of the period of guardianship for the benefit of the individual or of society? How has the answer to this question changed during the history of education?
10. What responsibilities as regards physical and moral, as well as intellectual growth, does the school necessarily assume under the lengthened school day and school year?
11. What factors in a society tend to prolong the period of dependence?
12. What provision should be made to insure to the individual a prolonged period of dependence, regardless of the economic and social status of the parent? Is society working in the direction of assuming the whole economic burden of child support and education?
13. What would be the immediate and the deferred economic effects of the universal extension of education to eighteen years of age?
14. What precautions should be taken lest the prolongation of the period of dependence should be accompanied by disinclination to bear social responsibilities?
15. In view of the significance of a prolonged period of dependence, should bright children be promoted more rapidly than their fellows, if formal education is to cease at the end of the college period?

PROBLEM 11

HOW IS EDUCATION CONDITIONED BY INDIVIDUAL DIFFERENCES?

How universal are individual differences? — How are differences distributed? — What are the causes of individual differences? — How do the sexes differ? — How do the races differ? — What is the relative importance of heredity and environment? — How do individuals differ in a single trait? — Why is each individual unique? — How do individuals differ in combinations of traits? — How does the distribution of traits nullify the theory of types? — How must the school recognize the fact of individual differences? — Why must universal education have a great diversity of aim? — To what extent must selective education have regard to individual differences?

How universal are individual differences? Every organism has characteristics which differentiate it from every other member of the same species. In the human race, the most complex product of the evolutionary process, these differences are especially pronounced. Whether the grosser physical characteristics of height, weight, and volume of body, or the more minute formations of skin-texture and thumb-prints be examined, the wide range of variation is apparent. Likewise in function, as in structure, the same phenomena are observed; in rate of heart-beat, speed of digestion, or physical endurance, individuality is expressed.

To these departures of the individual from the norm of the group biologists apply the name " variation." While in the study of biological traits this nomenclature is employed, those variations in which the educator and the psychologist are more particularly interested, are usually referred to as " individual differences." Thus the educator interests himself in the differences which exist, from individual to individual, in industry, courage, honesty, interest in his fellows, intelligence, executive ability, arithmetical facility, historical information, musical capacity, etc. All of these traits, and thousands like them, constitute a proper study for the educational psychologist. What is the extent of these differences? What are their causes? What is their significance? If the process of education is to be intelligently conducted, these questions must be investigated.

How are differences distributed? The discussion of these and other applied questions will be facilitated if attention is directed for a moment to the variation in a physical characteristic, such as height. In this case objective

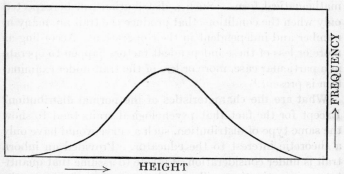

HEIGHT

DISTRIBUTION OF HEIGHT IN A LARGE UNSELECTED GROUP OF MEN
OF ANY RACE

measurement in terms of inches or centimeters is possible. If the problem is restricted to a consideration of differences found in a large unselected group of men of any race, reference to the accompanying diagram, in which the abscissa is the measure of height and the ordinate the frequency of the particular height, will reveal the nature of the distribution. There is a marked clustering around the average or median height of the group. The middle fifty per cent fall within

relatively narrow limits, and the remainder distribute themselves equally on either side, with diminishing frequency.
The greater the deviation from the mean, the fewer are the
individuals, until, at the extremes, only the dwarfs and
giants are found. If, for the same or other homogeneous
groups, the distribution of weight, length of index finger, or
chest measurement is investigated, a frequency curve of the
same general form is discovered. Within certain limits, so
generally do such distributions follow a typical and well-
known mathematical curve, called the normal probability
curve, that the distribution of such traits may be thought of
in terms of an approximation, more or less close, to its rigid
mathematical form. Such a distribution can be expected
only when the conditions that produce the trait are many in
number and independent in their operation. According as
more or less of these independent factors happen to operate
in a particular case, more or less of the trait under examination is present.[1]

What are the characteristics of the normal distribution?
Except for the fact that psychological traits tend to show
the same type of distribution, such a curve would have only
a theoretic interest to the educator. Provided an inborn
trait is under consideration, it is safe to assume that quantitative investigation will reveal an approximation to the
normal curve. Such indeed might be expected in view of
the relation of psychological function to physiological process. In acquired traits, such as achievement in school
subjects, any unselected group whose members have been
submitted to somewhat similar training influences, will
exhibit a distribution of like nature. Whenever problems of
individual differences are under consideration, continuous

[1] If, on account of a lack of statistical theory, the reader has difficulty in
understanding this statement, he must content himself with an examination of the curve.

reference to this typical form of " bell-shaped " distribution is necessary. Its study brings out the following three important facts, which aid clear thinking in this field; first, the variations or differences found in any single trait are usually continuous; second, these variations cluster around a single type; third, any classifications into types are essentially arbitrary in their nature and find their only justification in practical convenience.

Each one of these points may be illustrated by reference to a trait of basic significance to education, namely, the unanalyzed grouping of abilities commonly known as " general intelligence." For purpose of illustration, we shall assume that " general intelligence " is measured by a single scale, such as the Binet-Simon test or by some other examination which makes no attempt to analyze the relatively independent components of this complex trait. Under these conditions, from the lowest type of idiot to a level of intelligence possessed by a Socrates or a Newton, there is continuous progression; in spite of the wide differences, the extremes are connected by imperceptible gradations of capacity. In this trait there is but a single type from which all individuals may be regarded as deviating — the hypothetical average man. Furthermore, any classification of men into idiot, imbecile, moron, dull, average, superior, very superior, genius, and super-genius is essentially a matter of definition. Since such lines of cleavage are not found in nature, these divisions are the arbitrary creation of man.

What are the causes of individual differences? Any wide sampling, such as the population of a large cosmopolitan city, provides the material for the study of the various causes which account for the differences in human traits. These variations can all be classified under the following five divisions: 1. race differences; 2. family differences; 3. sex differences; 4. age differences; 5. environmental and

educational differences. Each individual of the group possesses a unique quantitative combination of properties
because of membership in a certain race, because of an
hereditary endowment through his immediate ancestry,
because of sex, because of degree of maturity, and because
of certain special environmental and educational conditions.

How do the sexes differ? With reference to sex and race
differences, a passing mention must be made of the experimental evidence which has been collected. While there are
great differences between the sexes in physiological structure, and in emotional and mechanical traits some divergence, the distinction in intellectual traits seems slight. In
emotional traits the scales are very insecure, but we may be
sure from the fragmentary evidence that in social tact,
companionship, and so-called intuition there is no outstanding superiority of one sex over the other. In intellectual traits, such as those measured by an abstract intelligence test, the evidence is still clearer, and here the two
sexes manifest about equal capacity. Such differences as
strike the observer must be traced rather to differences in
environmental force playing on one sex, rather than to any
fundamental difference in mechanical, social, or intellectual
capacity. Recent researches, published by the Vaertings,
into the physical and psychological traits exhibited by the
two sexes in a civilization where women rather than men
are dominant, suggest, and in fact almost prove, that those
traits which we customarily regard as masculine are really
the traits of the dominant sex. These are manifested by the
women in those groups in which the female sex plays the
dominant rôle. Similarly, under such conditions, men assume many of the characteristics of the women of western
civilization. Both observational and exact results are in
striking contrast with the popular notion that men and
women, in their inborn social and intellectual capacities,

are, as classes, poles asunder.   Even allowing for the fact
that the experimental evidence has been obtained in somewhat artificial situations, we can certainly say that, under
the test conditions of the school and the laboratory, the
differences in social, mechanical, and intellectual reactions
within either of the sexes is so great, compared with the
differences between the average achievements of the two
sexes, that there is an almost complete overlapping of the
two groups.   Certainly differences are not sufficient on the
intellectual side to justify the segregation of the boys and
girls in instruction.

How do the races differ?   In the matter of race differences the results are somewhat similar to those found in
the case of sex.   If we restrict our attention to unselected
groups of all but the obviously backward races, there
is but little evidence of great superiority of one race over
another.   The question is of course complicated by the
different climatic, cultural, and occupational forces which
play upon different races in different parts of the globe.
Until these environmental forces can be made more nearly
equal, or their effects more exactly measured, it is premature to assume very marked differences in social and intellectual traits.   The variation found within any one race is so
great as compared with the difference in achievements of the
various races as to make any sweeping assertions with reference to racial superiority very precarious.

Contrasting the colored population of the United States
with the white population, after allowing for the difference
in the opportunity, motivation, and tradition of the two
groups, we may legitimately assume that the white population is, on the usual intelligence scale, a year or a year
and a half superior to the pure stock of the colored race, but
the overlapping in intellectual status of the two races is so
great as to nullify the popular conception of the extreme

differences of the two groups. A further common idea that
the colored population develops mentally at just about the
same rate as the white population, and suffers from arrested
development in the early years of adolescence, also fails to
receive any significant experimental support.

Summarizing, we may say that sex differences and race
differences exist, but that they are much less than is commonly supposed. With reference to the former it is safe to
say that, with the introduction of more refined methods for
measuring the social and emotional reactions, greater differences than those which have been found in intellectual traits
will be revealed, but, until such instruments are available,
the degree of the difference must remain unknown.

**What is the relative importance of heredity and environ-
ment?** To assign weight to each of the five factors producing individual differences would carry us into the realm
of profitless controversy. However, the ever-recurring
problem regarding the relative potency of hereditary as
opposed to environmental forces may well be considered.
Since the days of Galton's pioneer work, much evidence
bearing on this question, so fundamental for education, has
been gathered. A review of the large amount of careful
experimentation in this field leads to the conclusion that the
earlier hypothesis of the almost complete efficacy of the
environment must give way to a less comforting theory.
The educational process, both on the social and the intellectual side, is much limited by the native differences in
men. Without a range of vision denied to mortals no one is
able to state dogmatically that the evidence shows native
equipment to be more potent than environment in shaping
human behavior. So closely interdependent are the two
factors that such a bald statement is meaningless. But
that the native endowment has not, up to the present, been
given due weight in educational theory may be said with

confidence. Any system of education or any system of social control which assumes the almost complete omnipotence of environmental forces is doomed to failure. As the civil engineer takes into account the inherent properties of the materials with which he works, so the human engineer must control his activities in the light of those inborn properties of men which environment is powerless to create or to destroy.

How do individuals differ in a single trait? Individual differences in a single trait should always be regarded as quantitative, rather than qualitative. The complete absence of a particular trait, such as lack of knowledge of Sanscrit, which is ordinarily regarded as a qualitative difference, is only the limiting case of zero ability on a scale for measuring acquaintance with this ancient language. Among individuals who have studied Sanscrit for a definite period of time, a distribution approximating the normal type would be found. While objective scales for the measurement of many of the more important social and moral traits are still lacking, this should not prevent thought regarding these traits from being guided by quantitative concepts. At the present moment, we see emerging more or less satisfactory instruments for the measurement of a certain narrow type of intelligence, particularly that form upon which a bookish and intellectualized type of school is dependent. The increasing popularity of these instruments, and particularly their wide use in practical affairs, have hastened and encouraged quantitative thinking with reference to this most important group of human capacities. For measuring persistence, emotional stability, moral integrity, coöperative ability, and a host of other fundamental human traits, no reliable scales are as yet available; nevertheless, the distribution of these traits presumably follows the normal probability curve. A few are highly endowed, many are moderately gifted, and a small number have but little capacity.

Why is each individual unique? The development of personality through the modification of original nature by a slow process of habit-formation is conditioned by the unique combination of traits with which the individual is endowed at birth. If we consider, firstly, those loose groupings of behavior-reactions known as instincts, it is patent that every individual is endowed, to a certain degree, with each tendency. But if the repertoire of instincts permitted sufficiently clear definition, and then permitted correspondingly precise measurement, we should discover that each individual had varying amounts of each of the tendencies. The complexity of this compounding of elements precludes the possibility of identical original natures.

The number of combinations which can be formed from a few tendencies, showing wide quantitative differences, is infinite. When we consider how numerous are the original tendencies, it is little wonder that nature never repeats herself. As an essential property of the action system, though not separate from the instincts themselves, the plasticity upon which habit formation is dependent must also be mentioned. Men differ as much in their plasticity as they do in any other respect. In the ability to make those more refined integrations which accompany reflection, still greater differences exist. If dissimilar environments are allowed to act upon these differences in original structure, extremely wide variations in personality and character may be anticipated.

How do individuals differ in combinations of traits? This introduces us to one of the most important problems raised by the phenomena of individual differences. Not only is the manner in which a single trait distributes itself among the population a subject of concern to us, but, of even greater interest, is the way in which various traits are combined and related in the same individual. Extensive quantitative studies of the distribution of important mental traits, in large groups of children, have shown that high endowment in one desirable tendency is apt to be accompanied by more than the average endowment in others. While no definite law can be stated, the correlation between desirable intellectual and social traits is certainly positive. When the elements are mixed to form a man, nature tends, on the whole to be uniformly generous, uniformly moderate, or uniformly niggardly. The old comforting theory of compensation, which assumes that meager gifts in one direction are compensated for by superior endowment in some other equally valuable quality, is not in accord with facts. Notwithstanding some superficial evidence to the contrary, intellectual ability, mechanical skill, emotional stability, persistence, and other desirable qualities seem to be positively associated.

This does not mean that the same individual may not be much more highly endowed in one direction than in another; statistical investigations have merely proved that one form of superior native talent is, as a rule, the accompaniment of other forms of original excellence. Of course, specialized training may develop one capacity at the expense of another, and thus tend to give the impression that a principle of compensation operates. For example, a man of intellectual pursuits, brought up in an atmosphere of leisure, may never have the opportunity nor the occasion to cultivate his mechanical aptitudes. Under these conditions his mental agility may be in marked contrast with his manual disability. Such a case, of course, proves nothing. To establish the theory of compensation it would be necessary to prove that he, or men of his class, had their circumstances necessitated the gaining of manual dexterity, would have shown themselves incompetent in this field. The available experimental evidence indicates, that persons of superior mental endowment, if given adequate training, would also be superior, as a rule, in mechanical achievement. The old assumption of the existence of clearly defined mental and motor types, in one of which every individual must fall, finds no experimental support.

How does the distribution of traits nullify the theory of types? On account of the positive correlation in the various desirable traits, any attempt to divide individuals into a few recognized types is futile. False theories of educational guidance, based on the erroneous doctrine that all individuals tend to conform more or less closely to one of the several clearly marked types, have long been championed. The claim has been made that around each one of these hypothetical types a large number of individuals cluster. According to this doctrine, the particular type to which an individual conforms may be quickly determined by examining a few basic traits. If the main characteristics of each of these types are discovered educational procedure may, with advantage, be adjusted to each of these relatively few natural groupings. A doctrine of this kind, with its consequent simplification of many of the problems of instruction, is so attractive that, even though the experimental evidence proves it in error, educators have been loath to abandon it.

In one form or another this theory crops out again and again in all thinking on social and educational theory; it is rampant in popular writing, on classification of pupils, and vocational guidance. In the days of Plato, it was the philosopher, the warrior, and the artisan which formed the natural classifications and determined political theory and education. Yesterday it was the visual, auditory, and kinæsthetic types which must be segregated and given separate instruction. To-day a recrudescence of the same idea is exhibited by those who insist that children can be separated into two groups, those who " work with their heads " and those who " work with their hands." Recent studies in which the mechanical aptitude and the intelligence of children are measured show that, in certain cases, high ability of the former order may be the concomitant of relatively low intelligence. But, however true the observation may be that in particular individuals marked intellectual ability is combined with an equally marked manual disability, or the reverse, such cases can never establish the type theory. In combinations of traits, as in single traits, men vary around one and only one type, the human type. The only type which can be postulated is the hypothetical average, commonplace, mediocre human from which every individual diverges to a greater or less degree.

Why must education treat each individual as unique? Abandoning the theory of types, we are driven to study each individual by himself to discover the measure in which he is endowed with various human traits. Particularly must those which he possesses in relatively larger degree than his other traits be singled out for special attention. Each individual must be treated as a separate problem; no resort can be made to any false simplification. An uncritical acceptance of the fact of positive correlation between desirable traits should not lead to a pessimistic and deterministic attitude with regard to the possibilities of education. Having explored the capabilities of a particular child in a few directions, only to find him deficient in each, one is always tempted to follow the generalization and come to the hasty conclusion that he is correspondingly poorly endowed in every trait. We find him poor in certain traits, which the present school values highly, and we assume that he is poor in all other respects.

The cure for this fatalistic manner of thinking is found in two directions, strangely opposed in their emphasis: firstly an eternal optimism regarding the possibilities of human nature; secondly, a more adequate understanding of the statistical significance of correlation. Optimism is necessary to motivate the search for those traits in which the child is relatively strong; a more adequate understanding of the significance of correlation shows that, however uniform may be the general tendency to positive correlation between desirable traits, within this general trend individual cases will diverge markedly from the rule. The very statistical studies to which appeal is made when discarding the theory of compensation prove with equal conclusiveness that in every individual some traits stand out favorably from his general level of capacity. Even though, with reference to the general population, an individual may be relatively low in all traits, certain of his powers raise themselves above the rest. Through these the individual should find a mode of expression and gain a recognition which his average level of attainment could never earn. The financial failure may have a gift for friendship, and, in a specific direction, the village dullard may show a reliability and a faithfulness which genius might envy. The large problem raised by the special abilities and disabilities which are found to exist within the same individual demands the careful consideration and minute study of the educator.

How must the school recognize the fact of individual differences? The school must have a diversity in its objectives and methods which is comparable with the diversity in human nature. The recognition of individual differences calls for a differentiation and a flexibility of curriculum and procedure which are limited only by the social and individual needs to be served and by the teaching resources of the school. As long as the school was a purposefully selective agent and opened its doors only to those who were later to form a learned class, there was some reason for the glorification of an intellectual ideal. To-day, under totally different conditions, there is no justification for such a narrow conception of aim.

We are in the greatest peril of measuring every individual and every process by a single standard. " Either learn or depart, there is no third way here," may be a sound motto to inscribe on the gates of the common school; but the connotation of the word " learn " must be carefully and critically examined. If to learn includes growth in mechanical skills, in the formation of health habits, in social habitudes, in the power to coöperate, in the recognition of the obligations of group life, in the enjoyment of companionship, in the love of music, in the appreciation of art, in an attitude of willing service, then the motto is an excellent one; but, if to " learn " signifies merely the gaining of facility in certain intellectual studies, such a motto is vicious. A school system with the single intellectual objective has much to answer for in the discouragement, thwarting, badgering, and heckling to which it submits a portion of its population — that portion which does not happen to possess the powers demanded by its relatively narrow disciplines. Many a child leaves school with an " inferiority-complex " which, if it does not color his whole life, only vanishes as a result of several years of successful experience in the more catholic and tolerant contacts of the everyday world.

Unless the common school is willing to set up other objectives than those of high academic attainment, the question may well be asked whether compulsory attendance to the age of sixteen is good for all. If, for a considerable number of the pupils, such attendance means continuous coercion in externally imposed activities under conditions of anti-social competition, perchance the moral disintegration brought about by such a process may more than counterbalance the small amount of book knowledge gained.

Whether the experiences incident to the gaining of a livelihood, even under our present industrial conditions, would
not be for many more educative than those of the typical
academic school is a debatable question.

As a people we have an abounding confidence in the good
that is derived by every child from mere bodily presence in
the precincts of the school. Whatever the quality of the
teacher, whatever the content of the curriculum, whatever
the nature of the motivation, whatever the social organization of the school group, we believe that only good can
eventuate from attendance. A more critical examination
of the results of the educational process, especially in the
later years of adolescence, might well make us restless in
this comforting belief. The obvious benefit derived by
some of the more intellectually gifted pupils should not
blind us to the equally obvious futility of imposing this type
of education on all. While it may be going too far to state
that, in the upper levels of the system, the total influence of
the school on a portion of its population is negative, we are
on firm ground in asserting that, in comparison with the
possibilities, the school is failing lamentably.

**Why must universal education have a great diversity of
aim?** If universal compulsory education is to justify itself,
educators, recognizing the intellectual limitations imposed
by nature, must embark on fearless experimentation in the
attempt to make the activities of the school more meaningful and more serviceable to its diverse clientele. Different
aims, different curricula, different social organizations must
be tried. Particularly joint activities must be sought
through which children of modest intellectual capacity may
acquire those mechanical skills, those elements of information, and those social attitudes which form the entrance requirements to the simpler walks of life. Particularly also
must be stressed actual participation in those concrete ac-

tivities whereby a socially enlightened community will induct the individual into a fuller physical, family, economic, civic, recreational, and religious life.

Intellectual snobbery and the educational spirit go ill together. Each separate curriculum which is derived from the careful study of the needs of any group in the school population should carry a dignity and receive the support and recognition which must always attach to any activity having as its objective the betterment of mankind. Let no one be so bold as to assign final relative values to these various types of educational activity; there is no room for intellectual pharisaism so long as each activity has an absolute and intrinsic worth to the individual who pursues it. Superiority, except with reference to certain objectives, is without meaning; industry regards as superior the man who plays its game; the school, the man who has intellectual talent; the family, the man who has the gift for affection; the church, the man who is capable of self-sacrifice; society, the man who is willing to give social service. The world of which the school forms a part calls for such varied abilities, for such a wide range of talents, for such a host of services, that it ill befits the school to laud one somewhat narrow type of superiority at the expense of the rest. A tolerant catholicity must permeate all our thinking about the functions of the common school.

To what extent must selective education have regard to individual differences? What has just been said applies more particularly to the period of compulsory education. Beyond this stage, in so far as the population of the school is unselected, *mutatis mutandis*, the same principles apply. When, however, special institutions are created with specific aims which plan only to cater to particular groups, the whole situation is changed. A study of individual differences in these cases would merely be helpful in devising effective instruments for selecting those who might reasonably be expected to benefit from the special instruction and to succeed in the particular calling. Education is much too expensive, both in money, and, more especially, in the more important direction of human effort, to allow ill-sorted individuals to clog and retard the working of such specialized agencies. Even within these institutions a certain amount of choice should be offered in the form of electives, for, however strict may be the process of selection, the individual differences that may be expected in such a group are, of necessity, great. These should be allowed that limited expression which is consonant with the main objectives of the institution.

What is the social significance of individual differences? This discussion of individual differences may be closed and summarized by stressing the following six points:

(1) The need for accurate knowledge of the extent of individual differences.

(2) The necessity for wider aims in the school and in society.

(3) The need for adapting the methods of education to these differences.

(4) The importance of cultivating in each person those traits in which, compared with the general level of his equipment, he is more richly endowed, provided these traits are socially useful and capable of yielding satisfaction to the individual.

(5) The importance of attaching a dignity and worth to many and different types of activity and occupation.

(6) The importance of instilling into each individual the conviction that there are some special services which, on account of inborn difference or peculiar environmental circumstances, he, and he alone, can render.

ADDITIONAL PROBLEMS FOR DISCUSSION

1. What definite administrative practices, in recent education in this country, can be traced directly or indirectly to a recognition of the importance of individual differences?

2. How can the fact of individual differences be reconciled with a democratic conception of education and social life?

3. What is the distinction between a qualitative and quantitative difference in human traits? Criticize the statement that differences in human personality are qualitative as well as quantitative?

4. Suppose the absurd attempt were made to equalize the term achievement of all members of a class in algebra, what devices would have to be employed?

5. How has the idea of the normal distribution of traits shattered many of the old theories based on clearly differentiated types?

6. What justification is there for the statement that the concept of the distribution of traits according to the normal probability curve is perhaps the most fertile concept in the field of the social sciences? Show its significance in the field of education?

7. What arguments would you adduce in favor of the theory that moral differences are much more the product of environmental forces than are intellectual differences?

8. What are the advantages and disadvantages of giving to children information as to their relative standings in intelligence and educational tests?

9. What arguments can be adduced to justify the expenditure of public funds for the extension of unusual and costly educational privileges to: (a) the mental defective; (b) the intellectual superior?

10. What are the factors in the ordinary school situation which make extremely difficult the adequate recognition of individual differences?

11. To what extent, in the existing economic order, do individual differences actually determine vocational choice?

12. What bearing have the known facts of individual differences on the proposed extension of universal compulsory education to the age of eighteen?

PART THREE

WHAT ARE THE SOCIOLOGICAL FOUNDATIONS OF EDUCATION?

An understanding of the sociological foundations of education requires the discussion of the following questions:

THROUGH education the child acquires control over the instrumentalities of civilization, and learns to participate in the life of his time. Therefore the only guide to a sound educational program is to be found in a critical analysis of this life. Such an analysis shows that there are six great interests about which human life revolves, and through which human nature is given expression. Men must always care for their bodies, rear their children, secure the economic necessities, organize for civic action, engage in recreation, and satisfy their religious cravings. Since the modes in which these needs find expression are the product of the cumulative experience of successive generations, the advance, and even the conservation of culture, depends on their successful transmission. Hence, from the beginning of human history, skills, knowledges, and ideals — the slow product of action, thought, and feeling — have by a process of tuition been passed from parent to child. Thus the social heritage has been conserved and youth has been inducted into the life of the group. In the past the major portion of this educational burden has been borne by the informal agencies; the school has touched life only at those points which to minds of scholastic temper seemed of the greatest moment. To-day, in almost every field of human interest, owing to the growth of knowledge, the expansion of human society, and the formulation of social purposes, grievous maladjustment abounds and achievement lags far behind possibility. The task of moderating this maladjustment and of bringing practice abreast of knowledge, having become too heavy for the incidental educational agencies, must be performed in increasing measure by the school. Because of the differentiation in modern society, the discovery and conservation of knowledge may leave the lives of the masses unaffected; through specialists this possession may remain from age to age an esoteric and relatively inert body of experience. The school, at all levels, must abandon its narrow literary and scholastic tradition and steadfastly associate and intimately identify itself with the activities of a people searching for a democratic mode of living. It must seek to further the physical and mental health of the population, to promote wholesome family relations, to order and humanize industry, to advance and purify the civic interest, to enrich and make significant the recreational activities, and to foster an ethical and enlightened religious life. Such an education would, to the limit of his capacity, fit each man "to perform justly, skillfully, and magnanimously all the offices both private and public" of a world citizen.

An understanding of the sociological foundations of education requires the discussion of the following problems:

PROBLEM 12. HOW MAY EDUCATION FURTHER HEALTH?
PROBLEM 13. HOW MAY EDUCATION PROMOTE THE FAMILY LIFE?
PROBLEM 14. HOW MAY EDUCATION ORDER AND HUMANIZE THE ECONOMIC LIFE?
PROBLEM 15. HOW MAY EDUCATION ADVANCE THE CIVIC LIFE?
PROBLEM 16. HOW MAY EDUCATION ENRICH THE RECREATIONAL LIFE?
PROBLEM 17. HOW MAY EDUCATION FOSTER THE RELIGIOUS LIFE?

PROBLEM 12

HOW MAY EDUCATION FURTHER HEALTH?

Why should health be the first concern of education? — How has man sought to control disease? — What degree of health do the American people enjoy? — How does civilization modify the conditions of healthful living? — Is a more healthful world possible? — Why does health practice lag behind health knowledge? — Why must the school bear larger responsibilities in the promotion of health? — How may the school provide for the formation of health habits? — How may the school impart health information? — How may the school develop a health conscience? — How must the school modify its program?

Why should health be the first concern of education? Health, the basis of both individual and social welfare, is the essence of life. Only a virile people is able to develop and maintain a high type of civilization, and only a robust individual can in fullest measure make actual his potential gifts. Since health is the condition of balanced and normal functioning of the life processes, in so far as it is impaired, life itself is compromised. The close dependence of mental on physiological processes and changes makes health almost essential to happiness and large intellectual achievement. While there are many isolated instances that suggest the contrary, the very attention they attract indicates their exceptional nature and goes far to prove the soundness of the principle of dependence.

Recent investigations of school children have exploded the popular notion that extraordinary mental development is usually accompanied by physical weakness, and have confirmed the opposing hypothesis of a positive correlation between these two phases of growth. Health holds the distinction of being a good in itself and a means to all else.

This suggests the oft-quoted statement of Spencer that " To be a good animal is the first requisite to success in life, and to be a nation of good animals is the first condition to national prosperity." And it must have been in the mind of Hippocrates when he said, " Wherever there is love of mankind, there is love of the medical art."

How have men regarded health? By all peoples that have not been influenced by some unnatural philosophy which exalts the mortification of the body and seeks to promote the spirit at the sacrifice of the flesh, the fundamental rôle of health in human affairs has been recognized. Throughout the ages men have yearned for health and life, and have dreaded disease and death; they have gone on innumerable quests for the fountain of perpetual youth, whose waters would break the hold of years; they have sought the elixir of life, with which to prolong their days on the earth; they have created Fausts, who in their old age sell their souls for the return of youthful vigor; they have imagined Utopias, where there is neither sickness nor want; they have even denied death, and dreamed of worlds beyond the skies in which they hope to live the life of eternal youth. Any new cult, however fantastic it may be, that promises relief from suffering and disease is almost certain of a large following; any nostrum, regardless of the nature of its ingredients, that is widely advertised for the curing of a common malady is sure to interest thousands. The ubiquitous drug store in our cities is a striking witness to our great concern about disease. Two hundred years ago " a pox upon you " was one of the common curses; to-day the ordinary salutation is merely a formalized query concerning health, and the farewell usually carries a wish for the continuance or the improvement of bodily vigor. Men have long recognized that with health are interwoven all the fortunes of life.

How has man sought to control disease? During his long career on the earth man has learned much about disease. From the beginning of his upward struggle through savagery and barbarism to civilization sickness has attracted his earnest attention. Time and again plagues and scourges have visited him, carrying off with little warning great numbers of the population; while in less spectacular fashion the minor ailments have quietly exacted their toll of human life. In his efforts to gain control over these destroying forces man has evolved a vast array of hypotheses concerning the nature and causation of disease. For centuries at a time, in blind faith, he has followed some seemingly promising lead only to erect superstitions to bar the way to genuine progress. He has thought to see relations that do not exist, and endeavored to promote health through a study of the courses of the stars; he has assumed the working of forces that are but the creatures of his imagination, and made propitiatory sacrifices to evil and unfriendly spirits. Until quite recent times it was customary to regard disease as either a diabolical visitation or a divine punishment. In the Middle Ages amber was worn upon the person with the assurance that it was a certain protection against fevers, and to-day among certain elements of the population there is a naïve faith in the efficacy of drugs.

Not all the premises, however, on which man has worked have proved false. Some have been found true; and from these, sifted out from the false through the slow process of trial and error, in which error frequently meant death, there has gradually evolved the science of medicine. With the coming of the modern world men began to study the human organism with greater and greater care, and thus developed the sciences on which medicine is based and through which the medical art is being improved. As a consequence, within the last three or four centuries man has practically banished certain diseases, such as bubonic plague and smallpox, from the civilized regions of the earth; he has greatly reduced the prevalence of others, such as typhoid fever and diphtheria; and he has increased the average length of life from twenty to more than forty years. This achievement has been possible through the formal education of a few specialists and the incidental education of the masses of the population — a marvelous achievement in view of the fact that no great collective effort has been made to utilize, for the benefit of the race, all available knowledge.

What degree of health do the American people enjoy? The entire harvest of these past sowings, therefore, has by no means been gathered. We obviously stand to-day only at the beginning. Much remains to be done. Our knowledge greatly outstrips our practice. Consider for a moment the present situation as regards physical defect, illness, accident, lowered vitality, and premature death. As a people we come from a vigorous racial stock and we live in a relatively healthful climate, yet physical defect is all but universal and preventable disease passes no one by. The late World War disclosed an unexpectedly large amount of physical impairment in that portion of the population which is supposed to be most robust. Approximately thirty per cent of our young men between the ages of twenty-one and thirty-one years, who were called in the draft, were disqualified for active military service because of physical defects. In some of the great industrial centers this percentage rose to a much higher figure, while in certain other sections of the country it was cut in half.

That defects of this order are not confined to our adult population is shown by the examination of school children. According to competent investigators, about three fourths of the children enrolled in our schools are in need of attention for physical defects which are partially or wholly remediable. During the next ten years six millions of people in the United States will probably die from preventable disease. The annual cost in dollars and cents of such ailments exceeds the entire expenditure for the support of our schools, and the cost in human happiness is incalculable. While the prevalence of the communicable diseases is declining, there are other diseases, notably cancer and the chronic organic diseases affecting the heart, blood vessels, and kidneys, which are on the increase. Because of ignorance, poverty, or indifference there are many people in the nation who, even in cases of serious illness, have no medical care whatsoever. The percentage of such persons is, of course, difficult to determine with any great degree of accuracy, but the findings of various medical surveys, conducted in different parts of the country, indicate that it is far from negligible. To the burden of illness and physical defect must be added that of accident. Annually in the United States there are about 2,000,000 accidents of sufficient severity to keep the individual from work for a period of at least four weeks. Of these, 75,000 are fatal. But, altogether apart from the spectacular misfortunes of defect, disease, and accident, human life may be greatly deepened and invigorated. Because of the operation of a wide variety of forces, to be considered shortly, the great majority of people to-day suffer from lowered vitality. Through the application of knowledge already available the general physical efficiency of the ordinary individual could be greatly increased. Finally, as a consequence of physical defect, disease, accident, and lowered vitality, there is much premature death. Although the average length of life is greater than in times past, it is still from six to eight years less in the United States than in certain other countries, such as Denmark, Norway, and Sweden; and medical authorities tell us that it could be increased at least ten years by adopting hygienic reforms already proven entirely practicable.

How does civilization modify the conditions of healthful living? The tendencies toward physical impairment in its various aspects are greatly aggravated by the changed conditions under which man lives. If any organism suffers a striking alteration in its environment or mode of life, it is a well-known fact that there follows a period during which it is especially subject to disease. An illustration of this process is furnished when a primitive race comes into contact with a highly developed civilization, and succumbs rapidly to strange diseases for which it has no special immunity. The organism requires time to work out a biological adaptation to the new conditions, and it may perish in the process. Civilized man to-day is in a position not wholly different from that of the primitive race to which reference has just been made. He is living in a new environment to which adaptation cannot be effected through the alteration of the biological inheritance, because this environment is constantly changing. Man finds himself at present in an artificial environment which is in large part his own creation — an environment which is very different from that in which the human organism was evolved. As we have already noted, through control over disease and the food supply the conditions of life have been eased somewhat and the length of life has been increased, but there are many factors in modern life that tend to offset these gains.

We are apparently leaving forever the old world whose dominant elements were earth, sky, trees, streams, mountains, prairies, sunshine, storms, snow, rain, winter, summer, wild animals, raw food, footpaths, abundance, scarcity, floods, droughts, starvation, early marriage, violence, relaxation, hunting, and fishing; and we are moving into a world of clothing, houses, chairs, artificial heat, electricity, cooked foods, spices, locomotives, trolleys, automobiles, aeroplanes, telephones, books, newspapers, microscopes, machines, late marriage, prostitution, hospitals, sanitariums, poorhouses, schools, libraries, drugs, doctors, dentists, opticians, obstetricians, birth control, suicide, cities, sewage systems, slums, wealth, theaters, churches, continuous employment, uninteresting occupations, factories, sedentary life, and specialization. This new world creates its own mental and physical diseases and defects.

While for many the approach of death may be postponed by removing the dangers to life and making it easier to live, there is no guarantee that this is not purchased at the price of a weakened race and a reduced zest in living. A race of men is needed that can live in this man-made world, and, since we cannot wait for the slow processes of organic evolution to produce such a race, there remains only the method of education. But if this method is used, the educational program should be of sufficient scope to attack the problem in its twofold aspect. On the one hand, we should give to the individual those habits, knowledges, interests, and ideals which fit him to live a healthy life under the conditions of civilization; and, on the other, we should strive so to modify these conditions that they will tend to conserve rather than destroy human life.

Is a more healthful world possible? There is no good reason for believing that the task which education is here asked to undertake is an impossible one, provided that very intelligence can be brought to bear upon it which has brought civilization into being. The progress of the past in controlling disease, in spite of no general and conscious effort on the part of society, suggests that this important portion of the problem is easily soluble. Something over a generation ago Pasteur said that " It is within the power of man to rid himself of every parasitic disease." In the case of certain diseases the truth of this statement has already been demonstrated, and in speaking of tuberculosis, one of the most stubborn of this class of human ailments, Earl Mayo has declared:

> If the members of the medical profession were given a free hand to deal with this disease, backed by adequate provision for the care of existing cases, tuberculosis could be practically stamped out within a single generation.

The work of Gorgas in the Panama Zone shows what is possible. In the course of ten years one of the most disease-ridden spots of the earth was made healthful; yellow fever, the scourge of the tropics, was completely rooted out; and the general death rate was reduced about ninety per cent. Equally striking have been the achievements of the naval medical service in certain islands of the Pacific, where the authorities have been unhampered in their efforts to grapple with the health problems of the population. The National Safety Council has proved that three fourths of industrial accidents are preventable; the work of the army has shown that many physical defects are amenable to treatment; and in innumerable instances the efficacy of the rules of personal hygiene has been established. The President of the American Medical Association has recently said: [1]

> If doctors could apply all they know to all the people, not only would life be prolonged and human happiness increased, but the whole aspect and order of life would be altered.

Why does health practice lag behind health knowledge? Here is a great body of knowledge which man has been slowly accumulating through the centuries and which can usher in a much more healthful world than the one in which we live. Why is it not being utilized? Various answers to

[1] Wilbur, R. L.: Convention of Tri-State Medical Association, Des Moines, Iowa, November, 1923.

this question suggest themselves. The development of science has been so recent that as yet society has made no genuine and systematic effort to find a place for it in the general social economy. It is not strange that scientific method, assailed so bitterly for generations by all the forces of the established order, and hardly tolerated to-day in many quarters, receives no adequate appreciation. In other words our customs do not adequately recognize the importance of this body of knowledge or the method by which it has been derived. As habits tend to persist in the life of the individual, customs resist change in the life of the group. We have but lately emerged from savagery, and our entire system of thought and belief shows only too plainly its origin. Vestiges of the superstitions of forgotten ages cling to us as the accent of his native tongue clings to the outlander long after he has lost touch with the homeland.

Moreover, the origin of our schools antedates the development of any carefully sifted knowledge about the nature and causation of health and disease. For the main part our formal educational agencies were established either to transmit orthodox interpretations of sacred Scripture to coming generations, or to insure the mastery of the tools of knowledge — reading, writing, and arithmetic. As a consequence the school has been identified from the first with a tradition of naïve faith in the perfection and finality of a Scripture which, as interpreted, fostered a pathological unconcern about health, promoted a morbid interest in other-worldliness, and in extreme cases even exalted the mortification of the flesh. We have therefore had no great popular institution whose clearly recognized function has been that of keeping social practice abreast of our knowledge about health and disease.

This condition has been exaggerated somewhat, perhaps, because of the persistence in the popular mind of a certain fatalism with respect to disease and physical misfortune — a fatalism that disappears only on the higher levels of sophistication. Man is inclined to regard the visits of these unwelcome guests as occurring quite independently of his own bidding; there seems to be a psychological principle operating which on the recovery of health banishes the memories of suffering: " Vows made in pain, ease will recant." In the matter of health man is notoriously improvident. While most people recognize in their more thoughtful moments the fundamental importance of physical well-being, they are so absorbed in their immediate interests that they give little attention to the conservation of health until the processes of physical impairment are well advanced. Each is confident that the adversity which has overtaken his neighbor is not stalking him. Members of the human species, though self-styled *sapiens*, are only a degree more subtle than the fur seal of the Pribilof Islands that watches with perfect composure the killing and skinning of his mates, even though all the facts in the case suggest that in another moment his own blood will be mingled with theirs. It is perhaps one of the ironies of fate that man appreciates health, the basic and greatest gift that life has to offer, only when he comes to sense its loss.

Why must the school bear larger responsibilities in the promotion of health? Nevertheless there are many signs that indicate an awakening interest in the application of our available knowledge to the promotion of health and the prevention of disease. Our medical schools have received increased and even enthusiastic support during recent years; and much is being done through boards and departments of public health, great private foundations, life extension institutes, insurance companies, industrial plants, libraries, newspapers, magazines, and a host of other agencies. Various organizations have waged aggressive warfare on tuberculosis, syphilis, typhoid, malaria, hookworm, cancer, and other diseases. Guarding the health of the people, our cities have their building laws and sanitary regulations, their playgrounds and public parks, their water and sewage systems, their quarantine rules and hospital facilities; and governments have seen fit to control the sale of alcohol and narcotics and to regulate the manufacture and sale of foods.

All of this work must continue, but it is the school, which touches the lives of the masses, that must bear an increasingly large share of the burden. No other agency reaches all classes without distinction. And since in a political democracy the efficiency of the public control of health and disease is a function of the entire population, no class can be ignored. The autocratic methods adopted and carried through by Gorgas in Panama cannot be repeated in our own Commonwealth. Unless the masses of the people are vitally interested in promoting health and combating disease, little can be done.

Furthermore, if conditions are to be improved, this knowledge must not only be passed on to the people, but it must also be made a part of themselves through the formation of habits and the inculcation of ideals. In order to accomplish this result it is clear that the process of health education must begin during those early years of life which are characterized by a high degree of plasticity and suggestibility. The school alone is in a position to produce the desired results. If the coming of a more healthful world is forced to depend on some other institution, it will be infinitely delayed. This should not blind us, however, to the fact that even for the school this will be a difficult task. The inertia of old customs lies heavy, and the school can have the child for only a fraction of his life. The school, together with other educational agencies, must carry the home and the community along at least a portion of the road that it would take the younger generation. In time this institution will come to be regarded as the agency through which society works into the lives of its members those truths about health and disease which its specialists discover.

How may the school provide for the formation of health habits? If the school is to make any genuine and adequate contribution to the furtherance of health, it must set up three objectives which, while closely related and often overlapping, merit separate attention. It must provide for the formation of health habits, the imparting of health information, and the development of a health conscience. The first of these is fundamental to the other two, for habits are the foundation on which the superstructure of life is erected. Habits determine disposition, they fix the objects of interest and attention, and they set the boundaries to a philosophy of life.

From the moment the child enters the school, therefore, effort must be centered on his forming desirable habits in the fields of both personal and social hygiene. He must form correct habits of posture, diet, elimination, sex, exercise, rest, play, work, sleep, clothing, cleanliness, breathing, ventilation, and of guarding the health of others. Paralleling and supporting these habits, in which the physical aspect is prominent, must go habits of mind which tend to conserve rather than dissipate energy. Early in life the child should form the habits of avoiding worry, of banishing groundless fears, of frankly recognizing the limitations of his own powers, of refusing to seek in fantasy refuge from the demands of living, of taking the necessary time to do the work of the day, of facing the realities of life unafraid; he should form habits of patience and decision, of wholehearted and courageous action, of serenity and happiness.

In the school this process of habit formation will be greatly facilitated by providing environmental conditions that call forth the desired reactions. All who come in contact with the child should possess these habits; the building should be clean and properly ventilated; work and play should take place under careful supervision; the equipment should not only make possible, but should also strongly encourage cleanliness and sanitary behavior; school lunches should serve to establish habits of diet; and school nurses, dentists, and physicians, in order to fix in the child the habit of consulting the specialist, should see to the regular correction of physical defects. The decisive character of the environmental factor deserves special emphasis, because the school in the past has been so highly artificial as to hinder the formation of the habits necessary to the promotion of health. We have often imparted knowledge of hygiene, and at the same time forced the formation of unhygienic habits. We must clearly recognize the indubitable fact that only as we train children in the ways of health will they actually prefer these ways to others.

2) **How may the school impart health information?** Habits, however, as the term is usually understood, are not enough. They do not provide that elasticity in behavior which is essential to the continuous adaptation of the individual to a shifting environment. These habits must be raised to the level of consciousness and made meaningful. The facts which lie back of them must be grasped, the basic principles must be understood. In a word, the individual must be informed, he must be made intelligent. Through definite instruction those superstitions regarding health and disease which have come down to us from a pre-scientific age, and which grow luxuriantly in almost every stratum of the population, must be eradicated.

In the past we have fostered a disease consciousness, we have waged a defensive warfare, we have assumed that nothing is to be done until the disease appears, we have emphasized cure rather than prevention; in the future we must develop a health consciousness, we must wage an offensive warfare, we must consciously develop virile and resistant bodies, we must emphasize prevention rather than cure. The men and women of the next generation must know that both health and disease have their causes, that these causes can be discovered and understood, and that through the application of knowledge the one can be promoted and the other prevented. Ready to rely upon themselves wherever expedient, but prepared to call in the specialist when necessary, they must recognize both their powers and their limitations and avail themselves intelligently of the medical resources of the community. In days of health, through hygienic living and regular medical examination, the approach of disease and physical impairment must be forestalled. The great desideratum is a new orientation with regard to this entire matter. The realization of this part of our program will entail the introduction into the formal curriculum of carefully selected and graded materials, designed to give to our children a sufficiently thorough understanding of the laws of health to serve as a guide to conduct.

How may the school develop a health conscience? But habits and information, however valuable they may be, are not sufficient to the task. The school must imbue its pupils with a profound concern for the promotion of their own health and that of the community, and must inculcate an earnest desire to eliminate disease and defect and privation from the life of men. The individual must be given a health conscience, he must be made to display a will to health, he must be encouraged to develop a moving sentiment for health. The very idea of health should arouse in the ordinary individual that emotional warmth which attaches to every cherished interest of life.

The development of such a positive attitude towards health is possible only under the guidance of teachers who themselves possess it in full measure, who appreciate the significance of their work, and who grasp the meaning of the struggle of the race for a more abundant physical life. Under such instruction our children must enter imaginatively into this age-long struggle of mankind, and thereby come to appreciate for themselves the worth of this portion of the human heritage. As in the past they have lived with the heroes of war and politics and finance, so in the future they must be made to live with those heroes who, in spite of discouragement and the most bitter opposition, have fought for the race the battles of medicine. Thus an increasing number of each generation may be induced to recognize and feel the obligation to carry forward the work of the past, and to enter enthusiastically into those great collective undertakings through which alone complete advantage can be taken of the discoveries of medical science.

How must the school modify its program? The program here outlined, involving the threefold task of forming habits, imparting information, and developing a sense of obligation, calls for a radical departure from the program of the conventional school. In three respects in particular does the ordinary school fall short. In the first place, for reasons already given, it has shown but little concern about health. Only in recent years have there been any thoroughgoing efforts to relate the work of the school to human need at this central point. In the second place, in those few instances where the school has embarked on an ambitious health program, there has been a tendency to place the great emphasis on the acquisition of information and to disregard the other and equally important elements of the program. The school has been led to assume a naïve faith in the complete efficacy of knowledge to regenerate the individual and society. While this view contains much truth, if considered with reference to great stretches of time, it is a relatively sterile educational doctrine. In the third place, the occasional school that has recognized these different aspects of the educative process has tended to make the mistake of erecting artificial barriers between them and of setting the school off from the rest of life. To be truly effective the instruction of the special institution must be made to influence the behavior of boys and girls as they mature and take their places in the ranks of the Great Society. If formal education is to function, it must be made an integral part of the process of living; for habits, information, and interests are given vitality and unity only as the forces of life flow through them. A more healthful world is possible; but, if the school is to have any large share in giving it birth, it must establish contacts with the world of the present and contribute to the making of those changes which bring into being the world of the future.

ADDITIONAL PROBLEMS FOR DISCUSSION

1. Show how man's instinctive equipment is utterly inadequate to promote health and combat the more serious causes of disease.

2. Justify Herbert Spencer's statement: "To be a good animal is the first requisite to success in life, and to be a nation of good animals is the first condition to national prosperity."

3. To what extent has the dissemination of knowledge about health and disease been hindered by the medical profession in the guarding of its vested interests?

4. What is the probable effect on the elimination of the unfit of the advance in medical and surgical skill and knowledge?

5. Which of the following factors has been most important in placing responsibility for health instruction on the school: (1) the decline of other institutions, such as the home; (2) the increase of medical knowledge; (3) the change in attitude towards health and disease; (4) the change in the conception of education?

6. What opportunities and obligations for the promotion of health does the development of compulsory education automatically create?

7. In addition to the formal health instruction of the school, how can

this institution coöperate with other agencies concerned with the promotion of health?

8. How do the authorities of our colleges justify the relative absence of health instruction in their institutions?

9. From the standpoint of the promotion of health, list the advantages and disadvantages resident in urban and rural communities. How should these differences affect the school program?

10. To what extent is a school board justified in overriding the opinions of minorities in enforcing various health measures, such as vaccination, the Schick test for diphtheria, and medical inspection?

11. Why is there such irrational dread of consulting a physician, visiting a medical clinic, or going to a hospital? How could specific instruction in the schools deal with this situation?

12. Explain the extraordinary expenditure by the American people on quack medicines and fake remedies. What can the school do to meet this condition?

13. What methods are or may be used in the school for the development of a health conscience?

14. In the formation of health habits, the imparting of information about health, and the development of a health conscience, show the contribution of each of the following: academic instruction in hygiene, gymnastics, sports, medical inspection and correction of defects, school lunches, open-air classes, and nutrition classes.

PROBLEM 13

HOW MAY EDUCATION PROMOTE THE FAMILY LIFE?

Why is the family the basic social institution? — How has the function of the family changed? — What are the primary functions of the modern family? — What is the trend of the modern family? — What educational problem is presented by modern family life? — Shall education recognize an evolving family institution? — What forces in modern society foster an unnatural sex life? — Is the family safeguarding the biological inheritance? — Are parents equipped to care for their children? — Can science replace taboo? — Should the school assume responsibility for sex instruction? — What should be the educational program?

Why is the family the basic social institution? Through the family the race has achieved civilization; through the home the individual finds his way into the complex world of the present. The family is the most ancient of human institutions, and is found to-day in some form among all peoples. It is the only self-perpetuating institution, and is perhaps rooted more firmly in the original nature of man than any other. Although the particular form the family takes is apparently dependent in large measure on circumstance, man's basic instincts drive him into some sort of family relationship. No other institution has been so closely identified with the interests and welfare of mankind during its long upward struggle.

Developing about the helpless infant, the family has fostered those social tendencies and virtues which have led to the partial substitution within a limited field of the principle of coöperation and mutual aid for the harsher principle of competition and strife. It has consequently furnished the pattern for the expression of our highest ethical and religious conceptions. The prophet, in his search for the ideal that should govern the relations between God and man and between man and man, has been able to do no better than point to the family and apotheosize the relations generated there. The Fatherhood of God and the Brotherhood of Man are two conceptions that make a universal appeal to the conscience of mankind. About the family cluster the tenderest of human sentiments, and all peoples guard with jealous solicitude the particular form of the institution which they have inherited.

How has the function of the family changed? The primitive family was an undifferentiated institution through which were performed all the functions necessary to the race, and in which was contained the whole of social life. In the patriarchal family of our own early ancestors the father was the priest, the governor, the warrior, and the hunter, while the mother was the nurse, the teacher, the agriculturalist, and the manufacturer. The children as they gained strength assumed the tasks appropriate to the sex. But, as time passed, the family expanded into larger kinship groups; the simple processes of savage life increased in scope and complexity; and an amorphous social group gradually became differentiated into definite forms and structures.

Without important interruption this process has continued until the family to-day subsumes only a small portion of society, and carries on but a fraction of the functions for which it was originally responsible. In one important realm after another the authority of the family has relaxed; it has given ground to the church, the state, the factory, the school, the hospital, and the theater; and function after function has been surrendered to some special agency. The consequence of this contraction of the family dominion is that the family has evolved from a very generalized institution into one that is highly specialized. During recent generations this change has proceeded so rapidly that its stability has been greatly impaired. Much of the foundation on which the family rested in times past has been carried away. On account of the weakened hold of the family on the individual, and because of its own altered and uncertain status, some definite educational effort must be directed to the task of fitting this institution for the effective performance of its functions.

What are the primary functions of the modern family? While the family continues to make vital contributions to the economic life, especially in the field of consumption, its work has been largely reduced to the central and basic function of generating and nurturing the race. This function, which is second only to the preservation of the life of the individual, presents a threefold aspect.

In the first place, the modern family provides for the expression of the sex impulses, the normal and controlled functioning of which is an important part of the individual's life. Of course, it is assumed that the physical union of the sexes, though of basic importance, does not constitute the whole of a balanced sex experience. With the development of civilization and the wide adoption of monogamy, the psychic union, involving both the sexually complementary elements and others of a non-sexual character, has become increasingly significant.

In the second place, the family is the socially recognized agency for bringing children into the world. Without doubt, this biological function is the most important one fulfilled by the family. Since the character of the germ plasm of a race is apparently largely determined, from generation to generation, by the number and quality of children born into the world, to the family is entrusted the heavy responsibility of guarding the most precious resource of any people — its biological inheritance.

In the third place, the family remains to-day the most

important agency for the care of children during their earliest and most impressionable years. Its functions here are both nutritive and educative. It is charged with practically sole responsibility for the physical and mental growth of the child during the first six years of life. If the child is hungry, the family feeds it; if the child is thirsty, the family gives it drink; if the child is weary, the family gives it rest; if the child questions, the family supplies the answer. And very early the family brings the child into contact with the life of the Great Society. These three functions are so vital to both individual and social welfare that no society which values its own prosperity can afford to neglect them. We shall, therefore, after considering the present condition of the American family, pass to the task of evaluating it from the standpoint of its success in performing each of these separate functions.

What is the trend of the modern family? The most superficial observation of the situation to-day reveals the fact that in the United States the family is undergoing a process of reorganization, if not of disintegration. It is clearly no longer the fixed and stable institution of a few generations ago. The divorce rate has mounted so rapidly during the last half-century that divorce and remarriage have become the most common occurrences. In the proportion of marriages thus dissolved the United States, having passed Japan, its only competitor, during the last decade, exceeds to-day not only the Christian world, but the non-Christian world as well. At least one marriage in every eight ends in the divorce courts, and in some communities the number of divorces in a single year approximates the number of marriages. Moreover, divorce is by no means a complete measure of the extent of maladjustment within the family.

Owing to the operation of a wide variety of forces, some of which go to the heart of the Great Society, the essentially patriarchal family of a hundred years ago is rapidly passing away, and is apparently being replaced by an institution with less centralization of authority. In the social mind there has been a gradual reappraisal of the relative values to be assigned to the several functions performed by the family. This reappraisal has tended to recognize the personal rights within the family group.

What forces are changing family life? The causes of these changes are not difficult to discover. The coming of the factory system, taking the father and sometimes the mother out of the home throughout the working day, has practically destroyed the family as an economic unit in vast elements of the population; the development of transportation and communication and the growth of cities have loosened the hold of the family and the community on the individual, and thus greatly weakened those forces which make for social control in primitive society; the rise of science has led to the shattering of so many time-honored customs and beliefs that not a few individuals have openly and actively questioned the sanctity of the family institution itself; the wider and wider opening of the door of economic opportunity to women has freed many from the necessity of becoming housewives, and given them all an independence which was formerly lacking; the extension of the opportunities of higher education to women has made many intolerant of conditions that their grandmothers accepted as a necessary part of their lot; and the whole feminist movement, culminating for the moment in the political enfranchisement of women and working towards the abolition of the double moral standard, seems to assure for woman a complete individual status.

What educational problem is presented by modern family life? This is obviously no place to discuss at any length the problem that has been raised, except to point out that it is essentially an educational one. We cannot, even should we desire to do so, go back to the patriarchal family of the pre-industrial world. We cannot discard our inventions, we cannot forget our science; in short, we cannot turn back the clock of human experience. But there should be little desire to return to the earlier family form with its ironclad conventions and its partial denial of the rights of personality to one half of the population. In spite of all the perversions that flow from diseased and impoverished minds, the sensational excrescences that here and there find their way to the surface of our family life, and the narrowly selfish violation of the larger social interests on the part of misguided individuals, the basic trend is clearly toward a relation based upon mutual consent rather than autocratic domination. This, of course, means that, just as in the fields of politics and economics we are endeavoring to solve problems that are much more complex and intricate than those faced by our forefathers in the eighteenth century, so in the realm of family relationships we are attempting a much more difficult task than they encountered in their age.

The real tragedy, therefore, does not consist in the domestic scandal, reports of which perpetually crowd the columns of our newspapers, but rather in that blindness with which modern society strives for a more wholesome type of family relation. Driven in this realm by the most powerful impulses, and relying almost wholly on the primitive and wasteful processes of trial and error, our population, while struggling to make its adjustments to the present, stumbles on in search of a better world. This blindness of organized society is only equaled by that of the youth who, caught in the grip of passion and guided by no foresight of consequences, lays the foundations of his family and marks the boundaries of his career. The nature of the educational task, revealed by the existing situation, is manifest. Society must see to it that every individual is equipped for the discharge of those responsibilities which he assumes when he enters into the family relation; responsibilities which cannot without disadvantage be delegated either directly or indirectly to the group.

Shall education recognize an evolving family institution? In carrying out the program necessary to the accomplishment of this educational task the mistake of postulating a static social order must be avoided. Peculiarly needful is the sounding of this word of caution, because there is always serious temptation, when thinking of the family or any institution so vitally concerned with human interests, to assume the finality of the existing arrangement. Except in the most general way, just what form the family will or should take in a future generation defies prediction. The one certainty is that, if the life of society is to continue, certain functions must be performed. Provided these functions are well cared for, the particular social structure which is set apart for their discharge is in the main a matter of indifference.

The family, as we have already observed, has rendered many services in the past which it no longer performs, and, possibly, it should not carry the entire burden which it bears to-day. Many of our domestic troubles, in fact, may be traced to lack of harmony among the three functions for which it is responsible. There are points of genuine conflict; but, so long as the family bears this threefold responsibility, its purposes should be achieved as well as clashing interests permit; and, where conflict is unavoidable, the less important should be sacrificed. This means that each generation, while trained to discharge these functions through the family institution as it is, must receive that wider equipment which will make possible the gradual and intelligent modification of present practice in the direction of a more wholesome family relation. Since it is impossible to-day to retire into the sanctified defenses of sex and family taboos of earlier generations, these facts must be frankly recognized in the formulation of any educational policy.

What forces in modern society tend to foster an unnatural sex life? We are now in a position to proceed to the evaluation of the American family from the standpoint of its success in providing for the temperate expression of the sex impulses, in guarding the biological inheritance of our people, and in caring for the needs of children. Mankind possesses no impulse, with the exception of the desire for food itself, which is more imperious than that of sex. Provision for its adequate and temperate expression is therefore a necessary concern of every people. The development of civilization with its complexities and artificialities has tended to promote, for a large section of the population, an unnatural sex life. The period of social infancy has been greatly lengthened, while the period of biological infancy has suffered relatively no change. In other words, while legitimate exercise of the sex functions is postponed for the majority of the population until the time of marriage, in the middle twenties, these functions mature in the early teens. For many, in fact, the opportunity of giving them direct expression is deferred to a much later period, and to others it is denied altogether. Owing to the relative stabilization of the food supply and the practical independence of climatic changes, the problem is further complicated by the substitution, in the case of the human species, of a more or less continuous sexual interest for the condition of periodic or seasonal sexual excitation which characterizes the functioning of this impulse in the lower forms of life.

Furthermore, our economic system, since it includes many occupations of a casual nature that require those engaging in them to live roving and homeless lives, denies to many individuals the satisfactions of normal family life. This body of shifting and migratory ne'er-do-wells, constantly recruited from unadjusted youth as well as the unemployed and unsuccessful, can be numbered only by the hundreds of thousands. In addition to these educational and economic unfortunates there are many persons engaged in commerce, transportation, and professional service for whom the demands of the occupation render impossible a settled family life. At the upper extreme of the social scale is another group, small in numbers, but influential in setting the standards of social conduct, and drawn from the classes of leisure and wealth, whose lives reveal an abnormal exaggeration of the sex interest.

To be properly understood and evaluated all of these facts must be projected upon that complex social background created by modern civilization. There is to-day an unnatural stimulation to sexual excitement caused by the wide and intimate contacts between the sexes which take place continually in every center of population, as men and women daily perform the tasks of the Great Society in office, shop, and factory. The congestion of population in many quarters of our larger cities so narrows the living accommodations that family is no longer segregated from family, normal home life is rendered impossible, and the ordinary physical barriers which separate the sexes are destroyed. Out of this situation the development of loose and perverted sex habits is certain; and unnatural attractions between child and parent, which may create serious conflicts within the self, are often set up. Moreover, the satisfaction of civic, recreational, and even religious interests bring the sexes together in close association. These contacts, occurring for the most part between comparative strangers, add to the relationships of the primitive community an element of novelty and adventure. All of these associations, too, take place quite outside the range of those forces which made for social control in the smaller societies of the past.

How is this problem aggravated by an ascetic tradition? This entire situation is greatly aggravated by the persistence of an attitude toward the sex function which makes it extremely difficult to arrive at an enlightened solution of any problem in which this function is involved. One is reminded of the observation of Samuel Butler:

Mankind has ever been ready to discuss matters in the inverse ratio of their importance, so that the more closely a question is felt to touch the heart of all of us, the more incumbent it is considered upon prudent people to profess that it does not exist, to frown it down, to tell it to hold its tongue, to maintain that it has long been finally settled so that there is now no question concerning it.

We have a tradition that exalts celibacy and regards the sex impulse as essentially unholy, and therefore outside the pale of intelligent discussion. With this ascetic tradition, which in spite of the passage of centuries still receives the sanction of social respectability, the actual practice of the vast majority of men and women is necessarily out of harmony. This gives rise to violent conflicts within the self, puts a premium upon hypocritical behavior, and dissipates the energies of the individual. The negative attitude toward sex receives support from vocal opinion expressed and legislation enacted by individuals who, for the most part, are either past the age of maximum sex interest or have been denied normal sex experience.

It is not surprising, therefore, that the pathology of sex is attracting an increasing amount of attention from those interested in social and educational problems. Perhaps the most spectacular product of this unnatural sex life is prostitution, with its degradation of character and its accompaniment of venereal diseases. The spread of these highly malignant affections, with their long train of misery and suffering, has been the object of much concern in recent years. That they can be controlled and stamped out, if society cares to set itself seriously to the task, is certain; but this will involve a parting with our tradition of sex taboo and the careful and open consideration of the problem in all of its aspects. Also, as a result of illicit sex relations under our existing legal and social system, children enter the world with the stamp of shame and inferiority ineffaceably placed upon them. This dwarfing of personality at the source, this denial to individuals of the elementary rights of birth, is one of the most tragic consequences of our refusal to deal frankly and intelligently with matters of sex.

But prostitution, venereal disease, and illegitimacy are not the only fruits of our failure to grapple with this problem. Attempts to suppress violently and completely such a powerful impulse are certain in many cases to lead either to perverted sex habits or to the direction of the impulse into subterranean channels, there to inhibit and warp the development of character. From this source the ranks of the incompetent and the neurasthenic are recruited. One of our larger educational tasks, therefore, is to equip the members of the coming generation to view with clear and undistorted vision the function of sex, and to recognize the fundamental rôle which it necessarily plays in the lives of men and women. If society is to be so organized as to provide for this impulse normal and legitimate expression, or adequate sublimation, such an understanding is necessary.

Are the physical aspects of sex overstressed in modern society? Continuing our discussion of the sexual life, we should make the explicit statement at this point that there must be no disposition to place exclusive emphasis on the physical aspects of sex. What has just been said, while appearing to apply more especially to the impulse toward physical union, has direct bearing on the entire scope of sex experience. The physical act is the core about which may develop the complete union of man and woman. In this union the contribution of the one is complementary to that of the other. One of the tragedies of prostitution is its reduction of sex life to its barest physical dimensions, and the denial to many individuals of that richer psychical life which is the possible product of sexual union. Unfortunately, after the first bloom of mating has passed away, in much of our family life, the psychical is made so subsidiary to the physical that this relationship comes to bear a resemblance to prostitution.

Quite unwittingly, through our policy of suppression and taboo, we have identified the sex impulse almost exclusively with its physical expression. Then we become alarmed when young men and women, drawn into the marriage bond by this primary urge of sex and an ephemeral physical attraction, awake to the slender basis of their union and seek fulfillment elsewhere. Clearly the family relationships should be established on the broadest possible foundation, and their exceptional potentialities for enriching the life of the individual should be more fully realized. Since life is becoming mechanized and depersonalized in so many realms, the home should seek especially to conserve and cultivate its primary emphasis on personal values. Every individual, regardless of his rating in other directions, can make a unique contribution in the cultivation of human relations. Through the family he should find in its highest form the opportunity of developing this capacity for companionship.

Is the family safeguarding the biological inheritance? Having appraised the family from the standpoint of its efficiency in the performance of the first of its three functions, namely, that of providing for the expression of the sex impulses, we come now to a consideration of the bearing of the family on the most important concern of any race, the conservation of the biological inheritance. In comparison with the guarding of this basic possession, most of the other tasks of society are of secondary importance. In this inheritance are the potentialities of the race. If they are lost, they are probably gone forever; while, if they are not fully utilized in any single generation, a people merely fails to realize its possibilities. Provided the talent of our people is conserved, we can perhaps look with equanimity on the exhaustion of our mineral resources, the depletion of our forests, and even the impoverishment of our soil at some distant time; for then we could expect a high order of intelligence to discover and invent substitutes to take the place of these important natural resources. Obviously, therefore, if there is a shred of evidence to indicate that this basic possession is suffering the least impairment, corrective measures, in so far as they lie within our knowledge and power, are imperative.

While it is not possible to speak with absolute assurance on this matter, because of the limitations of our knowledge of the forces of heredity and the facts of social life, there is reason for believing that we are losing from our stock some of its most talented and vigorous strains. Various influences are at work in the modern world that run directly counter to natural selection, and which tend to perpetuate the weak and incompetent. Our charitable institutions and the medical art enable many individuals to survive and propagate their kind who in a harsher age would have perished without offspring. Many thoughtful students of the question have maintained that the total effect of modern war on a race can only be dysgenic, since the most capable and virile men, being sent into battle, are destroyed before becoming parents.

What is the probable effect of the differential birth rate on the biological inheritance? The phenomenon, however, which concerns us chiefly here is the differential birth rate. During the last century, one of the most significant tendencies in western civilization has been the decrease in the number of children per family — a decrease to be traced to the desire on the part of many elements of the population to maintain a higher standard of living, and to the wide dissemination of knowledge of ways and means of birth control. Children are no longer an economic asset, and the parental instincts may receive adequate expression through the lavishing of affection on a small number of offspring. Hence ambitious and foresighted parents, in order to provide their children amply with the comforts, conveniences, and opportunities of life, consciously limit the number of their children. As a consequence this decrease of the birth rate has not affected all classes alike. On the contrary, as might be expected, it has shown itself particularly in the more intelligent and gifted portion of the population. Thus is reversed the condition that characterized the race in primitive times. Then, through the competition for sexual satisfactions and in the absence of any effective efforts to limit births, the very strains that are to-day hardly reproducing themselves probably appeared in numerous offspring. Moreover, the appearance of the differential birth rate in a society such as ours, in which individuals of talent born into the lower ranks of society are able to rise through their own efforts into the higher, is especially dangerous. These superior individuals, on entering the middle classes, tend to limit the number of their offspring and thus reduce their proportional representation in the population. If this continues from generation to generation, there is reason for believing that we shall gradually lose from our population those elements that achieve success in the fields of finance, politics, and intellectual accomplishment.

The conclusion, however, to be drawn from this analysis is not that we are advocating a general increase in the birth rate, a return to the conditions of a century ago when the only restraint placed on the coming of children was the natural one of sexual impotence or sterility. Rather should we desire fewer children from those who have many and more from those who have few. Let there be no misunderstanding here. An uncontrolled birth rate, under modern conditions of living, can only mean misery and want for a large section of the population. It would but contribute to the perpetuation of poverty, disease, and war. The thesis that, under the existing condition of economic efficiency, the total population of the earth is too large to be comfortably maintained, could be easily defended. The need is for an understanding on the part of all members of society of the nature of sex, and the laws of heredity. As man has mastered other forces of nature he must learn to control, in his own interests, the forces of human reproduction.

Are parents equipped to care for their children? The third important function performed by the family is that of caring for the child. In the minds of most people this is naturally regarded as its most valuable contribution to the life of society. But it is patent that for rendering efficient service here the great majority of parents are very inadequately equipped. We have proceeded on the assumption that an unenlightened and therefore ignorant girl, on giving birth to a child, immediately and mysteriously is endowed with sufficient knowledge not only to take care of its physical wants, but also to guide its mental and moral development. As a matter of fact, about the only legitimate expectation is that this young mother will love her child and will want to care for it properly. No more can be expected from the maternal impulses, and in many individual mothers the native strength of these impulses is not great.

The case of the young father is somewhat more disconcerting, since a corresponding natural impulse of equal strength cannot be postulated.

Are the physical needs of children cared for? Among the masses of the population, ignorance regarding the care of infants during both the ante- and postnatal periods is almost incredible. Perhaps in no other field so vital to the welfare of the race does superstition of the darkest type come so near to reigning supreme. Old wives' tales, credulously passed from mouth to mouth, savor of the absurd magic of primitive peoples. In every community there are numerous busybodies, dominated by a morbid interest in all matters pertaining to sex and childbirth, who insure the perpetual circulation of false and unscientific notions about the care of infants. Principles of feeding are not infrequently derived from the food habits of adults, and the simplest laws of hygiene receive no recognition.

The importance of the application of scientific knowledge to the care of children is already recognized by those fortunate classes capable of securing expert service. The differences in the infant mortality rate at the various levels of society give some indication of the appalling waste of human life at this period. Investigations in America have revealed an infant-mortality rate of 240 per 1000 among the very poor, in contrast with a rate of but 50 or less among the well-to-do in the same community. For the entire Registration Area of the United States, the lowest rate thus far attained is 76, while in New Zealand, in 1920, this figure dropped below 50, and in certain communities in our own country a rate of less than 40 has been reached. If the standards achieved by certain classes and communities here, and by all classes and communities in certain other countries are generally attainable, this means that from one third to one half of the infant deaths in America are pre-

ventable. Furthermore, vital statistics show that, except-
ing the period of extreme old age, the first year is by far the
most precarious period of life. Regarding the physical care
of children, of which sickness and mortality constitute a
relatively accurate measure, the mothers and fathers of the
present have but little effective knowledge.

Are the psychical needs of children cared for? In ministering to the psychological needs of their charges, in providing the environment which gives the earliest and most
important direction to the development of character and
personality, the shortcomings of parents are of a yet more
blighting nature. We have no means of knowing, with any
degree of accuracy, how many individuals carry through
life mental and moral scars which may be traced directly to
the unwise but well-meant treatment of ignorant parents;
but we may be fairly certain that mental ailments and in-
juries are as frequent as those in the physical realm. When
one considers the enormous potency of the educational influences of early years, one can only view with a heavy
heart the intellectual, æsthetic, and moral limitations of the
average home. At seven years of age, what a gigantic task
the child brings to the school! How thorough must be the
short period of formal education, if the accumulated errors
committed in the days of infancy are to be effaced! Especially is there grave danger that the child will have to pay a
costly price for that psychological friction generated by
those domestic quarrels and differences which appear so
frequently in the modern family. As one realizes the ignorance of the great majority of parents, and their totally
inadequate equipment for the care of children, one understands why the greater evils of society persist so stubbornly
from one generation to another, and wonders if too great a
price is not being paid for the maintenance of the primitive
family circle.

Can science replace taboo? We have surveyed the present situation, and have found much evidence of incomplete and unsatisfactory functioning on the part of the American family. Although the future of the race is more directly dependent on the family than on any other institution, its performance of each of its three primary functions leaves much to be desired. The improper functioning of the sex impulses causes both mental and physical diseases, the gradual dissipation of our biological inheritance is probably occurring, and the welfare of children is often sacrificed by the ignorance and neglect of parents. If this condition is to be improved, the entire question of sex and family relations must be approached in a new spirit. A re-orientation of mind and heart is required. We have tried the method of ignorance, we have tried the method of repression, we have tried the method of taboo — all have failed. During recent years the work of psychologists has shown the unwisdom of this negative policy, the policy of repression, in dealing with any powerful impulse. Experience suggests that the taboo is no safer guide in morals than it has proved to be in medicine and dietetics. There is every reason for believing that the one method which has proved especially fruitful to man in his efforts to solve other problems will serve him here. This is the method of the careful collection and critical examination of the available facts — the method of intelligence. But the removal of the taboo is but the beginning. Man does not possess an inborn equipment that is at all adequate to guide him in the exercise of the sex impulses, in the conservation of the biological inheritance, and in the nurture and care of children in the modern world. The needs of the situation necessitate the adoption of a constructive educational program.

Should the school assume responsibility for sex instruction? Since there is no other institution that reaches all classes of the population, the school will have to assume the major educational obligation. Some have suggested that the responsibility for this work should rest on the home; but it is only necessary to mention this suggestion in the light of the earlier analysis to realize its complete absurdity. If the home were functioning perfectly to-day this method would be successful, for the child would in most cases acquire the requisite habits, knowledges, and ideals, either incidentally or under the direct tuition of the parents. But since the family is not functioning properly, it clearly does not hold within itself the power necessary to its own regeneration. Others have maintained that this is the function of the church; but the authority of any church, or of all churches combined, is far from universal. Moreover, as an educational institution, the church is pitifully ineffective to-day, and it must bear no small portion of the responsibility for the perpetuation of the sexual taboo. Yet there are some phases of the problem which, under ideal conditions, could be solved more satisfactorily by the church than by the school. The latter lacks the ceremonial atmosphere possessed by the church, an atmosphere which is eminently favorable to the inculcation of ideals. Nevertheless the fact remains that, however great may be the contribution of the church or any other institution, a vigorous treatment of this question will require the coöperation and best energies of the school.

Is the school cognizant of the need? At present the program in operation in the average school is of little value. Over sixty years ago Herbert Spencer, commenting on the absence of any attention to this important division of human activities in the English schools of his day, made the following observation: [1]

If by some strange chance not a vestige of us descended to the remote future save a pile of our school books or some college

___
[1] Spencer, Herbert: *Education*, p 40.

examination papers, we may imagine how puzzled an antiquary of the period would be in finding in them no indication that the learners were ever likely to be parents. "This must have been the curriculum for their celibates," we may fancy him concluding. "I perceive here an elaborate preparation for many things: especially for reading the books of extinct nations and of co-existing nations (from 'which indeed it seems clear that these people had very little worth reading in their own tongue), but I find no reference whatever to the bringing up of children. They could not have been so absurd as to omit all training for this gravest of responsibilities. Evidently then, this was the school course of one of their monastic orders."

While the school of to-day shows some advance over that of Spencer's time, the improvement is by no means commensurate either with the need or with the growth of knowledge. The present program in those schools where a program may be said to exist is characterized either by sentimentalism, or by great timidity and lack of vigor.

What should be the educational program? In attacking this problem those principles should be followed which were outlined in the discussion of health. An adequate program must provide for habit formation, the acquiring of information, and the development of attitudes, interests, and ideals. Attention to sex hygiene, beginning in the first grade of the elementary school, should lead to the formation of correct sex habits. Ideally, this attention should be extended back to the earliest years of infancy. The nature study and biology of the grades and the high school naturally lead to an understanding of the function of sex. Before the maturing of the reproductive functions the child should be given a healthy attitude toward these processes. He should be made to comprehend the fundamental rôle of reproduction in the economy of nature, and to recognize it as the great creative force through which life is constantly renewed. Later he should be introduced to the more intricate and delicate problems that are involved in the expression and temperate control of the sex impulses.   In the high school every child should be required to take sufficient work in biology to acquaint him with the forces of heredity.   Here especially will it be necessary to inculcate ideals that will lead to an improvement of the racial stock, and to the adoption of a voluntary resolve by the individual to refuse, where feasible, to transmit or allow the transmission of mental or physical defect.   We must instill into the youth the feeling of genuine obligation towards the coming generation.

Finally, either in the later years of the high school or in continuation schools especially adapted to the purpose, courses of instruction must be organized that will fit young persons very definitely for the responsibilities of marriage and parenthood.   They must be made to recognize fully the obligations they assume, as well as the difficulties, disappointments, and even disillusionments that experience will in all probability bring.   They should be informed regarding the physiology and psychology of sex and the sexual processes.   While being taught to recognize the importance and naturalness of the purely physical attraction, they should know that a permanent union can hardly be formed on such a basis.   In a word, as they launch themselves on one of the most difficult and momentous undertakings of life, they should receive all the aid that can be given them by a sympathetic and enlightened society.

ADDITIONAL PROBLEMS FOR DISCUSSION

1. What sociological problems of the first magnitude are raised by the biological fact that the *urge* which brings children into the world is in many cases not equalled by the tendencies to parental fosterage?

2. What is the patriarchal family?   Criticize this family from the standpoint of: (a) its democracy; (b) its educational possibilities.

3. How has the lengthening period of dependence in modern society, and the elevation of the standard of living, tended to reduce the number of offspring?

4. Show how the large proportion of children from homes with foreign traditions has required the school to perform functions which are performed in most societies by the home.

5. What educational problems are created by the social forces which play upon the immigrant family on coming to this country? Contrast the foreign-speaking immigrant family with the English-speaking immigrant family.

6. In what respects is the typical rural family more primitive than the typical urban family?

7. Show how the taboo on sex has made the most elemental discussion of sex matters by parents with children practically impossible.

8. What is the original function of the taboo? How is a taboo created in the social mind? How may a taboo be broken? What would be the effect of the disappearance of the sex taboo?

9. Discuss the boarding school from the standpoint of the emotional and intellectual effects on: (a) the children; and (b) the parents. Discuss also the effects of the orphan asylum on children.

10. What are the advantages and disadvantages of committing the education of children to the hands of those who have only a professional interest in them as individuals?

11. What objections have been raised to giving practical and theoretical instruction in child nurture to girls attending our secondary schools and colleges?

12. How would you answer this argument: Since sex knowledge is peculiarly dynamic, it is highly undesirable and even dangerous to impart sex knowledge to children in the schools?

13. Discuss the effects of coeducation on the sexes at: (a) the elementary school level; (b) the secondary school level; (c) the college level.

14. What are the probable effects of the feminist movement on the care of children in the home?

PROBLEM 14

HOW MAY EDUCATION ORDER AND HUMANIZE THE ECONOMIC LIFE?

Why does the economic life occupy a strategic place in society? — How in modern times has man transformed the economic life? — How have mechanical inventions modified social life? — How has education been influenced by these economic changes? — How is current economic education defective? — How may production be increased? — Does education foster an equitable distribution of economic goods? — Does education foster wise and temperate consumption? — Does education foster conservation of natural resources? — Does education seek to humanize the economic life? — Is there a necessary conflict between economic and human values? — Can education infuse a new spirit into the economic life?

Why does the economic life occupy a strategic place in society? Food, clothing, and shelter constitute the material basis of human life and culture. The development of civilization itself, with its finer flower of science, literature, and art, waits upon the solution of the elementary problems involved in securing these necessities. So universal, persistent, and compelling are these wants that in every age the great majority of men and women have spent the larger portion of their waking hours in efforts to satisfy them. Economic forces, therefore, lie at the root of much of human behavior. As savages wander from place to place in quest of food, so civilized peoples migrate from one country to another in search of higher wages; and as the former engage in deadly combat over hunting grounds and berry patches, so the latter wage world wars for markets and raw materials.

The disposition of population over the earth to-day reflects in large measure the beneficence or niggardliness of nature. To the fertile regions man has ever tended; and in these fairer spots he has reared his great states and empires.

To-day, in spite of the pressure of population in many countries, there are vast and easily accessible areas which are practically uninhabited because they do not provide the necessary means of subsistence. In the modern world great cities grow up in certain places rather than in others, neither because these spots are regarded as beautiful nor yet because they are thought healthful, but because they prove to be well-situated for the promotion of the economic life. All human institutions, even religious ceremonies and ethical codes, are profoundly influenced by the methods followed by a people in gaining a livelihood. Political parties usually represent great economic interests, and famous institutions of learning may become powerful bulwarks for the defense of social classes in their enjoyment of special economic privilege. Because of the time and energy it requires, the very occupation in which an individual or group participates is a powerful factor in determining the mental pattern and in shaping the philosophy of life. While the woof and dyes may be derived from other sources, the economic life is the warp of the social order.

How has man shown his economic superiority over the animal? Without clothing, artificial shelter, or tools, for ages man sought his food much as do the lower animals to-day; and in his struggle for survival his superiority over them hung long in the balance. Through invention and discovery he has forged an endless variety of tools, and by means of machinery has harnessed the forces of nature; he has accumulated knowledge of innumerable industrial processes, and has developed the highly differentiated occupational life of modern society; he has domesticated plants and animals, and has even created new and more useful forms of each; and thus he has forced the earth to yield an ever increasing harvest of those material goods which satisfy his wants. So successful has he been in this respect that he has increased his numbers from a mere handful in some favored spot or Garden of Eden to approximately seventeen hundred millions dwelling in almost every land and climate. At the same time he has been so constantly adding to the number of his wants, and so refining his tastes, that he would almost prefer death to the barren and brutish life relished by his earliest ancestors.

How in modern times has man transformed the economic life? During the last century and a half the economic life of the western world has been transformed by a series of remarkable inventions and the general application of science to the productive process. The essentially rural civilization which, following the fall of Rome, was slowly erected in the course of more than a thousand years on the ruins of that ancient Empire, is now rapidly passing away and is being superseded by a compact urban economy. A revolution, more profound in its effects than any armed revolt that ever shook the foundations of a political State, has been achieved in the three realms of manufacture, agriculture, and communication. And these changes have been so radical and so unheralded that man finds himself in a new economic order without being altogether certain of the route he followed in his journey, or quite sure of where he is or whither he is tending.

How has manufacture been transformed? Beginning in the textile industry in the last half of the eighteenth century, power-driven machinery, displacing human energy and the hand methods of an earlier age, has been introduced into practically every phase of manufacture. This change, while greatly increasing the productivity of labor and enabling one man to do the work of hundreds or even of thousands, has had other far-reaching social effects. It has produced the factory system, with its thousands of operatives and its minute division of labor; it has separated the workman from his tools, and created the conflict between labor and capital; it has contributed to the growth of cities, with their great collective enterprises and their glaring extremes of poverty and riches; it has with the seductive promise of easy and fabulous wealth, tempted men of strength to the grievous exploitation of their neighbors; it has developed the wage system, with its emphasis on pecuniary rewards and its dehumanization of work; it has exalted the acquisitive impulses, and given the color of commercialism to the entire social fabric.

How has agriculture been transformed? In agriculture the changes have been only less thorough-going than in manufacture. Following the making of the first steel plow, in 1837, there have come in rapid succession the gang-plow, the harrow, the planter, the cultivator, the reaper, the threshing machine, and the automobile tractor. At the same time there has developed an applied science of agriculture which has given man increased control over nature. As a consequence, much of the drudgery of farm life has disappeared, while one man with the assistance of modern machinery, power, and methods can do the work formerly done by ten.

How have the means of communication been transformed? Neither the revolution in manufacture nor that in agriculture could have proceeded, however, without that series of brilliant inventions in transportation and communication which have bound country to city, nation to nation, and continent to continent. Thus has been made possible that division of labor and that degree of social integration characteristic of the modern world. Within a century man has developed rapid and effective means of travel by land, water, and air. In the early part of the nineteenth century steam power was successfully applied to motor vehicles and to navigation. Later came the trolley car and the automobile, with their dependence on electricity and the combustion of gases; and, in yet more recent times, have come the triumphs of aviation. The most striking inventions, however, have probably been made in the field of communication in its narrower aspects. With the advent of the telegraph in the second quarter of the nineteenth century, to be followed by the telephone, the phonograph, and the radio, both space and time have practically ceased to be conditioning factors in the transmission of thought. And its diffusion has been greatly facilitated by advances in the arts of printing and photography.

How have mechanical inventions modified social life? The life of to-day, and especially the economic life, may not be understood without constant reference to these inventions. Though satisfying some of man's most ancient needs, they have nevertheless magnified others and even brought many new problems into existence. Because of them he finds himself in a great coöperative society which is far removed from the small, isolated, and independent community of a half dozen generations ago. In the words of Robinson and Beard: [1]

These inventions explain the world in which we live, with its busy cities, its gigantic factories filled with complicated machinery, its commerce and vast fortunes, its trade unions and labor parties, its bewildering variety of plans for bettering the lot of the great mass of the people. The story of the substitution for the distaff of the marvelous spinning-machine with its swiftly flying fingers, of the development of the locomotive and the ocean steamer which bind together the uttermost parts of the earth, of the perfected press, producing a hundred thousand newspapers an hour, of the marvels of the telegraph and the telephone — this story of mechanical invention is in no way inferior in fascination and im-

---

[1] Robinson, J. H., and Beard, C. A.: *Development of Modern Europe,* vol. II, p. 31.

portance to the more familiar history of kings, parliaments, wars, treaties, and constitutions.

How have these inventions ushered in an age of material abundance? The advantages of this new society in promoting the economic life are many and obvious. As one of Ferrero's characters exclaims [1] in defending this new civilization:

What has man dreamed of since the beginning of time but the Earthly Paradise, the Promised Land, the Garden of the Hesperides, the Age of Gold, Arabia Felix, one and the same thing under different names: the Empire of Nature and Abundance? And has not the great myth, the wild fantasy of a thousand years, at last taken form and shape in those enchanted lands (America) beyond the ocean?

Through the employment of tools and machines the work of men is made more effective; through the utilization of mechanical power human energy is conserved; and through the division of labor many economies can be achieved. Consider for a moment what has been accomplished in the field of agricultural production. The labor required to produce a bushel of wheat was reduced from three hours in 1830 to ten minutes in 1896; and it has been estimated that fifty men, employing modern farm machinery and the new methods of agriculture, can do the work of five hundred peasants toiling under the conditions of the eighteenth century. The energies of the remaining four hundred and fifty are thus set free to engage in manufacture and commerce, and to produce that great variety of commodities found today in every village and city market.

In the manufacture of goods the increased efficiency has been even more pronounced than in the raising of farm products. In the making of screws, to take a somewhat extreme illustration, the ratio of machine to hand produc-

[1] Ferrero, G.: *Between the Old World and the New*, pp. 98–99.

tion is 4491 to 1. Through the use of mechanical power man is able to accomplish tasks that are utterly beyond his own unsupplemented efforts, tasks beside which those wonders of the ancient and primitive world, such as the pyramids and the hanging gardens, seem but the work of children.

The development of the existing modes of transportation and communication has likewise saved much time and energy, and has greatly widened the scope of human operations. This advance is responsible for the growth of commerce and man's greater independence of the vicissitudes of time and place. The division of labor between one part of the world and another, and even between one part of a great factory and another, would not be possible in the absence of the locomotive, the steamship, the telegraph, and the telephone. The great plains States of our own Middle West, for example, could not confine themselves to the almost exclusive raising of cereals if they were not connected by an efficient system of transportation with other sections of the world from which they could obtain, by exchange of their surplus of grain, the food, clothing, lumber, machinery, and luxuries required for the maintenance and enrichment of life. In like manner a great factory, covering several square miles of floor space and exhibiting an extraordinarily minute division of labor, could hardly be operated efficiently without some form of relatively instantaneous communication through which the work of the whole may be constantly integrated. Efficient means of transportation and communication are as necessary to the life of a complex society as are the circulatory and nervous systems to the physical life of man.

From this analysis it is clear that these inventions are among the finest of the many great gifts that have come from the mind and hand of genius. Here are revealed the possibilities of drafting intelligence into the service of common men in the common undertakings of daily life, rather than into the service of kings and priests and aristocrats in their quarrels with one another and their struggles for domination. A rate of producing the necessities of life, of which the mediæval world could hardly have dreamed, has actually been achieved; while the experience of a century suggests that, if man but cares to bend his energies to the task, he can provide an abundance of the material goods of life to even the humblest member of society, and banish poverty and want from human affairs.

How has education been influenced by these economic changes? The development of this highly complex industrial society has made necessary the establishment of vocational and professional schools of great variety and has even greatly modified the content and method of liberal education. The knowledge and technique which were generated by and adequate to the economic life of the Middle Ages have been refined and increased. The very preservation of the inventions and processes which support the industrial society of to-day is wholly dependent on the effective transmission of this body of experience. There has grown up a host of highly specialized callings, quite unknown a few centuries ago, which demand more or less of formal education for their efficient execution. As a field of knowledge necessitating long and rigorous training, engineering in all of its many divisions has been added to the learned professions; while the numerous managerial, commercial, and clerical occupations imply preparation of every degree of thoroughness. Furthermore, the methods of training skilled artisans have changed with the changing order, and in the field of agriculture there has been gradually accumulating a vast amount of applied science with which the modern agriculturalist must be acquainted.

Because of these numerous and insistent needs technological schools appeared in the early part of the last century, and schools of collegiate and professional grade followed in many fields. The Federal Government, through the Morrill and subsequent acts, has promoted this movement by subsidizing state schools of agriculture and mechanic arts; and the great universities have added departments and colleges of engineering, commerce, journalism, and graduate schools of applied research. In the field of secondary education the ferment has likewise been working for a hundred years and more. Both the academy and the high school, in their origins, recognized the changing demands of the new order. More recently we have seen the establishment of business, trade, corporation, manual training, and other types of vocational schools. Within the conventional secondary school itself the program of studies has undergone radical reorganization during the last generation; and numerous vocational curricula which point toward the clerical, commercial, industrial, agricultural, and household occupations have been introduced in rapid succession.

How is current economic education defective? The present educational program, however, is a half-hearted and inadequate attempt to meet the needs of the situation. It is the product of the blind drive of necessity, rather than the result of an intelligent consideration of the principles involved. It is based in large measure on an incomplete and incorrect analysis of our economic life. It has centered too exclusively on vocational preparation in the narrow sense of the term; it has placed disproportionate emphasis on those highly specialized skills and knowledges which are peculiar to a particular calling. Assuming that the productive process alone constitutes the whole of the economic cycle, it has been too largely concerned with this division of the problem. Failing to recognize the full import of the very forces that have brought it into being, it has tended to perpetuate an anachronistic individualism which is out of place in the modern world.   The present program lacks vision.   Current practice in education does not reflect an understanding of the fact that every important industry is a great coöperative enterprise sustaining a host of intimate and interdependent relationships with other industries and with the larger society of which it is a part.   The fact has been overlooked that the economic life itself is merely society at work, and not a self-generating process carried on in a vacuum.

What should be the objective of economic education? The object of an adequate program of education must be an economic efficiency, balanced by a recognition of the broader and more permanent interests of society and tempered by an unequivocal exaltation of human over material values.   Such a program must seek (1) to increase production; (2) to secure an equitable distribution of goods and services to the masses of the people; (3) to foster wise and temperate consumption of these benefits; (4) to conserve those basic natural resources on which the economic life depends; (5) to organize industry so that it will quicken rather than destroy the intellectual and moral life; and, finally, (6) to inject into industry a new spirit which will call forth the will to serve in place of the will to exploit. Society can afford to omit no one of these values from its educational program.   To a brief consideration of each from the standpoint of the educational needs and principles involved we shall now pass.

How may production be increased? Although the economic conquest of the North American continent in the course of a single century must be regarded as one of the greatest achievements of its kind in human history, it is well known to-day that the productive possibilities of our people are far from realized. Vast quantities of human energy are being wastefully dissipated, and great stores are but waiting to be released. The recent investigation of the Federated American Engineering Societies [1] showed industry to be but fifty per cent efficient, when judged by no criterion of perfection but rather by attainments actually achieved in certain plants and at certain times. According to the findings of this study, production might possibly be doubled without the invention of any new devices or the discovery of any new processes.

But the prevailing type of vocational education, even if greatly improved in quality, could hardly be expected to make any large contribution to the realization of this possibility. The customary program assumes that waste in industry is due to defective acquisition of the narrower skills and knowledges; it assumes naïvely that, provided we train carpenters, compositors, engineers, farmers, machinists, salesmen, and weavers in these special aspects of their respective callings, economic efficiency will be achieved. But this assumption is faulty, for the reason, paradoxical as it may seem, that these narrower functions are the *sine qua non* for industrial participation. Consequently, they are certain to be acquired in one way or another — on the job, if not through some special educational agency. Obviously, increased efficiency is not to be secured by giving major attention to that type of training which is necessary if industry is to run at all, for that is already provided more or less well and will be provided in any event. Industry, in the promotion of its own selfish interests, cannot afford to neglect these obvious instrumental needs. The great savings and the great gains will come from focussing the attention of the school on those aspects of our economic life that

[1] *Waste in Industry;* a Report by the Committee on Elimination of Waste in Industry of the Federated American Engineering Societies.

are in danger of being neglected, namely, the less obvious, the less insistent, and the more remote.

What are the causes of waste in production? If the greatest contribution of education to economic efficiency is not the skill involved in driving a nail, or the knowledge required in running a lathe, what is the goal toward which the school should strive? This question can only be answered by noting the great causes of waste in industry. The committee of the Engineering Societies found these to be faulty material control, faulty control of design, insufficient provision for research, labor turnover, normal unemployment, seasonal unemployment, industrial depressions, labor disturbances, overequipment, voluntary restriction of production by either management or labor, sickness, physical disability, and industrial accident. The most cursory and superficial examination of this list reveals the fact that the economic life of to-day is so novel and complex that man lacks the knowledge and power necessary for its direction. Education for economic efficiency must recognize that the division of labor within an industry, and the dependence of one industry on another for supplies or for markets, have made economic efficiency increasingly dependent on the successful coöperation of individuals and groups.

Since the obvious need is for more attention to the articulation and the coördination of the parts of our industrial machine, rather than to the perfection of the parts themselves in isolation, our educational program must give large attention to ways and means of securing effective coöperation. This will entail, however, a radical re-orientation in the realm of vocational training. In the past the object of this training has been individual success, and the motive to which it has appealed has been that of individual advancement. From the standpoint of great collective achievement, the type of achievement on which success in modern industry rests, a more thoroughly disintegrating force can hardly be imagined. In so far as our schools have exalted this conception of the successful life they have increased, rather than diminished, the influences responsible for waste in our economic order.

Who is responsible for productive inefficiency? Not only are the causes of productive inefficiency complex; they are also widely distributed in their incidence. Responsibility for waste must be borne by management, labor, and the public in the ratio of about four, one, one. To each of these three factors attention must therefore be given in our schools. In the education of those who are to fill managerial positions, especially is it needful to teach the lesson of coöperation. Unless the management can keep the industrial machinery running to capacity throughout the year, however effective may be the training of those who perform the manual labor and specialized tasks, there is little hope for greatly increased productive efficiency.

But the direction of industry is not wholly in the hands of those who technically constitute the management. The rank and file of workers participate more or less in the control of production under almost any condition of industry, and will apparently participate in a rapidly increasing measure in the future. If in no other way, they take part in the direction of industry by voluntarily slowing up the productive process, by quitting work individually, or by striking in a body. By such methods particularly do the workers contribute to economic waste. They must therefore be given that breadth of view and interest which will enable them to see and appreciate their industry as a whole and its place in the larger society. Only by a more adequate understanding of the economic, sociological, and psychological factors involved can labor contribute to that type of efficiency which will best serve its own more lasting interests and those of society.

Management and labor, however, cannot bear the entire burden of economic waste. At many points the interests of those engaged in an industry come into conflict with the larger interests of society. On the one hand, we should strive for such an organization of industry as will reduce this area of conflict of interests to the lowest possible minimum; and, on the other, we should endeavor so to inform the public as to enable it to protect itself from the attacks of predatory industrial groups. There are also certain wastes that can be prevented only through the collective action of an enlightened public. Industrial depressions, for example, can hardly be banished by the solitary efforts of individuals or economic groups. Likewise the operation of seasonal influences in many industries can be mitigated only through general social action. Public opinion must become informed in economics, as well as in politics.

Does education foster an equitable distribution of economic goods? If the problems of production are solved, however, the achievement of economic efficiency is only in its initial stages. As a matter of fact, a perfectly working industrial mechanism, in which there is neither open friction nor unnecessary dissipation of energy in the production of goods, is by no means to be desired for its own sake. This condition is as often an indication of successful coercion as of genuinely harmonious relationships. Economic slavery and ignorance on the part of the masses of the population are certainly not incompatible with such a limited ideal of economic efficiency. Even a great aggregate production of wealth by a people, since an exceptionally high rate of production may be attended by actual poverty and economic misery among vast elements of the population, is not in itself sufficient cause for satisfaction. This is well illustrated in our own country and in the other great industrial nations at the present time. Various studies of the distribution of income and numerous investigations into the cost of living show large sections of the people living on a level well below the minimum required for health and decency. What is more, they show that many are actually living on the poverty and pauper levels. This, it should be noted, is the condition that exists in the richest country in the world, a country favored above all others by a bountiful nature, a country that prides itself on its economic efficiency, a country that even boasts of its humanity. It exists in spite of an era of unprecedented mechanical invention, an almost miraculous mastery of natural forces, a huge accumulation of capital and the tools of production, and an enormous increase of wealth.

Our educational program, therefore, if it is to guard the interests of the entire population and not serve as a bulwark of privilege, must recognize the distribution of income as equal in importance to production itself. The central function of the economic order is that of distributing food, clothing, shelter, and some of the luxuries to all members of society. In the simple life of primitive times increased production meant greater material prosperity for all, but to-day no such natural relationship is found. Production might conceivably be greatly increased without appreciably improving the lot of the masses. Much more efficient production in American industry is certainly not inconsistent with the perpetuation of economic misery.

So long as each producer owned and controlled all three factors of production, namely, natural forces, labor, and capital, the problem of the equitable distribution to individuals and groups of an income produced in coöperation did not arise; but, since the coming of modern industry, with its minute differentiation of the productive process and its complicated system of exchange, this problem has insistently forced itself on the attention of society as one of the most

difficult confronting our race.   About it to-day there rages
the great industrial conflict, a conflict that seems to grow
ever more bitter as the years pass.   If the solution of this
problem is to be a peaceful one, it must come through enlightenment.   And the school, potentially the greatest of
all agencies for enlightenment, cannot refuse to carry the
major portion of this burden.   Up to the present time, educational authorities have shown no great concern over the
relation of vocational education to the distribution of income.   They have tacitly assumed that, whereas production
may be greatly increased through voluntary effort, distribution is a function to be left entirely in the hands of fate or to
the mercy of natural law.

Does education foster wise and temperate consumption?
The educational program, however, must not confine its
attention solely to production and distribution.   These two
processes are not the whole of the economic cycle.   The
gains derived from the more efficient production of economic
goods and the more equitable distribution of income may be
completely wiped out by wasteful methods of marketing
and unenlightened consumption.   In a very real sense the
consumer is the beginning and the end of the economic
process.   Whether natural or artificially stimulated, his
wants provide its motivation.

While some effort has been made in the teaching of the
household arts to look after the needs of the consumer, the
school has been inclined to adopt as its own the ancient
doctrine of *emptor caveat*.   At the same time it has been
exhibiting increased interest in equipping the salesman with
that technique which will enable him to sell goods and
services to the consumer, irrespective of the latter's need.
The new psychology of salesmanship, for example, is calculated to relieve the timid and uninformed of their income
as painlessly and effectively as possible.   This helplessness

of the ordinary individual is the more complete because of the rapid growth, in recent generations, of commercial enterprise. About the marketing of goods there has grown up a highly complicated system that in many instances separates the producer from the consumer by months and years of time and thousands of miles of space. There is thus substituted for the personal connections of an earlier age the impersonal relationships of to-day.

For the maintenance of this system for the exchange of goods, which is clearly necessary and advantageous on the whole, a considerable share of the individual and social income must be set apart. Nevertheless, at strategic points along the highway over which goods are transported from the producer to the consumer, adventurers and brigands are wont to establish themselves. Here, lying in ambush and holding up the caravans that carry both the necessities and luxuries of life to the masses, they divert a portion of these goods to their own uses without rendering adequate service in return. The writers, of course, have no intention of conveying the impression that the service of the middleman is unnecessary to the economic life. There is, however, much dissatisfaction with the way in which this function is performed at the present time. Obviously, we have not made progress here equivalent to that achieved in increasing the efficiency of the productive process. Furthermore, the medium through which exchange is carried on is far from stable, and is consequently the cause of much injustice. In recent years we have learned that, at least under those extraordinary circumstances which merely accentuate the tendencies of normal times, income, debt, or fortune may be halved or doubled within the course of a few months through fluctuations in the value of this medium. These are all problems of large magnitude whose solution waits upon the appearance of an economically enlightened people.

Is education responsible for extravagant consumption?
For bearing the narrower responsibilities of consumption
the individual is likewise unequipped or malequipped. The
American people are notorious throughout the world for
their thoughtless and extravagant consumption. This is
probably due in part to the relative abundance of goods in
the United States, and the consequent diminished need for
thrift. But there are other reasons. On every hand there
are temptations to unwise and intemperate expenditure.
By the importunities of the ambitious salesman, the suggestion of the ingenious advertisement, and the breadth of
social contacts, the wants of folk are artificially stimulated
to a greater extent than ever before in the history of the
race. Furthermore, in the practical absence in America of
aristocratic orders erected about other principles, an aristocracy of wealth has had little difficulty in securing the general acceptance of its own badge of excellence and in imposing on an unresisting society the standards of a commercial
civilization. As a consequence, a disproportionate share
of the energy and talent of the nation is expended in the
competition for pecuniary rewards; and the success of an
individual or family is commonly measured in terms of
financial achievement. The ambitious young man, therefore, seeks membership in an exclusive club, or the elderly
matron jockeys for social position through conspicuous consumption. All too frequently the expenditures for food,
dress, houses, entertainments, automobiles, jewels, servants,
travel, and even education are dictated by considerations of
display rather than utility.

This prostitution of the process of consumption, which
bears no relation to the legitimate satisfaction of the
æsthetic impulses, and which can only dissipate the economic resources of the nation, is by no means confined to the
wealthy classes. In fact it seems that the members of each

class strive to emulate in conspicuous waste those of the class slightly more fortunately situated. Even a large increase in income may be dissipated in a more ambitious program of expenditure which contributes nothing to the economic stability of the family. Children drop out of high school because they cannot maintain the standards of consumption for which the high school ostensibly stands. As a fitting climax to this mad competition in display, those who indulge most freely in the vice comfort themselves with the economic superstition that extravagant consumption creates work for the poor and promotes prosperity. They fail to recognize the obvious truth that luxurious consumption, instead of creating a greater demand for labor, merely gives a different direction to the productive energies of a nation.

In the face of this situation the school is permitting young men and women to pass through its doors to assume the responsibilities of parent, worker, and citizen almost totally uninformed about markets and the quality of goods, about the snare of the advertiser and the vanity of social emulation, about savings and the keeping of accounts, and about the larger rôle which consumption plays in determining the character of the economic life. Furthermore, in the formation of wise and temperate habits of consumption, as well as in the inculcation of corresponding ideals, the lack is yet more nearly complete. Before attention is given to the correction of these defects we cannot claim to have embarked on an educational program that is seriously concerned with the promotion of the economic life.

Does education foster conservation of natural resources? Closely related to the question of consumption is that of the conservation of natural resources. Any nation is plainly building on the sands, if it is not instilling in the minds of its children through the process of education a feeling of the essential sacredness of these resources. If a people fails to concern itself with the conservation of its soil, minerals, forests, and other limited sources of power and materials, it is in no wise superior to the individual who, without thought of the morrow, squanders his patrimony in riotous living.   For how many generations the race will be dependent for its very existence on the continuance of these resources, in much their present form, is a matter of speculation; but there is good reason for believing that it will require them for many generations, and perhaps even for centuries to come.   Hence the necessity that the youth of each age pay homage to the principle that the earth and its resources belong to no single generation of men, but to the unborn as well as to the living.   They must be made to realize that the wasteful exploitation of these gifts of nature is nothing short of pillage.

In the light of traditional and present practice, the educational needs of the American people in this realm are great indeed.   The impoverished soil in many regions, the depleted mineral resources, and the fire-blackened forest areas tell their own tale.   This heritage of nature has been regarded by ambitious, enterprising, able, and unprincipled individuals as providing opportunities for the rapid and easy acquisition of wealth.   Lands of unsurpassed fertility three hundred years ago have lost much of their responsiveness to cultivation; the loss in coal, gas, and oil occasioned by faulty mining, careless transportation, and wasteful use exceeds the actual consumption; and in three centuries two thirds of the great forests of our country, originally unrivaled among civilized nations in both extent and value, have been either cut or destroyed by fire.   According to Van Hise, the exploitation of our timber resources has proceeded with a recklessness and a wastefulness that cannot be matched in the history of the world.   The educational campaign for the conservation of our resources, initiated by far-seeing men and women in the early part of the present century, and carried forward through the press, the platform, and specially organized agencies, must be incorporated into the program of the school.

Does education seek to humanize the economic life? Up to the present point attention has been directed chiefly to the material aspects of economic life and efficiency. Although the discussion is ordinarily pursued no further, a total disregard of the other values involved represents an essentially false emphasis in an educational program. "The formidable judgment industrialism has to face," writes Santayana, "is that of reason, which demands that the increase and specialization of labor be justified by benefits somewhere actually realized and integrated in individuals. Wealth must justify itself in happiness." Our economic institutions must not only concern themselves with the material interests of present and future generations, but, in addition, must promote directly the humane and moral life. Little imagination is required to see that the latter may be needlessly sacrificed to the former.

We must recognize that even food, clothing, and shelter merely condition living and are not life itself. There is excellent authority for the statement that life is more than meat and the body more than raiment. Moreover, from this same source has come the injunction to seek first the less tangible and more immaterial values, with the assurance that all things shall be added. At this point, since material considerations furnish the motive power which drives the wheels of the industrial order, our economic life falls farthest short of the ideal. Here also is the work of the school, in its one-sided attention to vocational efficiency, and in its strong predilection to reflect the conditions of industry, most shortsighted and even pernicious.

Is there a necessary conflict between economic and human values? In times past a conflict in the experience of the common man has usually existed between the economic and the intellectual and moral life. The gaining of a livelihood has been regarded as having nothing in common with the more humane interests of mankind. Work has been looked upon as evil, as something to be escaped, as always involving drudgery and the negation of freedom and spontaneity. The unfavorable connotation which this short word carries is clearly suggested by the fact that the three words offered by Webster as synonyms of *work* are *labor*, *toil*, and *drudgery*.

This attitude toward work goes far back into antiquity. In the third chapter of the first book of the Hebrew sacred scripture it finds perfect expression. " In the sweat of thy face shalt thou eat bread "; so runs the ancient curse laid upon man as he was driven from paradise. Here is a most interesting and illuminating effort on the part of man to account for the fact that work is well-nigh universally a disagreeable experience. The necessity of work is clearly looked upon as a great misfortune, that can be explained only in terms of divine wrath. It is regarded as punishment for some early transgression of the race. And interestingly enough one of the most powerful dogmas of the Christian Church postulates the return of a purified race to a paradise from which all toil is banished, and in which the redeemed enjoy eternal rest. The hard conditions of life through which the race has passed, rather than any inherent quality of work, is reflected in this tradition. While the lot of the masses of the people has usually included much drudgery, many occupations in every age have furthered the growth of personality. These callings the privileged and fortunate classes have ever sought to monopolize for themselves and their children; and not improbably these favored groups have had much to do with the perpetuation, if not with the origin, of the tradition which they rigorously and even conscientiously apply to other classes, that man is condemned to degrading toil because of ancestral sins.

How has modern industry intensified the problem? The revolution in industry, to which constant reference has been made in this discussion, has given added force to the doctrine that, for the great majority of men, work is necessarily identified with drudgery. The minute division of labor, with the pace of operations set by power-driven machinery and with the more elastic functions of management, buying, and selling assigned to specialists, has reduced the factory operative to a mere cog in a great industrial mechanism and taken from him all freedom of action.

The need for intelligence and the opportunity of developing his social instincts are thus denied the ordinary workman, and are concentrated in the offices of the superintendent, the commercial agent, and the efficiency expert. Little wonder that the rank and file have resisted bitterly this encroachment of industry on the rights of personality, and have feared the ultimate effects of those tendencies which imply yet greater specialization and the more complete separation of the workman from the knowledge and technique underlying his work. Much of the unrest in the economic world to-day may be traced to this dehumanizing process that has been promoted by the uses to which mechanical inventions have been put. The attitude of the management toward the routine worker has been greatly influenced by his reduction of status. In many instances, being worn out and finally scrapped in the interests of production, he is rated and treated as a machine. Workmen through their organizations have been forced to wage constant warfare against the doctrine that labor is but a com-

modity.   Even a great Federal Board has recently given
out the pronouncement that the demand for a living wage
should not receive serious consideration at the hands of
those responsible for the direction of our system of railway
transportation.

What solutions are offered?   For the purpose of meeting
this situation two divergent proposals have appeared in the
Great Society.   The one we may style the doctrine of leisure, the other the doctrine of work.   Those who adhere to
the former doctrine are many, and are found in positions of
power and influence.   Perhaps rationalizing their own desires that the present industrial system will remain sub-
stantially as it is, they assume that this tendency toward
the degradation of labor is an inevitable consequence of
mechanical invention, and suggest that the only salvation
of the common man is to be found in shorter hours of labor
and a compensating leisure life.   They would deny to him
the possibility of expressing himself in his work, but would
be willing to pay him well for it.   They would insist that he
sell his birthright for a slightly gilded bowl of pottage.
This view implies no fundamental social change, but recognizes as final the apparently inexorable logic of the industrial
revolution.

The other doctrine would seek salvation through work
rather than leisure, and consequently implies a radical
reconstruction of the economic order.   The champions of
this view maintain that, if we care to give to the problem
the time and energy and the heart and mind which are so
freely given to the increase of profits, the economic life can
be so reorganized as to foster the growth of personality.
Their argument assumes the following form.   In modern
industry, with its inventions and its countless applications
of science, this elevation of work is most easily possible.   The very diversity of the economic life should

make possible a cultivation of individual aptitude, capacity, and interest not conceivable in the past. In a more primitive age it would have been difficult to make of industry a great educational enterprise, for the foundations upon which it rested were little understood. In that day there was some basis in necessity for the interpretation given in the third chapter of Genesis, but the conditions of life today make possible a more humane philosophy of work. The situation is greatly changed. There is no longer need of continuing the cruel paradox of civilization that the very activities in which men engage for the purpose of maintaining physical existence must tend to impoverish the spiritual life. For such a condition there is small excuse, since through mechanical invention, so it is suggested, man can dominate nature and compel it to do the drudgery involved in the support of human life. The machine may be made the slave rather than the master of man.

Which solution must education champion? As to the relative merits of these two doctrines there is much dispute. That the second is the more attractive must be admitted. It should therefore be supported in so far as the native equipment of men makes it possible and the conditions of productive efficiency permit. In the field of industry the greatest educational task of this generation is that of so organizing our economic life that the area of conflict between the demands of productive efficiency and the personal growth of the worker will be reduced to the minimum. The existing economic order in its concern for profits has shown such a ruthless disregard for the lives of the workers that in the long run it would undermine its own foundations. That monotonous work, however, can be wholly eliminated from industry is probably an idle dream. By giving to each individual the knowledge underlying the process in which he is engaged, much that is now the most meaningless routine can be made significant; by rotation from task to task, where the work of industry has become minutely differentiated, the monotony may be relieved and the adaptability of the worker preserved; and by participation in the management of the enterprise the highly specialized operative can be given some feeling of his own worth and an opportunity to give expression to his creative and social impulses. In a word, even the simplest of callings can be made to take on complexity and meaning to the degree that its relations to the rest of life are appreciated.

But while saying this we must be on guard against the intellectualistic and pathetic fallacy that so easily creeps into this discussion of the relation of vocation to the growth of the self. There is a natural tendency for the critic of our economic life to make universal his own reactions to the narrower types of work, and to assume that they are as limited in their intellectual possibilities, and as uninteresting and disagreeable, for the ordinary workman as they are for him. Both of these assumptions contain but partial truths. The present situation is perhaps not so bad as the imaginative observer thinks it is, nor does it contain the possibilities of improvement that he believes and hopes it does. Any sound educational program must recognize the profound differences in individuals and be prepared to accept the limitations placed by nature on the ideal. The most that we can hope to do is to give to each individual who works in industry as wide an appreciation of the scientific and social meaning of his task as his native equipment permits. Nevertheless, the educational possibilities are far in advance of present industrial practice. In this direction education can render a humanitarian service of which at present it scarcely dreams.

Can the will to serve be made to motivate the economic life? If education at its various levels is to accomplish some small part of the program outlined in this discussion, if it is to increase our productive efficiency, if it is to secure a more equitable distribution of the goods and services produced, if it is to develop habits of wise and temperate consumption, if it is to promote the conservation of our natural resources, if it is to bring industry into harmony with life itself, it must seek to promote the organization of industry about a new principle.   The principle of service must be enthroned in place of the principle of profits.   So long as profits determine the course of the economic life it is mere rhetoric to champion the larger and more permanent interests of the individual and society.   The unbridled desire for profits is a divisive force in the industrial order which generates the strife and misunderstanding that to-day are shaking the foundations of western civilization.   That there are other motives to which appeal can be made is clear to him who is familiar with the various forms which economic institutions have taken in the course of human history.

We find ourselves then in an anomalous position, partly because the notion of service has been so narrowed that it covers only the more unusual and spectacular forms of achievement, such as are rendered by the statesman, the soldier, the physician, and the clergyman.   This has made necessary the reliance in the more ordinary fields of endeavor on some other motive.   No attempt is made to pay the soldier or the statesman what he is worth in dollars and cents, but each is satisfied because he is rewarded by the knowledge of worth-while accomplishment and by the esteem in which his service is held.   " I offer neither pay, nor quarters, nor provisions: I offer hunger, thirst, forced marches, battles, and death.   Let him who loves his country in his heart and not with his lips only, follow me." Thus Garibaldi, in 1849, appealed not in vain to the youth of Italy.   In the economic sphere, on the other hand, there has been no extra-financial recognition of valuable service rendered. Hence society is driven to the impossible and fantastic attempt to dole out to each workman the exact financial measure of his performance. In the absence of the least tinge of idealism we have exaggerated the importance of the acquisitive impulses, and have thereby induced the sickness from which the industrial world is suffering. This malady can only be cured by raising the humblest phases of the economic life to the level of valuable service rendered to an appreciative society.

Can education infuse a new spirit into the economic life? If such an attitude toward occupation can be developed, the individual, regardless of the nature of his task, will derive satisfaction from its successful performance. Apparently the first demand of man is that his efforts be adequately appreciated by the members of the group to which he belongs. In most cases, even in instances of great achievement, unless this appreciation is forthcoming the successful performance of a task is but gall and wormwood. In times of war the digging of a trench or the preparing of bandages assumes an unwonted significance because it is part of a great collective enterprise involving the welfare of the group. A British war correspondent, during the World War, well expressed this change when he wrote of the men in the trenches:

It is a wonder that never palls, but is always new: the spirit which these men of ours possess, from no matter what corner of the Empire they may have come. One wonders where the grumblers, the cowards, the mean people whom one thought one met in ordinary life, have gone. They are not here. Or, if they are, they are uplifted and transfigured. They doubtless, many of them, could not explain or express it, but some wind has blown upon them, the inspiration of a great cause has come into them, some sense of comradeship and brotherhood inspires them, something has made true soldiers and gallant men of them all.

In times of peace the running of a sewing machine or the cleaning of streets is potentially just as significant as many of these war-time activities, if we but possessed the traditions and the imagination so to regard it. In fact many of the ordinary tasks of the economic world assume heroic proportions when viewed in proper perspective.

This then is the supreme task of education as it touches the economic life — to inject a new spirit into vocation, to give to the coming generation a wider appreciation of economic activities, to get men and women to see and feel that through the economic institutions the race is wresting from a somewhat hostile nature those basic goods on which human life and civilization rest.

ADDITIONAL PROBLEMS FOR DISCUSSION

1. What relationship exists between the rapid economic growth and the unrivaled expenditures on public education in North America? In whose interests has been the rapid extension of the opportunities for education?

2. In what respects has the industrial revolution made necessary the modification of the earlier form of training artisans by apprenticeship?

3. Justify the statement that the extraordinary advance in the material prosperity has not been accompanied by any corresponding advance in the principles of living upon which human happiness depends. How can the absence of this advance be attributed to false emphases in education?

4. To what extent has the development of our vocational schools and curricula been determined by the interests of special industrial groups, rather than by considerations of the general social welfare?

5. To what extent is economic health and the curing of economic ills dependent upon the possession on the part of the population of common rather than special knowledges, dispositions, and ideals?

6. What school practices hinder the development of those coöperative habits and dispositions which are essential to the growth of a better industrial order?

7. From what quarters may we expect opposition to the giving of serious attention, in our educational institutions, to a more equitable distribution of wealth and to the conservation of natural resources?

8. What practices in: (1) elementary school; (2) secondary school; (3)

state college; and (4) private college, contribute to the growth of habits of wasteful and extravagant consumption?

9. From the standpoint of motivation, how is play to be distinguished from work? What are the reasons in modern society for the clearly marked distinction?

10. What fundamental criticism would you make of the social theory that would give but little attention to improvements of the social conditions of work, but would rather reward the worker with increased leisure?

11. What is the ideal of success set before the student of the secondary schools and colleges of the country? Does the nature of this ideal explain the reduced ranks of some of the more humane professions?

12. How have the social and economic facts of our industrial life been overlooked as a rich source of material for a general education? What has been the reason?

13. What is the error in the theory that the great majority of men will only work effectively for hire? What light did the war throw on this question?

14. Contrast the position taken in these pages with the assumption underlying the following statement: "The only possible defense for the expenditure of public funds for educational purposes is found in the increase of economic production."

15. What are the controlling purposes of vocational training when this training is in the hands of private interests, whether employer or labor union? How do these purposes differ from those advocated in these pages?

16. Critics of this section maintain that such a discussion of the economic life as is here presented is not pertinent in a text-book on the Principles of Education. How would you justify its relevancy?

PROBLEM 15

HOW MAY EDUCATION ADVANCE THE CIVIC LIFE?

What is the function of civic institutions? — What was the early faith in political democracy? — Has this faith been realized? — Has social kept pace with material progress? — Why must the nature and purpose of civic education be changed? — What kind of a society should education seek to create? — What is a democratic society? — What must be the objectives of civic education in a democratic society? — How may the school encourage the formation of basic civic habits? — How may the school develop an appreciation of the social heritage? — How may the school inculcate a progressive civic attitude? — How may the school develop respect for orderly methods? — How may the school impart precise civic information? — How may the school cultivate a scientific civic temper? — How may the school develop a broad social consciousness? — Can the school educate for world citizenship?

What is the function of civic institutions? Since the first days of group life man has found it both wise and necessary to resort to collective action in the pursuit of social ends. By means of such action the material and moral welfare of the community and the good of the individuals composing it have been promoted. Men have associated together to insure safety against external attack, to preserve order and security within the community, to guarantee justice through the impartial adjustment of disputes, to curb anti-social tendencies by the punishment of offenses, to administer efficiently the common affairs of the group, to assist the individual citizen in the achievement of his own legitimate purposes, and to guide him in the development of his own capacities. They have organized for the purpose of realizing the faith that the world can be remoulded closer to the heart's desire.

To attain these and other ends man has created political

institutions of great variety and complexity. But not infrequently these agencies for the public good have become so powerful and productive of injustice in the hands of individuals or classes that thoughtful men have regarded them as wholly evil. Monarchs have enslaved entire peoples, and for generations have demanded heavy tribute for every service rendered. Men and women have even been required at times to fall down and worship the State, and to offer up to this political divinity a perpetual sacrifice of wealth and human flesh. Only through eternal vigilance is it possible to thwart the efforts of the servant to assume the rôle of master.

What was the early faith in political democracy? In order to control these institutions in the general interest and to make them responsive to the common needs, there have appeared, at various times and places in human history, and more particularly in recent centuries in western Europe and America, popular governments based on a wide suffrage. In the eighteenth century men began a vigorous assault on the crumbling despotisms and tyrannies of feudalism which has led to the almost universal adoption among civilized peoples of some form of political democracy. At that time there was a tendency to ascribe all the evils to which man is subject to the maleficence of kings and queens and emperors, and to the selfish greed of the various hereditary ranks of the feudal state. There was a naïve faith in the perfectability of human nature. Many believed that the perfecting of mankind would naturally and quickly follow the abolition of these restraints of privilege. In anticipation of the great changes that were coming and the fond hopes for the early establishment of a new social order to be dominated by the ideals of liberty, equality, and fraternity, the enthusiasm of the period is well described in the memorable lines of Wordsworth:

"Bliss was it in that dawn to be alive,
But to be young was very Heaven! O times,
When Reason seemed the most to assert her rights,
A prime enchantress — to assist the work,
Which then was going forward in her name!
Not favored spots alone, but the whole Earth,
The beauty wore of promise — that which sets
The budding rose above the rose full blown.
What temper at the prospect did not wake
To happiness unthought of?"

To these eighteenth-century advocates of political democracy man was a rational being who, always seeing and pursuing the more abiding interests, would, if given the opportunity, make short shrift of the social ills of the time. To them political democracy was the philosopher's stone through which an ideal society would be shortly brought into being. Bryce has thus described the community which it was conceived unfettered human nature would create: [1]

In it the average citizen will give close and constant attention to public affairs, recognizing that this is his interest as well as his duty. He will try to comprehend the main issues of policy, bringing to them an independent and impartial mind, which thinks first not of his own but of the general interest. If, owing to inevitable differences of opinion as to what are the measures needed for the general welfare, parties become inevitable, he will join one, and attend its meetings, but will repress the impulses of party spirit. Never failing to come to the polls, he will vote for his party candidate only if satisfied of his capacity and honesty. He will be ready to serve on a local Board or Council, and to be put forward as a candidate for the legislature (if satisfied of his own competence), because public service is recognized as a duty. With such citizens as electors, the legislature will be composed of upright and capable men, single-minded in their wish to serve the nation. Bribery in constituencies, corruption among public servants, will have disappeared. Leaders may not be always enlightened, nor assemblies always wise, nor administrators ef-

[1] Bryce, James: *Modern Democracies*, vol. I, pp. 53–54.

ficient, but all will be at any rate honest and zealous, so that an atmosphere of confidence and goodwill will prevail. Most of the causes that make for strife will be absent, for there will be no privileges, no advantages to excite jealousy. Office will be sought only because it gives opportunities for useful service. Power will be shared by all, and a career open to all alike. Even if the law does not — perhaps it cannot — prevent the accumulation of fortunes, these will be few and not inordinate, for public vigilance will close the illegitimate paths to wealth. All but the most depraved persons will obey and support the law, feeling it to be their own. There will be no excuse for violence, because the constitution will provide a remedy for every grievance. Equality will produce a sense of human solidarity, will refine manners, and increase brotherly kindness.

Has this faith been realized? This was the anticipation. How cruelly have the hopes of these idealists been thwarted! At the very time when political democracy has triumphed, at the very time when four once powerful empires have crashed to the earth in war and revolution, great masses of men scoff at popular governments and even speak of the general failure of parliamentary institutions. Political democracy has not ushered in the millennium. A glance over the modern world reveals all too much of corruption, inefficiency, coercion, poverty, crime, bitterness, strife, frustration, fear, hate, ignorance, violence, tyranny, and vice. Bryce, writing near the close of his life, thus summarizes human experience with democratic institutions: [1]

As respects progress in the science and art of free government, experience has established certain principles that were unknown to those who lived under despotisms, and has warned us of certain dangers unforeseen by those who first set up free governments; but when it comes to the application of these principles, and the means of escaping these dangers, the faults that belonged to human nature under previous forms of governments have reappeared. Some gains there have been, but they have laid more in

---

[1] Bryce, James: *Modern Democracies*, vol. II, pp. 607–08.

the way of destroying what was evil than in the creating of what is good; and the belief that the larger the number of those who share in governing the more will there be of wisdom, of self-control, of a fraternal and peace-loving spirit has been rudely shattered. Yet the rule of Many is safer than the rule of One, — as Cavour said, that however faulty a legislative chamber may be an ante-chamber is worse — and the rule of the multitude is gentler than the rule of a class. However grave the indictment that may be brought against democracy, its friends can answer, "What better alternative do you offer?"

Why has political democracy fallen short of the anticipation? This estimate of the success that has attended political democracy, coming as it does from one who gave his life to its study and promotion, can afford but little comfort. When compared with the expectations of its eighteenth century advocates, its limited accomplishments appear the more striking. The hopes of these zealous reformers and idealists have by no means been realized. We cannot say that political democracy has failed. We should rather say that the social salvation of a people cannot be achieved merely by the adoption of a political philosophy. The problem of human living is far more difficult than our forefathers imagined; and those inventions and discoveries which have led to the transformation of the physical basis of social life have not made it easier. Their faith was based on all too simple a formula, namely, that the gift of suffrage would create the will to use it, and that an elementary education consisting chiefly of reading and writing would create the capacity to employ this gift aright. Both of these assumptions have proved unsound. Many individuals refuse to exercise the franchise, and the ability to read may merely make the citizen more amenable to propaganda. A society based on universal suffrage is certain to reflect the limitations and defects of mind and character resident in the population.

It was also unforeseen that even popular governments, by making the school an instrument for the inculcation of pious political dogma, may blind its youthful citizens to reality. In many quarters to-day critics are saying that the possibilities of education are much more restricted than was believed in the early days of the Republic. That we can place little hope in mere literacy is certainly true; but there is no support in experience for the view that the limitations set by human nature are sufficient to render all forms of education ineffective. As yet no genuine effort has been made to attack the problems of civic life through a broad educational program. Such a program, the only hope of human society, must be consciously derived from an analysis of man's social nature and the conditions of life in the modern world.

Has social kept pace with material progress? In the nineteenth century were laid the material foundations of a new civilization. The great task of the twentieth is the erection on this base of a social and spiritual superstructure of commensurate pattern. Until this is accomplished the times will be out of joint, and the full harvest of man's brilliant achievements in the domain of physical nature will not be garnered. Many of our institutions, customs, attitudes, and ideas are adjustments worked out for a simpler type of social life than is possible to-day. There are yoked together, therefore, two divisions of the social inheritance in different stages of evolution and manifesting contradictory attitudes toward the world. In the realm of mechanical invention, where progress has been rapid, there is a constant and socially stimulated search for improvements; while in the field of social invention, where advance has been slow in the past, new discoveries far from being encouraged are, if radical in their nature, even regarded as dangerous. We cling as fondly to an outworn institution or

prejudice as the savage clings to his stone hatchet or the
mediæval peasant to his wooden plow. Nevertheless, as the
sickle has given place to the reaper, the shuttle to the power
loom, the horse to the locomotive, and the signal fire to the
telegraph, so must many of the social conventions of the
present, survivals of a by-gone age, give place to more useful and efficient adaptations. The function of education is
to facilitate rather than hinder this process of adjustment.

How have the problems of social life been complicated?
Mechanical invention has brought into existence a world for
which the race is not fitted by nature and for which it can
be fitted only through an elaborate educational experience.
The ordinary citizen would make a fairly good member of
the small kinship group of primitive times in which life is
simple and direct and his relations to others are intimate
and face-to-face. Under these conditions the results of his
actions are apparent to himself and others and the determination of responsibility is not difficult. His allegiance is not
divided by membership in divers groups whose interests
conflict at many points. With the welfare of this small
primitive group therefore he identifies himself completely,
and finds little difficulty in giving to it a natural and un-
questioned loyalty. But when this same individual is
placed in a nation of a hundred millions of people, or in a
world of many hundreds of millions, in which the results of
behavior are difficult to trace and in which there are countless groups supporting every conceivable interest, groups
within groups and groups beyond groups, groups forming
and reforming in endless variety — when this same individual is placed in such an environment he finds himself
facing problems which he cannot solve, and constantly in
the presence of problems which he does not perceive. The
cost of living rises, or the scourge of war visits his country,
and he curses some malevolent spirit resident in a great

financial center or in the capital of a foreign nation. Man becomes lost in the mazes of the labyrinth of his own construction and wanders blindly on in search of some passage that will lead him out of confusion.

Why must the nature and purpose of civic education be changed? This situation sets the educational task. The methods of the past require supplementation and modification. To the incidental education, which comes in the discharge of the ordinary responsibilities of living and which was adequate to the needs of earlier times with their limited possibilities and hopes, must be added conscious educational guidance of the most enlightened character. The fundamental purpose of civic education, however, if it is to render any important service in promoting the civic life, must undergo radical change. As we contemplate the spirit of mistrust and hate that broods over the modern world, a spirit that our own and previous generations have created, a feeling of profound humility is the only attitude which we may fittingly assume in the presence of the more difficult and complex social problems. Pathetic indeed is the practice, current among the nations of the world, of assuming the great purpose of education to be that of authoritatively teaching the youth to become like their elders. The achievement of such an objective can only mean the perpetuation of the failure, the limitation, and the bewilderment that beset the world to-day. Our fear should rather be that, in spite of all that can be done, the next generation will give only too clear evidence of its parentage. If we are to rely upon authority, upon whom shall we place the mantle of the prophet?

The present condition of the race suggests that the whole of mankind, the middle-aged and the old, as well as the young, should go to school. But such an heroic measure, except to a very imperfect degree, is obviously impracticable.

The most for which we may legitimately hope is that educational leaders, recognizing that their ignorance is only less complete than that of their followers, will regard their task as largely that of leading men and women, and especially the younger generation, in a spirit of comradeship on a quest for a better world. If the school is to take an active part in that general reconstruction of human society for which mankind wistfully watches to-day, from men and women of large vision, broad sympathy, and inquiring mind, must the ranks of the teaching profession be recruited.

As Bryce well says: [1]

Whoever attempts to forecast the course systems of government will take must therefore begin from the two propositions that the only thing we know about the Future is that it will differ from the Past, and that the only data we have for conjecturing what the Future may possibly bring with it are drawn from observations of the Past, or, in other words, from that study of the tendencies of human nature which gives ground for expecting from men certain kinds of action in certain states of fact. We cannot refrain from conjecture. Yet to realize how vain conjectures are, let us imagine ourselves to be in the place of those who only three or four generations ago failed to forecast what the next following generation would see. Let us suppose Burke, Johnson, and Gibbon sitting together at a dinner of The Club in 1769, the year when Napoleon and Wellington were born, and the talk falling on the politics of the European continent. Did they have any presage of the future? The causes whence the American Revolution and the French Revolution were to spring, and which would break the sleep of the peoples in Germany and Italy, might, one would think, have already been discerned by three such penetrating observers, but the only remarks most of us recall as made then and for some years afterwards to note symptoms of coming dangers were made by a French traveller, who said that the extinction of French Power in Canada had weakened the tie between the American colonies and Great Britain, and by an English traveller who saw

---

[1] Bryce, James: *Modern Democracies,* vol. II, pp. 598–99.

signs of rottenness in the French Monarchy. Men stood on the edge of stupendous changes, and had not a glimpse of even the outlines of those changes, not discerning the causes that were already in embryo beneath their feet, like seeds hidden under the snow of winter which will shoot up under the April sunlight. How much more difficult has it now become to diagnose the symptoms of an age in which the interplay of economic forces, intellectual forces, and moral and religious forces is more complex than ever heretofore, incomparably more complex than it had seemed to be before discovery had gone far in the spheres of chemistry, physics, and biology, before education had been diffused through all classes, before every part of the world had been drawn into relations with every other part so close that what affects one must affect the rest.

The slender basis on which any dogmatism regarding the future of society must rest is here delineated. It is for this reason that the methods commonly employed in civic education are apt to be either sterile or productive of evil. Leaving those things that are behind and pressing on to that which is before, it is the inescapable task of each generation to confront with openmindedness the problems of the future.

What kind of society should education seek to create? If this analysis is at all correct civic education must include much more than the knowledge of political machinery. It must provide for the modification of the current political modes in which human nature has expressed itself. While the individual citizen should know something about the forms of government, the organization of political parties, and the methods of voting, this is only the beginning of civic understanding. He must see beyond these mechanisms to the purposes of political institutions and the possibilities of associative living. He must be given a vision of a better social order and at the same time the will to achieve it. He must be made to realize that these institutions are but instruments, and very imperfect instruments at that, to be employed in giving reality to such a vision. While it is impossible to lay down the plans and specifications for the social order which is implicit in, and made possible by, the great changes of recent centuries, there are certain controlling principles or ideals that must guide the development of the educational program.

Our children must be equipped more effectively than are their elders for living together in the Great Society without friction or the sacrifice of personality. But this is a negative statement of the ideal. Our aim must be that of bringing into existence a social system that centers about and promotes the growth of the individual, a system in which frustration is less common and life is more abundant. Friction, though symptomatic of maladjustment, is not the greatest of social ills, for it is often generated by individuals or classes in their efforts to escape from bondage. In the past there have been many instances of group life in which open conflict has been reduced to a minimum; but this condition has usually meant an unabashed sacrifice of personality for all but a privileged minority, and probably a less obvious, though equally injurious, warping of the character of the members of this minority. In primitive times, and throughout the greater part of human history, repression has been the lot of man. Liberty has always been a plant of tender growth, apparently exotic to the conditions of human society. Even to-day, after a struggle of centuries for freedom, there are many who look with favor on a strict regimentation of society. But outward tranquillity can be bought at too great a price. The friction that so characterizes modern society must be reduced by furthering a more rational ordering of life and not by clumsy resort to repression, the age-long tool of incompetence.

What is a democratic society? The concept of democracy as commonly referring to a set of political institutions based upon popular elections must be expanded to include a way of living. The worth of social life must be measured in terms of its contribution to the growth of human personality and to the development of the potentialities latent in original nature. The ideal of Immanuel Kant, that every man should always be treated as an end and never as a means merely, is essentially democratic. According to Dewey, society is democratic in so far as the individual member of a particular group shares intelligently in all its activities and interests, and in so far as each group within the larger society sustains intimate and varied contacts with other groups. To the degree that the lives of individuals are made barren by the arbitrary subordination of their needs and interests to those of others, and to the degree that groups are isolated from one another by social and artificial barriers, society is undemocratic. In a society that is democratic, when measured by these criteria, there exist the greatest opportunities for personal growth; only in such a society are the educational resources latent in social life offered freely to the individual whatever the condition of his birth. The educational program, while keeping its feet firmly planted in the life of the present, must derive its inspiration from some such ideal conception of a better social order.

Bertrand Russell, at the close of his discussion of *Proposed Roads to Freedom*, thus holds the ideal before us; [1]

The world that we must seek is a world in which the creative spirit is alive, in which life is an adventure full of joy and hope, based rather upon the impulse to construct than upon the desire to retain what we possess or to seize what is possessed by others. It must be a world in which affection has free play, in which love is purged of the instinct of domination, in which cruelty and envy have been dispelled by happiness and the unfettered development of all the instincts that build up life and fill it with mental delights.

[1] Russell, Bertrand: *Proposed Roads to Freedom*, p. 212.

Such a world is possible; it waits only for men to wish to create it. Meantime, the world in which we exist has other aims. But it will pass away, burned up in the fire of its own hot passions; and from its ashes will spring a new and younger world, full of fresh hope, with the light of morning in its eyes.

Perhaps the most difficult of all educational tasks will be that of bringing into existence a generation of men who sincerely yearn for such a world. Many living to-day do not wish it; especially is this true of the great majority of those occupying positions of responsibility and power. They lack the drive, the courage, or the wisdom to bend their energies to the task; or, hugging to their breasts the puny satisfactions of privilege, they make the " great renunciation " and turn their backs on the venture of democracy. " Hatred in the past and trepidation for the future effectually block the way of social advance." Yet the response given by the people of all lands to the idealism expressed in the closing years of the World War indicates the presence of a deep reservoir of good will that may yet be harnessed to the task of creating a more humane world.

What must be the objectives of civic education in a democratic society? We have now considered in a general way the nature of the educational problem which the school must face, if it is to make any effective effort to promote the civic life. The principle of growth must find conscious expression in the life of the individual and in the life of society. Civic education must be looked upon as a process that begins with birth and ceases only with death. For the purpose of increasing and refining the happiness of all the members of society, education must seek the continuous reconstruction of the social order and human relations. It must ever strive to give the lie to the cynical jest made twenty-three centuries ago by Sophocles that " The best thing for a man is never to have been born at all, and the next best

thing to return swiftly to that darkness whence he came."
Our program, reflecting this wide view of civic education,
must take into specific account each of seven objectives.
It must provide: (1) for the formation of certain basic civic
habits; (2) for the development of an appreciation of the
worth of our social heritage; (3) for the adoption of a progressive attitude towards civic questions; (4) for the growth
of a disposition to rely upon orderly methods in the attainment of social ends; (5) for the acquisition of precise information about the more important problems of contemporary
life; (6) for the cultivation of a scientific temper in the field
of social relations; and (7) for the development of a broad
social consciousness.   An adequate program must plan for
the achievement, at the various levels of instruction, of all
these objectives.   We shall now pass to a brief examination
of each of these aims, and shall consider the educational
means necessary to its attainment.

How may the school encourage the formation of basic
civic habits?   In the first place, the formation of civic
habits must receive attention.   Through active membership
in many groups the individual citizen should form those
dispositions necessary to life in a democracy.   Beginning
in the home, the child should progressively assume responsibility for the performance of certain tasks necessary to the promotion of the family welfare.   Through
actual participation in this simple form of social life he
should learn to respect the rights of others, to find pleasure in performing acts of simple kindness, to render willingly within the home the various services appropriate to
his age, to be honest, truthful, and fair in his dealings
with other members of the family.

These habits formed in the home should be extended
naturally to an ever-widening group.   In the school and on
the playground children, passing and enforcing laws in the

interests of the group, should participate in the control of
their own affairs.   The life of the school, recognizing no
social classes and permitting special privileges to none,
should approximate as closely as possible the ideal of a
democratic community.   At the same time the school
should maintain an intimate contact with the community
of which it is a part, and should stimulate the formation of
those habits which are required in the adult civic life.
Since each of the other seven objectives can be translated
partly into terms of habit, since in fact each can be given
expression only through habits of action, feeling, and
thought, the remaining discussion will, in some measure,
elaborate and give more definite form to this first point.   In
a sense, they are dispositions which, supplementing the
more simple expressions of virtue in primitive groups, must
be cultivated with especial care in the Great Society.

**How may the school develop an appreciation of the social
heritage?**   In the second place, provision must be made for
the development of an appreciation of that priceless social
heritage which comes as a free gift from the lives and labors
of that long and varied line of human forebears, linking man
with the rest of animate nature.   In spite of its imperfections, we must not forget that this heritage represents the
struggles and sacrifices of countless generations of men and,
in the last analysis, is all that stands between us and the life
of the brute.   Our young people must be made to realize
fully what our institutions have cost in human energy,
travail, and blood.   Especially necessary is this to-day
when the older and more arbitrary sanctions of morals and
religion are so rapidly losing their authority.   The younger
generation must be made to value the high privilege of living
in this age in which they so freely enjoy the fruits of the
achievements of past generations.   The thoughtless attitude towards this heritage which is characteristic of the

ordinary citizen is playfully described by Robinson in the following words: [1]

> In every age the prevailing conditions of civilization have appeared quite natural and inevitable to those who grew up in them. The cow asks no questions as to how it happens to have a dry stall and a supply of hay. The kitten laps its warm milk from a china saucer, without knowing anything about porcelain; the dog nestles in the corner of a divan with no sense of obligation to the inventors of upholstery and the manufacturers of down pillows. So we humans accept our breakfasts, our trains and telephones and orchestras and movies, our national Constitution, our moral code and standards of manners, with the simplicity and innocence of a pet rabbit. We have absolutely inexhaustible capacities for appropriating what others do for us with no thought of a "thank you." We do not feel called upon to make any least contribution ourselves. Indeed, we are usually quite unaware that a game is being played at all.

How may the school inculcate a progressive civic attitude? In the third place, a progressive and positive attitude towards the problems of social life must be fostered in the youth of the nation. This is perhaps the only effective way in which the individual may give expression to his appreciation of what the daring, adventurous, and creative spirits of earlier generations have bequeathed to him. He must be made to realize that every particle of our social inheritance has been created by men, that at one time every habit, idea, or invention was an innovation and constituted a departure from customary practice. Paradoxical as it may seem, the true disciple of the inventors and prophets of the past is not the man who blindly clings to their inventions or reverently repeats their dogmas, but rather he who, giving expression to their spirit and making intelligent use of the fruits of their genius, improves upon their efforts. Commenting on the great lesson that history

[1] Robinson, J. H.: *The Mind in the Making*, p. 57.

teaches in this connection, the writer from whom we have just quoted has thus criticized current educational practice:[1]

> If what has been said above is true, or any considerable part of it, is not almost our whole education at fault? We make no consistent effort to cultivate a progressive spirit in our boys and girls. They are not made to realize the responsibility that rests upon them — the exhilaration that comes from ever looking and pressing forward. They are still so largely nurtured upon the abstract and the classical that we scarcely yet dare to bring education into relation with life. The history they are taught brings few or none of the lessons the past has to offer. They are reared with too much respect for the past, too little confidence for the future. Does not education become in this way a mighty barrier cast across the way of progress, rather than a guidepost to betterment?

It is a sad commentary on the character of education that some of those social changes which have proved most wise were opposed from the start by the educated classes. Instead of firing the youth with a zeal for making happier the lot of man, education has rather developed the mind of timid and reactionary mould. The school has often striven with success to produce the unprogressive citizen with, in the words of John Morley, " his inexhaustible patience of abuses that only torment others; his apologetic word for beliefs that may not be so precisely true as one might wish, and institutions that are not altogether so useful as some might think possible; his cordiality towards progress and improvement in a general way, and his coldness or antipathy to each progressive proposal in particular; his pygmy hope that life will one day become somewhat better, punily shivering by the side of his gigantic conviction that it might well be infinitely worse." Obviously an education of this type, since it can serve only a privileged class and this class only in narrow fashion, does not merit attention, still less deserve public support.

[1] Robinson, J. H.: *The New History*, pp. 265–66.

Another aspect of this problem is the need of developing a willingness and even a desire on the part of the citizen to give freely of his time and energy to the common good. An appreciation of the benefits of which one partakes is of social value only in so far as it results in works. For the individual to be progressive avails but little, if his powers are wholly absorbed in the pursuit of strictly private ends. No small part of our civic failure may be traced directly to the indifference of large sections of the population. Each individual is so concerned about " getting ahead," — the great ideal of American life — that he is willing to spare but a small part of his time for the purification and advancement of the social interest. The public service does not stand high in the estimation of the ordinary citizen. The economic life has drawn more than its share of the talent of the nation. Consequently, for the most part, only second-rate men enter the field of politics, and many who enter the public service do so for private ends and in the very spirit in which they would engage in a profit-making enterprise. In direct contrast with the condition prevailing in certain other countries, the term " politician " carries to most American ears a distinctly sordid connotation. Clearly, an education that does not place the highest premium on the life of the man or the woman who gives his energies unselfishly in the service of the Republic falls far short of the needs of the time. Unless democracy can enlist a fair proportion of its finest capacity in the public service, such a form of government can be neither enlightened nor righteous, and in the end cannot endure.

How may the school develop respect for orderly methods? In the fourth place, the educational program must inculcate in the citizen the fixed disposition to rely upon orderly methods in the attainment of social and civic ends. In the United States, this objective is of especial importance, because the American people are apparently possessed of a powerful strain for violence. Although we have been experimenting with free institutions for almost a hundred and fifty years, we have not learned to place confidence in the orderly processes of law. That we are an extraordinarily criminal people, is shown by the fact that, in the ordinary year, there are approximately as many homicides in either New York City or Chicago as in the whole of England, Scotland, and Wales. Racial antagonisms from time to time give rise to bloody conflicts in which millions of dollars worth of property are destroyed, and men, women, and children are brutally killed. In many sections of the country bands of " respectable " citizens, without any compunctions of conscience whatsoever, take the law into their own hands and, following some farcical legal procedure, flog, lynch, or burn their victims. Our industrial disturbances are frequently marked by a degree of violence that is seldom seen in other civilized countries. In recent years, persons and classes of high authority have connived at the open violation of law and the use of illegal force in their own interests. They speciously argue that in destroying the law they preserve it.

That this tendency toward mob behavior may be explained in terms of the survival of frontier influences or the heterogeneity of our population is entirely beside the point. Whatever the cause, the situation is altogether deplorable and requires the most serious educational attention. Vigorous measures must be introduced into the school and society for the purpose of instilling into the minds of our people a meet and proper respect for orderly methods of adjusting social conflict.

How may the school impart precise civic information? In the fifth place, our youthful citizens must be informed concerning the more important problems and issues of contemporary social life. In a political democracy this is a basic need. Much of the conflict in the world to-day is due to failure at this point. The founders of free government, assuming that the masses of the people would know their own best interests and would elect officials to give these interests effect, believed that on important issues the voters would be essentially right. But experience has shown that public opinion can be trusted only if it is based on adequate and accurate information. With the growth of a complex society, and with the development of the press and agencies for propaganda, such an equipment has become a rare possession. One of the two great dangers threatening all modern democracies, a leading publicist writes, is:

the irresponsible power wielded by those who supply the people with the materials they need for judging men and measures. Dissemination by the printed word of untruths and fallacies and incitements to violence which we have learnt to call propaganda has become a more potent influence among the masses in large countries than the demagogue ever was in the small peoples of former days. To combat these dangers more insight and sympathy, as well as more energy and patriotism, are needed than the so-called upper and educated classes have hitherto displayed.

The same point is made by Lippmann when he suggests: [1]

that when full allowance has been made for deliberate fraud, political science has still to account for such facts as two nations attacking one another, each convinced that it is acting in self-defense, or two classes at war each certain that it speaks for the common interest. They live, we are likely to say, in different worlds. More accurately, they live in the same world, but they think and feel in different ones.

Due to the operation of many forces the truth about events and issues is obscured, but the individual citizen, unconscious of the limitations under which he lives, naïvely

[1] Lippmann, Walter: *Public Opinion*, p. 20.

assumes the perfect trustworthiness of his own picture of the world.

If the school were to conceive its function aright, much could be done to bring relief to this condition. It should in the first instance inform its pupils concerning the nature of public opinion, the way in which it is formed, and the agencies at work upon it. Beyond that, with a degree of thoroughness adapted to the level of maturity and capacity of the individual, the school should take up in turn each large social issue and bring the student in touch with the information upon it suitable to his understanding. Hitherto we have been very meticulous in our concern over issues that have been dead for decades and even for centuries. We have demanded acquaintance with the fabled doings of fabled peoples. We have insisted that our children know all about the forces that brought Athens and Sparta into conflict, or that led to the murder of the Gracchi. While much can be learned from the distant past, our first consideration, following perhaps a general survey of human achievement, should be given to those matters about which conflict surges to-day. Our young people should be informed concerning the causes of poverty and crime, the forces that make for political corruption, the inefficiency of the administration of justice, the ways and means of controlling economic power in the interests of society, the conflict between labor and capital that is shaking the foundations of western civilization, the working out of adjustments between races and classes and religious sects, and the abolition of war and imperialism. An indefensible policy is pursued when youth are permitted to assume the responsibilities of citizenship in relative ignorance of these questions, or, what is even worse, in possession of a repertoire of prejudices, half-truths, and fallacies, nicely calculated to aggravate the evils under which the world now labors.

How may the school cultivate a scientific civic temper?
In the sixth place, effort must be made to cultivate a scientific temper in the field of social relations. It is not enough that we possess the findings of science. New problems are constantly arising which, as they are attacked by the citizen, demand reliance on the methods and spirit of science. Each individual, to the limit of his capacity, should be taught to approach these social perplexities with the single minded desire to learn the truth. He should be freed, in so far as possible, from that dogmatic attitude toward social questions which now characterizes our society. Especially do the American people need to develop a tolerant attitude toward new ideas, for even the shrewdest of men will make mistakes in evaluating new and untried theories. Intelligence, not force, must test the validity of social ideas.

The reception accorded creative thought in the realm of physics is thus contrasted by Bertrand Russell with its reception in the realm of social politics: [1]

We have had in recent years a brilliant example of the scientific temper of mind in the theory of relativity and its reception by the world. Einstein, a German-Swiss-Jew pacifist, was appointed to a research professorship by the German Government in the early days of the war; his predictions were verified by an English expedition which observed the eclipse of 1919, very soon after the armistice. His theory upset the whole theoretical framework of traditional physics; it is almost as damaging to orthodox dynamics as Darwin was to Genesis. Yet physicists everywhere have shown complete readiness to accept his theory as soon as it appeared that the evidence was in its favor. But none of them, least of all Einstein himself, would claim that he has said the last word. He has not built a monument of infallible dogma to stand for all time. There are difficulties he cannot solve; his doctrines will have to be modified in their turn as they have modified Newton's. This critical undogmatic receptiveness is the true attitude of science.

What would have happened if Einstein had advanced something

---

[1] Russell, Bertrand: *Free Thought,* pp. 16–19.

equally new in the sphere of religion or politics? English people would have found elements of Prussianism in his theory; anti-Semites would have regarded it as a Zionist plot; nationalists in all countries would have found it tainted with lily-livered pacifism, and proclaimed it a mere dodge for escaping military service. All the old-fashioned professors would have approached Scotland Yard to get the importation of his writings prohibited. Teachers favorable to him would have been dismissed. He, meantime, would have captured the government of some backward country, where it would have become illegal to teach anything except his doctrine, which would have grown into a mysterious dogma not understood by anybody. Ultimately the truth or falsehood of his doctrine would be decided on the battlefield, without the collection of any fresh evidence for or against it.

While this statement is perhaps extreme and may seem to some a gross exaggeration, its sting resides in the fact that it contains so much of truth. It shocks because it is lucid and turns the light on areas commonly and protectingly shrouded in darkness. There is thus revealed in its true form a social practice which is customarily clothed in the deceptive garments of respectability. As this quotation suggests, the scientific spirit has little in common with the methods that usually prevail in dealing with matters touching on the nature of man and his social relations. Here, slight indeed is the premium placed on the exercise of intelligence. We exhibit no hesitation about entertaining an unverifiable opinion or clinging to an unfounded prejudice. In fact we feel duty-bound to defend it, and we show great industry in searching through our experience for reasons that will enable us to remain of unchanged mind. The individual who thus holds to his convictions in the face of the repeated assaults of fact, however carelessly these convictions may have been formed by himself or his ancestors, is looked upon as having given evidence of character, and receives the social approval of his group. It is commonly regarded a commendable trait to present a closed mind to the more important and difficult problems of life. The world to-day requires a new type of courage, the courage to observe and to think, and to use the results of observation and thought for further observing and thinking.

The possibilities of improving our social life are probably without practical limit, but, so long as truth remains an unwelcome and despised intruder, the road to progress is barred. Advance, which is always difficult, is thus needlessly obstructed. Another generation must be taught to seek enlightenment here and fittingly reward those who can illumine its forward path. Especially is this necessary to-day when, as General Smuts has said, " Humanity has struck its tents and is once more on the march." Contemporary civilization is seething with new and strange social ideas and doctrines. Some of them contain much that will prove of value to mankind, while many hold nothing of worth for the race. But to distinguish truth from error is always difficult. It is never easy to measure in their germinal state the potentialities of strange forms of life. In a scientific temper our youth must learn to approach every contribution in this field. Without regard to the source from which it comes or its effect on some cherished but less serviceable notion, each social invention must be calmly evaluated in the light of the evidence. An effort must be made in our schools to cultivate the open mind, the mind that is eager for a continuous revelation, the mind that holds all conclusions more or less tentatively, the mind that remains ever youthful, inquiring, and hopeful.

How may the school develop a broad social consciousness? In the seventh place, the development of a broad social consciousness must be promoted through the school. Improvements in transportation and communication have destroyed the barriers that formerly separated kin from kin, community from community, nation from nation, race from race. Almost within the span of a generation the whole world has been crowded into a single parish. In this parish must live all the races of mankind. Although the evidence from the late War indicates that, if they would dwell long upon the earth, they must dwell in peace, whether they will live together in peace or in conflict is to-day an unanswered question. The growth of man's power for doing evil has marched hand in hand with his mastery over natural forces.

Without exaggeration it may be said that he is to-day able to destroy himself, or to impoverish life to such a degree that he would not care to preserve it. But, as man is constituted to-day through training and education, we are forced to concede that he cannot be expected to live in peace with his neighbors. Either he does not want peace, or else he wants those things which are only compatible with war. By every virile race, war, the product of narrow minds and selfish interests, is glorified in song and story. Through this body of tradition, in which the figure of Mars all but reigns supreme, the imagination is led back, from generation to generation, to a legendary and mythical past. In our histories the hero of war is accorded the place of highest honor among those who have served the State. Love of country has ever been identified with willingness to follow the national flag with little regard to the cause in whose name it is raised. We question the patriotism of the man who loves peace and seeks to promote it, the man who strives to understand the point of view of another political, economic, or religious group. As Europe hung in the balance between war and peace in 1914, one of the most powerful figures on the continent making for peace was murdered. The assassin was later acquitted in the national courts on the grounds of patriotic intent. An individual may be instrumental in driving two nations into conflict and yet be lauded as a patriot, and even given the highest political office with which his country can honor him. A politician can secure a large following by circulating the vilest of slanders regarding the motives of a neighboring people, and a journalist can build up a powerful paper by appealing to the narrowest of class, religious, and race prejudices.

Our ignorance of the orientals is not so great to-day as it was in the Middle Ages, when scholars speculated on the character of the Antipodes, but it is much more prolific of harm. Then whether one people understood another mattered little, because they were so completely separated by geographical barriers that at the very worst they could but engage in a war of brigandage or piracy. To-day all is changed. Yet we nurse our misconceptions and prejudices about other groups as fondly as the Mediæval theologian cherished false notions about the stars and the planets. We are inclined to repeat the folly of the critics of Galileo who, in order that they might persist in their denial of the existence of Jupiter's moons, steadfastly refused to place their beliefs in jeopardy by viewing the heavens through the telescope.

All the facts indicate that as a people we possess an all too limited social consciousness. The world of to-day is divided into races, nations, sects, classes, communities, and families. He who lives therein is not only a member of the small kinship group characteristic of primitive times; he is also a member of a local community, of a great nation, and, finally, of the human race. He must be made to feel genuine membership in the larger societies. The parochial spirit must be expanded into a world spirit. We already recognize the immorality of the man who places the welfare of his family above the good of the community; but little imagination is required to see that it is just as immoral to subordinate the interests of mankind to those of race or nation. Much of the unhappiness from which

mankind suffers is due to the fact that the social consciousness of the ordinary citizen is not sufficiently broad to sub-
sume the responsibilities that the wider citizenship involves.
To a small group alone does he feel responsible, but his
actions affect the welfare of millions. The criminal who
robs that he may divide the loot with his gang, the politician who seeks political office that he may give a city
franchise to a friend, the manufacturer who exploits the
children of others that he may transmit a fortune to his own,
the teacher who misrepresents the actions of nations that
he may inspire a love of country in the hearts of his pupils,
the ecclesiastic who circulates half-truths regarding the
beliefs of rival sects that he may enhance the prestige of his
own denomination, the statesman who defends his country
in its pursuit of a wrong course of action that he may kindle
an unreflective loyalty, and the saint who would damn un-
believers that he might advance his own doctrine — all are
exhibiting a social consciousness that is too narrow to serve
the larger needs of associative living.

Can the school educate for world citizenship? In order
that the school may make important contribution to the
development of this broad social consciousness, in order
that the pupil may be brought to feel some allegiance to
groups other than those small groups into which he happens
to be born, our educational program must be derived from
fundamentally different principles. In the first place, the
citizen of the Great Society must be given an impartial
though sympathetic account of the history and achievements of his own group, whether it be his family, his community, his economic class, his religious sect, his nation, or
his race. Every time virtues are exaggerated or vices condoned, forces that lead to misunderstanding and conflict are
certain to be generated.

In the second place, having due regard for the limitations

set by capacity and the period of formal education, we must give him a similar account of other groups. It is the height of national unwisdom to permit our youth to grow into maturity with the perverted notions which they possess about other religions, other nations, and other races. They should be made eager to see, know, and understand their brothers and sisters brought up in strange lands and nurtured in foreign cultures. They should be made to realize that modern civilization is not the product of the genius of any one people, but rather the fruit of the coöperative and cumulative efforts of many peoples working through thousands of generations. Of those that have contributed in the past our knowledge is but fragmentary; of those that will contribute in the future nothing is known.

In the third place, each member of society must be given an adequate appreciation of the supreme value of the works of peace and the relative futility of the resort to arms in advancing the genuine interests of the race. The heroes of war must be eclipsed by those less arresting figures who have made the positive contributions to civilization. Honor must be rendered where honor is due; especially must homage be paid to those who have promoted the more abundant life — the statesman, the reformer, the prophet, the teacher, the scientist, the inventor, the physician, the engineer, the organizer, the poet, the artist, the philosopher, the good workman, the delightful companion, and the wise parent. The activities and interests which all peoples hold in common must be emphasized. While recognizing in our histories the distinction between offensive and defensive wars, between wars of aggression and wars of liberation, we must place primary stress on the evolution of peaceful culture. Our citizens must see that this is the culture of true grandeur, the culture which offers unlimited opportunities for noble and heroic service. A spectacular heroism will meet the perils of war, but a steadfast heroism must meet the perils of peace. An educational program organized in this larger spirit cannot fail to lead an increasing fraction of our people to that vision of the world and that feeling of true kinship with mankind which in the past have been vouchsafed only to the prophet.

ADDITIONAL PROBLEMS FOR DISCUSSION

1. Why can we not leave the solution of social problems to highly trained social engineers, as we leave the solution of mechanical problems to mechanical engineers?

2. How has the growth of the Great Society made more necessary and at the same time more difficult the intimate feeling of social responsibility in the individual?

3. How has the increased complexity of society made the incidental civic education gained through unguided participation in social life inadequate? Evaluate, from the standpoint of civic responsibilities, the life of a savage, the life of a citizen in a city-state of Ancient Greece, and the life of a citizen in the metropolis of a modern industrial state.

4. Were the schools of the past, when they took as their function the giving of the tools of learning, correct in the assumption that the knowledge and interest in civic affairs would later be acquired by the individual in the normal process of living?

5. What are the arguments for and against the common notion that the stability and perpetuation of democratic institutions depend, more than do the conservation of aristocratic institutions, on the universal extension of education?

6. What are the disadvantages to the individual and society which flow from the fact that the ordinary citizen accepts, as quite natural and inevitable, the prevailing conditions of social and national life?

7. What are the fears entertained by those who object to giving to the student a genuinely progressive and evolutionary conception of the working of society?

8. What radical changes would you expect to occur in the German system of education as a result of the democratic revolution? How should the formal education of a democracy differ from that found in an autocratic state?

9. In the light of Dewey's two criteria of a democratic society, criticize the typical school system from the standpoint of: (1) general control by society of the school; (2) relations between teachers and administrators; (3) relations between teachers and pupils; and (4) relations among the pupils themselves.

10. How should the accessibility of political office in a democracy motivate interest in an active participation in and understanding of civic affairs? Why is there a tendency for educated and high-minded citizens to refuse to run for political office?

11. How can the general spirit which animates American life and education be blamed for the disposition to rely on disorderly methods in the attainment of civic and social ends?

12. Compare the better school with the better type of newspaper as an effective agency in acquainting the citizen with the more important problems of contemporary social life.

13. To what extent has the teaching of American history and civics hindered the development of the spirit upon which harmonious international relations depend?

14. From the standpoint of achieving the objectives set forth in this section, what are the shortcomings of history and civics as taught in most schools?

15. Why is there apparently a greater faith in the extra-curricular activities than in the formal curriculum of the school, in fostering the formation of those dispositions required in social life? In what way can the formal curriculum be made to take on the effectiveness of the extra-curriculum?

16. Criticize the statement that it is impossible for the ordinary educational institution, in treating controversial questions, to do more than reflect the effective opinion prevailing in the community.

17. To what extent is the school responsible for the lack of interest exhibited by college students in social and political events?

PROBLEM 16

HOW MAY EDUCATION ENRICH THE RECREATIONAL LIFE?

What is recreation? — What is the psychological significance of recreation? — What determines the value of a recreational activity? — How should the educational program be derived? — What is the dominant interest of modern life? — What is the character of American folk-life? — Is recreation accorded a secure status in American life? — How has recreation been commercialized? — Is the recreational life in America superficial? — How have institutional changes modified the recreational problem? — What is the recreational problem of rural life? — What are the special recreational problems of urban life? — Can recreation be made to lend significance and beauty to the common activities of life? — What has been America's contribution to the fine arts? — How may the school enrich the recreational life through the conventional formal curriculum? — What are the possibilities in the extra-curriculum? — What changes are essential to the inauguration of this program? — What is the wider opportunity of the school?

What is recreation? Even under the most primitive conditions of existence the whole of man's time and energy is not consumed in those activities directly related to the maintenance of life and the satisfaction of family, economic, civic, and religious interests. After these needs are met a margin of leisure remains. In periods of plenty the savage may have opportunity for giving expression to those impulses which but lightly condition existence; and during the inclement seasons, when the ordinary routine of life is suspended, he may turn his mind to the pursuit of congenial interests. In these moments of leisure man may elaborate the common life and weave into it meanings and appreciations which are not derived from external necessity. Thus grow up in the life of every group the recreational arts — songs, stories, games, dances, ceremonials, and festivals.   Among the earliest of human records are the crude drawings of animals scratched on the fragments of bones, or painted on the walls of caves.   These were the diversions of the primitive huntsman as in moments of leisure he relived in imagination some exciting adventure of the chase or contemplated the thrills of future exploits. Through activity as well as through rest the re-creation of life proceeds.

What is the place of recreation in life?   The place and function of these recreational activities in the general economy of life require careful consideration.   The primary object of recreation is not the promotion of health.   Neither is it to be regarded as an appendage to the economic, the family, the civic, or the religious life.   It must not be confused with those activities whose main object is to bring about some definite and pre-determined change in the external world, although it may be associated with and grow out of such activities.   Its function is not instrumental.   A recreational activity is a genuinely leisure activity, an activity in which one engages without thought of reward, either in this world or in the next.   But since the word leisure frequently carries too wide a connotation, it must be used with caution.   Leisure is often contrasted with economic labor, and thus uncritically made to embrace all activities that are not directly related to gaining a livelihood.   When used in this way it includes many health, family, civic, and religious interests which naturally cannot be followed during the hours devoted to the pursuit of vocation.   They represent duties, however, that must be performed; responsibilities that should no more be escaped than those centering in the economic life.   Regardless of convenience or inclination, a definite time should be allotted to their performance.   The essence of recreation, on the other hand, is freedom.   One does not engage therein from a sense of duty, but rather for the sake of the activity itself. This, of course, does not mean that recreation may not promote health or further the social life in its various aspects. Much less does it mean that the non-recreational activities must always be entered into either under external compulsion or from a self-imposed feeling of obligation. The point to be distinctly understood is merely that recreation is not ancillary to any other interest whatsoever. It must always enjoy an independent status.

What is the relation between play and work? The line between recreational and other activities, however, cannot be rigidly drawn, because by imperceptible gradations the one type of activity shades off into the other. Recreation may incidentally advance every legitimate human interest; and, in the measure that its own special purpose is not sacrificed, this is desirable. Likewise those activities which are directed towards the modification of some aspect of the environment may contain a large element of freedom. This also is much to be coveted. In all departments where the operation of external and arbitrary authority is reduced to a minimum, activity partakes of the nature of recreation. This is often true of the promotion of health and the fostering of the family, civic, and religious interests.

Even in the field of vocations there are many cases where, because the individual expresses himself fully in his calling, work becomes identified with play. But this is the exception to-day. For the great majority of men the gulf that separates vocation from recreation is so great that the two have little in common. This unfortunate state of affairs is due in part to an economic system in which the individual workman is a means to production, in part to an education that exalts routine over freedom, in part to a native endowment that limits the powers of appreciation, and in part to the conditions imposed on mankind by natural forces.

Happy indeed is the individual whose vocation gives expression to a wide range of impulses and thus satisfies the craving for recreation. The ideal of a social order in which work will continuously re-create rather than exhaust the life forces of the population should be constantly before us. But the immediately practical problem in the world as we know it, is that of equipping the individual to supplement his hours of labor with a rich recreational life.

What is the psychological significance of recreation? While recreation requires no justification in terms of the other great goods of life, the use to which man puts his leisure time must always be of great significance. Says Dewey:[1]

> Play and art are moral necessities. They are required to take care of the margin that exists between the total stock of impulses that demand outlet and the amount expended in regular action. They keep the balance which work cannot indefinitely maintain. They are required to introduce variety, flexibility, and sensitiveness into disposition.

Recreation promotes a wholesome development of the capacities and functions; it prolongs the period of youth by creating the conditions necessary for both physical and mental health; it serves as a tonic to the organism by adding to the zest of living; and above all it lends color and sweetness and beauty to life. Since recreation takes place under the conditions of freedom, it provides opportunity for the manifold expression of personality; and, all constraining influences being relatively absent, the self is permitted to develop according to the laws of its own being and in response to its own potentialities.

It is for this reason that art sustains such an intimate relation to the recreational life. The conditions of recreation are in large measure the conditions of art. When man

[1] Dewey, John: *Human Nature and Conduct,* p. 160.

plays he becomes an artist. This suggests the great educational significance of recreation; in play the inhibitions are cast aside, the spirit is exalted, attention is undivided, and the individual loses himself in the activity. Hence the modification of the organism, the formation of habit, the growth of disposition, the process of education advances at the maximum rate. To a peculiar degree, therefore, what man does in his leisure hours shapes his personality and moulds his character.

What activities are re-creative? Recreation cannot be identified with any particular type of activity. It has assumed multitudinous forms among various peoples and at different times in human history. To-day its form changes with individual and with circumstance. Indeed, the possibilities of recreation are almost as numerous and as varied as the number and variety of human impulses and activities. A canvass of the population in an American community would reveal a diversity of leisure activities, the mere listing of a few of which will try the patience of the reader. Many would be found attending social gatherings, going to the theater, appreciating music, watching athletic contests, reading newspapers and fiction, and engaging in out-of-door sports. Others would be employing their spare time in visiting museums, collecting stamps, motoring into the country, hunting rabbits, gambling in stock, " shooting craps," making extended vacation trips, walking in the parks, swimming in the pools, playing billiards, retailing community gossip, going on picnics, making home-brew, writing books, discussing the failings of other people's children, lying in the sunshine, flirting with the other sex, enjoying the companionship of friends, quarrelling with neighbors, writing letters, adorning the person, window shopping, experimenting with radio, playing cards, attending teas and dinners, using carpenter's tools, smoking tobacco, painting china, " bossing " servants, dozing in chairs, studying birds, reading philosophy, indulging in daydreams, collecting bottles, visiting the poor, tinkering with machinery, making gardens, or spinning theories of education.

Some of these activities are primarily intellectual, others contain a large æsthetic element, others are essentially social, others emphasize the physical, and yet others are avocational. The assignment of relative values to these activities is most difficult. Of course, those which are clearly anti-social or harmful to the individual merit no support. Others which, besides being worth while in themselves, contribute to health or advance some important social interest, may be argued to possess greater worth than those which do not perform these added functions. But in the passing of such judgments care must be taken lest the recreational life be subordinated to other concerns.

What determines the value of a recreational activity? Disregarding any instrumental value which a recreational activity may have, let us now return to the basic question: Apart from differences in intensity is one type of enjoyment better, or nobler, or finer, or more worthy than another? For example, is the satisfaction that comes from the appreciation of grand opera of a higher order than that which accompanies attendance at a wrestling match? The common answer is an affirmative one. Although the case is not quite so clear as it appears, with this answer the writers are in agreement.

The superior position which is so readily accorded grand opera by the uncritical is largely a product of tradition. It is to be explained in no small measure by historical accident. Grand opera has somewhat better social connections and carries greater respectability than wrestling. The appreciation of the former, since its development requires careful and sustained cultivation as well as generous financial support, is a more difficult form of satisfaction to secure. Consequently its acquisition has been largely restricted to the classes of leisure and means, and has come to reflect the prestige of these classes. On the other hand, most people, regardless of ancestry, experience, or education, have no difficulty in appreciating a wrestling match. The enjoyment of this amusement, with all similar forms of appreciation, being derived rather directly from certain powerful inborn tendencies, is primitive. In so far as the recreations of a people are of this relatively unlearned type that people is under-developed and is ill-prepared for a life of leisure. But this in itself is not a serious criticism of the enjoyment involved in the watching of a wrestling match, nor does it elevate the appreciation of grand opera to a superior status. A particular leisure interest might be very difficult to acquire, and even sanctified by an intimate association with aristocracy, and yet be tedious and unproductive of genuine satisfactions. We must therefore seek elsewhere for the test whereby the relative value of a recreational activity may be measured.

If grand opera deserves a higher rank than wrestling, and we believe it does, it is because, in the majority of cases, grand opera offers to the individual a wider range for the development of interest and because its potentialities for future and varied satisfactions are without practical limit. In our schools efforts should be centered on those forms of recreation that show some promise of a long and varied growth, and that at the same time are dependent for their enjoyment on an educational training which can be economically given.

What has been the attitude of the school towards recreation? In the past the public school has either assumed that the recreational needs of the population are adequately cared for through the incidental education of the home and the community, or that play is an unimportant part of life. Our elementary education, greatly influenced in its origins by a narrow religious conception, carries a tradition which is hostile to recreation. Moreover the curriculum of this institution, designed to meet the educational requirements of the common people, was reduced to that barest minimum which was thought essential to the successful performance of the simpler economic and political functions. The life for which this school was supposed to prepare was harsh, impoverished, and bereft of leisure. The conventional secondary and higher education, though planned to fit into the life of the privileged and favored classes, has also neglected the recreational interests. Dominated from the first by a narrow scholastic tradition, it has been reluctant to grapple with the problems of human society. Hence the program for enriching the recreational life, in both the lower and the higher schools, is as yet very imperfectly developed.

How should the educational program be derived? The nature of the educational program required must be determined by a careful study of human nature in its present social situation. Hence it will be necessary to consider the current status of the recreational life in our own country before making the more concrete educational proposals. A program borrowed from some other country or some other age cannot be expected to function in modern America. And, since the minor characteristics of the situation shift from community to community, the program for a particular school must be developed in response to local needs and shortcomings. Owing to the limitations of space, the discussion here will be confined to the most general analysis of the existing leisure activities. Only the more significant facts pertaining to the recreational life in the United States, facts not to be disregarded in the construction of the educational program, can be noted. Attention will be directed, in the first place, to certain features that generally characterize the recreational life in America; in the second place, to conditions that are peculiar to the rural community; and, finally, to some special problems that are appearing in urban and industrial centers. This survey, by conveying to the reader some conception of both the magnitude and the diversity of the task, will make clear the nature and the extent of the educational program required.

What is the dominant interest of modern life? Before considering those conditions of recreation which are peculiar to American life, it will be well to note certain general characteristics of that modern civilization of which our own culture is a part, and of which it is at the same time a peculiarly extreme expression. Each civilization has had its marked characteristics. As Ferrero has remarked:[1]

Every epoch directs all its efforts towards a supreme goal, which for it is the all-important one. There have been epochs ablaze with religious fervor, whose chief aspiration it was to diffuse and to defend the faith. There have been epochs with a profound sense of the ambition for glory, which fought great wars. Others again have turned their attention to the fostering of the arts and sciences. Our civilization aims, in the first place, at the mastery over nature, and the intensive exploitation of all the riches of the earth.

That this is the controlling purpose of our age, few will deny; and likewise, that within limits this purpose may legitimately enlist the energies of any people, all will agree. But our relatively complete absorption in the production and exchange of material goods will seem extravagant to the critic of a later generation. Into the task of making the world beautiful, of making life sweet and agreeable to those who live it, but little of our energy is directed. " So feverish and yet so mechanical, so interesting and yet so unlovely,"

[1] Ferrero, G.: *Ancient Rome and Modern America*, p. 171.

the age in which we live subordinates living to the process of gaining a livelihood, regards artistic creation as a superfluous frivolity, and considers industry, commerce, inventions, and wealth the only serious occupations of men.

How is quality sacrificed to quantity? The reward for our great interest in extending the dominion of man over the forces of the natural world has been an abundance of the material goods of life which surpasses the wildest dreams of earlier ages. But for the moment, at least, quantity has been secured at the sacrifice of quality. We are insensitive to beauty and, whether in the building of a city, the exploitation of forests, or the selling of drugs, the demands of commercial enterprise override æsthetic considerations. Borrowing again from Ferrero: [1]

The artistic mediocrity of our epoch is surpassed only by the superficiality and confusion of its tastes. Each succeeding year sees that which used to appear the height of elegance and beauty to its predecessors, despised, neglected, and forgotten. All the styles of the past and all the styles of the different countries swirl around us, before the fickle gusts of fashion. Every picture which excites admiration for a moment is quickly forgotten by the fickle taste of an age which ransacks every corner in search of the beautiful, because nowhere can the beautiful be found. . . . Nobody can explain how it happens that so rich, so wise, and so powerful a civilization does not succeed in being beautiful, and shows itself powerless to infuse a breath of beauty into anything it creates, be it big or little, into its cities or into the small objects of daily use. . . . Our age produces in great quantities, but maybe not a single one of the buildings and material objects produced by it in such abundance can hope to conquer the ages. Everything is precarious, ephemeral, destined to live a few months or a few years; destined to a premature death from the very first hour of its birth."

How does the competitive spirit make excessive demands on human energies? As de Coubertin has so forcefully pointed out, the modern world is a restless and fitful world,

[1] Ferrero, G.: *Ancient Rome and Modern America*, pp. 52–55.

a world of flux and of change. Nothing is stable and secure; all is uncertain and provisional. The development of rapid means of transportation has made of man an essentially mobile creature, and the equalization of opportunity has made possible the rapid rise to power and fortune. Both geographical and social barriers which formerly limited the actions of men have been swept away. In social position, as well as in space, an individual may proceed far from the place of his birth. Hence the appetites and ambitions of the masses have been excited to a point unknown in the past. At any moment of time man may either fear or hope everything. Both failure and success are ever-present possibilities which lend power to the competitive spirit, and hold the mind in a condition of continuous excitation. So rapidly do conditions change, and so often are opportunities altered, that modern society is in a " state of incessant ebullition."

All of this puts a strain on personality which was not known to earlier civilizations. The individual, caught up in the overmastering whirl of uncontrolled events, is so pushed and driven by circumstance that his obligations always exceed his capacity. Consequently, in facing the daily task his state of mind is not unlike that of an impecunious debtor awaiting the visits of his creditors. To him is perpetually denied that " divine ambrosia " which has been man's source of strength in ages past — healthy sleep and peace of mind. For the excessive demands made on the mental energies of men by the cruel uncertainties of the future and the savage competition for success, compensation is sought in some form of equally stimulating diversion which will momentarily induce a sweet forgetfulness of the world of serious things. Thus to the long list of factors which produce strain and exhaustion, which dissipate the life forces of the population, are added the pursuits of leisure hours.

What is the character of American folk-life? From a consideration of modern civilization in its more general aspects, attention may now be directed to the special form which it takes in the new world. Perhaps the most outstanding feature of recreation in the United States is the relative absence of that rich folk-life which is characteristic of the older civilizations. There is a cultural barrenness about the American community that challenges attention. It is this spiritual poverty that has called forth from the adverse foreign critic the unflattering comment that America lacks a soul. While such a wide judgment can hardly be passed on any age or people with justice, since the precise meaning of soul is somewhat obscure and reflects the bias of him who uses the term, this estimate only too obviously contains a painful sting of truth.

Whether one goes to the great metropolis with its teeming population and its frenzied haste, or to the rural hamlet with its broader spaces and more measured tread, the same fundamental deficiency is apparent. In the former, to be sure, the leisure hours are crowded with activity; but the character of this activity reveals more clearly than does the colorless tedium of the village the cultural immaturity of our people. In the superficial, vulgar, hurried, and exhausting diversions which abound in the urban center, there is reflected no artistic heritage that has grown out of the life of the folk. Rather are they the product of commercial enterprise bent on deriving a profit from amusing an harassed population.

Why is American folk-life barren? The more important reasons for the relative absence of a folk-life in the United States are not difficult to discover. The fundamental explanation lies in the fact that America is a new country, settled under circumstances that are somewhat unique in the history of the world. Our population has been drawn from all the nations of Europe, and in some measure from all the races of mankind. But the significant point is that America has been peopled, not by clans or tribes, as the great land areas in the past were settled, but by individuals who, dissatisfied with conditions in the homeland, decided to try their fortunes in the new world. Only very rarely have communities or organized groups migrated to America. Hence the cultural tradition has usually been broken, and the efforts to reconstitute the folk-life of the old world in the new have met with but little success. Even where immigrants have settled in distinct quarters in our great cities, and have enjoyed conditions somewhat favorable to the maintenance of a degree of cultural unity, through the work of the public school and the influence of other contacts the second generation usually drifts away from parental control, and comes to despise those elements of the foreign culture which mark its own people off from the native population. Being unable to distinguish the good from the bad in the culture of other peoples and unconscious of our own cultural deficiency, we have unwittingly encouraged this process and have even called it Americanization.

This unenlightened form of Americanization is well illustrated by Lippmann's description of a pageant, which a friend of his attended: [1]

It was called the Melting Pot, and it was given on the Fourth of July in an automobile town where many foreign-born workers are employed. In the center of the baseball park at second base stood a huge wooden and canvas pot. There were flights of steps up to the rim on two sides. After the audience had settled itself, and the band had played, a procession came through an opening at one side of the field. It was made up of men of all the foreign nationalities employed in the factories. They wore their native costumes; they were singing their national songs; they danced their folk dances, and carried the banners of all Europe. The master of

---

[1] Lippmann, Walter: *Public Opinion,* pp. 86–87.

ceremonies was the principal of the grade school dressed as Uncle Sam. He led them to the pot. He directed them up the steps to the rim and inside. He called them out again on the other side. They came, dressed in derby hats, coats, pants, vest, stiff collar and polkadot tie, undoubtedly, said my friend, each with an Eversharp pencil in his pocket, and all singing the Star-Spangled Banner.

Poverty stricken though our own spiritual possessions are at some points, we have taken them as the criterion of excellence and have required the immigrant to conform. As a consequence we have cut ourselves adrift from the achievements of the past and have banished from the life of the folk that warmth and beauty which enrich the cultures of other peoples.

Other important factors, however, have contributed to this defect in our civilization. Various religious and economic forces have left their mark on American culture. The austere influence of Puritanism, with its belief in the righteousness of a barren emotional life, as reflected in the absence of ritual, and the sternness of its social discipline, has hindered the development of normal recreational interests. Indeed it has often driven this life into subterranean channels and into the hands of the less scrupulous and more vicious elements of the community. With the development of our civilization and the advent of a commercial age, this cramping tradition of religious origin, forming an alliance with the growing economic and industrial forces, has accentuated that subordination of the more humane to the more material interests of men which generally characterizes the modern world.

This tradition has also been reënforced by the influence of the frontier on American life. Before the appearance of modern means of transportation and communication the wide reaches of a great continent separated man from man and family from family. A life of comparative isolation, fraught with danger and hardship, was thus substituted for the more compact and secure life of the old country. The frontier made difficult, if not impossible, the perpetuation of customs and traditions that had grown out of a mode of living in which groups of men lived together and enjoyed a common life. This tendency towards isolation was perhaps fostered by the famous Homestead Act which, though admirable in so many respects, added to the difficulties attending the development and organization of social interests. Furthermore, the constant westward trend of the population until the close of the nineteenth century, to the fertile lands of the Mississippi and beyond, increased the instability of the family and the community. Each generation in the East would send its quota of youth to found new homes and cities and States in the West. Thus the line by which traditions descend from age to age was broken again and again.

Finally, should be noted the operation of those basic forces which were generated in the process of gaining economic mastery of an undeveloped continent. To-day the severity of that primitive struggle with savages, forests, great distances, mountains, rivers, and soil cannot be fully appreciated; but its ineffaceable mark has been stamped on American life and culture. There was little leisure for the men and women of that day. The age of the pioneer was an age of unremitting toil, the strain of toil was cruelly exhausting, and the hours of toil were long. Into this great task of subduing a continent the energies of our people have necessarily been poured. A splendid material civilization has resulted, but this achievement has been attended by certain spiritual sacrifices.

Is recreation accorded a secure status in American life? The American people have not learned to play. Life is organized about other interests, and from these its standards of value are derived.   Because of the relative absence of contrary traditions, the logic of modern civilization has come to dominate existence in the United States more than in the countries of the old world.   So obsessed are the men of to-day " by the frenzy of work " that they no longer have time to live.   Play is often regarded as childish and as having an insecure place in the adult economy.   Hence the adult feels that he must defend every lapse into childhood in terms of some good which his companions will recognize as legitimate.   The professional man, for example, if he plays golf, passes an hour in a social gathering, attends the theater, or reads poetry, thinks he must justify what may be considered a form of dissipation by maintaining that his health requires the golf, that his personal success is furthered by the social gathering, that he draws a moral from the play, or that his mind is improved by the poetry.   In thus curiously rationalizing his conduct he preserves his respectability, obeys the conventional American code, and at the same time gives expression to his play interests.   In a world that requires the healing effects of recreative play more than any world of the past, play is not welcome. Yet only play can serve as " a balancing force, a counterpoise to the intellectual excesses of a sedentary, nervous civilization which is agitated by a perpetual excitement."

How has recreation been commercialized?   Another serious defect in our recreational life is our relative inability to amuse ourselves.   We are, moreover, even exhibiting a tendency to lose what small capacity we possess in this direction.   In the absence of some specialist on whom we can depend for entertainment, we are helpless.   An English writer, describing conditions in his own country before the War, says: [1]

[1] Welton, J.: *The Psychology of Education*, pp. 487–88.

Every class in this country has lost the habit of amusing itself artistically. The poor as well as the rich look to professionals to amuse them, and have a profound distrust of their own artistic powers and a false shame in exercising them. The artist, whether actor, musician, or dancer, is regarded as a peculiar person, half admired and half despised. He is not, as he once was, merely a man who can do what everyone does, only better. He is a professional entertainer with mysterious powers of his own, which ordinary people do not share and cannot understand; and they would think it indecent presumption to attempt to compete with him.

If this is a sound characterization of England, how much more so it must be of the United States, where the commercialization of amusements has been carried farther than in any other country. The American family, since its members lack the powers of recreational self-direction, looks forward with little zest to an evening spent at home. The movie theater, the café, the dance hall, and the skating rink all exist that this strain may not be put on family life! Both parents and children have little interest in artistic creation, they know how to play but few games, they have very limited powers of conversation, they are poor companions. Incidentally it may be noted that, without appreciably increasing its satisfactions, this helplessness adds greatly to the cost of living. The school could hardly render a more welcome or valued service than that of increasing the competence of the individual in the field of self amusement.

Is the recreational life in America superficial? Recreation in America is not only expensive; in large measure its appeal is primitive and superficial. This is due in part to the commercialization of amusements and in part to the undeveloped character of our people in the realm of recreational interests. Where well-developed standards of artistic appreciation are lacking, satisfaction must come from variety. A superficial but transitory interest in the new, whether in the field of industrial products or in that of musical creation, is characteristic of American life. The entrepreneur in theatrical enterprises, interested naturally in increasing his profits, seeks a production that makes a wide appeal; and, since his prospective patrons are uneducated for dramatic appreciation, he relies with success on the presentation of some simple and melodramatic story based upon adventure, sex, tragedy, and mystery. Goethe must have had a premonition of one of our peculiarly American theatrical products, the *revue*, when he thus satirized the dramatist:

> But above all, give them enough of action;
> He who gives most, will give most satisfaction;
> They come to see a *show* — no work whatever,
> Unless it be a show, can win their favor:
> Therefore, by their taste be thou admonished,
> Weave brilliant scenes to captivate their eyes:
> Let them but stare and gape, and be astonished,
> Soon as a dramatist your fame will rise.
> A show is what they want; they love and pay for it;
> Spite of its serious parts, sit through a play for it;
> And he who gives one is a certain favorite.

America is peculiarly the land of the cinema, the local chautauqua, the athletic spectacle, and the circus. Our interest as spectators in athletic contests of every description, from throwing horseshoes to prize-fighting, would be difficult to duplicate in any other civilized country. But neither primitiveness nor superficiality is to be condemned. There must be no mistake about this point. No absolute condemnation is placed on these lower forms of recreation. Rather it is the over-emphasis which they receive in contemporary American life that merits criticism. These interests are good, but they are not enough. Nevertheless, only through them can the elevation and refinement of taste be promoted. They are the medium through which the present is transformed into the future. From them the educational program must take its point of departure and derive its vitality. Recreationally we are undeveloped; but, if our educational institutions genuinely concern themselves with the problem and coöperate with other agencies in its solution, these primitive and superficial activities may be instrumental in leading us to a higher type of recreation. If the schools fail to make this contact with reality, they will contribute nothing to the improvement of standards of appreciation.

How have institutional changes modified the recreational problem? The changed condition of certain institutions, which in the past have made valuable contributions to the recreational life, has added to the task of the school. At least in many districts, the hold of the church on the population has weakened. While the primary function of the church is religious, this institution has always been a center of recreation. Even under the reign of Puritanism the church was a center for social gatherings, a place where people met from week to week to worship God *together*. Among other sects the camp meeting, a religious festival of a primitive type, undoubtedly served to brighten the barren stretches of a pioneering existence. While not to be likened to the coming of a circus, it served in some measure the same functions. The saloon also has practically disappeared, and its decease was extraordinarily sudden and unexpected. Whatever the evils associated with this institution, and they were many, in the life of the American workman it satisfied cravings in addition to those for liquor.

The home likewise, as we have observed repeatedly, has been undergoing a process of disorganization since the advent of the industrial revolution. In many parts of the country, and especially in the industrial centers, the family has ceased to exist as a stable social unit.   It is therefore no longer a natural center for the expression of leisure interests. This situation has been somewhat aggravated by the reduced birth rate, which limits the possibilities for pleasant and agreeable companionship within the home.   Where a family of ten is recreationally self-sufficient, the family of three, or four, or five is dependent.   The commercial interests have been quick to take advantage. of these social changes, but education has made no corresponding advance.

What is the recreational problem of rural life?   Passing from the examination of the general social situation in the United States, we may now consider in turn the special problems of rural and urban life.   In that radical reconstruction of rural civilization which is one of the most urgent needs of our time, the enrichment of the recreational life must play a leading rôle.   The rapid drift of population to the cities in the last half century has caused alarm in the minds of many thoughtful citizens.   This increase of the city at the expense of the country, however, provided the population which remains on the farms is not negatively selected, should give rise to no uneasiness.   The growth of cities has been the inevitable product of improved agricultural production, the industrial revolution, and inventions in the realm of transportation and communication.

There is much evidence, though, to indicate that a process of negative selection is going on, and that the more vigorous and talented strains of the population are being attracted to the cities.   The significant fact to be noted here is that the recreational poverty of rural life is a very important factor in producing this result.   The ambitious and gifted individual, dissatisfied, either for himself or his children, with the cultural barrenness of the farm, moves to the city.   A rural education that places its attention exclusively on improving the economic side of farm life can only hasten this depletion of the rural stock. It is not wholly without significance that tenancy is extraordinarily high in certain of our richest agricultural States. This means that the economically successful farmer leaves the land to live in town or city and rents his holding to a tenant. Where a farm can support two families, it frequently supports one *in absentia*. To youth rural life must be made attractive and humane, if a virile population is to be held on the land. The agricultural community must become a pleasant place in which to live. The achievement of this end is one of the fundamental tasks of rural education.

What are the special recreational problems of urban life? Our great industrial and urban centers have problems of the recreational life that are peculiarly their own. Hand in hand with the growth of the factory system and the differentiation of processes there have come an increased monotony of labor and a shortened working day. Even in the steel industry, long the stronghold of reactionary forces, steps have recently been taken to adopt the eight-hour day. These two changes, the monotony of labor and the reduced hours of toil, are closely related, the one perhaps being in part the cause of the other; and they both have important educational implications. Perhaps we may look forward in the more or less remote future to an economic life so ordered as to make the work of production interesting and meaningful to all who participate in it. Towards such an ideal we should strive, but in the mean time we cannot shirk the responsibility of equipping the population for a wise and temperate use of leisure hours. If the joy of living is to be preserved at all under the conditions of modern industrial organization, with its regimentation and mechanization of the workers, it must be preserved through a rich and abundant recreational life. Our industrial populations must be taught to play. This alone can insure for the routine worker those experiences which give life significance, experiences to which every individual has an inherent right.

The educator should do more than haltingly apply a remedy for the temporary relief of an intolerable condition. He should recognize, in the reduced hours of labor, an opportunity for launching a recreational program that would change the whole aspect and order of life. At present, great masses of the population are but ill-equipped to use with profit, either to themselves or to society, the increased leisure which through bitter struggle they have won for themselves. They therefore become the victims of a system of commercialized amusements in which the appeal, if not actually vicious, is frequently primitive and unproductive of personal growth. Through the development of the play life and the refinement of our æsthetic sensibilities the current system of values might conceivably be subjected to critical reappraisal. A new rating might be placed on the accepted notions of success; the gold standard for measuring all values might be found inadequate; the push and pull of contemporary life might be moderated; our cities, homes, factories, and industrial products might be required to take on a certain beauty; quality as well as quantity might find a secure place in our folkways; *bigger* might no longer be regarded as synonymous with *better;* and the creative impulses might be exalted over the acquisitive and possessive tendencies. The leaven appearing first in recreation might work itself into and transform the economic life.

Can recreation be made to lend significance and beauty to the common activities of life? If recreation is to become this leavening force, it must maintain a close connection with the rest of life. Normally, play and art, while freeing men from the limitations placed on desire by the dictates of utility, nevertheless glorify, idealize, beautify, and make significant all the great interests of mankind — love, industry, politics, war, religion. They have always drawn the outlines of a finer world, but a world projected from the one men know. To-day recreation is constructing an isolated world of its own to which individuals go in order to escape the tedium, monotony, and strain of ordinary existence and to find a compensation for its deficiencies.

As revolting as many of the features of industrial civilization are to the sensitive mind, the natural tendency of the population to flee from reality should be checked. If we live with this civilization, we will be forced to improve it. The modern city is huge, crude, and ugly; but it abounds in vitality. An old civilization has been shattered, and there is no chance of its return; a new civilization has been born, and it is certain to live and grow. Although some would say that the Paradise of Beauty was buried with the remains of the old and is lost forever, the facts hardly warrant this extreme pessimism. The ancient patterns of beauty are gone, and cannot be restored; but new patterns, which are in harmony with the changed conditions of life, will be generated. The need of the time, therefore, in the realms of art and play, is for a type of creative work which takes into account machines, science, and democracy. Into the home, the school, the factory, the street, the city, the village, the legislative hall, and the church the creative spirit must go. The common tasks and interests of men must know the refining touch of the artist's hand, the idealizing vision of the poet's mind, and the vital glow of the prophet's heart.

What has been America's contribution to the fine arts? In concluding this survey of the present social situation in America, one last consideration which may serve to clinch the argument should be noted. The final fruitage of the recreational life of a people is to be found in its creative work in the fields of literature, music, and art. America has produced a poet or two of first rank, but there her contribution to the fine arts rests.   In contrast with the achievements of certain other peoples, the poverty of our own achievements is most striking.   The following observation by Carleton Parker is to the point: [1]

In Florence around 1300, Giotto painted a picture. . . . The day it was to be hung in St. Mark's the town closed down for a holiday, and the people with garlands of flowers and songs escorted the picture from the artist's studio to the church. . . . We probably produce per capita one thousand times more in weight of ready-made clothing, Irish lace, artificial flowers, terra cotta, movie films, telephones, and printed matter, than these Florentines did; but we have with our 100,000,000 inhabitants yet to produce that little town, her Dante, her Andrea del Sarto, her Michael Angelo, her Leonardo da Vinci, her Savonarola, her Giotto, — or the group who followed Giotto's picture.

How is our limited achievement in this field to be explained?   The reason for our limited achievement in the fine arts is not difficult to discover.   The fundamental fact is that the American people are not genuinely interested in literature, music, and art.   The whole trend of our civilization is toward the practical, the useful, and the remunerative.   Hence art is either definitely subordinated to and made to serve these material ends, or is regarded as one of the frills of existence.   It has therefore been customarily left to women of leisure and been regarded as predominantly a feminine interest.   So strong is this tradition, in some sections of the country, that a man is suspected of being a bit " queer " if he directs his energies to poetry, music, or art.   And if a boy is attracted to these fields he is often ridiculed as effeminate by his associates.   In common opinion the fine arts should be left to girls, and taught in finishing schools for young ladies.   Under these conditions

[1] Parker, Carleton H.: *The Casual Laborer, and Other Essays*, pp. 58–59.

the energies of our people are directed into other channels and the fine arts languish.

The significance of this cultural deficiency, for the present discussion, is that the absence of great creative work in the fine arts means more than an absence of artists. It means a lack in the life of the people. As Parker points out, with all our numbers and wealth we cannot begin to match that long line of brilliant artists which is the glory of Florence. But of far greater significance for education is the fact that we have failed to reproduce that group of forgotten men, women, and children, who with flowers and songs followed Giotto's picture.

After full allowance has been made for the capacity of the genius for individual and independent achievement, the basic fact remains that he is greatly influenced by the social *milieu* into which he is born. Hence, wherever there is great creative work, there is a cultivated people to provide the stimulus; and wherever such work is absent, the explanation can usually be found in a people undeveloped on the æsthetic side. For its immature members the group provides the foci of attention; it sets the goals to be striven for; it determines the direction taken by genius in expressing itself. If talent is born into an inhospitable world, there is reason for believing that it is distorted, dwarfed, or altogether lost. The highest peaks do not rise abruptly out of the plain; so the great creative geniuses do not appear in those societies which lack the artistic tradition and fail to stimulate the development of the lower levels of talent.

What is the educational significance of the absence of artistic creation? Chafing under the caustic comment of the foreign critic and desiring to work a speedy cure of our defect, we have sometimes been tempted either to imitate an alien culture or to produce artists by an educational *tour de* *force.* The first leads to superficiality and the second to failure. Ferrero well says: [1]

In order to create and foster art it is necessary to educate generations of artists to do good work and generations of amateurs to understand and appreciate it. Neither the artists nor the public taste can be educated without a spirit of tradition and of æsthetic discipline, which induces the public to allow the artists the necessary time for the perfecting of their respective arts in all their details; which induces the artist to recognize the legitimate requirements of the public for which he works, and to seek to satisfy it by adapting his own work to those requirements.

This analysis, therefore, drives us back to the fundamental recreational defect of our civilization — the absence of a rich folk-life. As a people we have no great interest in the æsthetic side of the world in which we live. Few of us have had from the cradle that intimate contact with fine poetry, song, and pictures which is necessary for the development of the highest standards of appreciation. This contact comes only with the rich folk-life which penetrates every recess of society. These standards can come only as we live with the beautiful, and only as these standards become the possession of an increasing portion of the population will there be provided in America that social stimulus to creative work which is essential to truly great achievement. The great educational task is not that of training the genius; rather is it that of creating and fostering in the masses, the source and inspiration of talent, a growing consciousness of and interest in beauty. As we have just said, the great aim cannot be that of producing a genius, but rather that of producing a group that will recognize and acclaim a genius. Totally disregarding any preconceived ideas regarding ultimate standards of artistic appreciation,

[1] Ferrero, G.: *Ancient Rome and Modern America*, p. 188.

education must begin on the humble plane on which the people live.

How may the school enrich the recreational life through the conventional formal curriculum? This is the situation that confronts those interested in the promotion of education. At many points our recreational life is barren and unsatisfactory. What is the school doing to enrich it? On paper it is apparently doing much. An examination of a conventional school program gives the impression that not a little of its work is justified on grounds that fall under this general heading. Consider for a moment the formal curriculum. Literature, music, and art all receive attention in the schools. They are presumably taught for the purpose of increasing the interest of our people in an important aspect of the play life. But if this is the real purpose, we must confess that much of the seed is either non-viable, or is sown on very infertile soil. So little of it germinates or takes root in the lives of children.

We must keep in mind that our success in ministering to the needs of the recreational life must be measured in terms of the persistence beyond the school of the interests and activities fostered under its guidance. If, as a result of tuition, our children do not love literature and music and art, if they are not made to feel a need for these things, we must admit failure. In such an event something is wrong with our instruction. As a matter of fact, we have made the mistake of applying to the teaching of these subjects methods and principles generated in the teaching of wholly different kinds of materials.

What are the possibilities in literature? Since literature has long been an important subject in the curriculum, let us consider the treatment which it receives in the school. By insisting on a deadening analysis and by clinging to an ideal of abstract scholarship, vital interest in this field has been nipped in the bud.   Literature has too often been murdered by dissection.   Analysis has its place in the process of education, and so has the ideal of scholarship, but they must not be set up as the sole ends of instruction and permitted to tyrannize over all the work of the school. Where its approach should be through the feelings and the emotions, education is dominated by intellectual concepts. All education has been forced into the same moulds, and with tragic consequences the spirit has been sacrificed to the form.   In our examinations we test for a pedantic knowledge about literature, and confuse this knowledge with a genuinely appreciative æsthetic experience.   Little wonder therefore that, instead of creating interest and developing a love of beauty, we have put literature in bad repute among children and have taught them to look with suspicion on everything carrying its label.   In our impatience to reach the goal we have been loath to follow the one road that leads to it; we have violated the fundamental pedagogical principle of always beginning the process of education at the point attained by the pupil; we have insisted that the pupil show from the outset an interest in literary classics, and that he display the conventional reaction toward them; we have demanded mature appreciations from youngsters, and have consequently placed a premium on hypocritical behavior.   Standards of appreciation cannot be handed from teacher to pupil, like physical objects, neither do they appear unheralded and in mature form at the behest of desire.   They are creatures of growth, products of life, gauges of experience.

What are the possibilities in the fine arts?   Wherever we have attempted to teach either music or any of the fine arts we have sinned in similar fashion and even more deeply. We have tried to teach the grammar of an art before teaching the art itself.   Music is frequently buried under its technique, and is seldom resurrected. We have perhaps had our eye too much on producing the artistic genius, failing to realize that, if we develop genuine standards of appreciation among the masses of the people, and thus create a demand for artistic creation, the latter will take care of itself. The great object of instruction in this field should be that of developing an appetite for the fine arts. This will require the temporary sacrifice of conventional standards. But this sacrifice is more apparent than real, since standards that exist only in the minds of teachers and find no expression in the lives of pupils are without educational reality. If taste for the fine arts is stimulated, even though it is established on a humble plane, the gradual elevation of standards will inevitably follow. But in order to register this initial victory the teaching of an art must begin on the level of appreciation which the pupil brings to the school.

This means that we must frankly introduce into the curriculum courses in literature, music, and art with the definite purpose of arousing interest and stirring the emotions of children. In some fields it may be possible to compel pupils to master subject-matter; to compel them to like the experience is impossible. In our efforts to enrich the recreational life we must in some way get children to like the fine arts, and to like them so much that, bereft of them, life would be robbed of much of its sweetness and charm.

What are the possibilities in reading? Other subjects in the formal curriculum may supplement the fine arts. Reading, for example, has become one of the most important of our recreational activities. Of the two forms, silent reading is of much greater importance than oral reading. The school should acquaint the pupil with the wealth of satisfactions which this field holds for him, and develop interest in those types of reading which are of greatest recreational value. Besides opening up the inexhaustible resources of the world's literature, it should introduce children to the popular magazines and to current fiction of the better sort. But, since reading fits in so well with its conventional purposes, there may be a tendency for the school to overemphasize this interest as a recreational activity.

What are the possibilities in science? Another field that should be made to yield much larger returns in the development of leisure interests is that of natural science. Yet one hesitates to use the term "Science" in this connection because, through school practice, it has come to be associated with a thoroughly desiccated and devitalized type of material. The world of nature has always been a source of interest and wonder to the race. It is therefore nothing short of a tragedy that our increase in knowledge should, in the hands of teachers, become an obstacle to the development of an appreciation of the stars and the planets, the seas and the rivers, the mountains and the valleys, the plains and the forests, the soil and the rocks, the animals and the plants, and all the wonders of natural creation. By unimaginative instruction the romance, the poetry, and the mystery of this stupendous achievement in matter and energy, and of man's fascinating adventure within it, have been destroyed. How often has a boy or a girl brought to a course in botany, zoölogy, physics, or chemistry a genuine curiosity about natural phenomena, only to have it destroyed by laws, formulæ, and classifications! We have flooded the immature student with such a mass of abstractions as would overwhelm a seasoned scientist. The latter has always and rightly insisted on following in his own researches the lead of curiosity.

If the teaching of science is to be successful, it must rekindle the interest out of which science itself sprang. But this we have denied the child. As a consequence, in order to secure attention in a field to which every normal child, without interference from his elders, willingly devotes a portion of his leisure hours, we are forced to resort to the most artificial motivation. Materials derived from the sciences, aiming directly at conserving and developing the interests of pupils in the phenomena of nature, must be introduced into our schools. We must abandon the all-too-common method of requiring the student to commit to memory a systematic treatise which presents the discoveries and speculations of scientists in a highly condensed and abstract manner. Of course, where the mastery of a particular science or a portion of a science is necessary for the specialist, the problem assumes quite a different aspect. With this question, however, we are not here concerned. Our contention is that the field of natural science offers large opportunities for the enrichment of the recreational life, but that the methods usually followed in teaching it are not conducive to the realization of these opportunities.

What are the possibilities in the extra-curriculum? Although certain other subjects of the program of studies contain large recreational possibilities, space does not permit their consideration. Outside the formal curriculum, where the pupils themselves have been given a measure of freedom, we have probably been most successful in caring for the needs of the recreational life. Perhaps here is our most fruitful suggestion for the further evolution of the program. We may reasonably assume that the most effective way of developing recreational interests is to provide the pupil with a certain amount of free time within the school day, during which he is expected to participate in any one of a great variety of activities. The only training for leisure is leisure.

The school must provide as effectively for play as for work. There should, of course, be no disposition to place complete emphasis on the fine arts, or on any other single type of activity. The school cannot afford to shape its program in accordance with principles which underlie the education of an aristocracy of either birth or talent. Every level of interest or aptitude must be reached. After all, the intrinsic worth of an experience can be determined only by him who lives it. If the potentialities of a youngster are exhausted in the playing of marbles or the spinning of tops, by all means let him shoot his marbles and spin his tops. But the ordinary child possesses varied capacities, and should be stimulated to develop not one but many interests. He should be encouraged to participate in intellectual activities, to play games, to read literature, to appreciate music and art, to converse, to engage in some avocation, to go hiking, to dance, and, in a word, to develop any line of wholesome activity toward which he has an inclination. Likewise, the individual of superior and diversified talents should be urged to give expression to his rich natural heritage, and should also be stimulated to attempt artistic creation. In the field of recreation there is no room for that Pharisaism which would foster a self-righteous spirit among those endowed with any special gift.

What are the possibilities in companionship? In this connection, special mention should be made of the need for developing capacity for companionship. Few of us, dominated as we are by the demands of haste and the crowd, are good companions. We pay scant attention to the formation of friendships, and, when formed, we give but little thought to keeping them in repair. Many of us become embarrassed and unnatural on entering even a small group. Yet most of us possess large possibilities of development in this direction. The value of companionship in making life pleasant, agreeable, and significant has never been neglected by the aristocracies. There is no good reason why the ordinary citizen of a democracy should be a poor companion, nor why crude and boorish manners should be associated with democratic institutions. Writes Arthur Ponsonby, in his *Decline of Aristocracy:*

Democracy must be on its guard in its very natural prejudice against traditions of refinement and leisure which have been so much misused by the aristocracy. It must be careful not to insist on a general average type characterized by the self-satisfied mediocrity of a bourgeoisie, devoid of dignity or noble aspirations . . . and only educated in a purely utilitarian sense toward a standard of brute efficiency.

In the cultivation of the simple associations of men particularly must democracy profit from the experience of aristocracy. Hence, in our schools, social gatherings in which the capacity for companionship may be fully developed, and in which the amenities of social life may be acquired, should be encouraged and provided in great abundance. All the work of the school should be carried on so as to promote the refinement of manners, the formation of friendships, and the growth of simple kindliness. Especially through those activities, which at present are unwisely called extra-curriculum interests, social life may be refined to the point of exhibiting a certain artistic beauty.

What changes are essential to the inauguration of this program? What has been suggested in the foregoing paragraphs would obviously require fundamental changes in the conventional school. Although in the more progressive communities much has already been accomplished, the physical equipment of the school would have to undergo great modification. Any attempt at the promotion of recreational interests will entail ample playgrounds, gymnasia, play rooms, auditoria, museums, and the utilization on the part of the school of the facilities of the community. The school day will have to be lengthened. At this point, particularly, the boarding school of the well-to-do has an advantage over the day school of the public. The success of the famous English " Public Schools " in ministering to the recreational needs of their boys has rested, in no small measure, on the fact that they are boarding schools. The leisure of the students is spent under the supervision of the school. It is this supervision of leisure which is needed for the great masses of children in our cities — children whose playground is the street and whose leisure is perforce passed in questionable surroundings, and in many cases under the direction of ignorant, if not vicious, older companions. The practice which is often followed to-day in our more populous centers of running two alternative sessions daily for two groups of children, and thus shortening the time spent in school, is much to be deplored.

But if we are to attack this problem of recreation successfully, the greatest change must be wrought in the attitude of teachers, parents, and members of school boards toward the play life. There is a deeply entrenched conviction that school is a place for work and not for play. Certain changes which have already appeared and which are fundamentally recreational have been contemptuously styled " fads and frills " by adverse critics. Such opposition is to be expected; it is but a symptom of the disease which has been diagnosed and which American society must cure. If our people sufficiently valued the play life there would be but little opposition to such a program as has been suggested; in fact it would already have found expression in the schools. The great desideratum then is a change of heart, a spiritual rebirth, on the part of the taxpayer.

What is the wider opportunity of the school? In conclusion we should point out the wider social implication of the program. The adult community must be included as well as the children. The time is past when we can think of education as limited to the years of childhood, and of the school as concerned only with children. The school must reach out to embrace the old along with the young. In every section of the country it should become a community center, a meeting place for the interests of the entire citizenship. Particularly should it be made a center for satisfying the recreational needs of the community. The effective school is eager to touch the parents. Can it approach them at a more strategic point, and be less accused of trespassing on forbidden territory, than in attempting to foster, satisfy, and elevate their desires for recreation? And as adults learn to play they will see more clearly the value of play for their children.

ADDITIONAL PROBLEMS FOR DISCUSSION

1. What religious, economic, and social factors operated in the early history of this country to dwarf the recreational life?
2. It is stated in the text that recreation has no ulterior purpose. If this is the case, what principles must govern the relation of recreation to the serious activities of life?
3. What are the differences between work and play from the standpoint of: (1) motivation; (2) complexity; (3) product? From these three viewpoints examine the activities of the following: (a) a professional baseball player; (b) an actor; (c) the millionaire amassing his tenth million; (d) a primitive huntsman; (e) a boy playing football on the corner lot; (f) the gridiron star in a big varsity game; (g) the politician; (h) the university professor of independent means; and (i) the average pupil in a high school algebra class.
4. What is the fallacy of identifying leisure with all activities which fall outside the narrow vocational calling? In what respects do many of the health, family, civic, and religious activities approximate vocational rather than recreational activities?
5. Show how, because of its peculiar nature, recreation influences the growth of character out of all proportion to the time actually spent in the activity.
6. Criticize the following activities from the viewpoint of their possibilities of affording a growing recreational satisfaction: marbles, golf, horse-shoes, cards, music, literature, stamp-collecting, automobiling, radio, wrestling, tennis, swimming, theater, moving pictures.
7. What are the more important advantages and disadvantages which

have arisen from the extension of recreational facilities through commercial agencies?

8. How has the growth of applied science, during the last hundred years, increased the time available for recreation and modified its modes?

9. What recreational activities should be stressed by the rural school? How would these activities differ from those stressed in the city school?

10. How has the domination of the school by a narrowly academic and intellectually minded class tended to overstress reading as a recreational activity for the major portion of the population?

11. How has commercialism artificially stimulated rivalry in the leading athletic events of our colleges, and thereby impaired their educational function?

12. Why has gambling been associated so frequently with recreational activities? How does gambling reveal a relatively impoverished recreational interest?

13. How may the school and other agencies raise the level of one important form of recreation — human companionship? What relationship has this question to the teaching of oral composition in the schools?

14. From the standpoint of the development of recreational interests and pursuits that will function throughout life, what are the serious objections to the nature and mode of conduct of the athletic sports emphasized in high school and college?

15. Without imperiling the recreational values involved, what steps could be taken to enhance the wider educational and social values that inhere in the following: the newspaper; the theater; the motion picture; the radio?

16. What would be the objection to introducing into the formal curriculum instruction in the orderly undertaking of the following games: checkers, basketball, baseball, dancing, rudiments of card playing, fireside and parlor games, charades, dominoes? How would a knowledge of these games as a common possession affect the family and community life?

PROBLEM 17

HOW MAY EDUCATION FOSTER THE RELIGIOUS LIFE?

What is the relation of religion to adjustment? — Why do men crave a general interpretation of the universe? — What is religion? — To whom should men go for religion? — What is the relation between religion and morals? — How may religion motivate conduct? — Is moral education dependent on religion? — What evils have flowed from historical religion? — Can intolerance be minimized through education? — Can formalism be checked through education? — Why is religious faith uncertain? — Does contemporary education meet the need? — What are the defects of current efforts at religious education? — How may the religious life be fostered? — Can religious instruction have definite objectives?

Does the foregoing analysis embrace the whole of life? The relation of education to health, family, economic, civic, and recreational interests has now been considered. Not a few engaged in the work of education would say that these five departments embrace the whole of life. Because of the sins committed in the name of religion, and because of the amazing triumphs of science in the modern age, minds have become confused. The dogmatism of religion contending with the arrogance of science has presented a spectacle which has distorted the judgment of two generations. But refusal to place the secular interests in the wider setting which transcends the bounds of sense and the limits of exact knowledge, is as unsatisfying and superficial as that primitive cosmology which accounted for the stability of the earth by assuming it to rest on the back of an elephant which in turn was supported by a tortoise.

Those who, while recognizing the necessity of making the general interpretation of life, would confine public education to the five great needs of men already considered, sometimes defend their own position by contending that the separation of Church and State automatically relieves the public school of responsibility in this field. They maintain that, by disregarding the claims of religion, no general philosophical stand is taken, or need be taken, concerning the nature of the universe and the destiny of man. They keep silent, and in so doing believe that they are exhibiting a detached impartiality. This is a most naïve assumption, for, by ignoring the question, a most decided answer is given. And the answer which through evasion is thus unconsciously given, is of doubtful value, partly because it is made in ignorance, and partly because it is for the most part a negative rather than a positive answer. Certainly, this problem cannot be escaped. In every far-reaching decision the individual starts from certain basic propositions whose truth is implicitly assumed. If he fails to recognize the existence of these assumptions on which his life rests, he is of all men most to be pitied. Born conceivably to be a spectator of all time, like an ostrich he buries his head in the sand.

What is the relation of religion to adjustment? Throughout this volume the view is consistently maintained that education is a form of adjustment. If this conception is accepted, the educator must be perpetually watchful lest the adjustment be merely to the more immediate, superficial, and ephemeral aspects of the environment. In so far as the experience of the race can serve individual men in their efforts to adjust themselves to the deeper and more abiding realities of existence, that experience should be incorporated into every educational program meriting the support of a serious-minded people. The central aim of education should be to help the individual to that wider interpretation of existence which holds the largest possibilities for service and the greatest support in fact.

The introduction of the child to this interpretation should

be marked by none of that dogmatic intolerance which has been so commonly associated with religious practice. Or, to speak more guardedly, such intolerance, which seems to be the unfortunate but inevitable accompaniment of this interest, should be reduced to a minimum. Since knowledge accumulates and life bursts the moulds of earlier years, the interpretation must change from age to age. Yet certain broad principles, dynamic in their character, have stood the test of time, and around these there should be no insuperable difficulty in getting the great majority of enlightened men to rally to-day. Against the superficial intellectualism of the hour man must constantly appeal to the wisdom of the ages. This wisdom conditions the more fundamental adjustments to life, and without it there can be no unity in the educational program.

How may this problem be attacked? So important is the subject under consideration, and so overlaid with misunderstanding and prejudice, that, at the risk of tiring the reader, certain questions must receive attention which, though not immediately related to narrow educational practice, are essential to the wider educational theory. The scope of this discussion will therefore be somewhat broader than the treatment accorded the previous problems. The following topics will be touched upon, in order: first, the common craving of men for a general interpretation of the universe; second, the nature and variety of religious experience; third, the relation of religion to conduct and morals; fourth, the evils which flow from institutional religion; fifth, the great need in the modern world for an accepted body of religious principles; and finally, the educational program itself in its more concrete aspects. Although a more condensed treatment may for certain reasons be desirable, it seems impossible to exclude from the discussion any one of these points.

Why do men crave a general interpretation of the universe? The demand on the part of men for a general interpretation of the universe, touching human destiny and the purpose of existence, is well-nigh universal. Consider the following quotation from Tolstoy who, at the age of fifty, faced the eternal problem of existence and sought anew the meaning of life:

> What will be the outcome of what I do to-day? Of what I shall do to-morrow? What will be the outcome of all my life? Why should I live? Why should I do anything? Is there in life any purpose which the inevitable death which awaits me does not undo and destroy? These questions are the simplest in the world. From the youngest child to the wisest old man, they are in the soul of every human being. Without an answer to them, it is impossible for life to go on.

If man were privileged to ask of an infinite mind one question, and only one, with the assurance that it would be truthfully and completely answered, what riddle would he propound? Would he seek to satisfy his curiosity regarding some fundamental question of science, such as the biological origin of man, the possibility of creating living tissue in the test tube, the dimensions of the universe, the ultimate constitution of matter, or the relation of body and mind? Or would his query center on some interest of human welfare, such as the increase of the span of human life, the control of the forces of biological heredity, the banishing of poverty and economic want from the catalogue of human ills, the peaceful organization of the common life of the nations, or the development of artistic genius?

While recognizing the great significance of each he would, if wise, ask no one of these questions. Rather would he seek to penetrate more deeply into the mysteries of life. He would want to know something of the forces that lie at the heart of the world and determine its destiny. He would ask, perhaps: Is the universe friendly? Is there a purpose working itself out in the world of nature and in the lives of men? Does this purpose recognize moral distinctions, or does it merely discern differences in size and distinguish strength from weakness? Does it manifest a deep oblivion of the laws of right and wrong? Is it beyond good and evil? Do the thoughts and feelings and actions of men obstruct or facilitate the realization of this purpose, or are they but the impotent sparks that fly from the anvil of the forces of creation? On the answer to this question rests in large measure the significance of life; and every man must answer it, if not through taking thought, at least in the life that he lives.

In a familiar passage in the Preface to his *Heretics*, Chesterton writes: [1]

There are some people — and I am one of them — who think that the most practical and important thing about a man is still his view of the universe. We think that for a landlady considering a lodger it is important to know his income, but still more important to know his philosophy. We think that for a general about to fight an enemy it is important to know the enemy's numbers, but still more important to know the enemy's philosophy. We think the question is not whether the theory of the cosmos affects matters, but whether in the long run anything else affects them.

This view, though not popular to-day, contains and will always contain fundamental truth.

What is religion? This brings us to that special division or aspect of human experience which has ordinarily been styled religious. In the very widest sense, religion may be identified with man's conception of and his attitude toward the primal values of life. In the words of William James. [2]

[1] Chesterton, G. K.: *Heretics*, Preface.
[2] James, William: *Varieties of Religious Experience*, p. 35.

Religion, whatever it is, is a man's total reaction upon life, so why not say that any total reaction upon life is a religion? Total reactions are different from casual reactions, and total attitudes are different from usual or professional attitudes. To get at them you must go behind the foreground of existence and reach down to that curious sense of the whole residual cosmos as an everlasting presence, intimate or alien, terrible or amusing, lovable or odious, which in some degree every one possesses. This sense of the world's presence, appealing as it does to our peculiar individual temperament, makes us either strenuous or careless, devout or blasphemous, gloomy or exultant, about life at large; and our reaction, involuntary and inarticulate and often half unconscious as it is, is the completest of all answers to the question, "What is the character of this universe in which we dwell?"

Why is religious interpretation always limited? While recognizing the logical necessity of thus imputing religious attitudes to all men, even to the cynic and the libertine, and of acknowledging the affinity of the religious with the irreligious, James goes on to limit his discussion of the religious life to " the feelings, acts, and experiences of individual men in their solitude, so far as they apprehend themselves to stand in relation to whatever they may consider divine." In this discussion a similar course will be followed. Instead of denying the religious quality to any honest effort to interpret the deeper experiences of men, instead of attempting to establish the absolute truth or falsity of any religious beliefs, we shall rather take the position that certain religious interpretations, because they reflect more faithfully the fundamental facts of life, are more serviceable to man than others. Because of the limitations inherent in a temporal and highly circumscribed existence, every attempt on the part of man to apprehend the full meaning of life must fall far short of finality. For but a moment each man stands on the banks of the river of time, and his estimate of its source, its destination, and its power must al-

ways reflect the narrow range of his vision. Since the world of knowledge is ever shrouded in mystery, a large element of uncertainty must characterize even the most careful interpretation, and every evaluation, being a reaction of a finite mind upon an infinite problem, must betray the restricted confines of that mind.

How varied are religious interpretations? In spite of the difficulties which attend the task, man has in all ages and in all places meditated on the ends of life and sought its central meaning. He always has, and he always must, seek an answer to the question: What is good? Likewise, his destiny, whether in this world or another, must always agitate him. Groping after an understanding of those forces which give him birth, condition his life, and inevitably cause his death, he has endeavored to solve the riddle of life. In his efforts to control these forces which beset him he has used cajolery, attempted compulsion, uttered defiance, pronounced curses, offered up prayers, granted submission, and pursued truth. In his reaction to the facts of life he has run the entire gamut of his emotions. He has known love and hate, joy and sorrow, fear and anger, elation and dejection, wonder and disgust. His knowledge of the world of nature has ranged from darkest superstition to most exact science.

Consequently, man's religious beliefs and practices, since they must always be bound by the data of experience and knowledge of the world, have shown the widest diversity. So varied indeed have they been that students have often hesitated to include them all in a single department of human experience. At one time or another man has worshiped almost every object and aspect of creation. He has bowed down before birds and beasts, fishes and reptiles, shrubs and trees, sticks and stones, rivers and mountains, and the sun, the moon, and the stars. He has trembled before the storm and sought to appease the thunder and the lightning. He has rendered homage in spring to the forces of reproduction. He has even made sacrifices to images graven by his own hands. Because religion has so frequently taken primitive and degenerate forms, because the great religions have all evolved by gradual changes from humble beginnings full of error and delusion, some have sought to discredit the religious experience. But all human institutions develop from humble origins. Science, in whose name these critics so often speak, must trace her own lineage back to the magical practices of savage peoples. Whether religion was given to man direct from the hand of the creator or was evolved from the worship of nature, its worth in refining and making meaningful the lives of men remains the same.

To whom should men go for religion? In his efforts to discover his essential relation to the universe man has perpetually searched and evaluated his experience. His interpretations of life have been many and diverse. Because of this diversity and because of the absence of any objective check, from certain quarters has come the suggestion that all forms of religion are equally true and equally false, equally good and equally bad, equally wise and equally foolish. Consequently, it is argued, each man should choose entirely according to his taste. While every individual has a right to the interpretation that satisfies him, we might well be guided here by the same principle that serves us in other fields. As we go to the great scientists for science, to the great artists for art, to the great composers for music, to the great philosophers for philosophy, and to the great poets for poetry, so we should go to the great religious prophets for religion and to the great mystics for mysticism. In our search for the deeper meanings and purposes of life we must go to those blessed with the prophetic strain. There is no more, but rather less, reason for following the tyro here than in other fields. We may certainly assume that the widest differences in philosophical interest and religious insight exist among men. From those highly gifted in this last respect the leaders in the religious life of mankind have been recruited. As we cast the eye over the course of history we see standing out in bold relief certain gigantic figures, possessed of extraordinary spiritual power and deeply concerned over the purpose of life — men who have placed their stamp on peoples and cultures and whose thoughts and teachings have entered into the social inheritance of all races. We see Zoroaster, Amos, Buddha, Confucius, Jesus, Mohammed, Saint Francis, and other rare spirits. Clearly, to these men of vision we should turn for spiritual insight, and for an estimate of the nature and worth of the religious life.

What is the vision of the prophet? In the following simple statement of the great religious teacher is set down an interpretation of life and an ideal of conduct to which the response is all but universal:

> Then one of them, which was a lawyer, asked him a question, tempting him, and saying: Master, which is the great commandment in the law? Jesus said unto him: Thou shalt love the Lord thy God with all thy heart, and with all thy soul, and with all thy mind. This is the first and great commandment. And the second is like unto it. Thou shalt love thy neighbor as thyself. On these two commandments hang all the law and the prophets.

The first commandment assumes that at the heart of creation there is a power working for righteousness and a power worthy of love. It assumes that even the most humble member of our race is of infinite worth. The second commandment is "like unto" the first, and is indeed merely a corollary of it. For, if all men, regardless of race or condition, are the objects of this wide solicitude, then, perforce, it behooves each man to place a high estimate on the worth of his neighbor. In these two commandments resides that finest of all religious faiths, the belief in the Fatherhood of God and the Brotherhood of Man.

Does religious faith lie within the domain of science? But with reference to all these wider interpretations the skeptic will say that the evidence is inconclusive. He will stoutly maintain that he has never seen this power back of creation, and, since he prides himself on living the life of reason, unless it is brought within the range of either the microscope or the telescope or made to reveal itself in the test tube, he confuses faith with superstition. He admits the possible existence of such a power, but, as the men of old waited for a sign, he too waits for the evidence of the senses.

Let us at once grant the contention that there is no scientific proof of the presence of this force in the universe. We shall even go farther. Since this power is not a part of the world of phenomena, the world with which the scientist necessarily and rightly deals, it will never be discovered with the instruments of science. Nothing but confusion can arise from the notion so commonly encountered to-day that the scientist must discover God. Man but postulates God in his attempt to understand the universe. This interpretation, while it must be perpetually modified by the findings of science, can neither be proved nor disproved by the technique which conforms to its canons. It is a faith that transcends the world of sense — a faith whose worth can be determined only by him who believes it. In certain of its aspects it is neither objectively given nor objectively derived, but rather a goal to be achieved. "The criterion of the material world," says Hall, "is objective existence; the criterion of the spiritual world is subjective need." A wide acceptance of a particular interpretation of experience

is probably necessary to make it true in the fullest sense.
The man who waits for proof before accepting any positive
evaluation of the universe will wait in vain, for it is the
product of a creative act. It will come only when sought,
and then only to those who dare a venture of faith.

What is the relation between religion and morals?
These two commandments, it should be observed, bring
together in intimate union two aspects of life which had
long followed different courses, namely, religion and morality. In their origins these two divisions of experience were
widely separated, but their final close association was inevitable. So interwoven in the thoughts and actions of
men have they become, that to distinguish the moral from
the religious is now difficult. Indeed religion in its highest
form has been aptly defined as morality touched with emotion, and, perhaps one might add, with meaning. In all
the great religions this association is found. The Hebrew
prophet Micah has thus pronounced the supreme interest of
Jehovah in righteousness: "He hath shown thee, O man,
what is good; and what doth the Lord require of thee, but
to do justly, and to love mercy, and to walk humbly with
thy God?" The Buddhist sacred scripture urges a way of
life which suggests a familiar passage from the New Testament:

> Let us live happily, then, not hating those who hate us!
> Let us live free from hatred among men who hate.
> Let a man overcome anger by kindness, evil by good;
> Let him conquer the stingy by a gift, the liar by truth.

In the *Zend Avesta* of ancient Persia a similar emphasis on
morality is found: "Purity is for man, next to life, the
highest good; that purity, O Zarathustra, that is in the religion of Mazda for him who cleanses himself with good
thoughts, words, and deeds." And in the Golden Song
of Hierocles, representative of the later Hellenic religion,

occurs the same teaching: "Purity of soul is the only divine service."

How may religion motivate conduct?   The association of religion and morality is of extraordinary significance.   Being raised above the plane of mere expediency, morality is given a divine sanction.   Since the individual in the act identifies himself with that central purpose which moves through the universe, the performance of duty becomes a joy.   It exalts and idealizes and lends warmth to those principles of action which, if the Kingdom of Heaven is to come on earth, must find expression in the lives of men. This elevation of moral behavior is described by James in the following words: [1]

When all is said and done, we are in the end absolutely dependent on the universe; and into sacrifices and surrenders of some sort, deliberately looked at and accepted, we are drawn and pressed as into our only permanent positions of repose.   Now in those states of mind which fall short of religion, the surrender is submitted to as an imposition of necessity, and the sacrifice is undergone at the very best without complaint.   In the religious life, on the contrary, surrender and sacrifice are positively espoused: even unnecessary givings-up are added in order that the happiness may increase.   *Religion thus makes easy and felicitous what in any case is necessary;* and if it be the only agency that can accomplish this result, its vital importance as a human faculty stands vindicated beyond dispute.   It becomes an essential organ of life, performing a function which no other portion of our nature can so successfully fulfill.

How may religion give stability to conduct?   Another important consequence of the union of religion and morality is the greatly increased authority which it gives to the moral law.   No aspect of human life is trivial.   Even the most petty act must carry a serious mien to him who lives in the sight of God and in the hope of eternity.   The great

[1] James, William: *Varieties of Religious Experience*, pp. 51–52.

moral function performed by religion in society is thus described by Bryce, in his discussion of the influence of religion in the American Commonwealth: [1]

If we ask how far religion exerts a stimulating influence on the thought and imagination of a nation, we are met by the difficulty of determining what is the condition of mankind where no such influence is present. There has never been a civilized nation without religion, and though many highly civilized individual men live without it, they are so obviously the children of a state of sentiment and thought in which religion has been a powerful factor, that no one can conjecture what a race of men would be like who had during several generations believed themselves to be the highest beings in the universe, or at least entirely out of relation to any other higher beings, and to be therewithal destined to no kind of existence after death. Some may hold that respect for public opinion, sympathy, an interest in the future of mankind, would do for such a people what religion has done in the past; or that they might even be, as Lucretius expected, the happier for the extinction of possible supernatural terrors. Others may hold that life would seem narrow and insignificant, and that the wings of imagination would droop in a universe felt to be void. All that need be here said is that a people with comparatively little around it in the way of historic memories and associations to touch its emotions, a people whose energy is chiefly absorbed in commerce and the development of the material resources of its territory, a people consumed by a feverish activity that gives little opportunity for reflection or for the contemplation of nature, seems most of all to need to have its horizon widened, its sense of awe and mystery touched, by whatever calls it away from the busy world of sight and sound into the stillness of faith and meditation. . . .

No one is so thoughtless as not sometimes to ask himself what would befall mankind if the solid fabric of belief on which their morality has heretofore rested, or at least been deemed by them to rest, were suddenly to break up and vanish under the influence of new views of nature, as the ice-fields split and melt when they have floated down into a warmer sea. Morality with religion for its sanction has hitherto been the basis of social polity, except under military despotisms: would morality be so far weakened as

---

[1] Bryce, James: *The American Commonwealth*, vol. II, pp. 597-98.

to make social polity unstable? and if so, would a reign of violence return? Standing in the midst of a great American city, and watching the throngs of eager figures streaming hither and thither, marking the sharp contrasts of poverty and wealth, an increasing mass of wretchedness and an increasing display of luxury, knowing that before long a hundred millions of men will be living between ocean and ocean under this one government — a government which their own hands have made, and which they feel to be the work of their own hands — one is startled by the thought of what might befall this huge but delicate fabric of laws and commerce and social institutions were the foundations it has rested on to crumble away. Suppose that all these men ceased to believe that there was any power above them, anything in heaven or earth but what their senses told them of; suppose that their consciousness of individual force and responsibility, already dwarfed by the overwhelming power of the multitude, and the fatalistic submission it engenders, were further weakened by the feeling that their swiftly fleeting life was rounded by a perpetual sleep. . . . Would the moral code stand unshaken, and with it the reverence for law, the sense of duty towards the community, and even towards the generations yet to come? Would men say "Let us eat and drink, for to-morrow we may die?" Or would custom, and sympathy, and a perception of the advantages which stable government offers to each one, replace supernatural sanctions, and hold in check the violence of masses and the self-indulgent impulses of the individual? History, if she cannot give a complete answer to this question, tells us that hitherto civilized society has rested on religion, and that free government has prospered best among religious peoples.

Is moral education dependent on religion? At this point before continuing the main line of thought it is perhaps well for us to consider a question of major educational importance. Whether this supernatural sanction is necessary to the control of conduct, as Bryce suggests, is a matter of speculation concerning which there is no general agreement. As yet the evidence on either side of this question of profound social significance is inconclusive. That the authority derived from a consideration of social expediency may be sufficient to insure the formation of desirable habits and ideals is certainly a tenable hypothesis. At some time scientific experiment may prove its truth; but until this proof is forthcoming, it would be the height of educational folly to abandon gratuitously a force which has served so powerfully to control conduct in the past. At present human experience indicates that any program, designed to foster the development of morals, can hardly afford to ignore religious influences.

That our schools, therefore, which have always displayed at least a theoretic interest in the growth of character, should exclude religion from their program is as unfortunate as it is surprising. Because of the probability of some measure of dependence of morality on religion, the latter should be accorded a high place in the educational curriculum. From this discussion, however, the conclusion must not be drawn that the only justification of religious instruction is to be found in the sanction which it may give to moral conduct. Religion, no less than beauty or companionship, is required by men in the simple fulfillment of life. While possibly of great instrumental value in the promotion of other interests, and particularly morals, the essential value of religion is unique.

What is the significance of religious devotion? Another result of the union of religion and morality, equal in significance to the sanction which it gives to conduct, deserves consideration. It seems to be a psychological fact that happiness comes to the individual only to the degree that he throws himself whole-heartedly into some great activity. He who seeks happiness directly seldom finds it. "For whosoever will save his life shall lose it; and whosoever will lose his life for my sake, the same shall save it." This paradox, having its root in human nature, lies at the heart of the religious life. In its psychological aspect religion is devotion, and consequently it has not failed to move men by demanding sacrifice and self-denial. There is a rugged element in the nature of man which responds to such an appeal. In those heroic episodes of human experience, when men deliberately choose the more difficult and dangerous course, this strain shows itself. Religions not only require devotion from their converts, but they also require devotion to certain ends. The great religions require devotion to great ends. The prophet says: "Whosoever will be great among you, let him be your minister; and whosoever will be chief among you, let him be your servant." Here is a religion which adjures its adherents to devote themselves to the service of their fellow-men, to lose the narrow life of animal selfishness in the broader life of human brotherhood.

How may religious faith unify personality? Furthermore, this unwavering devotion of the self to the service of forces and ends of transcendent worth and permanence cannot fail to elevate character and to color the entire attitude toward life. In the rapidly shifting scenes and fortunes of the immediate world, this devotion to the ideal resolves the conflicts of personality and gives to the religious soul stability and poise. In the course of his life man must endure with equal fortitude the calms and storms encountered on the seas of experience. Unless viewed in proper perspective these vicissitudes must make existence intolerable. Man craves a security which material and temporal things can never afford. This need of anchoring in a changing world to the unchanging realities of life has been recognized by the prophets of all ages. How wise is the admonition of Jesus:

Lay not up for yourselves treasures upon earth, where moth and rust doth corrupt, and where thieves break through and steal: but lay up for yourselves treasures in heaven where neither moth nor rust doth corrupt, and where thieves do not break through nor steal: for where your treasure is, there will your heart be also.

An almost identical passage from Buddhist scripture stresses the same point:

> The treasure thus laid up is secure, and passes not away; though he leave the fleeting riches of this world, this a man takes with him, a treasure that no wrong of others, and no thief, can steal.

And Rousseau gives expression to a similar thought: "Every man goes down to the grave carrying in his clutched hands only that which he has given away." Through the religious life man attains that tranquillity of mind which comes only to him who is in accord with the universe.

To summarize we can do no better than quote from Drake: [1]

> Religion, in the best sense of the word, is the devotion of the heart and will to some great ideal in life. It is the universal war against sin and wrong, greatly and imaginatively conceived. It is the divine urge in the human breast — "the life of God in the soul of man." It summons men from their haphazard, animal life, rescues them from their passions, is never without the sense that they need correction, adjustment, salvation. Its presence means emancipation from the cares and fears of worldliness, release from anxious burdened moods, a new tranquilization, poise of spirit, power; a widening of horizons, an easing of strain, an inner resourcefulness and stability. The individual loses himself in a larger life, and thereby finds that life has more dignity and worth than the natural man knows.

What evils have flowed from historical religion?

From such a pure and unalloyed religion as we have described, nothing but good can come. But institutional and historical religion has been prolific of both misery and error. Under the banners of religion no small part of the evil in the world has been worked. Almost every crime has received the blessing of the priest in the name of God. That which

[1] Drake, Durant: *Problems of Religion*, pp. 225–26.

has so often been regarded as the finest thing in life has brought untold suffering in its train. The practices of religion have fostered strife and injustice. Times without number the cross, symbolic of the Prince of Peace and good will on earth, has become "the handle of the sword." Religion has set father against son and brother against brother; it has burned cities, destroyed nations and stoned the prophets of mankind. Religious institutions have shackled the minds of men and thus enabled the despot to shackle their bodies. The most grievous forms of exploitation have been sanctified by holy water and protectingly covered by the priestly cassock. The doctrine of immortality has been prostituted to make men tolerant of injustice on earth, in the hope of securing reward beyond the grave. Religion has been used as an instrument by powerful and privileged classes to hold the weak and the poor in subjection.

Popular revolutions have not infrequently identified religion with those reactionary and tyrannical forces against which revolts were aimed. More than a century ago revolutionary France burned all the gods of religion, proclaimed the Age of Reason, and set up a Goddess of Reason to worship. Recently analogous ceremonies have been observed by the young Communists of Russia. The charges against religion are indeed grave. Little wonder that thoughtful and sincere men have vigorously maintained that the net contribution of religion in the past has been evil.

What are the evils of intolerance? The evils which have been associated with religion cannot be condoned, but they may be explained. And, if they are understood, through enlightened educational measures their virulence in the future may be reduced. In the main these evils may be traced to two causes: first, the tendency of religion to breed intolerance; and, second, the necessity of making religion assume an institutional form.

Let us consider first the question of intolerance. To its adherents every great faith in its entirety bears the stamp of divine authority. From this fact has come much of its virility as well as its tendency to make mischief. In the thought of the religious devotee his beliefs take on the character of absolute certainty. He is willing to concede no possibility of error or imperfection in either practice or doctrine. As a consequence, he rather naïvely divides religions into two groups, the true and the false, his own and all others. He therefore does not hesitate to resort to the sword in order to establish what he in his bigotry believes to be absolute and final truth. The man, certain that he is right, is only a step away from the persecution of others. Under these conditions he naturally attaches transcendent importance to his own religious beliefs and practices. When weighed in the balance with other values, they seem of incalculable worth. Hence in this field the most extravagant behavior may to the zealot appear necessary and right. The religious fanatic may have so such confidence in his own formula that out of love for other men he is willing to destroy their bodies in the hope of saving their souls.

Can intolerance be minimized through education? The correction of this intolerance can only be found in an educational program in which the problems of the religious life are frankly faced. In this program an effort should be made to emphasize those fundamental truths which make a common appeal to the majority of the enlightened and earnest members of diverse sects. Those religious elements which unite peoples rather than divide them should be singled out for emphasis. The fugitive and local features of religion should give place to the abiding and universal. All religious instruction should exhibit that humility of attitude which man must ever feel as he sincerely ponders the meaning of life. Representatives of a great religious sect, visualizing the need for a universal religion which would be acceptable to all men, have suggested that such a religion will be one

surcharged with the universal, ethical principles enunciated by the Hebrew prophets rather than based on ancient or mediæval doctrines, customs, and practices; a religion compatible with all scientific truth rather than based on the miraculous; a religion that conforms to the ideal of constant revelation rather than a single act of revelation; a religion without mysteries,[1] without dogmas, hence without superstitions, without hatreds; a religion in principle so true, in belief so simple, in spirit so humane, and in action so inspired by love that it will guide its followers into that brotherhood which is the hope of man.

What are the evils of formalism? We may now pass to a consideration of the second set of forces which may distort religious expression. Many of the evils which are ordinarily associated with religion are products of the growth of religious forms and institutions. There is always the danger of confusing religion with the social structure that bears its name. In times past the institution has frequently been the bitter enemy of genuinely religious experience, just as the school has often been the unconscious opponent of a truly educational experience. Especially in the realm of religion does the form tend to kill the spirit. Moreover, when an institution comes under the influence of some privileged class or vested interest in society, the inevitable result is that sacerdotal forms and customs are brought into the service of non-religious ends. The uncritical member of a religious sect, losing touch with the spirit, often shifts his allegiance to an empty form. Under these conditions it is a simple task for unenlightened or unscrupulous inter-

[1] *Mysteries* here refers to those rites and ceremonies which in most religions have been kept esoteric by a priestly class. An appreciation of that mystery which must always shroud life and the universe must remain a vital part of religion.

ests, by manipulating the form to which he is loyal, to force his life into narrow or vicious moulds. With the appearance of organized religion it becomes respectable and narrowly profitable to repeat creeds and observe ceremonials; but at the same time it becomes increasingly difficult to make these forms serve as channels through which the religious life may freely flow. Religion, if it survives this treatment, is apt to lead an attenuated existence as an isolated part of experience completely dissociated from the rest of life. Ceasing to affect moral behavior, and no longer carrying an intelligible interpretation of the cosmos, religious practice degenerates into meaningless ornament.

From time immemorial there has been a conflict between the prophet and the priest. The former is a man of vision, and is the embodiment of living religion; the latter through accepted forms follows some prophet of the past, and is the exponent of the religion of the dead. The former cares nothing for creeds and ceremonies, but much for conduct; the latter shows little concern about conduct, but is meticulous in his observance of forms. The voice of the true prophet is heard in these words of Amos:

> I hate, I despise your feasts, and I will take no delight in your solemn assemblies. Take thou away from me the noise of thy songs; I will not hear the melody of thy viols. But let judgment roll down as waters, righteousness as a mighty stream.

Isaiah thus enunciates the same principle:

> Trample my courts no more, bring no more vain oblations. I cannot endure wickedness coupled with worship. . . . Your hands are full of blood. Wash you, make you clean; put away the evil of your doings from before mine eyes.

And one would search the literature of religion long before finding anything to equal the scathing denunciation poured out by the Christ on those who in his day presumed to stand in the place of God on earth. Like the waters of a spring, religion tends to become corrupted as it proceeds farther and farther from the basic experience out of which it flows.

Can formalism be checked through education? The aim of religious education should be to secure for the individual an intimate religious experience, rather than to inculcate a narrow observance of the outward forms of ritual. Its object should be to touch the life of the pupil at the center rather than to adorn the periphery with an easy skill in the practice of genuflexions, with a becoming grace in the wearing of robes, with a faultless manner in the observance of ceremonials, and with a perfect intonation in the recital of creeds. As James Martineau says: [1]

If I see a man living out of an inner spring of inflexible right and pliant piety; if he refuses the colour of the low world around him; if his eye flashes with scorn at mean and impure things which are a jest to others; if high examples of honour and self-sacrifice bring the flush of sympathy upon his cheek; if in his sphere of rule he plainly obeys a trust instead of enforcing an arbitrary will, and in his sphere of service takes his yoke without a groan, and does his work with thought only that it be good; I shall not pry into his closet or ask about his creed, but own him at once as the godly man. Godliness is the persistent living out an ideal preconception of the Right, the Beautiful, the Good.

The vitality of a conception of life can only be measured in terms of its effect on conduct. The professions and formal observances of the individual are of small consequence. Yet the central purpose of the program of religious education has been that of preparing children to make such professions and observe such forms, and this, in spite of the fact that the latter were without basis in their lives. The only fault of most of the so-called religious education is that it is not religious — it is ecclesiastic.

[1] Martineau, James: *Hours of Thought*, vol. I, p. 247.

Why is religious faith uncertain? The peculiar need for religious education to-day cannot be understood without reference to the great changes of recent times. The intimate contacts of diverse cultures and civilizations have shaken the confidence of peoples in the sanctions of the inherited moral codes. Old religious beliefs have been seriously undermined by those changes in social organization and social thought which have accompanied the growth of science and the spread of knowledge. Religion, having formed its associations with a relatively primitive culture, and with unscientific conceptions about the world, has been reluctant to seek new affiliations. From this fact has appeared in certain quarters the tendency to regard religion as a superstition, as a survival from early times, as a portion of the swaddling clothes required by the race in its infancy but hampering in its maturity. And it must be confessed that those who have been delegated by society to guard the religious interests have in large measure grossly misconceived their function, and have shown no small disposition to keep religion securely tied to those conceptions of the natural world which modern science has rendered obsolescent. In their more unenlightened moments they have even sought to identify religion with magic and necromancy, and to-day, they do not hesitate to dispute the field of natural phenomena with the scientists. From each of these engagements science emerges unscathed and strengthened, while dogmatic religion retires in confusion and dishonor. The great injury done is that a growing number of the spectators of this unequal contest are convinced that religion has lost its erstwhile vigor. Many are being led to believe that religion has no special province of its own into which the scientist may not enter and exhibit his superiority. In refusing to recognize their own limitations and their dependence on the work of others, and in refusing to give up territory to which they have no right, the avowed defenders of religion are temporarily in danger of being driven from their own legitimate dominion.

As the development of science has given man a new conception of his place in the natural world, so the industrial and political revolutions have transformed the social world in which man lives. To this changed social world religion as an institutional force has failed to adapt itself. Because of the blindness with which we worship, because of the comparative isolation which separates religious practice from the rest of life, because of the cult of authoritative revelation which dominates theological doctrine, religious practice is perhaps the most backward portion of our social heritage. For the most part the creative period in the history of religious inspiration and thought antedates the coming of the industrial era and the rise of the democratic ideal. To be sure, the basic principles of the great religions, transcending the bounds set by the time and place of their origin, breathe a universal spirit, but many of the customary applications of those principles reflect the conditions of a semi-barbaric and tribal culture. Religious expression, therefore, because it clings to the shibboleths of a past age, is forced into a secondary place in society and constrained to become the handmaiden of the political and economic interests — the vital forces of the modern time. Even its friends can only say that the religion of our own day is a powerful stabilizing force in society which, by serving as a brake on human passion and by reconciling the individual to his lot, bars the hasty introduction of radical social doctrine and slows down the pace of social change. As a great positive agent for integrating the life of mankind and for ushering in the Kingdom of Goodness, religion does not function. The great desideratum to-day is a reinterpretation of life and a restatement of the destiny of man which take into account the development of science and the profound social changes of recent centuries.

How does mankind suffer from this uncertainty? Already mankind has waited too long for this re-synthesis of experience. Religion has consequently lost much of its authority and the sanctions which it gave to conduct are rapidly falling away. In relative aimlessness, and unconscious of its destiny, the modern world drifts into the future. Having sailed beyond those limits in both space and thought which hemmed in and sheltered ancient culture, the barque of civilization is now in the open sea of doubt and uncertainty. Never before in human history has this vessel been more in need of a compass, never before have its sails been filled by such contrary winds, never before has its crew so seriously threatened mutiny. To abandon the figure, out of the welter of recent change there has come a condition of intellectual and moral bewilderment. The present confusion of ideals and values supplies no common ground on which men may meet to resolve their difficulties, no accepted standards to which they may appeal in the adjustment of conflict. In a world that has achieved physical unity, division marks the minds of men. Over a stout barrier of ignorance, prejudice, and misunderstanding, each guarding with jealous and watchful eye its own narrow interests, Labor faces Capital, Youth faces Age, Pagan faces Christian, Black faces White, East faces West. No body of ethical principles or common interpretation of life exists to which the various races and peoples, classes and sects, swear fealty and own allegiance. The development of such a spiritual heritage out of the wealth of materials at hand should be the first task of the educator. For this reinvigoration of religious practice and this reinterpretation of life we cannot, as in times past, rely on the authoritative revelation of an occasional prophet. This function, which

sense by Dr. Nathan Krass,
of Temple Emanu-El, Sixty
Street and Fifth Avenue.

Dr. Krass explained that alth
the scientist was neither an
dox or reform Jew and althoug
did not accept all the teachin
Judaism, his beliefs were in f
mental harmony with the Je
faith.

"The religion of Albert Ein
will not be approved by certain
tarians," Dr. Krass said, "b
Jews. Judaism never shackle
devotees with a creed and neve
sisted on measuring with a
stick the thoughts of its follo
As long as a man believes that
man service is the goal of man
he should be deemed a Jew.

"Einstein has no sense of rel
in the sense the professional
ligionist uses the term, nor eve
the sense of awe at the mys
of the universe is but a mo
translation of the songs of the e
Biblical psalmists. This metaphy
base of religion, this quest of
ultimate, is present in the de
as well as in the scientist.

"But religion even expressed a
code of morals is not antagon
to Einstein's ideas. The great
pounder of relativity is no hedo
no pleasure-seeker, not one of th
who believe that comfort and ha
ness are the goals of man's
deavor. He worships goodness
beauty and truth and believes w
the Jew that our conduct should
be motivated by fear of punishm
or hope of reward. His goal is in
peace and satisfaction, which is
has been the goal of the truly
ligious.

"Only the mechanist, the scien
who scoffs at the notion of a u
verse explained by any but mech
ical means, can be called anti
ligious. The relativist like Einste
who expresses his inability to und
stand the vitalistic principle of li
is profoundly religious."

EINSTEIN'S ARTICL
SCORED AND PRAIS

Dr. Felix Adler Charges
Views Are Not Those of
Religious Philosopher.

DR. KRASS UPHOLDS TH

Asserts "Cosmic Sense of Aw
Mystery of Universe" Is in H
mony With Judaism.

Professor Albert Einstein's au
ity to discuss religion was challe
yesterday by Dr. Felix Adler, fou
and senior leader of the Societ
Ethical Culture, in a sermon i
society's meeting house, Central
West at Sixty-fourth Street.
Adler said Einstein's article
"Science and Religion" in THE
YORK TIMES, on Sunday, Nov.
vealed the mind of a methem
physicist and not that of a reli
philosopher. For this reason
Adler said, the article was u
vincing.

Einstein was described as a
foundly religious man" and he
belong to Judaism in its la

essentially different from the answer a Greek would have given in the time of Plato. He would have said nothing about the importance of compulsory Egyptian or Sanskrit, and equally nothing of a knowledge of simples or metal working. But he would have said that the backbone stuff must be a clear and critical knowledge of oneself in relation to God and to the universe.

If this view is broadly interpreted, and if the necessity of adjusting instruction to the different levels of ability receives proper regard, this religious aim should be the basic concern of the education, not only of the public man, but of the private citizen as well. Education must take much of its inspiration from the pressing need of to-day for a more adequate adjustment of the individual to the totality of existence.

What should be the educational program? Concerning the need for this synthesis and evaluation of experience all far-seeing educators agree, but, weary of sectarian quarrels and suspicious of ecclesiastical bickerings, and in spite of their realization of the need, these same individuals view with apprehension the inauguration of a program of religious education. How is the need to be met? In answering this query attention should perhaps be first directed to what is being done at the present time. An examination of current and suggested practice will reveal the nature and magnitude of the difficulties which must be faced. Numerous experiments in religious education are in progress in our own and in other countries. The churches, of course, have always made some provision for instruction in creed and doctrine. For more than a hundred years the Sunday School has formed an integral part of the religious organization of a number of sects. More recently in certain instances the Sunday School has provided for religious instruction at regular periods during the week. Religious authorities have also established daily vacation schools for the study of the Bible.   But more important for our consideration is the proposal, already given practical expression in certain communities, that clergymen should be admitted at stated times to the secular schools for the purpose of giving religious instruction to the children of their respective denominations.   Throughout the Commonwealth of Australia ministers have the right of entry in the public schools. And in those countries in which the school and the church have never been completely separated, some form of coöperation in promoting religious instruction has always been maintained.

What are the defects of current efforts at religious education?   In all of these experiments there are three defects or dangers.   In the first place, if the responsibility for religious instruction is left entirely in the hands of the several churches, vast numbers of children will receive no spiritual training.   Only one-fourth of the children of the nation attend Sunday or church schools; and, since many boys and girls come from homes which have established no religious affiliation, a large proportion of the pupils would remain untouched even though clergymen were admitted to the schools.

In the second place, whether religious instruction is provided through the Sunday School or under denominational auspices during the course of the week, the learning of creeds is emphasized, the spirit is sacrificed to the letter, sectarian differences are magnified, and those very forces which have so frequently stifled religion in the past are given free rein.   Much of the motivation back of these movements and experiments takes its rise from denominational rivalry and the interest of each sect in holding its own children within the church.

In the third place, all of these practices and proposals suffer from the common defect of identifying religion with the interests of a special professional class, and of making complete the separation of religion from the school. If divorced from the currents of life, neither religion nor morals can be successfully taught. The inevitable consequence of every attempt at this type of instruction is that the religious experience appears but a pale and ethereal phantom amid the riches of that colorful world in which the child plays and works and feels. From the standpoint of fostering the religious life this can only be disastrous.

How may the religious life be fostered? If religious instruction is to be effective, the entire life of the school must be penetrated through and through with the religious spirit. This spirit must be reflected in the classroom and on the playground, in the formal curriculum and in the freer activities of the school. While certain religious forms and ceremonies might well find a place in the program, experience suggests that the worth of their contribution may be easily overestimated. Their observance may be unattended by genuine religious experience, and without them such an experience may be gained. Then, too, where the spirit might bind sects together, the form will keep them apart. The religious way of viewing the world must grow out of the life of the school as naturally as participation in social undertakings.

How may the humanities be utilized? The life of the child can be particularly enriched through the humanities of the regular curriculum. In story, history, biography, literature, and music the child should live through and identify himself with the finest religious experiences and aspirations of men. He should be led to see in its fullness the struggle of the race, through its prophets and seers, for a clearer perception of the meaning of life. No account of human history can omit this growth of mankind in religious stature; no survey of human thought can overlook the masterpieces of religious revelation; no study of human poetry can ignore the beauties of religious expression; no report of human courage can disregard the devotion of religious heroes; no contemplation of human destiny can neglect the fruit of religious meditation. From an intimate and sympathetic contact with the religious life of mankind, religious prophets will take their place in the ideal gallery by the side of great leaders in the fields of secular interest, the taboos which so often restrict and inhibit the religious life to-day will be banished, and the religious side of the child's nature will grow and expand.

How may science be utilized? Even the study of the world of nature, provided this world is constantly viewed as the home of man, should make large contributions to the growth of the religious life. This does not mean that science should be confused with mythology and taught for the purpose of contributing to the " greater glory of God " and of revealing marks of "His infinite wisdom" in nature. Equally it should not be taught for the purpose of chasing God out of the universe. Rather should science be taught for what it is, a most fascinating and fruitful inquiry of man into the world of phenomena, an inquiry which does not presume to fathom the depths of the world, an inquiry whose province lies outside the domain of human values, an inquiry whose fundamental postulates touch but the surface of life. Science as well as religion has its fanatics.

In the last analysis science can never tell men what is Beautiful and Good, nor even what is ultimate Truth. It can count, measure, and catalogue anything that lends itself to enumeration, measurement, and classification. It can even draw generalizations from these observations, but it can do no more. Because science has pushed back the veil of ignorance which formerly blinded the eyes of men in the immediately practical affairs of life, because man has conse-

quently become more independent of drought, storm, and
pestilence, the thoughtless conclude that religion has been
superseded by science. As a matter of fact, faulty science
has merely been superseded by less faulty science. In
those great crises which from time to time visit both individuals and groups, man realizes his final helplessness in the
universe. Generations of scientific inquiry have but added
to the mystery of existence. If, in our study of the world of
nature, these limitations of science be ever kept before us,
instead of appearing to be in conflict with religion, science
will but reveal the need for the wider interpretation of life
and serve as an indispensable instrument in the realization
of human destiny.

How important is the spirit of the school? More important to the growth of the religious life than the introduction of formal materials, either from the field of the humanities or from that of the natural sciences, is the general spirit
of the educational agency. To be truly effective all the
work of the school should bear a religious aspect, it should
purposefully reflect an interpretation of life. This, of
course, does not mean that both the child and the teacher
should be perpetually weighted down by a grave contemplation of the infinite, nor that they should forever carry a
lugubrious and doleful countenance. Whether the general
tone of life is melancholy or joyous, agitated or serene, depends on the nature and quality of one's religion rather than
on its presence or absence. If an elevated form of religion
is to work its way into the life of the child, all of the activities of the school should be in harmony with it. The Folk
High School of Denmark affords a splendid illustration of
an educational institution that has unified its program by
faithfully adhering at every point to a religious interpretation of life. The unity of purpose which this institution has
thus achieved has probably been responsible, in no small

measure, for the unrivaled services which it has rendered in promoting the social and economic reconstruction of this Baltic State during the last half century.

How important is the character of the teacher? Of decisive importance is the attitude and equipment of the teachers. To a large degree they form the traditions of the school and create its atmosphere. If they are religious men and women, the boys and girls who come under their influence will partake of their character. But if they pass lightly over, ignore, or, as is sometimes the case, mock at the deeper meanings of life, or if they are embarrassed when faced with a religious problem, no amount of theoretical religious instruction can set at naught the perpetual operation of the silent forces of example. Those in charge of our schools, therefore, must themselves frankly wrestle with those great problems of life which are styled religious. Until this defect is remedied, until our teachers are given a thorough religious training, the school cannot foster the religious life.

Can religious instruction have definite objectives? If the public school is to have any share in religious education, the practical difficulties which must be met are enormous. Our long tradition of the separation of church and school makes all but impossible any general agreement on objectives. Yet, if the work of the school is to be effective, there must be objectives. In the ordinary community they would of necessity be confined to those basic and relatively noncontentious elements which the great religions hold in common. This suggestion possesses the double merit of being most feasible and of covering the greatest need.

Following the analysis suggested by Bobbitt, the school should strive to give to every child the ability to see the natural environment "as a vast and restless sea of forces and phenomena, infinite in number, extent, subtlety, and complexity"; a faith in the benevolence of the cosmic order toward those who seek to understand and conform to its laws; a feeling of intimate kinship with nature and the whole of the phenomenal world; a lifelong wonder in the presence of the marvelous manifestations of life and nature; a conviction that the feelings, sufferings, and aspirations of men are weighed in the scales of the forces of creation; a faith that righteous conduct is the finest product of the universe; a confidence in the power of men to choose between good and evil; a sense of membership in a universal brotherhood of men; a firm resolve to live in accord with that purpose which moves through the universe to fulfillment; a cheerful acquiescence in the demands for personal sacrifice in the promotion of the greater good; a feeling of deep security in the future which lies beyond the grave; a habit of thoughtful meditation on the meaning and value of life; an eagerness to engage in the eternal quest for the True, the Beautiful, and the Good; and, finally, a clear perception of and faithful allegiance to that ideal kingdom of peace and good will which for ages has been the hope of man, a kingdom in which justice will " roll down as waters, righteousness as a mighty stream."

ADDITIONAL PROBLEMS FOR DISCUSSION

1. Show how the harmonization of the health, family, economic, civic, and recreational activities is dependent on an interpretation of existence which transcends the bounds of any one of these realms and which is essentially religious.

2. How have the changes in the other agencies which are concerned with moral and religious instruction, particularly the church and the home, affected the responsibilities of the school for instruction in this field?

3. Justify the statement that the absence of religious instruction in the school is not to be traced to indifference to religious matters on the part of the various groups of the community, but rather to an extreme regard for religion which gives rise to the fear that their own particular beliefs will not be taught.

4. Why do we attach such an extreme value to human life? Show how

this conception which influences all human relationships depends upon an interpretation of human existence which lies outside the confines of science.

5. Show how the data of science must be taken into account by religion, but that science can never take over the religious function.

6. Why is science, because of its very nature, unable to determine the ends of human activity? How, then, does science serve man in the attainment of his ends?

7. Why is the proposed search for a religion without mystery a vain quest? What is the distinction between mystery in religion and superstition in religion?

8. In what respects is it true that religion touches morality with emotion, and at the same time gives to morality an added significance?

9. In the absence of those religious sanctions which have been such potent forces in the control of behavior, would it be possible, through a purely secular education, to provide effective substitutes for these guiding forces in human conduct?

10. Why is the separation of the school from the church and from religious instruction, which is ordinarily regarded as the solution of the problem of religious education, in actual fact an ostrich-like refusal to face frankly a pressing problem? Suppose similar treatment were accorded to debatable social and economic problems, what would be the outcome?

11. What are the outstanding pedagogical difficulties in carrying out a program of religious instruction in which, of necessity, the factual elements are subsidiary to the appreciations and orientations involved?

12. Show the dangers inherent in the conception of religion as a force which encourages man in docile fashion to accept, as inevitable, evil conditions which through his own efforts could be ameliorated?

13. What are the religious and social causes which bring into existence clearly differentiated sects? How does sectarianism make but limited use of the wealth of the religious heritage of mankind?

14. What criticism would you make of the general educational practice of failing to acquaint the pupils with the lives and teachings of the great religious leaders and prophets? How would such acquaintance defeat the narrow purposes of sectarianism?

PART FOUR

WHAT PRINCIPLES GOVERN THE CONDUCT
OF THE SCHOOL?

To further health and conserve human life, to enable man to direct, improve, and enjoy the activities of the family, industry, citizenship, recreation, and religion, the formal educational agencies have been created. Through the elementary school, the secondary school, the college, and the various vocational and professional schools, society supplements the informal agencies and gives conscious direction to human effort. The determination of the proper function, place, and procedures of each of these institutions is becoming the major problem of each generation. Without a sound educational practice a sound educational philosophy is barren. Only as the curriculum is well chosen, only as effective methods are employed, only as the opportunities of education are adequately extended, only as provision is made for differences in capacity, only as the more gifted individuals are selected for the advanced educational privileges, only as teachers of superior talent and training are employed, only as the educational enterprise is liberally supported, only as the school is controlled by wise and disinterested counsel, can formal education succeed in fashioning a better order of humanity. The achievement of this task, the adjustment of education to the needs of society at any time and at any level of culture, requires a most carefully analyzed and organized system of instruction. But as social life becomes increasingly complex and as the educational agencies grow in number and variety, the administration of education becomes correspondingly complex. Human happiness, human achievement and human destiny become intimately dependent upon a wisely conceived and effectively administered educational system. In a modern society, a society which is committed to science, industrial specialization, and democracy, how can the fuller educational aims be consummated? What are the means for realizing these ends? How can society guarantee that each member may have life and may have it more abundantly? What are the fundamental principles which should govern the conduct of the specialized educational agency?

The consideration of these issues requires a discussion of the following problems:

PROBLEM 18. WHAT CONSTITUTES THE VALUE OF A SCHOOL STUDY OR ACTIVITY?

PROBLEM 19. WHAT IS THE FUNCTION OF THE ELEMENTARY SCHOOL?

PROBLEM 20. WHAT IS THE FUNCTION OF THE SECONDARY SCHOOL?

PROBLEM 21. WHAT IS THE FUNCTION OF THE COLLEGE?

PROBLEM 22. WHAT IS THE RESPONSIBILITY OF THE SCHOOL FOR VOCATIONAL EDUCATION?

PROBLEM 23. WHAT METHODS SHOULD CONTROL THE CONDUCT OF INSTRUCTION?

PROBLEM 24. TO WHOM SHOULD SOCIETY DELEGATE THE EDUCATIONAL FUNCTION?

PROBLEM 25. HOW SHOULD SOCIETY SUPPORT AND CONTROL THE EDUCATION?

PROBLEM 18

WHAT CONSTITUTES THE VALUE OF A SCHOOL STUDY OR ACTIVITY?

Why is the question of values so important? — Why does educational practice force evaluation? — Why must the school articulate with social life? — Why is the school expanding its curriculum so rapidly? — How does this expansion demand the recognition of the principle of relative values in curriculum construction? — What are the criteria for judging the worth of a school activity? — How can the school avoid duplicating the work of other agencies? — How does capacity of the individual control the selection and conduct of activity? — How must interest control the selection and conduct of activity? — What are the important activities of life? — How do the six basic life interests provide the materials for education? — How should the common activities of social life affect the curriculum? — How does the theory of mental discipline give a false simplicity? — How can the theory of mental discipline be restated in modern terms? — Are all subjects equal in forming intellectual habits? — To what extent do habits transfer? — What are the conditions of transfer at the higher levels? — What is the relation of interest, content, and procedure? — How are content and procedure values regarded in present educational practice? — How may these ideas be applied to the elective system? — What are the dangers of abstract discussion of values?

Why is the question of values so important? In view of the limited time given to formal education, the importance of the problem of selecting for any particular individual the most advantageous school activities in which he shall participate is patent. Upon the nature of these activities, upon their breadth and thoroughness depend the satisfactions which the individual will derive from his own life, and the satisfactions which he will afford to others. But to give a final answer to the question as to what constitutes the value of a school study, or, as we prefer to call it, a school activity, is impossible. To answer this question at all profoundly would carry us into the dim region of philosophical speculation, where the ultimate values of life are investigated. In this discussion we shall have to limit ourselves to practical aspects of the problem and in so doing we shall lay ourselves open to the criticism of being both superficial and dogmatic. But even though we attempt to confine our attention to some of the simpler aspects of the problem, we shall from time to time be forced to recognize the more profound implications.

Why does educational practice force evaluation? In view of the great individual differences in original nature, in view of the intense specialization of modern living, it is futile to attempt the general evaluation of an activity without reference to the specific individual who is to undertake it. An activity only has value, for a particular person at a particular time, with a particular biological and educational history, and with a particular future. An activity cannot be judged *in vacuo*, it is always the activity of a definite person taking place in a peculiar setting, and having certain consequential effects on the activities of others. In spite of this, the educator is compelled to select subjects of instruction and organize programs of studies for various groups of children, and thus to assign values to the various activities of the school. When for the whole population a series of activities, or, in other words, a certain portion of the course of study, is made compulsory, there is the definite assumption that the resulting educational product, regardless of the divergent and varied future careers, is of value to each individual of the group. Whenever, on the other hand, participation in a series of activities is made optional, the implicit assumption is that these activities are not sufficiently universal to justify submitting all persons to the training they afford. When we consider the multitude of activities that have some claim to inclusion in the courses of study of our various educational institutions, and when we realize that relative values must be assigned to these studies for the guidance of the student, we see the enormous responsibility which the framers of the curriculum and the advisers of the students must assume, if they are to perform their work in a manner calculated to yield the best results to the body politic.

Why is there such need for the intelligent determination of values?   Overwhelmed by the complexity of the issue, knowing full well that many of his decisions will reflect a limited vision of the nature of the individual and of the society for which men are striving, the educator is tempted to adopt the present *laissez-faire* attitude toward the curriculum. He refuses to be the arbiter in matters which are so surcharged with human happiness and he is reluctant to make decisions upon which social welfare and destiny depend.   The period of compulsory education is being extended; increasing demands are being made upon higher education by large groups of individuals whose needs and powers are unknown.   Never have the opportunities of higher education been offered to persons of such varying backgrounds and diverse futures.   Obviously there is need for rigorous and sincere thinking on every phase of the curriculum problem.   Whether or not the responsibility is welcome, decisions of great moment have to be made; to refuse to act is, in effect, not to reserve the judgment, but to make a positive decision for the generation in our schools that our present procedures, devised to meet a very different situation in the past, are adequate to-day.

Why must the school articulate with social life?   Inertia, tradition, self-interest and ignorance have all been operative to prevent the courses of study of our various educational institutions from keeping pace with and reflecting the changing conceptions of education, the changing conditions of our civilization and the changing relations of social life. There is always a lag between the adaptative devices of education and the demands of the social situation. The progressiveness of a society varies inversely as the extent of this lag. Over any long period of time the health of society is most intimately dependent upon the close articulation of the activities of the school with those of life. As the school activities are well chosen, relatively efficient individuals will assume the tasks and forward the ideals of a better social order; as they are poorly chosen, initiates who have failed to realize their own possibilities will enter adult life inadequately equipped to understand its needs or perform its labors.

Why is the school expanding its curriculum so rapidly? The vast number of studies which are clamoring for admission to the curriculum of the school is a product of four allied social phenomena:

(1) The decline in the effectiveness of the unspecialized educational agencies.

(2) The development of scientific knowledge with reference to life activities.

(3) The growing belief that organized and systematic instruction is superior to casual and desultory learning.

(4) The increasing faith that the school can reduce the gulf that exists between the activity as it is pursued under present conditions, and the activity as it might be pursued under more favorable conditions — the creation of these favorable conditions constituting the problem of education.

How does this expansion demand the recognition of the principle of relative values in curriculum construction? In spite of this crowding of activities upon the formal agency there is a common idea among those who frame the curriculum of our elementary and high schools that, provided a subject can be demonstrated to be of value to the proposed learner, perforce, a place must be found for it in the curriculum. This is fundamentally wrong; the problem is not one of absolute but of relative value. Few activities which have received the serious consideration of the framers of school curricula are without value. The question that should be asked is: For the group of individuals involved, has the particular activity under consideration sufficient value to justify its inclusion in preference to other possible activities which it will displace?

What are the criteria for judging the worth of a school activity? In view of the pressure brought to bear by limited time on the scope of the activities of the school, it will be well for us to examine in a general way some of the more important considerations which determine the worth of a school activity. The criteria controlling the selection of the studies must be carefully chosen and then fearlessly applied. The following four principles suggest themselves:

(1) The activity must be one not provided by the out-of-school training.

(2) The activity must be within the capacity of the individual.

(3) The activity must, as far as is consistent with criterion (4), be of interest to the individual.

(4) The activity must with the maximum economy of time leave behind it, in the form of habits, skills, knowledges, procedures and ideals, powers which will, with a high degree of probability, be employed by the individual in the important activities of his life.[1]

As we examine each of these tests, and as we combine them into a single composite measure of an activity, we shall

---

[1] Logical organization might suggest that the fourth criterion be placed first in the list. The justification for placing it fourth is found in the fact that the other criteria are simple and relatively easy of application. They can therefore be disposed of quickly, that the decks may be cleared for a consideration of the fourth criterion which involves a number of thorny issues.

realize how complex are the psychological and sociological issues involved in curriculum construction.

How can the school avoid duplicating the work of other agencies? The first criterion calls attention to the obvious fact that care must be taken lest the school, pressed for time, duplicate activities which are given adequate exercise in the out-of-school life. This would seem to be a perfectly straightforward criterion and one exceedingly easy to apply. It is patent that the mechanics of reading and figuring are activities which incidental training outside the school does not afford. In cases of this kind the application of the criterion creates no difficulty. Still less is there any degree of doubt, purely on the basis of this criterion, when the formal aspects of grammar, algebra, Latin, or botany are under consideration. The more specialized and advanced education becomes, the more obvious is the application of this principle. Passing from these activities about which there is little uncertainty, we get into regions of difficulty when we consider the advisability of introducing into the school program such activities as systematic physical exercise, health instruction, training in cooking, dressmaking and child rearing, the elementary facts of economic and civic life, the rudiments of numerous games and recreations, and the simple facts of the moral order. Does not the training outside the school produce the proficiency and provide the understanding which life demands in these activities? This question is still further complicated by the diversity in home and community conditions under which the out-of-school life is led. These conditions vary greatly from pupil to pupil in the same school. Unquestionably, children coming from the better homes receive training in certain directions which the school may duplicate wastefully. Under a strictly individualized instruction, for these favored pupils those activities for which the home training was adequate would be omitted.   But, in the school as it is now organized with its heterogeneous groups, such detailed valuation of each activity for each individual is impossible.   To use the classical phrase, we must predict on the uncertain basis of the greatest good for the greatest number.

The policy of the school has always been to refuse to undertake systematic instruction in any field where other agencies, particularly the family, the church and community life were capable of meeting the need.   But, it has, from time to time, because of functional changes in other institutions and on account of the growth of knowledge and increasing complexity of life at certain points, introduced new studies and activities into the curriculum.   This should be the consistent policy of the school as a specialized institution; a policy which, if effectively carried out, compels the educator to study very carefully the performance and potentialities of all the informal agencies of education.   Only in this way can there be any assurance that the school is neither duplicating effort nor assuming that other agencies are performing services which in point of fact they fail to render.   If these two errors are to be avoided, the school, as an institution integrating with all the other agencies, must keep in the closest sociological touch with all the external forces which play upon the citizen during his pre-school, school, and after-school life.

As education becomes more conscious of the essential conditions under which it must operate, there can be little doubt that large school systems will be compelled to organize much more fully than at present systematic means whereby the shortcomings of society in educational influence, and the needs of communal and home life are more adequately determined.   To what extent is the school duplicating the effective work of outside agencies?   To what extent are the children receiving adequate health and sex instruction?   To what extent are the trade, semi-professional and professional schools adapting their curricula to the needs of the social situation? To what extent is the civic, recreational and religious life being understood and appreciated? Where does formal education need to be extended? Increasingly, these and similar questions will have to be answered in the light of information carefully and laboriously collected by a Department of Sociological Research, supported by the various educational institutions or else maintained by outside foundations. Teachers, from the very nature of their task and the setting of their activity, cannot answer these questions. Special bodies of investigators are required, both to sense the problems and to procure the information necessary for their solution.

How does capacity of the individual control the selection and conduct of activity? The second criterion, that the activity must be within the capacity of the pupil, seems so apparent as hardly to need mention. This principle would not merit consideration were it not for the constant tendency on the part of educators to attempt (1) to curtail the necessarily long process of education; (2) to extend an intellectualized education to all individuals, irrespective of capacity. The exacting demands of his present life and the wider social life which awaits the child always press heavily upon those in charge of instruction. These demands, combined with the short period of formal training, and an ignorance of the intellectual capacity of the pupil, often cause the schoolmaster, in the interests of accelerating the necessarily tedious process of learning, to submit his pupils to processes which are so complex in their nature as to be ill-adapted to the stage of development of the pupil. The history of education abounds in illustrations of the violation of this second principle. Children have been treated as miniature adults and have been compelled to undertake studies far beyond their comprehension. In the field of education the longest way round is often the shortest way home. Not only must this criterion determine the sequence of educational activity, but, because of the enormous individual differences in learning capacity, it must be used to decide whether an activity can with profit be introduced at any time into the educational program of the pupil. Particularly is this necessary in a country which is in process of experimenting with universal higher education. Mere bodily presence while an activity is in progress is without potency; the value of the activity can be measured only by the dispositions which are left in the participator. When carefully constructed tests reveal that the pupil is not deriving benefit, the solution of the difficulty may not, as many assume, be more of the activity; rather what may be required is the abandonment of this particular study and a substitution of some activity which is proved to be within the capacity of the learner. Nothing is more conducive to discouragement and more deadening to the attitude upon which successful learning and living depend than submitting the pupil to a course of instruction which lies outside his capacity.

Impressed by the danger of thrusting the individual into activities which are beyond his powers, certain educators have gone so far as to deny that the activities of the wider social life are the guiding and assessing factors in determining the worth of school activities. They have denounced the doctrine that education should be regarded as a preparation for adult activities, and have stressed the notion that all the activities of the school should be measured in terms of their contribution to making meaningful the present experiences of the individual. As a reaction to a curriculum which is wholly adult in its conception, this plea for present meaning is valuable; it automatically prevents the selection of subject-matter which is beyond the capacity of the learner. But that the present limited and unintegrated life interests of the pupil can of themselves furnish the goal of the educative process is an unsound hypothesis. Furthermore, inasmuch as this theory provides no guidance in choosing the aspects of the present life of the pupil which should be elaborated and made meaningful to him, it is a relatively barren educational doctrine. If the exponents of this theory are sincere with themselves, they are compelled to admit that those aspects of the pupil's present experience, which in actual practice they isolate and to which they attempt to give meaning, are selected because of their value as a preparation for participation in the more mature activities of his group. The divergence between these two points of view is not so great as might seem, for the child, during the time that he is a learner, is living in close touch with many of the activities from which spring the problems of adult life. In spite of the fact that in certain circles scorn attaches to the conception of the aim of education as preparation for later life and in spite of the dangers already stressed attending this aim, we would claim that it is the safest criterion for judging the values of pupil activities. But to this point we shall return when we consider the fourth criterion of worth.

How must interest control the selection and conduct of activity? The third criterion of a school activity is that it call forth interest on the part of those who participate in it. The factor of interest must always be considered by those who control the studies and methods of the school; but interest as the major criterion for the selection of subject-matter is a pernicious guide. The fundamental assumption lying back of the philosophy of instruction which would have interest dictate the nature of the activity is in error; the immature individual, by reason of his very immaturity, cannot assess his interest in an activity in the light of its potential-

ities.   He will often show interest in an activity out of which
nothing can grow, and, on the other hand, for long periods,
will often fail to identify himself, of his own initiative, with
activities which are basic to successful adaptation in a complicated world.   Any system of education which sets up
child or student interest as its guiding star is doomed to
failure.   In the determination of the nature of the activities,
not the temporary and often misguided interest of a relatively ignorant pupil, but the requirements of a well-con-
ceived society constitute the final standard of value.   Provided the activity satisfies the other criteria, and especially
the fourth, the greatest ingenuity must be used in making it of
intellectual and social interest to the pupil.   This is essential,
not only because interest is in a way its own justification,
but, also, because numerous studies of improvement reveal
the enormous potency of interest in facilitating the process
of learning.   We would go even further and make the point
that, for the sake of ensuring a satisfied learner, minor
sacrifices of later values must be made to court interest.
But, at the same time, we would deplore the present extreme
tendency to allow the degree of sacrifice to be so great as to
imperil the great social function of the school.   The school
must follow the interests of the immature in order to create
interests which are more serviceable in the situations of
later life.   The special educational agency exists to create
interest in matters which are remote and do not appeal
naturally to the child mind.   On this account we would de-
nounce as ranting cant the sentimental doctrine that the
child must not be stimulated to join in activities which at
their inception and also during their prosecution cannot compete in interest with the more primitive play activities
naturally satisfying to the human.   The fact remains that
many activities of the school are so necessary to the organization and needs of social life, that, whether initially or

finally they are intrinsically as interesting as competing activities, the child must be required to participate in them. We may conclude the discussion of this criterion by making the broad general statement that particularly at the level of universal education considerations of the immediate interest of a study decide the methods which will be employed in presentation rather than settle the question as to its inclusion or exclusion.

How must the wider social life control the selection of school activities? The extreme importance of the fourth criterion has already been stressed. According to this criterion the activity must, with the maximum economy of time, leave behind it, in the form of habits, skills, knowledges, procedures, and ideals, powers which with a high degree of probability will be employed by the individual in important activities of his life. While this statement on the surface appears platitudinous, our discussion will show that its practical application forces us into the realm of bitter educational dissension. In what follows the reader can be introduced only to some of the more salient points around which this dispute centers.

If we assume that a school activity must prepare the individual for his important adult activities, two questions arise at once:

(a) What are the important common activities of life?
(b) How is it possible to predict, for a particular pupil, the nature of his specialized adult activities?

The impossibility of giving definite answers to either of these questions, both fundamental to the construction of a course of study, shows how hazardous is the undertaking of assigning values to the various school activities.

What are the important activities of life? The first question as to what are the important activities of life opens up a wide field of controversy. Only as colorless answers are given to this question can there be any agreement; and the answers are only agreeable because they are vague. For example, all would concur in the statement that an activity has value to the extent that participation in it yields a balance of human satisfaction. The narrow question has been answered, but others have been raised which are equally difficult. Must the satisfaction be immediate or deferred? How can satisfactions of the same individual in different activities be appraised? How can the satisfaction of one individual be evaluated in terms of the satisfactions of others? What constitutes the legitimacy of a satisfaction? Is an activity to be judged by the satisfactions which it brings in our present disordered society? These questions have been raised to show how profound are the issues involved. Let no man think that the problem of curriculum construction consists simply in cataloguing the activities of our present society, and on this basis — certainly a false one — assigning values to school activities. That no final answer can be given to these questions may be admitted at once. Only a mind that mirrors the universe can afford to be dogmatic on life values.

How do the six basic life interests provide the materials for education? In view of these difficulties we may be excused if we cut the Gordian knot of determining the important activities of life by reference to the discussion of the problems in Part Three. In a general way we examined the basic and significant activities of man as these are reflected in the great human institutions. One is forced to believe that as these activities are more intelligently conducted, mankind progresses; as they are undertaken without adequate training, mankind falters; as they are entered upon through an ill-conceived education, mankind regresses. In accordance with this philosophy of life, and at the risk of being accused of begging the question, we may say that the activities of the school must be selected and directed to give to each pupil a maximum share consistent with his capacity in the enterprise of improving [1] the conditions under which operate: (1) physical life; (2) family life;. (3) industrial life; (4) civic life; (5) recreational life; (6) religious life.

These basic life activities — activities in large measure common to all men — abound in problems which challenge education at all levels of instruction; whether in the elementary or secondary school, the college or professional school, there are habits, skills, knowledges, procedures and ideals which must be inculcated, if these six aspects of life are to be guided by intelligence. General elementary knowledge of each of these activities at the elementary levels, more advanced general knowledge of each at the intermediate levels, training for performing some specialized service or for coping with the more difficult problems of some specialized aspect of these life activities, at the highest levels — these are the bases for the selection of school studies. On this account these life activities which further health and find expression in the home, industry, citizenship, recreation, and religion must be critically examined to discover the material they afford and the problems they present to education. These activities must be scrutinized not only to ascertain the present modes of operation but also to elicit information with a view to their constant modification. In this way alone can they be made to satisfy more deeply the higher wants of an ever-widening circle of men. Unless education is to maintain a static society, it cannot assume that individuals must be trained to conduct these activities as they are now taking place in our society. Education must evalu-

---

[1] By "improvement" any particular writer can only mean that modification of the activity which, in all probability, will give greater opportunity to each individual to create and enjoy those human satisfactions which according to the theory of values held by the writer are most worthy.

ate present practices and future possibilities, and in the light of this evaluation proceed to fashion its course of instruction. The less profitable and even vicious elements in the various institutions must be eliminated while those elements which work for the conservation and advancement of human life must be stressed.

How must each study show its relationship to these basic activities? The curriculum of the school increasingly must demonstrate its obvious and direct contribution to the effective continuance and steady improvement of the six aspects of life which have been discussed. The words "obvious" and "direct" are purposely employed because the wide nature of these six aspects of life may serve as an excuse for the introduction of almost any activity. No activity, meriting serious consideration for inclusion in the curriculum of a school, could fail to be justified in terms of some indirect and remote contribution to some phase of life. When, however, those who champion the retention of a certain study, or the introduction of a new study, are made to assume the burden of proving the extreme likelihood that the activities included in the study will make an obvious and direct contribution to the individual participant when engaging in some important life activity, there will be a distinct step of advance. This obvious and direct contribution will have to be described in specific terms. The glittering generalities, which for too long a time have been employed to justify many studies, will be discounted in favor of definite objectives, sociologically evaluated, and shown by definite tests of achievement to be attainable by the pupils. It is the irony of fate that Latin, which for the larger section of its students has been justified in such vague terms, should be the first subject in the school curriculum to be compelled to submit itself to minute scrutiny as to its aims and to the possibility of their attainment. As critics or champions of other subjects voluntarily undertake similar studies or are driven to assume the responsibility for like investigations in their respective fields, a new era in curriculum construction and intelligent student guidance will arrive.

How should the common activities of social life affect the curriculum? The fundamental life activities which we have examined in Part Three must always serve as the final reference in the construction of the curriculum of educational institutions. Whether we consider the activities which are common to all men and women irrespective of their specialized occupations or those other activities which, while essential to the continuance of society are carried on by particular groups of individuals, the guidance which an examination of life activities provides is basic. But in considering the relation of education to these specialized occupations the further question must be faced: Is it possible to predict, for a particular pupil, the nature of his occupational activities in adult life? The undesirability and in fact the impossibility of answering this question at all early in the career of the pupil has led to the present practice of making the initial eight years or even sixteen years of school training essentially unspecialized in its nature, so unspecialized at times as to be disadvantageous.

How should the specialized activities of social life affect the curriculum? For pupils who are to leave school at fifteen it is generally agreed that little should be done in the way of specific preparation for narrow callings; beyond this age an increasing responsibility must be felt for making the education of those who are to leave school without attending college bear a direct and intimate relation to the basic life activities and in some cases to the probable future specialized occupation. At this level of instruction close articulation with special skills and knowledges of the occupation is only desirable where the calling is complex or preparation cannot be provided within the industry. For a smaller group of the school population the period of general education in our present unanalyzed practice is continued to the close of the college course. Only at the end of this period does the specific vocational training begin to function in the various professional schools, or in the vocation itself. The general nature of the education of the majority of students during the later period of the college course is not so much dictated by its superiority to a more specific education looking to the future career of the student, as by the impossibility of predicting for the student what will be the nature of this career. On account of this desire to leave every avenue open and to postpone definite vocational decision there is great waste in educational effort in our higher institutions. In the interests of making higher education more valuable, there are formidable arguments to be adduced in favor of making the student choose, much earlier than at present, his probable future calling. As society becomes more definitely organized it is a safe prediction to make that pressure will be brought to bear in this direction. This movement in higher education towards a training bearing more specific relation to vocation must be contrasted with the opposite tendency which should control the elementary and earlier secondary period. Here education should be increasingly freed from any narrow vocational dominance. Under conditions as they exist now for many students in our colleges who lack the intellectual interest necessary for the liberal course, the generality of the aim easily degenerates into aimlessness. The resulting deleterious effect on the work of these institutions is patent. Whether the disadvantages accompanying an early decision would not be much more than compensated for by the greater incentive to the student which would accompany a course having a closer relation to his future specific career is a matter for serious debate. Our colleges abound with individuals of limited capacity who are using their time to relatively little advantage because their courses of study are so general as to have little obvious and direct relationship to any specific life occupation. Whether America can afford to spend the effort and money on individuals as aimless as are many of the mediocre and inferior students of our colleges is a serious question that must be faced. If the introduction of a more concrete type of instruction centering about the basic activities of life and a more efficient mode of vocational guidance could do anything to quicken and give point to the activities of this growing group of mediocre and inferior students in their later education, any expenditure of effort in this direction would be well repaid. Certain it is that if our college course were longer than at present the moment of vocational decision would be delayed still further; no clearance of the air makes decision easy at the end of the four-year period; economic facts force the issue. How great would be the evils attending a compulsory decision earlier in the college course? This problem should receive the close attention of all students of higher education. The proposal would revolutionize for the group for which it is designed the content and spirit of the later years of instruction, and would leave the college of liberal arts free to perform its unique function. A general aim is unquestionably proper during approximately the first ten years of education; but an intimate knowledge of the conditions in higher education reveals the fact that except for the intellectual few, for whom a continued general education is definite preparation for future career, it is a distinctly dangerous objective.

How does the theory of mental discipline give a false simplicity to the problem? The difficulty of evaluating in any detail the activities of life, and the still greater difficulty of predicting the future career of the pupil, has led in the history of education to an ingenious theory by which these two difficulties are largely sidestepped. In the simple beginnings of formal instruction all subjects introduced into the curriculum showed with reference to social needs the obvious and direct contribution which has been stressed. As social life widened and assumed new forms and values, as the fields which gave scope to human activity broadened, as the basis on which the older disciplines rested was questioned, as the body of knowledge grew and expanded, the necessity for selection became pressing. This selection brought into question the value of certain studies which had long held undisputed sway in the schools; these studies, no longer making an obvious and direct contribution to life, had derived a vested interest in the school program and, consequently, refused to be lightly set on one side. The question became urgent at the period when the extension of education, the era of economic specialization, the breaking down of social barriers, and the enlargement of the choice of occupation in accordance with democratic principles were making prediction of future career very hazardous. Then arose the plausible theory that the main problem of curriculum content could be solved without facing, in any detail, the two troublesome questions: What are the important activities of life? What is to be the specialized career of the individual under training? Such a doctrine was so attractive that it was embraced with enthusiasm and defended with vehemence.

This doctrine, termed the theory of mental discipline, must now be considered. In a somewhat extreme form it may be stated as follows: Certain studies, partly because of their content and more particularly because of their forms, methods and procedures lend themselves so much better than do other studies to the creation of certain generalized intellectual powers that these studies must be included in the curriculum even though the reason for their introduction has long since disappeared and even though their content makes no obvious and direct contribution[1] to the life of the individual pursuing the study. In so far as this theory is followed, those responsible for curriculum construction are relieved from the necessity of giving any detailed consideration to social values or individual careers. At the various stages of instruction, whatever may be the nature of society, whatever may be the particular position that the individual is to fill, there is a general path which all may profitably pursue with the assurance that if followed with due diligence and toil it will lead most directly to effectiveness in the various and diverse avenues of life.

Why was this theory so attractive? Of course no school of educational thought has been so captivated by this theory as to assume that certain specific occupations such as medicine, law, engineering, etc., do not require specialized training: nor has any such school ever neglected to teach the language which serves as the vehicle of instruction. In fact at the two extremes, the early formal education of the child, and the late professional education of the student, there is little resort to any values apart from those of direct utility. The period which elapses after the first obvious tools of learning have been provided and before the period of vocational or professional education is embarked upon, is the time of educational doubt. Hence it is here that the theory of general mental discipline with its simple treatment of values is so acceptable.

Not only was the theory welcomed as introducing a sim-

[1] It may here be mentioned that no subject making an obvious contribution to effectiveness in social life is ever defended by these more remote considerations. When, however, due to changing conditions, a course of study ceases to make such a direct contribution, its supporters strive to establish it upon what they believe to be the higher and surer foundation of its discipline value.

plicity into curriculum construction but it was also supported by the current psychological concepts. According to the psychological ideas of the time, "the mind" which controlled behavior was made up of a number of isolated faculties, such as memory, imagination, observation, reasoning, etc. Further, it was assumed that each of these faculties admitted of training and was then capable of working in any situation and upon any material irrespective of the subject-matter employed in the training. In accordance with this concept, the function of education was to strengthen and discipline these faculties. In view of the importance of training each of these powers which, according to the theory, when once trained, were available generally, the problem of curriculum organization resolved itself at once into a search for those studies which in the surest way and in the shortest time would accomplish the accepted objectives. The uncritical assumption that these faculties when once trained would function in very diverse conditions led quite naturally to a willingness to disregard the social content of the curriculum. To train these powers was the major educational objective. In the belief that these generalized powers would be operating in the multitudinous situations of practical life, it seemed idle to debate any question apart from the direct issue: How does a particular subject contribute to the all-important aim of training the faculties? Having convinced themselves of the indisputable merits of certain subjects in accomplishing this aim, the proponents of this doctrine assumed that the curriculum, once for all, was established, and that while minor alterations might ensue, its general contour, whatever the changes in the social order, was finally fixed. Devised to meet the problems raised by the increasing complexity of educational material, and the increasing specialization of occupation, and finding justification in the prevalent theory of mental faculties, it is no wonder that this theory of general discipline has had staunch adherents, and, in slightly changed forms, still has its ardent supporters.

Is this theory dependent on the faculty psychology? If the theory of mental discipline depended upon the so-called faculty psychology for its validity, it could be given instant dismissal. All psychologists are now agreed that it is not legitimate to regard the mind as an aggregation of various independent faculties each of which can receive a separate training. Modern investigation shows that the mind is not departmental but unified in its activity. The "memory," "observation," "reasoning," "imagination" of the faculty psychologists are not separate powers which can be developed in isolation, but rather different aspects of the working of a mechanism which always functions as a unit. When the individual reasons, it is not some specialized faculty, analogous to a large muscle, which is in operation, but a host of connections involving a large part of the nervous system. The faculty theory has given place to the modern doctrine of a mind made up of a multitude of connections integrated together to control behavior. But the abandonment of the old faculty psychology does not shatter, as many believe, the theory of mental discipline. Our manner of statement makes it still a tenable theory, even though the faculty psychology is moribund. To restate the question, Do not some studies leave behind in the individual pursuing them certain intellectual powers of wide application which are so valuable, and so economically imparted through these studies that, quite apart from any direct and obvious relation of their content to life activities, they should find a place in the curriculum?

What are these intellectual powers? If we may assume for a moment that we may speak of generalized intellectual powers — and the legitimacy of this assumption will be examined later — the nature of these powers will be made clear by listing some of the more significant:

(1) *Habit of Inquiry:* the tendency to seek problems and explanations.

(2) *Habit of Concentration:* the tendency to concentrate all the available intellectual energy on a problem.

(3) *Habit of Persistence:* the tendency to work on a problem even though its solution is difficult and brings no immediate reward.

(4) *Habit of Reference:* the tendency to consult reliable authorities even though such consultation delays solution.

(5) *Habit of Openmindedness:* the tendency to discount prejudice.

(6) *Habit of Integrity:* the tendency to watch for, and avoid, illicit "Rationalization."

(7) *Habit of Disavowal:* the tendency to be willing to acknowledge one's ignorance whenever and wherever it exists.

(8) *Habit of Demonstration:* the tendency to differentiate desire, belief, and proof.

(9) *Habit of Analysis:* the tendency to reduce an experience to its component parts.

(10) *Habit of Generalization:* the tendency to reduce a series of experiences to a general principle.

(11) *Habit of Application:* the tendency to use general principles in later experience.

(12) *Habit of Self-reliance:* the tendency to rely on one's own judgment and mental processes.

How can the theory of mental discipline be restated in modern terms? As far as it affects the practical problem of curriculum construction, the question now becomes: Are all subjects in the curriculum, if well taught, of equal value in forming such intellectual habits? If the answer to this question is "No," the further issue arises: To what extent is it wise to sacrifice interest and direct relationship to life activities, for the purpose of establishing these habits? The answer to this last question depends not only upon the extent to which each subject builds up sound intellectual habits within its own domain, but also upon the extent to which such habits, acquired in one field of study, transfer over to other fields. On neither of these points is accurate quantitative information available. No one is in a position to state for the various studies what are the precise contributions of each to the growth of intellectual habits in a particular individual. No quantitative evidence is available to answer the question as to the degree of transfer that may be expected when the student, having built up a series of habits in one group of situations, is called upon to face groups of situations which are increasingly different from those in which the habits were acquired.

Are all subjects equal in forming intellectual habits? With reference to the first question as to the relative values of different subjects in inculcating sound intellectual habits it is idle to say that all subjects have equal value from this standpoint. For purposes of exposition these intellectual powers will henceforth be referred to as procedures. As far as the school or college curriculum is concerned to-day, one may almost venture the statement that the correlation between content values and procedure values is low. In the languages, in mathematics, and in the exact sciences, if loose thinking takes place, the erring student is at once brought to book. If, in German, a wrong case is used, if, in physics, a wrong method is employed, there is scarcely need to bring home to the student the consciousness of his failure to grasp the fundamental principles; his failure is writ large. To produce the same inner conviction of error in the descriptive subjects such as English, history, civics, and sociology is quite impossible. In other words, loose thinking can be punished in certain subjects in a much more effective way than in others. It is a mere platitude of psychology that the results of desirable connections must be readily recognizable by the student; likewise when undesirable connections are made they must be apparent. Hence a subject which brings these facts inevitably to the notice of the pupil has very great pedagogical value. Can it be seriously maintained that all subjects fulfill this fundamental law of learning to the same degree? The student who fails to solve a problem in geometry is cognizant of his own shortcomings — in such clear-cut fields there is no "shuffling." Lax procedure and lax thinking fail to yield the product desired, and nobody is more clearly aware of the fact than the student himself. The same student in other subjects, which are more speculative and therefore less exact, indulges in equally loose thinking, but from the very nature of the subject, he is not so painfully conscious of the lacunæ in the process. One idea is supported by a great name, so also, is the opposing idea; the student can accept either, and it is extremely difficult to tell whether the conclusion at which he arrives is the outcome of logical thinking or the result of hasty and ill-considered judgments. If it is contended that all subjects may be made to have the same inherent value in this respect, the methods of teaching many of the more modern subjects will have to be radically modified, if not revolutionized.

How is the problem of discipline still further complicated? Before we leave this question fairness demands that attention be called to an important but often neglected consideration. A school subject can only inculcate intellectual habits in those who wholeheartedly throw themselves into its activities. Many of the more difficult subjects are condemned, because pupils on account of their lack of capacity or interest shirk the responsibilities and burdens involved, and fail after being "exposed" to these subjects to show added powers. The fact that the student is unable to undergo the discipline *is* a reason for excusing him; the fact that the student is unwilling to undergo the discipline *may* be a reason for guiding his energy into other channels, but neither of these facts is a sound reason for the general condemnation of the subject as a discipline. Attention may now be directed to the second question.

To what extent do habits transfer? This concerns the extent to which a power acquired with one set of data can be employed with other data. Transfer takes place when habits, dispositions, and ideals acquired in one situation are used in other situations. The mediating factors of transfer may range from simple automatic habits, illustrated by a child who in learning to skate uses the walking mechanism, to complex language habits, illustrated by a scientist who having been taught to correct himself in his own field of study by saying, "I must avoid judging by superficial appearances and suspend my judgment until more evidence is available," uses the same formula to guide his behavior in other fields. At the risk of offending the behaviorist we may say that the first transfer is the result of the functioning of old mechanical habits in new situations, whereas the second transfer results from a comprehension of the "meaning" of the new situation. The first type of transfer is found in animal and man alike, the second, to any marked degree, only in man. The experiments that have been made in this field have been, in the main, confined to narrow, in fact almost semi-automatic functions, and the evidence points to the fact that while transfer is always present it becomes increasingly and surprisingly less as the situation to which the old habits are applied varies from that in which they were acquired.

What are the conditions of transfer at the higher levels?

Little work of a prolonged or significant order has been done to investigate that form of transfer which is dependent on meaning. We know nothing quantitatively concerning the manner in which any of the habits of intellectual attack, such as careful analysis, delayed judgment, looking for similarities, intense concentration, acquired with great pains in one study, will function in another field. The sizing up of a new situation or the attempt to get at its significant relation ships to old methods of response is obviously dependent on the intelligence, specific interest, and the factual equipment of the individual. The mind of a Newton or, as the behaviorists would prefer, the language mechanisms of a Newton (!) are required to relate the falling of the apple to the movement of the stars; the intelligence of a Watt is demanded to relate the mere lifting of the lid of a kettle to the performance of useful work; the genius of a Spencer is required to relate a principle of organic evolution to a similar principle operating in the realm of social institutions. Obviously the relating of the one event to the other takes place only in a mind that is exceedingly acute. The statement that this transfer takes place only to the extent that the content and procedure is the same in the two fields is an undue simplification and leaves out of consideration the most important factor, namely, the active intelligence which makes the transfer. A content and procedure which one individual sees to be directly applicable to a new problem, may not appear significant to another person. Transfer of this nature is never a mechanical process which can be expressed in terms of the objective similarity of two fields, it must always be regarded in the light of the generalizing capacity or intelligence of the individual. The point cannot be too vigorously maintained that whenever thinking takes place, transfer of training occurs.

What is known concerning transfer? Until careful

quantitative investigations such as are now being initiated
have been made, to determine the extent to which in individuals of differing mental endowment transfer of this more
subtle type takes place, educators will be ignorant of those
fundamental facts and principles which condition the selection of educational curricula and methods.[1] Until such investigations have been made great diversity of opinion is
inevitable.   Meanwhile we can do nothing more than interpret the limited evidence, both observational and experimental, which is now available.   Three somewhat dogmatic statements must suffice to summarize present knowledge.

(1) Transfer of procedure does take place.
(2) The extent of this transfer is so much less than *a-priori*
arguments would suggest, that in teaching transfer
must be an ever-present conscious aim.
(3) The amount of transfer is directly dependent on the
level of intelligence of the individual involved, and
upon his factual resources and degree of interest in
the field to which transfer is to be made.

What is the relation of interest, content, and procedure?
Accepting this summary as the answer to our question on
transfer, we may now raise a further point. To what extent
is it wise to sacrifice interest and direct relationship to life
activities, in order to establish sound and vigorous intellec-

[1] It is of interest to note that the school of educators who are contending
for a curriculum that shall center around the present life problem of the
child is also the school that would assure us that transfer of training is almost non-existent. The two positions are in direct conflict. Their first
position compels them to assume that the procedures acquired in pupil
problems will automatically transfer to the different problems of adult life.
If transfer, as they claim, does not take place in any marked degree, it
would seem that they would be driven to construct a curriculum around the
important activities of adult life.   Obviously it is impossible to maintain
that the present problems of the pupil are the guide to instruction and, at
the same time, assume that there is but little transfer of training.

tual habits — habits which the evidence suggests have a more or less general application? In weighing the merits of a particular study, there are three considerations that must be borne in mind: (1) interest value; (2) content value; (3) procedure value.

The values are so interrelated that convenience of thought alone justifies their separate discussion. By interest value is meant the power that the study has of awakening agreeable responses in the student. Interest is evidence that there is a voluntary identification of the self with the activity. The degree of interest is a measure of the felt significance of the study to the total life experience. The content of a subject is the factual basis. The content value of a study is measured in terms of the contribution which it makes to the furthering of the purposes of the individual. The procedure value of a study is measured in terms of the contribution which it makes in forming sound habits such as we have illustrated in a limited intellectual realm, — habits which may have a somewhat wide range of application. The interest factor has already received attention; we have noted its importance and the manner in which it should control the time and mode of presentation of subject-matter, but we have made it subsidiary to content and procedure values assessed from the standpoint of the degree to which the content and procedure lead to effectiveness in life activities. On this account, leaving the interest factor for the moment, we shall direct attention to the difference in practice which arises from the conflict of opinion as to the relative worth of the content and procedure values.

How are content and procedure values regarded in present educational practice? That content acquired in one field is useful in other fields is apparent to the most casual observer. Specific content elements which do not suffer the usual and proper fate of most school facts,— benign obliteration — if ever used in a subject other than that in which they were acquired, are subject to one hundred per cent transfer: thus many of the facts gained in history, geography, civics, economics, and arithmetic are used over and over again in the ordinary life of the individual. In the realm of procedure, under which are included general mental habits, attitudes, and even ideals, the whole problem of transfer is much more subtle. Those who construct the curriculum are facing their problem with these ideas of procedure and content values in mind. They are convinced that content transfers, but, since everything suggests that the procedure transference is small, they regard it as a precarious objective of instruction. Under such conditions, the alteration which has taken place in school studies is the logical outcome. Educators say, in the heat of the attack on the mental discipline theory, "We are sure of our content transference; let us therefore have content subjects rather than fly to those studies which have procedure for their primary aim, concerning the transference of which we know so little." In other words, the curriculum, at the present moment, is being crowded with content subjects, the confessed aim of which is to give content values. As a reaction against the old formal curriculum this may be advantageous, but it should be carefully noted that whereas content values only function in specific circumstances, procedure may be and usually is of generalized application. Thus, if an individual studies one subject carefully and continuously and develops sound intellectual habits in that subject, even supposing that these habits function, on the average, but five per cent as effectively in other fields of experience, this five per cent transfer may be of much greater value than a large amount of transfer in content. Though in advanced courses few further facts are acquired, the long period necessary for the interrelations of these facts may be of incalculable value, if it results in the formation of modes of intellectual attack which find application in a wide range of experience.

It may also be pointed out from the standpoint of social efficiency, in which is included interest in literature, esthetic studies and public affairs, and even from the standpoint of vocational efficiency, how little content is required. The large majority of people, if their education had provided them with the habits already listed, could acquire in a very short time all the facts which their business proper and their outside interests demand; furthermore these facts would not be acquired under artificial pedagogical conditions, but under the more natural and stimulating conditions of life. They would be acquired to meet present demands and necessities. Our educational institutions, therefore, especially at the higher levels, must devote a considerable part of their time to procedure values. This could be done without requiring the institution to lay itself open to the charge of neglecting important content studies introduced to widen interests and to guide the individual in his social relations.

How must the emphasis on procedure vary at different levels of instruction? To be more explicit, in the elementary school the direct content values may be safely stressed. Beyond this stage, in so far as pupils of mediocre or lower intelligence are under consideration, since any transfer of procedures at these levels is apt to be slight — direct content values should still be stressed. In the higher forms of education, especially for students of superior intelligence, procedure values must receive explicit recognition. But it cannot be too greatly emphasized that these procedures must be derived as far as possible from studies which have an obvious and direct relationship to the basic social activities that have been discussed in Part Three. This obvious and direct relationship to these activities must only be sacrificed in so far as the evidence is convincing that certain studies, owing to their more rigorous methods and greater intellectual demands, afford a discipline which cannot be obtained from studies of more direct social content; moreover, the type of discipline afforded must be such as will in the long run render the individual more capable in the important activities of his adult life.

How may these ideas be applied to the elective system? The chaotic state of our present sense of values is reflected in the workings of the elective system. If we consider the present state of educational theory, the task of those who are to guide the elections of students beyond the elementary studies is most unenviable. When the guide is on sands which he knows to be shifting, is it any wonder that he fails to point out the way with certainty? Where twenty years ago the adviser said, "You must," ten years ago he said, "You should," to-day the weak counsel is, "You may." The present state of affairs is due to the fact that we have not yet had time to weigh what evidence we have, or to collect further evidence on the question. We are perfectly aware that in the assigning of the relative value to any particular study, three considerations must be borne in mind: (1) interest values; (2) content values; (3) procedure values. It is possible that never will these three factors be fully harmonized. Conceivably in the process of time, a great educator may arise who will outline a course such that for large groups of individuals the procedure, interest, and content value will be a maximum. Meanwhile, we must not deceive ourselves that he has come. But admitting our ignorance, we must make each student realize the three outstanding factors from which a subject derives its value. No one factor should be emphasized to the exclusion of the rest. It is highly undesirable to have certain educators eulogizing interest, others eulogizing procedure, and others eulogizing content, each with a complete disregard of the legitimate claims of the others.

The elective system is too often justified by the erroneous theory that each subject, taught by a human teacher, is of equal value from the standpoint of training. If this system, demanding as it does great integrity on the part of the student, is not to work evil, certain warnings must be regarded. Beyond the elementary school, for those who pursue an academic course, a considerable portion of the work of each student must be directed along lines which involve continued and correlated courses of study. Continued, for it is only those subjects which are studied beyond the stage where data are collected and through the stage where methods are applied to the data, that anything approaching sound intellectual habits can be imparted. Correlated, for when a general method has to be acquired the soundest educational means is to insist that the method be used with many kinds of data. One is not fed, but merely puffed up by disorganized knowledge. For the quick and sure return which content teaching gives, we must not sacrifice the values accruing from an education which inculcates procedures of wide range of application in the important activities of life.

What are the dangers of abstract discussion of values? As we close this discussion which has necessarily been somewhat abstract, the reader must again be warned that the question as to the value of an activity can never be given a general answer. An answer only has significance with reference to a particular individual living his life under a particular set of conditions. Furthermore each separate activity can only be evaluated in so far as it is projected upon all the other activities which form the total experience of the individual. The differences in individual capacity, training, and expectation make mass decisions for the purpose of group instruction most perilous. Personality is not the result of a series of divorced experiences, it is the outcome of the total life experience. Each separate activity must be judged by the manner in which it will integrate with other activities. This integration must be such that it produces a balanced, creative, and happy member of society — a member who, to the limit of his capacity, is continually striving to change this society for the better.

ADDITIONAL PROBLEMS FOR DISCUSSION

1. What definite guidance does the commonly stated aim of education as "the harmonious development of the self" give in the selection of the activities and studies of the school?
2. How does the curriculum tend to foster a static form of society? How might the curriculum be changed to favor a dynamic form of society?
3. Contrast the effectiveness of the educational forces external to the school in the following: cultural vs. the illiterate home; immigrant vs. the native home; rich vs. the poor home; rural vs. the urban community; small vs. the large family.
4. What subjects in the high school and college curricula reveal the lag which exists between the adaptive devices of education and the demands of present-day society? What are the forces which serve to retain these subjects in the curriculum?
5. Show how the wide extension of educational opportunities and the lengthening of the time spent in school have been responsible for the radical alteration of the public school curriculum in both the elementary and secondary departments.
6. Show how formal education tends to select out for elaboration only those present experiences of the pupil which are significant from the standpoint of probable future responsibilities of the student. How does this selective force (dependent upon the level and type of their culture), operate in different ways among different peoples?
7. How would the extreme proponents of the doctrine of interest in education criticize and attack the statement that "any system of education that sets up interest as its guiding star is doomed to failure"?
8. What forces operate to reduce the direct and obvious relation to important life activities possessed by any study when first introduced into the formal curriculum?
9. Why was the older doctrine of general discipline styled the doctrine of *formal* discipline? What is the exact connotation of the word formal in this usage?
10. What is the distinction between method and content? What is the

fundamental philosophy back of the statement that it does not matter what you teach but how you teach it?

11. How do you account for the fact that in the beginnings of education in the elementary school and at the other extreme of education in the professional school there is little resort to the justification of study by their formal values?

12. Why must a consideration of *relative* rather than absolute values always determine the selection and elimination of subject-matter from a curriculum?

13. Justify the statement that all reflective thinking involves transfer of experience. How does all theoretical training, such as a course in principles of education, assume transfer?

14. How does the skillful and wise teacher insure the maximum of transfer (to other activities) of powers gained within a particular subject? How does the amount of specific attention devoted to active working for transfer vary with groups of different levels of intelligence?

15. Why has wide extension of secondary and higher education tended to stress content rather than procedure teaching?

16. How has the attack on the theory of general discipline favored the introduction of the elective system?

17. Illustrate from the curriculum of the elementary school how each of the four criteria governing the election of subject-matter (discussed in text) has made itself felt.

18. From the standpoint of the four criteria for the selection of school studies, criticize the inclusion of each of the following in the eighth grade curriculum: Algebra, Domestic Science for girls, Sex Hygiene, Latin, American History, English Grammar, Ethics, Astronomy.

19. Criticize the electives of a typical high-school or college student by reference to the four criteria for the selection of school activities given in this section.

20. Enumerate the major difficulties which are involved in answering the question: What constitutes the value of a school study?

PROBLEM 19

WHAT IS THE FUNCTION OF THE ELEMENTARY SCHOOL?

Why is the elementary school the basic educational institution? — What are the activities of the present elementary school? — Is the conventional curriculum an anachronism? — What are the criteria for the selection of the curriculum? — Why must the curriculum reflect group life? — Why must the curriculum recognize the capacity of the child? — Why must the curriculum recognize the interests of the child? — Why must the school consider the work of other agencies? — Why must the curriculum reflect the basic human activities? — How can educational experience be classified? — What provision should be made for concrete experiences? — How has the elementary school unconsciously furthered non-scholastic aims? — Why must the elementary school abandon its narrow intellectual emphasis? — How should the elementary school provide vicarious experiences? — How must concrete experience be made the vehicle of vicarious experience? — In what moulds has the social heritage been preserved? — How can this cultural experience be made available at the elementary level? — Why must the school keep in close sociological touch with the life of the community? — How should the elementary school provide for the acquisition of the tools of knowledge? — What major issues does the teaching of the language arts raise? — What is the relative importance of the several tools of knowledge? — What should determine standards of attainment? — Should the tools of knowledge be taught incidentally? — How must different levels of ability be recognized? — What is the function of the elementary school?

Why is the elementary school the basic educational institution? In 1920, according to a report of the Federal Bureau of Education, out of a total public school enrollment of approximately twenty-two million children, nineteen and one-half million were found in the elementary schools. For the most part these figures are based upon the conventional eight-four plan of public school organization. If from this total are subtracted the children of the seventh and eighth grades, since under the junior high school reorganization these two years fall within the limits of secondary education, there still remain approximately sixteen million boys and girls enrolled in the first six grades of the public school. Whether, therefore, elementary education is regarded as covering eight or six years, it is in this division of the school system that the great majority of the younger generation are found to whom society extends the privileges of a formal education. Practically all of the nation's children pass a longer or shorter period in this institution. Moreover, this experience comes to them in those early years of life which are so potent in determining the direction of later growth.[1] Hence the supreme importance of the question that heads this discussion: "What is the function of the elementary school?"

What are the activities of the present elementary school? A significant answer to this query is found in current curriculum practice. But this practice, since it varies much from place to place and is constantly changing, is difficult to describe. Any summary is in danger of conveying a wholly inadequate, if not a grossly erroneous, impression of the actual situation. Nevertheless, with these necessary cautions, it will be profitable to examine some of the more general findings of Holmes's investigation of the curricula of the elementary schools in fifty American cities in 1914.[2] The facts here revealed will serve as a basis for discussion and will aid in defining the problem. In these cities it was found that for this particular year the average number of

[1] It should be noted that the work of the elementary school is based upon some six years of pre-school life. That this early education, provided in the home, is of great significance various studies are beginning to show. Through the training of parents and through the extension of the kindergarten this pre-school age must be reached.

[2] Holmes, Henry W. "Time Distributions by Subjects and Grades in Representative Cities," *The Fourteenth Yearbook of the National Society for the Study of Education*, Part I, pp. 21–27.

hours given to each of the elementary school activities in
all eight grades combined was as follows:

	NUMBER OF HOURS	PER CENT
Opening exercises, including allotments in ethics, etc.	242	3.3
Reading, including phonics, literature, dramatics, story-telling, etc.	1311	17.9
Language, including composition, grammar, punctuation, pronunciation, etc.	849	11.6
Spelling	454	6.2
Penmanship	355	4.8
Arithmetic, including algebra, geometry, business arithmetic	981	13.4
Geography, including physical and commercial geography	474	6.5
History, including civics	360	4.9
Science, including nature-study, elementary science, physiology, and hygiene	262	3.6
Drawing, including picture-study, art, etc.	394	5.4
Music	359	4.9
Manual training, including industrial training, handwork, etc.	291	4.0
Physical training, including athletics, gymnastics, folk-dancing	316	4.3
Recess	452	6.2
Miscellaneous, including unassigned time, study	222	3.0
Total	7322	100.0

Why must the school work against odds? Before the details of this table are examined, attention may be directed
to the proportion of the pupil's time spent in formal education.   In these fifty cities, in which both the school day and
the school year are longer than in the average American
community, the child who attends every day the school is in
session, who progresses at the normal rate, and who completes the work of the elementary school in the expected
eight years, spends but seven thousand hours under the
supervision of the educational authorities.   This is but
slightly more than one tenth of his entire time and only

about one sixth of his waking hours. Furthermore, it is little more than two and one half hours a day throughout the school life of the pupil. That the power of the school is limited, therefore, and that the work of the school may be set at naught by forces which are operating beyond its range of influence, is only too apparent from these figures. The school, in so far as it seeks to correct and elevate the common and accepted practices of life, works against tremendous odds. The activities which children pursue in the purified and enriched educational environment constitute but a fraction of the activities in which they engage outside the school as they follow the call of interest or respond to social expectation. If the school, therefore, is to function positively as a social institution, if it is to do more than reflect and enforce contemporary social practice, if its work is to be effective in promoting social advance, its actual authority must greatly exceed its nominal authority. The instruction of the school must be so thorough, its activities must be so significant to children, that its power will shape and give direction to much of the out-of-school life of its pupils.

What is the position of the three R's in the curriculum? In order to discover how the more progressive elementary schools of the country are spending their time, a more detailed examination of the facts presented in the table will be necessary. Over forty per cent of the total time in these schools is given to formal instruction in the language arts — reading, language, spelling, and penmanship. If to these subjects is added arithmetic, well over one half of the time is accounted for. Whatever may be the impression to the contrary, the facts speak for themselves: the three R's still dominate the elementary school curriculum. History and science receive but little attention, and music and art are given only perfunctory recognition. One might expect an educational institution whose primary purpose is to meet the educational needs of the masses of the people would sustain through its curriculum a more obvious and direct relation to their interests. Either the analysis of the basic life activities and needs presented in Part Three is erroneous, or the present-day elementary school is at fault.

The activities of the American elementary school, if these curricula are at all representative, are highly literary and academic and are drawn from the more attenuated and marginal concerns of life. The dominant purpose of this institution is preparation for the more advanced work of a yet more academic nature provided in the conventional high school. Since the best public school practice is found in these cities, in all probability these tendencies are yet more characteristic of elementary education as a whole. Furthermore, in those first six years, which are coming to constitute the elementary school, formal reading, writing, and arithmetic occupy an especially entrenched position.

What was the origin of the conventional curriculum? The explanation of this extraordinary literary emphasis is not difficult to discover. It may be found in the growth of culture and in the history of the elementary school. As social life became more differentiated and consequently more dependent on effective means of communication and measurement, there arose the need in an increasing proportion of the population for the mastery of the elementary aspects of written language and number. Since the mastery of these elements of culture was difficult and since the school career of the individual was short and uncertain, a carefully organized and somewhat narrow educational program centering on these objectives was necessary. Thus in its origin the elementary school naturally and necessarily emphasized the acquisition of the tools of knowledge.

As a basic social institution the position of the elementary school at this time seemed far from secure and it played but a minor rôle in society. Its methods were unbelievably crude, attendance was irregular, the school day was short, the school year existed only in embryo, the wider educational objectives were not in sight, and a philosophy of popular education was yet to be developed. In consequence, the school was forced by circumstance to confine its attention to the most obvious educational needs. Moreover, the immediate ancestor of the elementary school throughout the western world was an institution designed largely by ruling classes to provide for the children of the masses the barest minimum of educational opportunities. Its primary purpose was to prepare the children of the humble to occupy a humble position in society. In accordance with the narrowness of its purposes the offerings in such a school were necessarily meager. The traditions of this early school, the vestiges of an outgrown civilization, cling to the elementary school of to-day. The school, lagging behind the demands of society, is slow and even reluctant to adapt itself to a changed conception of its function.

Is the conventional curriculum an anachronism? Since the establishment of the first reading and writing schools, society has continued to grow more and more complex and the demands for education have increased *pari passu*. Likewise, with the growth of democratic ideals the practice of making education in its various forms follow class lines has fallen into disfavor. In place of the narrow conception of the past the elementary school is coming to be regarded as the school for childhood. No longer is it to be looked upon as a school for the abolition of illiteracy, although it will guarantee a literate population; no longer is it to be viewed as a school for the poor and unfortunate, although it will look after the needs of these classes. Rather it is the school into which the community will gather its children from the ages of six to twelve. Here it will, as far as time and capacity allow, promote their growth into sturdy, dependable, and efficient members of society, capable of enjoying the privileges and desirous of carrying the lighter burdens and discharging the less arduous duties which fall to the lot of every citizen. Whatever is required to further the adjustment of children to the primary conditions of life, that must the elementary school be prepared to do. Whether this involves the formation of health habits, the inculcation of wholesome sex and family attitudes, the gaining of a simple understanding of human dependence on food, clothing, and shelter, the acquisition of coöperative social dispositions, the development of worthy recreational interests, or growth of religious insight and sympathy, this fundamental educational agency must not shirk the task. To all children, regardless of the circumstances of birth, society must extend these privileges and enforce these responsibilities. "What the best and wisest parent wants for his own child," writes Dewey, "that must the community want for all of its children. Any other ideal for our schools is narrow and unlovely; acted upon, it destroys our democracy." This is the only conception of the elementary school which a people, favored by material abundance, enlightened in its political traditions, and humane in its social ideals, can reconcile with its educational philosophy.

What are the criteria for the selection of the curriculum? Attention may now be directed to the original question which in modified form may be restated as follows: What are the activities in which *children* should engage under the supervision of those specially trained representatives of the community known as teachers? A general answer to this question may be given in terms of a few principles. There are five criteria that should guide the selection of those activities which should constitute this foundational education of the citizens of a democratic society. Although four of these principles have been discussed at some length in the immediately previous chapter on the value of an activity, each will be considered here with particular reference to its bearing on elementary education.

Why must the curriculum reflect group life? In the first place, the activities of the elementary school should serve to induct the child into the life of the group of which he is an immature member. They should equip him to carry on and improve that life. In whole or in part this first criterion has been recognized throughout the ages in both the informal and formal educational agencies; it is basic to the construction of any defensible educational program and is peculiarly pertinent to the organization of the life of the only educational institution which touches directly all the members of society. Since the perpetuation of the group is as dependent on an education which recognizes this principle as any education whatsoever is dependent on group survival, to any contradictory principle even a hearing cannot be granted.

Why must the curriculum recognize the capacity of the child? In the second place, the activities of the elementary school should be adjusted to the capacities and attainments of children. This is merely a recognition of the ancient pedagogical principle that all genuine learning must take its point of departure from the present position of the learner. To neglect this criterion in the selection and organization of subject-matter is educational suicide. Yet at the elementary-school level, because adults have forgotten the experiences of their own childhood and fail to realize how long is the educational road which separates them from children, this error is often committed. Moreover, so great is the task of inducting the child into the life of society and so short is the time for the performance of this task, that the teacher is often reluctant to wait upon the slow processes of growth.

Why must the curriculum recognize the interests of the child? In the third place, in so far as it is compatible with the other criteria, the activities of the elementary school should be drawn from the interests of children. There is a temptation to follow the lead of a certain school of educational thought and make this statement without qualification, but such a course seems hazardous and mistaken. At the elementary school level particularly, since the child's comprehension of his own needs is seriously defective, interest is a deceptive and dangerous guide in determining the content of the curriculum. As there are many things which children desire but should not learn, so there are others which they must learn whether they so desire or not. It is fortunately true, however, that in large measure the interests of children are mobile. On no other assumption can one explain the wide range of activities in which children spontaneously engage among peoples at various stages of culture. The desire for social recognition drives the child to participation in the life of his group, whether that group is a savage tribe or a modern industrial community. Under skillful teaching, therefore, the pupil can ordinarily be stimulated to take interest in the learning of those things which the conditions of life require; and in the service of economy this should be achieved wherever possible. The interests of children are a condition of efficient learning, but they do not furnish a sufficient and trustworthy guide in the choice of those activities on which the perpetuation and advancement of society rest. Educational authorities cannot thus abdicate their high office, shirk the responsibility of basing the elementary school program on a thorough understanding of the needs of social life, and shift their burden to the shoulders of children.

Why must the school consider the work of other agencies? In the fourth place, the elementary school should not duplicate the work of the informal educational agencies. There are many activities which serve to induct the child into the life of the group, which are adjusted to his capacities, and which appeal to his interests, which deserve no place in this institution. The elementary school, dedicated as it is to the purposes of education, is not the only agency for the education of children. The home, the church, and the community all bear heavy educational burdens; and wherever there is associated activity education as a social function proceeds. It has been said that the school is life, and there is a profound truth contained in this statement; but in a certain sense the school is more than life and less than life. It is a specialized agency. Its great function is to supplement and perfect life as it is conditioned by the immediate and pressing demands of the environment. And, unless it absorbs the functions of all other educational agencies and takes complete charge of the child, this will remain the great function of the school. At present, the school is a sheltered place from which certain of the rigors and severities, and perhaps some of the fullness, of life are banished. Here, without hindrance, adjustments may be made to the deeper, wider, more complex, and more permanent realities. Clearly, the leisure which nature has intended for children and which a wise society recognizes through its special educational agencies should not be consumed in aimless dissipation. The elementary school has a special function to perform which can be performed only through a most carefully selected and organized curriculum.

Why must the curriculum reflect the basic human activities? In addition to these four criteria which should be applied to the selection of the subject-matter to be taught in any educational institution, there is a fifth principle which must be recognized in the curriculum of the elementary school. For the most part, the activities of this school should be drawn from the great common interests of men. However essential to the welfare of society an activity may be, if it implies occupational specialization, it can have no secure place in the elementary school. While it is as necessary to provide for the varying capacities of children as for the differences among older persons, and while the pupils should be allowed freedom for exploring their aptitudes and for developing their recreational interests, there is little room here for that differentiation of the curriculum which points towards special careers and which characterizes the higher education. The central task of the elementary school is to insure the acquisition of those fundamental skills, knowledges, appreciations, dispositions, and powers which all members of the group must possess (at least in some degree) if they are to live together in a relation of mutual benefit and enjoy to the maximum the fruits of collective enterprise. This institution should provide that common culture through which the group is integrated and given direction.

How can educational experience be classified? The general criteria have now been considered. The way is cleared for the discussion of the more practical question: What are the specific activities which conform to these criteria and which are consequently entitled to a place in the elementary school? To this query, since conditions change from age to age and from place to place, no absolute answer can be given. The educational needs of a people can be determined only for a given level or stage of culture. Yet in every modern society the elementary school should include within its curriculum materials representative of each of the six great departments of human interest: health, family, industry, citizenship, recreation, and religion. In the presentation of these materials economical instruction demands that attention be directed to three aspects of educational experience or three types of subject-matter.

First, there are the simple, concrete, and purposeful experiences which bring the child into direct contact with the immediate world of sense and which are necessary to the formation of the elementary habits and dispositions. Through these activities is given the intimate personal experience upon which all further education depends. Second, there are those mediating activities which do not afford first-hand experience of the natural and social environment but which through symbolism and communication, oral and written speech, provide the wider setting, interpretation, and idealization of the concrete experiences gained in the first group of activities. Through them by means of language the pupil is introduced to the concrete experiences of others; and he thus participates vicariously in the essential experiences of the race. Third, there are the activities which are necessary for imparting those tools of knowledge upon which the successful pursuit of the first and second groups of activities is intimately dependent. It will be obvious that reference is here made to the language and number arts. To the extent that incidental learning in the home, the community, and the school fails to give the necessary facility in the use of these tools, they must receive the formal attention of the school.

While these three aspects of educational experience must be clearly recognized in the elementary school curriculum, care must be taken lest they be formalized. The threefold classification is made purely for purposes of exposition and not to suggest the organization of the course of study. The concrete activities, the vicarious experience, and the tools of knowledge should not be rigorously separated in the school. The contrary policy should be consciously pursued wherever possible. In sound school practice all three types of activities should be closely related and integrated into a unified educational program in which they are merely three different aspects of a single developing experience. With this caution in mind we may now proceed to consider the educational function to be performed by each of these classes of experience.

What provision should be made for concrete experiences? The fundamental principle on which all education rests is that the modification of behavior proceeds through the activity of the organism as it responds to the stimuli of the natural and social environment. The school, therefore, should be a center of abundant and eager activity. To be educative this activity must be purposeful; it must represent an effort on the part of the pupil to attain some legitimate educational end. Otherwise an acquired power may actually fail to integrate with the rest of the child's experience and to function in his life. Care must also be taken lest the aim of the pupil be different from that for which the school is working. Frequently the purposes of children are at variance with the purposes of formal education, although this disagreement is only apparent on careful analysis. For example, the educational aim of a game may be to teach the pupil how to coöperate with others, while the motivation of the pupil may be merely to dominate his classmates or to impress the teacher with his own power. In the elementary school, in those early years of childhood when the mental life of the individual is in its first stages of growth, it follows that, if the work of this institution is to find a place in the life of the child, these experiences should definitely originate from the concrete world of nature and society. There is no short cut to the deeper understanding which should belong to the more mature years. In its simplest and most primitive form knowledge means power to do; it means familiarity with men and things. Activity of a social nature which has not been rendered meaningless by divorce from the child's experience must therefore constitute the foundation for the development of a sound educational program.

How should the concrete experiences reflect the enlargement of social life?   In the past, before community life had been greatly affected by the advance of modern industry and the integration of society, children were incidentally supplied with a sufficient range of contacts of this simple and concrete order to furnish an adequate experiential basis for the formal work of the school.   At a very early age they entered into the life of the community and engaged in its occupations.   Since this life was neither complex nor highly differentiated, these experiences were ample for providing that simple understanding of the world which men required. The special educational agency therefore could assume the concrete knowledge necessary and confine its meager energies to the task of teaching the three R's.

But whether the school of the past met the limited needs of its day as well or better than the school of the present is meeting the larger needs of modern society, is a purely academic question.   The significant fact is that the school, if it is to perform its educational task, must supplement the simple activities incidentally provided.   Definite provision must be made for those concrete experiences which furnish the only route by which the child may gain an understanding of the world and adjust himself to the conditions of contemporary life.   In the early grades, constant care being taken lest the service of the informal agencies be duplicated, ample provision must be made for these basic and direct contacts with the world.   As Dewey and others have suggested, children should be given the opportunity of working with paper, cardboard, wood, leather, cloth, yarns, clay, sand, and metal; they should learn how to use the simpler tools, such as knife, needle, thread, fork, pan, stove, broom, hammer, saw, file, plane, and spade; they should become familiar with the processes of folding, cutting, pricking, measuring, moulding, modeling, pattern-making, heating, and cooling; they should participate in gardening, cooking, sewing, printing, weaving, painting, drawing, singing, dramatization, story-telling, and outdoor excursions; they should take part in a great variety of plays and games. All of these activities should proceed in an environment essentially social in its character.

How should these concrete experiences reflect the six great fields of human interest? All these concrete activities should center about the six great fields of human interest. They should not be chosen at random from all the possible simple experiences of children, but rather from the standpoint of their contribution to an understanding and appreciation of the forces which condition man's existence. A conscious effort must be made in the elementary school to introduce activities which provide opportunities for direct participation in all great life interests that come within the range of childhood. In the first place, much can be done at this level of instruction to further health. The basic task of insuring the formation of health habits is peculiarly the task of the elementary school. At every turn there is opportunity to stimulate children to form sound and to correct unsound health habits. This work cannot be started too early in the grades. In the second place, the promotion of the family life may be undertaken here in a simple way. Through coöperation with the home the school may contribute to the development of those elementary social dispositions necessary to a happy family life, and many of the activities of the home may be brought into the school either in work or in play. In the third place, from the economic life may be selected an unlimited number of valuable educational activities. This basic human interest, neglected in the past, merits close attention. Although conscious development of commercial skills should be postponed to a later period, through the introduction of various forms of vocational and economic activities and through experience derived from contact with the local industries valuable dispositions and attitudes toward the economic life can be formed. In the fourth place, many activities should be introduced into the elementary school for the purpose of advancing the civic life. It is perhaps in developing the ability to live together in groups that the elementary school provides the richest opportunities. Everywhere in the school we see groups of children. They work in groups and they play in groups. Here is an unrivaled opportunity for children to acquire those habits, dispositions, and attitudes that are necessary for adaptation to life in the Great Society. Here also, as the children of all classes, races, and sects mingle together on terms of equality, many of our social problems manifest themselves in simplified form. In this social life of the school is a body of experience which might well serve to give unity and direction to the entire elementary school program. In the fifth place, the enriching of the recreational life requires the introduction of a great variety of play activities. With a longer school day much more than at present can be done in developing worthy habits of recreation. In the past the recess period, although, as a rule, it has received but the most perfunctory attention from the educational authorities, has rendered a valued service. But in the main it has worked negatively in relieving the tedium of the school rather than positively in developing happy recreational dispositions. The short school day, however, does not justify the limited attention given to music, dancing, companionship, and the recreational arts. From the first grade to the last these activities should find a place in the school. In the sixth place, through simple and concrete experiences the program of the elementary school should foster the religious life. To what extent religious rites and ceremonies should be introduced into the public schools is a matter of dispute; but that the religious life of the child is greatly affected by what goes on in the school cannot be disregarded. The underlying atmosphere should certainly be deeply and sincerely religious. Only from such an environment may children be expected to develop those attitudes of reverence, and serenity, and gain that elevation of purpose and character which mark the religious nature.

How has the elementary school unconsciously furthered non-scholastic aims? This program of concrete social activities which has been outlined contains no radical principle. Already it exists in unorganized form or is implied in the practices of the school. The great need is merely to make purposive and effective that which circumstances have created. The growth of the elementary school and the extension of the period of compulsory education have conspired to produce a situation whose educational possibilities teachers have been slow to realize. The school conventions must be changed. To-day the emphasis is still placed on those traditional instructional practices which were the product of the narrowly circumscribed school and the limited educational opportunities of several generations ago. It should not be forgotten that the elementary school is a little community possessing some measure of stability and permanence. Into this institution are gathered all the children of a neighborhood, and here these children live together for a longer or shorter period. This situation presents the educational opportunity. Teachers, following the conventions, have consciously taught these children many things — reading, writing, and arithmetic — but unknowingly they have probably taught them more. At least, the boys and girls in our schools have been allowed to learn much that is not mentioned in the formal curriculum. Proper consideration has not been given to the implications of the fact that the child brings his entire self into the school and that whatever he does effects some change in his native and acquired equipment of instincts, habits, and dispositions. As a child learns to read he may form certain habits that either violate or conform to the laws of health; as he plays with his classmates he may develop certain sex tendencies; as he loiters in the halls he may acquire certain desires for extravagant consumption; as he competes for marks in spelling he may develop certain social dispositions; as he studies arithmetic he may form certain standards for appreciating mural decorations; and as he converses with his teachers he may acquire certain religious attitudes. Ever since schools were first established this process has been going on in some measure; the educational situation to-day requires that it be given conscious direction.

Why must the elementary school abandon its narrow intellectual emphasis? The view presented here is that the emphasis in the elementary school should be less intellectual and academic than has ordinarily been supposed. This is not because the value of intellectual interests and intellectual guides is discounted, but rather because their place in life is not so great as the procedures of the school imply. Only in academic haunts is it assumed that the core of human experience is intellectual; and only in scholastic cloisters is it taken for granted that society can be ruled by logic, or a group of men by rational motives. To an individual whose education has developed merely the intellectual side of his nature the behavior of men, and consequently the behavior of society, which is guided by love and hate, joy and sorrow, would be incomprehensible. Too great emphasis on intelligence makes intelligence itself sterile. Furthermore, although man may be said to possess an intellectual urge, intelligence is ordinarily instrumental in the satisfaction of other drives. The intellectual resources of the average individual are not great, the forces which control him are decidedly irrational, and the reflective processes are customarily the handmaiden of instinct, habit, and desire. All of these considerations make one very slow to set up purely intellectual standards for the common school. Because of the extraordinary contribution which intelligence makes to the solution of human problems, this institution must emphasize it as much as possible; but the school can emphasize intelligence only in the measure that its varying population possess it. Knowledge, at whose shrine the school has always worshiped, may be mischievous, barren, or fertile depending on the way in which it is used and the end which it serves. If the school is to function effectively, it must insure the formation of habits, dispositions, and attitudes. These cannot be economically formed unless activities which give them expression are introduced into the curriculum. Knowledge does not automatically eventuate in social behavior and influence the formation of character.

How should the elementary school provide vicarious experiences? The second group of activities which must be given a place in the program of the elementary school will now be considered. The child must be led to participate vicariously in the essential experiences of the race. The concrete personal experiences which are gained through direct and immediate contact with the world of men and things are insufficient in themselves. They alone cannot provide the education required by the conditions of modern life. They must be placed in a wider setting than can be obtained directly through the eye, the ear, and the hand; they must be given a deeper interpretation than the immediate experience contains. Habits must not be confined to their mere executive phase, but must be translated into ideals that they may find expression in conduct as new situations are faced. The concrete activity is only the beginning of mental growth, and the peculiar function of the school is to provide those optimum conditions through which this growth may proceed.

How must concrete experience be made the vehicle of vicarious experience?   The concrete experience must be made the vehicle for adaptation to the wider environment; the mental life of the child must not be confined in the narrow bounds of this experience.   The final educational outcome of such an activity, if it is not consciously related to the larger world into which the child should grow, may be exceedingly limited.   Through analysis and synthesis, and through communication with others, whether by oral speech or by the written page, the sensory experience should be expanded and filled with meaning.   In this way the observation and thought of others may be brought to bear on the solution of the child's own problems, and these problems with their solutions may be viewed in their more general aspect.   An illustration will make this point clear.   The civic life must be improved through the development of citizens in the schools.   In the attainment of this end certain civic habits must be formed through participation in the social life of the school.   But there is no guarantee that these habits, formed within the school, will function outside.   In fact in many instances, unless the most specific attention is given to the process, there will be little transfer from the one situation to the other.   It is the function of the school to take these concrete situations, involving the formation of civic habits, and show their intimate relation to situations of a similar nature in the larger world.   The immediate life of the school and the community must be systematically and conscientiously expanded.   This must be achieved lest habits of action, feeling, and thought, developed with great care within the confines of the school, are not available for use in the Great Society.

The activities included in this second group are those through which the child's own immediate experiences are enriched by the experiences of others. In adjusting himself to his environment and in adding to the meaning of life the individual must receive the assistance of the accumulated wisdom of the race. As soon as the child is capable of communicating with his elders, this process of vicarious learning begins. Of course, from the very first the infant, in the satisfaction of his wants, unknowingly receives the benefits of racial experience. His food may be selected in accordance with principles discovered by careful experimentation, his clothing may be fashioned in recognition of the laws of hygiene, the discharge of various bodily functions may be so ordered as to conform to some tested plan, and his whole environment may reflect the experience of countless generations. But in instances of this character the infant is the passive recipient of the benefits which flow from the social heritage. Through the experience of others his life is preserved, his wants are satisfied, and even his habits are formed, but that experience remains without intellectual significance to him. Only when the child begins to communicate with others is he enabled to utilize their experience in solving his problems and to enter fully into his social inheritance.

In what moulds has the social heritage been preserved? This social heritage, the product of ages of living, has been preserved through some form of language, through oral or written speech, through number, drawing, painting, moulding, or sculpture. It is crystallized in the material instrumentalities of civilization, in tools, machines, and dwellings, in museums, monuments, and libraries. It is woven into the thoughts, feelings, and actions of men. Much of this experience is transmitted to the child through the simpler natural and social contacts gained in those concrete activities which form the basis of all mental growth. But these contacts do not carry on their surface the total meaning which is resident within them, nor do they of themselves provide for the full utilization of the related racial experience. These simple activities must be elaborated and unfolded before the pupil in order that he may see their wider significance and appreciate their deeper meaning. For this the educator will have to go to the great human records in which knowledge, thought, appreciation, and aspiration are preserved: history, geography, science, literature, music, art, and philosophy. From these sources come those supplementary experiences which provide for the direct and simple contact, the wider setting, interpretation, and idealization. Through history the child may be led back to the beginnings of civilization, he may be a spectator of the origins and fortunes of nations, races, and institutions. Through geography he may travel from his own neighborhood into an ever-expanding world in which he sees diverse men and peoples adjusting themselves to the forces of nature. Through science, natural and social, he may be given a deeper and broader understanding of the natural and social phenomena about him. Through literature, music, and art he may be drawn into a world of beauty which has been created by the artists of the past. Through philosophy, gauged to the level of his understanding, he may be introduced to a consideration of the meaning and purpose of life.

How has the form of these moulds hampered elementary instruction? In the light of this analysis of the educational necessity of affording the child opportunity to enter vicariously into the experience of the race, we cannot do better than examinine the effectiveness of the present school. For transmitting to youth the essence of the social heritage, this agency has always been considered important. The achievement of this end has always been regarded as one of the primary functions of the school. But in performing this function it has been handicapped by the form in which knowledge is preserved. Only for purposes of economical conservation and reference and for the promotion of mature study and research has the racial experience been organized into separate bodies of knowledge which become increasingly numerous and increasingly isolated. It is only necessary to point out that all of these branches record a common body of facts — the thoughts, feelings, and actions of men. In this sense all knowledge is history and is unified through its common origin. The school is too prone to assume that the arbitrary lines of demarcation drawn by specialists must be followed in the teaching of children. Such an assumption can only be fruitful of educational error and devastating to sound educational practice. The school has consequently fallen far short of its opportunity in unlocking to the child the rich stores of human experience. Because they are taken out of the human setting which gives them meaning, history, geography, science and art remain isolated and abstract disciplines and assume an artificial aspect.

How can this cultural experience be made available at the elementary level? If this heritage is to be made available, particularly at the elementary school level, it must be removed from these logical containers to which it has been consigned for preservation. It must be aired in the breezes of experience and brought back into the currents of life. The child and his activities are at the center of the educative process. Hence materials drawn from these various bodies of knowledge can be made educative only as they expand and make significant concrete activities selected according to criteria set down in Problem 18. History, geography, science, and art are without meaning unless they serve to solve some problem or to satisfy some need. In the strict sense one individual cannot give his experience to another.

All that a teacher can do for his pupil is to prevent participation in certain unprofitable or harmful experiences and provide opportunity to engage in certain valuable activities with a minimum of wasted effort.   Insight, which is the precipitate of living, cannot be passed directly from teacher to pupil.   This does not mean that the heuristic method of instruction should be followed and that the child should be required to rediscover and re-create in his brief life the discoveries and products of the past.   Such a proposal is obviously absurd.   It does mean, however, that these vicarious experiences, if they are to possess any educational value, must develop out of those concrete experiences which must always serve as the basis for mental growth.

Why must the school keep in close sociological touch with the life of the community?   If we assume that the activities of the school, whether of the simpler or the more complex type, should center about the great human interests, there remains the difficult question: Since it is quite impossible to include them all, what particular activities should be selected?   The school must not attempt what is already well done by some other agency.   The social deficiencies of a people must therefore be discovered, and activities must be introduced into the elementary school accordingly.   This means that in a changing society, conscious of its own needs, the curriculum will be undergoing continual and intelligently directed change.   For the purpose of discovering its educational needs, the progressive community will conduct a perpetual survey of its activities.   The school will thus become the agency through which the practices of a people are gradually purified and adapted to the needs of the world.   According to this conception of elementary education the common school is the institution through which the best intelligence of society may operate to insure the most satisfactory adjustment to the basic conditions of life.

How should the elementary school provide for the acquisition of the tools of knowledge? The third group of activities remains to be considered — the language and number arts. Only through the mediation of these arts can the individual participate vicariously in the experience of others. Upon them therefore the successful pursuit of the first two sets of activities is intimately dependent. With the mastery of these tools of knowledge, as they have been styled, the elementary school from the day of its origin has been largely concerned. To-day this remains one of the primary functions of the elementary school; and so it must ever remain unless either civilization or human nature undergoes some profound change which would alter the whole basis of life. In the twentieth century our dependence on reading, writing, and arithmetic is much greater than it was in the seventeenth. In fact the modern world, with its complex industrial systems and its great political organizations, would fall of its own weight, if it lost the support derived from the possession of these abilities on the part of the great mass of the population. If the people of the United States were to forget the alphabet, this nation would rapidly break up into small primitive groups, famine would sweep the land from ocean to ocean, our great cities would soon be depopulated, society would be forced back into some simpler and less productive form of industrial economy, and the residents of New York State would be an alien race to the natives of the Mississippi Valley. The great significance of these acquisitions to the intimate personal life of the individual may also be stressed. Consider, for example, how reading makes possible an unlimited enrichment of experience. He who can read, wherever his physical lot may be cast, need not live in a narrow and circumscribed world. To him may come the thoughts, aspirations and experiences of mankind. Since these tools of knowledge are not readily acquired as incidents in the process of living, explicit attention must be given to their acquisition. The elementary school must teach the language arts.

What major issues does the teaching of the language arts raise? With regard to the position these language arts should occupy in the elementary school, there are three questions which merit consideration. First, what is the relative importance of the different tools of knowledge? Second, what standard of attainment should be set up for each as the goal towards which to strive? Third, to what extent should these arts be taught as separate and distinct subjects in the formal curriculum? These questions will now be considered in order.

What is the relative importance of the several tools of knowledge? Of all the language arts, oral speech is decidedly the most important in the life of the ordinary individual. It is the primary art out of which in the development of both the race and the individual all the rest are evolved. By means of this instrument man converses with his fellows and through its sub-vocal use he engages in the processes of reflection. But, in accordance with conventional school practice, many would maintain that it merits little attention in the school. They would argue that the normal child, by constantly participating in oral speech from earliest infancy acquires a high degree of proficiency during the pre-school age. While there is a measure of truth in this contention, we would take the unequivocal position that one of the major tasks of the elementary school is the development and refinement of oral speech. Nurtured, as he is, in a restricted and limited environment the ordinary public school pupil, particularly the child of immigrant parentage, brings to the formal agency an oral speech full of imperfections. At the best his practice abounds in vulgarities and grossness and is susceptible of much improvement. Especially should attention be directed to imparting facility in the uses of this art which further companionship.

Next to oral speech in importance stands reading. Concerning the general importance of this art sufficient comment has already been made. Ability to read differs from oral speech in that, only in the rarest cases, can it be acquired without the help of the school or some form of definite instruction. Furthermore, there are two forms of reading, oral and silent, which must be clearly distinguished. In modern life, with its practically unlimited demands on the reading abilities, the latter is by far the more important. In the school, therefore, much attention must be given to the cultivation of silent reading; and it must not be taught as a handmaiden or a companion of the oral form. Psychologically it is a different process, and the development of improper reading habits is the almost certain consequence of teaching silent reading through the oral approach.

The writing of the vernacular is probably the third of the language arts to be stressed in the elementary school. This complex ability presents the threefold aspect of penmanship, spelling, and composition. Composition, the essential part of the process, is dependent on the more mechanical abilities of penmanship and spelling. To all these processes attention must be given, but the common emphasis in the elementary school should be reversed. Handwriting and orthography should be definitely subordinated to expression.

Finally, there is the problem of arithmetic, the problem of acquiring the ability to manipulate number and quantitative concepts. This ability is clearly required by any one who would live successfully in the industrial society of to-day with its complicated system of exchange and its constant demands for a knowledge of numerical relations. It is doubtful, however, if there is any clear justification for the serious introduction of arithmetic into the early grades as is customary at present. The extent to which this ability enriches the experience of the child and the extent to which it fosters social coöperation, are extremely limited. This raises an important educational question, Would it not be wise to postpone the teaching of all but the most elementary arithmetic until the later grades or, in other words, until children have reached that stage of maturity at which number concepts can be adequately grasped and more rapidly taught. Teaching arithmetic in the early grades is an anachronism. It is a survival from an age when the school career of the child was much shorter and more precarious than it is to-day.

In summary the following propositions may be set down. The several tools of knowledge should not receive equal emphasis in the elementary school; the literary arts are of incomparably greater importance than arithmetic; the former, because of their great value in enlarging and enriching the world of the child, should be introduced very early into the curriculum; the manipulation of number concepts, on the other hand, should probably receive little emphasis in the lower grades; and especially oral speech and silent reading, the two basic instruments of social intercourse and thought, should be effectively and fully taught.

What should determine standards of attainment? The second question regarding the position of the language arts in the elementary school must now be considered. What standards of attainment should be set up as the goals towards which to strive? In the past there has been a distinct tendency for artless perfectionism to dominate the thought and practice of education. It has been assumed, for instance, that in oral reading every child should become a Daniel Webster, that in penmanship he should acquire a perfect and stereotyped hand, that in spelling he should spell all but the most highly technical words of the English language, that in written composition he should rival the masters of style, and that in arithmetic he should lay the foundations of a mathematical career. Such academic phantasy is disastrous to clear thinking on educational values. Standards of achievement must not be derived from the pious aspirations of pedagogues, but must rather be evolved from a close study of the conditions and demands of life considered in the light of the measured capabilities of children. In modern society the ordinary individual seldom indulges in oral reading, has little need for writing a perfect hand, is called upon to spell only the words used in his writing, is unqualified by both nature and circumstance for the creation of literature, and requires but the simple arithmetical processes in the customary transactions of life. It should be explicitly understood, however, that standards should not uncritically reflect present social practice. This practice is full of error and folly. Rather a wholly different principle must serve. Standards must be derived from a study of great common needs. In some measure present practice is the product of insufficient, unsound, and even bad education; the function of good education is not to perpetuate, but rather to modify and improve this practice. Defensible standards must be formulated in the light of the possibilities resident in human nature, the prevailing conditions of life, and an acceptable and critical social and moral philosophy.

Should the tools of knowledge be taught incidentally? A final question concerning the teaching of the language arts remains to be examined. To what extent should the language arts be taught as separate and distinct subjects in the formal curriculum? From our method of presentation the reader has perhaps been led to the conclusion that reading, writing, and arithmetic should be formally taught as separate and distinct subjects. Such a conclusion is without foundation. The different tools of knowledge have been given this separate treatment merely for the purpose of making explicit our position with reference to their importance. At this point we cannot discuss in any detail the methods which should be employed in securing the desired degree of mastery. We are rather insisting that these levels be attained. A word concerning method, however, needs to be said in order to clarify the issue which has been raised. It is our contention that, wherever possible, the interests of economy will be served by relating reading, writing, spelling, speaking, and figuring quite definitely to the more meaningful social experiences. Undoubtedly much time and energy has been wasted in the schools of the past by pursuing what superficially appears to be the economical course. By demanding of the child a slavish attention to the mastery of forms and mechanisms from which all significant content and purpose have been abstracted, the schoolmaster has unwittingly lowered the motivation of the learning process. Command over these tools is to be acquired economically only by employing them in an experience which is developing and which is worthwhile in itself. This does not mean that reading, for example, from the very beginning should be made purely incidental to participation in other activities. Certain studies of the rate of learning prove the contrary. The processes involved are far too complex to permit of such an easy solution. Reading is a very difficult art to acquire, and can only be developed efficiently under the most careful supervision of a trained teacher. A child might learn to read without such guidance, but the extended investigations of Judd and others show that in all probability he would form some very bad habits. The question therefore reduces itself to this: To what extent is it necessary to introduce into the elementary school under the conditions of artificial motivation direct drill on language and number forms? To this question, since much depends on the intelligence of the individual child, no single and absolute answer can be given. The indirect learning will be almost sufficient for the gifted, while a considerable amount of direct drill will necessarily have to be provided for the less fortunately endowed. In each case, with a view to securing the largest possible educational result with the smallest expenditure of energy, there will have to be a careful analysis of practice and a delicate weighing of values.

How must different levels of ability be recognized? According to the foregoing discussion, in the curriculum of the elementary school provision should be made for those concrete experiences upon which all mental growth ultimately rests, for those more complex activities through which the child enters vicariously into the essential experiences of the race, and for those more formal activities by means of which ordinary facility in the use of the tools of knowledge is acquired. Before leaving this discussion we must consider the basic question regarding the organization of this program for different levels of ability. The elementary school is frankly non-selective in its character. Within its enrollment may be found practically the entire gamut of intelligence and the whole range of capacity. Into the first grade of the school come the bright, the average, and the stupid, as well as the extremes of genius and feeble-mindedness. Such diverse individuals cannot all engage in the same activities on equal terms. The ideal procedure, according to some, would be to return to individual instruction; but this, at least for the present, is extremely difficult. In many types of activities, because of certain social values that flow from group instruction, it would be positively undesirable. The need for economy requires that children be taught in groups, and under these conditions sound instruction in some subjects can be given only in relatively homogeneous classes.

In response to the demands growing out of this situation the schools have been very roughly graded according to chronological age and different attainment levels. So crude has been this classification, however, that children of widely differing abilities, and even of very dissimilar ages and attainments, have been brought together and taught in a single group. Only by varying the rate of promotion has any formal provision been made for children of varying capacities. While in the smaller schools, in so far as individual instruction cannot be provided, differences of capacity will always have to be taken care of by thus advancing the brighter pupils to higher chronological age levels and holding the slower children in the lower levels, in the larger schools a different procedure should be followed. Here, variation in the rate of promotion should be strongly tempered by more homogeneous classification at each age. Under such a plan, age being defined as a composite of the stages reached in anatomical, physiological, psychological, and social growth, children would be admitted to the elementary school at approximately six years. At each age level, for the purpose of securing a relatively homogeneous grouping with respect to the particular trait or set of traits required in the learning processes involved, a careful classification would be effected. For the most part, a child would be promoted regularly from year to year and be kept with children of about his own age. The activities in which children would engage at each level would be adjusted to their abilities. There would be a minimum curriculum which all would be expected to master. Those in the slowest group would cover this minimum only. For each of the other groups, according to the endowments of their members, the program would be enriched.[1] The

[1] By enrichment is not meant the inclusion of a larger amount of the same

current meaning of grade would be destroyed. But, if the educational needs of children were more effectively met, this would be no serious loss. In many of the activities of the curriculum, in those of a purely social or recreational nature, in living the common life of the school, where the possession of intellectual gifts is not the decisive factor, children of different levels should be brought into association. Thus, the development of unwholesome social attitudes would be prevented; and children would come to recognize differences in mental endowment in the same objective way that they note differences in physical traits.

What is the function of the elementary school? In conclusion and in summary it may be said that an ideal elementary school would bring together for educational purposes, regardless of social status and native endowment, all the children of the community. Under the supervision of men and women carefully trained for their work these immature members would be inducted into the life of modern society. Through participation in activities which would insure the acquisition of those basic skills, habits, attitudes, dispositions, ideals, and powers required by all members of the group this central purpose of the elementary school would be achieved. The core of these activities, and the force which would give them reality, would be the concrete life of the school and of the community. The life of the former, as much as the life of the latter, would reflect the great fields of human interest. The enlargement and interpreta-

---

grade of material. To advocate such a practice would be to commit an educational crime. The brighter children must be provided with those experiences which develop their powers. This might well mean the introduction into their program of such special subjects as foreign language, advanced mathematics, or any branch of learning which requires long and rigorous study. On the higher levels this must be permitted, even though such practice may appear to violate the central purpose of the elementary school.

tion of these concrete activities would make necessary the elementary mastery of the language and number arts, and through them the reading, imaginative study, and appreciation of those human experiences which have found expression in history, geography, social science, natural science, literature, art, and philosophy. In the early years of the school the activities would be of a simple and direct character, while in the later years the emphasis would be increasingly on the more complex and ideational experiences. At first, there would have to be relatively complete dependence on the immediate environment; but it would be the purpose of education to lead the child step by step to the larger physical and social world and to the wider and deeper realities of life. Not only would age levels be recognized, but also ability levels at each age. In this institution children would remain for approximately six years, or until they reached the period of early adolescence. Throughout the elementary school the great emphasis would be placed on making those fundamental adjustments to life which are secured through habits, attitudes, and ideals. In a simple way, and in the measure possible, the elementary school would seek to further health, promote the family life, order and humanize the economic life, advance the civic life, enrich the recreational life, and foster the religious life.

ADDITIONAL PROBLEMS FOR DISCUSSION

1. How does the almost complete absence of competing agencies in America make the elementary school a powerful force for social integration and for the propagation of the democratic ideal?
2. Why is the conventional elementary school in America an eight-year school? What are the tendencies operating to reduce the elementary course to six years?
3. How may the changing conception of the function of elementary education be expected to alter the emphasis on the three R's in the curriculum?
4. How has the true purpose of elementary education been subordinated to the demands of preparation for secondary education?

5. How does the extreme heterogeneity (social, cultural, and racial) of the elementary school population make necessary the duplication of work which for some pupils is being performed effectively by other agencies? Is there an argument here for private education as well as increasing differentiation within the public elementary school?

6. From the standpoint of equipping the individual to perform the common and unspecialized activities of life, criticize the present practices in teaching: (a) arithmetic, (b) formal English grammar, (c) oral reading, (d) spelling, (e) silent reading, (f) physiology, (g) place geography.

7. How would you criticize the conventional curriculum of the elementary school from the standpoint of its contribution to effective participation in, and adequate understanding of, the six basic activities discussed in Part Three?

8. What can be said for and against the attractive educational doctrine that nothing should be taught a child until such time as he feels a distinct need for it?

9. Why is there grave danger that formal education on the elementary school level will, as the name signifies, be formal and unmeaningful?

10. How has the advance of our scientific knowledge of the processes involved in reading revealed the danger attending undirected "picking up" of reading outside the school? How does this factor apply to other fields of learning?

11. What are the reasons for the change in emphasis with respect to oral and silent reading?

12. Show how the undue influence of the intellectual ideal has been especially harmful to the true aims of a universal elementary scheme of education.

13. What educational objections may be raised to classification by intelligence levels? Can these objections be met?

14. In what respects should the content of instruction employed in the elementary schools of a democratic society differ from that used in the schools of an autocracy?

PROBLEM 20

WHAT IS THE FUNCTION OF THE SECONDARY SCHOOL?

Why is the public high school peculiarly a product of American life? — Why does the secondary school occupy a key position in the education of a people? — Why is the American secondary school at the crossroads? — What two sets of activities constitute the program of the high school? — What is the official program? — What is the old secondary school tradition? — How has secondary education been socially and intellectually selective? — How is the high school abandoning the selective principle? — How may universal secondary education be justified? — How does the extension of secondary education involve the abandoning of traditional notions? — What are the evils of college domination? — How should the conflict between secondary school and college be resolved? — What forces have created the junior high school? — What should be the criteria for the selection of the curriculum of the enlarged secondary school? — What can the secondary school expect of elementary education? — What must be the basic function of the secondary school? — What are the universal needs in the field of health? — What are the universal needs in the field of family life? — What are the universal needs in the field of industry? — What are the universal needs in the field of citizenship? — What are the universal needs in the field of recreation? — What are the universal needs in the field of religion? — What types of experience will satisfy these six basic needs? — What concrete experiences are necessary at the secondary level? — What provision must be made at the secondary level for vicarious participation in the racial experience? — What attention should be given to the tools of knowledge at the secondary level? What provision must be made for differences in interest and vocational expectation ? — What provision must be made for differences in capacity? — What is the place of the languages and the abstract sciences? — Why must these subjects be restricted to a few students ? — Why must the secondary school foster adult education ? — What is the function of the secondary school in American society ?

Why is the public high school peculiarly a product of American life? In the public high school,[1] more than in any other

---

[1] Owing to the fact that the American public-school system is undergoing a process of radical reorganization, the meaning of secondary education is somewhat ambiguous. Under the conventional plan of organization

educational institution, has the genius of the American people expressed itself.   This school is peculiarly the offspring of our democratic conception of society.   Particularly during the last generation have the American people exhibited an enthusiasm for this social agency which causes it to occupy a unique place in the history of our institutions.   The lower and higher divisions of our educational system have been greatly influenced by the practices and experiences of other peoples.   The kindergarten, the elementary school, the college, the university, and the professional school have been developed in other countries; but the public high school, with its revolutionary implications and its central position in the system, is indigenous to the United States.   No claim is made that the American secondary school has no historical connection with those older forms of secondary education which are the heritage of the entire western world. But the contention may fairly be made that this institution, though still embodying many practices and conventions borrowed from older civilizations, has been erected on the foundations of a radically different educational and social philosophy.

Why does the secondary school occupy a key position in the education of a people?   As opposed to the somewhat traditional course pursued in the development of elementary and higher education, American society has followed a relatively uncharted course in the field of secondary educa-

the secondary school is a four-year school based on an eight-year elementary school, while under the new plan secondary education embraces the upper six years of a twelve-year system, or possibly the upper eight years of a fourteen-year system.   These six or eight years are divided into a junior and senior division of three or four years each.   With this reorganization, though its precise form is still uncertain, the writers are in sympathy.   They consequently think of secondary education as covering at least a six-year period which roughly coincides with the period of adolescence.   But in this discussion, when reference is made to conventional practice, the term secondary education will be used.

tion.   The reasons for this fact will now be considered. The secondary school, more than any other educational institution, reflects the controlling ideals and purposes of the social order.   Radically different societies must have radically different conceptions of the scope and nature of secondary education.   To discover the deeper social philosophy of a people, the question may well be asked: Who is admitted to the secondary schools?   The response to this question will be illuminating.   The elementary school of a democratic people may resemble quite closely the elementary school of an autocratically governed state, but the secondary school in a democratic society must be essentially different in form as well as in spirit.   Through this institution the privileges of a higher education are extended to the masses, and through this agency American society has registered its attitude towards such fundamental matters of social concern as the equalization of opportunity, the inheritance of privilege, the stability of classes, and the sources of leadership.   Since the secondary school occupies such a strategic position in the social order and since American secondary education has evolved as yet no adequate or consistent philosophy, the problem which heads this discussion is of immense social import and of extreme difficulty.

Why is the American secondary school at the crossroads? In considering the function of the secondary school, we could follow the course pursued in the discussion of elementary education and attempt a somewhat detailed survey of current practice in curriculum construction.   But this mode of approach, since courses of study in the secondary school have but little uniformity, would not be especially helpful. The curriculum of this institution is in a state of rapid change.   It reflects two traditions, the one representing the past and occupying an entrenched position, the other representing the future and engaged in marshaling its forces.

" The old is out of date;
The new is not yet born."

The one is definite and embodied in a program, the other is
indefinite and without settled expression. The new tradition is marked by conflicts and inconsistencies, and is
driven by contradictory impulses. In the field of secondary
education our age is an age of uncertainty and an age of experimentation. From this uncertainty and experimentation
will come new purposes and new programs. The forces at
work in modern society have torn the secondary school
loose from those moorings to which it has been securely
anchored for centuries. On account of this insecurity new
subjects or new principles of curriculum organization are
often eagerly and uncritically welcomed. In certain quarters any suggestion that holds out promise of educational
stability receives a hearty welcome and gains instant support. But in the absence of an accepted philosophy each
new proposal has its day, ofttimes a very short day, and
passes on to be resurrected and rechristened by a later generation of teachers. With remarkable swiftness, in that
margin of the curriculum where experimentation is permitted, subject follows subject into oblivion. Because of
this condition any detailed description of the activities of
the present secondary school is impossible. But that we
may be able to see more clearly the nature of this conflict
between the old and the new traditions and to estimate the
strength of the forces ranged on either side, the general
nature of the curriculum will receive examination. This
will enable us to grasp that modern conception of secondary
education which is emerging out of the welter of confused
and chaotic practices of the present day.

**What two sets of activities constitute the program of the
high school?** In the typical high school there are two sets of
activities which engage the attention and energy of the

students. There is the official program which both teacher and parent customarily regard as including all the important work of the school. Records of the performance of each student in these official activities are carefully preserved, are reported to the parents, and are made the subject of solemn discussion at the meetings of the members of the school staff. On the other hand, there are the activities which may be described as unofficial. They have been created very largely by the students themselves and, in spite of the apathy and even hostility of the authorities, they have come to occupy a secure position in the high school. Into these activities the students throw themselves with an enthusiasm that is in marked contrast with their response to the official curriculum. With eagerness they follow the course of these activities, with a solemnity paralleling that of the faculty meeting they discuss their participation in them, and in their annuals and other publications they carefully preserve a record of individual and group performance. This unofficial curriculum of athletics, societies, clubs, parties, and dances has been developed by the student as a compensation for submission to the requirements of the more formal and abstract curriculum of a highly selective and academic education.

What is the official program? In the official program the great emphasis is placed on language and mathematics. English, Latin, French, German, Spanish, algebra, and geometry constitute the backbone of this curriculum. This emphasis represents the older tradition to which reference was made in an earlier paragraph. In addition, a year or two of abstract science and several years of political and military history will usually be found in the high school. In the science, attention is focussed on an academic content rather than on human problems; and in the history, emphasis is placed on the ancient and medieval rather than on the

modern world.   These more recent subjects have for the
most part been forced to capitulate to the earlier tradition
and become in both content and procedure as much like the
older "respectable" subjects as possible.   In the small high
school, and most American high schools are not large, little
else will be offered in the official curriculum.   After provision has been made for the inclusion of these accepted subjects, the narrow margin of time that remains is only sufficient to give a little play to the idiosyncrasies of the principal
or some other dominating personality in the school or the
community.   If the institution is a large one, the situation
is quite different.   The offerings are likely to be very wide
indeed.   Often they will include a range of subject-matter
that would have been regarded a generation or two ago as
altogether too ambitious for the ordinary college.   These
subjects are organized rather loosely into curricula which
presumably are bound together by some unifying principle.
A generation ago the tendency existed to take some line of
academic interest as this binding principle; to-day the tendency is to exalt a special vocational interest.[1]   Since in
each curriculum or individual course of study only a portion
of the program is definitely prescribed, the student is
given a measure of freedom in the choice of subjects.   In
some cases the amount of the prescription is so small that
almost complete freedom is given the student.   In general,
it is not too much to say that the boy or girl in the public
high school either pursues the narrow curriculum of the past
or the loose and shifting curriculum of the present.   In
either case he drifts through the high school without securing
the unified, integrated, and serviceable educational experience for which we have pleaded in Part Three.

[1] Examples of the first type are the Latin, English, and Latin-Scientific
curricula which are still found in some high schools; while examples of the
second type are the college preparatory, normal, commercial, agricultural,
and industrial arts curricula which are common in the high school of to-day.

What is the old secondary school tradition?   At this point the old tradition of secondary education from which the high school is endeavoring to break away may well be scrutinized.   In spite of the recent changes in the curriculum, the activities of the high school remain predominantly literary and mathematical.   Whence came this curriculum?   Why does it remain with us?   The answer is simple.   In its origin the function of the secondary school of Western Europe was to prepare for the higher education, and this required first a literary, and later, a literary and mathematical training.   The reasons for this emphasis cannot be elaborated; it must suffice to point out that the Latin grammar school, the school which the American colonists brought from Europe, originated at a time when Latin was not only the language of learning and culture, but also the official language of the church and the state.   Against this narrow curriculum and the domination of the college the American people revolted in the second half of the eighteenth century by creating the private academy which greatly widened the scope of secondary education.   But this institution, originating as a protest against the old tradition, rapidly fell under its spell and survives to-day as a college preparatory institution of the most conservative type.

Toward the close of the first quarter of the nineteenth century the popular demand for a broader conception of secondary education again made itself felt.   There resulted the public high school which in its inception set its face against the college preparatory tradition.   Again the story is repeated.   As the high school was established in communities in which it was the sole secondary school, the influence of the college gradually asserted itself.   It was only natural that the more powerful classes in such communities, the classes who support the higher education, should insist that their children be prepared for college.   Since the college, in its infinite wisdom, has never been averse to making very definite prescriptions covering the previous education of those seeking entrance, the curriculum of the high school has virtually been dictated by the college. Particularly has this been true of the small school in which the limited teaching staff and the slender financial resources necessitate a narrow program. Whereas in the larger high school the new subject can simply be added to the old, in the smaller school, if the new is introduced, the old is perforce abandoned. Other forces, however, have been influential in perpetuating the tradition of language and mathematics. High-school teachers have been trained to teach such a curriculum, and its administration, since classes may be large and no elaborate equipment is required, can be made relatively inexpensive. For a certain highly selected type of mind it provides subject-matter which bears some relation to future needs. But even for the intellectually gifted it is a narrow curriculum; while for the masses of students now enrolled in the secondary school it can furnish but the travesty of an education — a travesty because it fails to make any obvious and direct contribution to the more intelligent and appreciative participation in the enterprise of improving the conditions under which man seeks to satisfy his physical, family, economic, civic, recreational, and religious needs. This somewhat severe arraignment of the older tradition brings us to a consideration of the changing conception of secondary education in the United States.

How has secondary education been socially and intellectually selective? Throughout the history of western Europe secondary education has been socially and intellectually selective in its character. Ordinarily, where education has reached an advanced stage of development, there has appeared in some form a dual system of schools. The two divisions of the system provide separate and parallel educational facilities for two groups of children of corresponding ages. The one division, from which the elementary school has developed, was designed to take care of the limited educational needs of the masses and provided but the barest rudiments of an education; and the other, composed of the secondary and the higher schools, was intended to provide an education for the classes. The object of the latter was to prepare the favored children of the aristocracy for those positions of leisure and leadership which they were destined to occupy. Between the two halves of this system there was no articulation. Hence, the opportunities of an advanced education were forever denied those whose educational careers were begun in the school of the common people. But secondary education has not only been socially selective, it has been psychologically selective as well. Its standards have been set well above the capacities of the average, and those who could not meet the requirements have been eliminated. To those who are fortunate both by nature and by nurture, the secondary school has been dedicated in the past.

Contrary to the common belief the public high school, as exact studies have revealed, is still decidedly selective. But both theory and practice are carrying us away from the selective principle. Early in the development of our educational institutions the dual system of education with its two distinct parallel divisions was abandoned. In its place, through the organization of a secondary school that articulated with the elementary school at one end and with the college at the other, a single continuous system was established. This revolutionary change will, in the history of intellectual and social emancipation, be regarded as one of the greatest, if not the greatest, cultural achievement of the American people. The significance of this change is, as yet, hardly realized, and is only just beginning to bear fruit.

The expansion of secondary education which was implicit in this departure from tradition was somewhat slow in coming. In fact, it is only within our own generation that the increasingly heterogeneous population of the high school has forced on the attention of educators the complete inadequacy and unsuitability of the old academic practices and conventions.

How is the high school abandoning the selective principle? During the last thirty years the four-year public high school has been developing at a rate without precedent in the history of educational institutions. Expenditures on secondary education have increased many fold since 1890; the number of high schools has grown from about twenty-five hundred to more than fifteen thousand; the high-school building has developed into the most imposing edifice found in many a community; the number of teachers has increased approximately nine hundred per cent; and in the more populous centers the curriculum has been greatly enlarged. Considered in isolation no one of these changes is especially important, but in combination they are extremely significant. They are symptomatic of that fundamental transformation which is radically altering the character of the high-school population. So extensive is this change in the student body that secondary education is being rapidly shifted from its old base to an essentially new foundation. In 1890 there were in the public high schools of the nation but two hundred thousand boys and girls; to-day there are well over two million. That this registration, however impressive it may be, does not represent universal secondary education, is apparent: there are between eight and nine million children of high-school age in the nation. For the most part the twenty-five per cent enrolled in this institution are selected from the fortunate classes and from those children possessing superior mental and moral endowments. These are the current facts, but in principle and in reality America is moving swiftly away from the conception of a selective secondary education toward the conception of a universal secondary education which without regard to either social status or native talent enrolls the adolescent. The ramparts erected by an aristocratic order for the defense of hereditary privilege have been forever swept away and the wider extension of educational opportunities at this level merely awaits a program. Already in some of the more progressive communities universal secondary education is all but realized, and in certain of the states legislation is breaking with the tradition of compulsory education for the elementary period only and is pointing towards the extension of some measure of secondary education to all.

How may universal secondary education be justified? This new conception which regards secondary education as the education for adolescence, in the same universal manner that elementary education is the education for childhood, requires some elaboration and defense. It means a definite move in the direction of the realization of one of the most commonly accepted American ideals, namely, the equalization of those opportunities which in the past have been so dependent on family circumstance. This is the defense offered by him who thinks in terms of individual rights. There is an equally powerful argument that may be advanced from the standpoint of social welfare. Society has become so complex that the limited and narrow education which was adequate in the past fails to fit the citizen to cope with the problems of the Great Society. In our somewhat extended analysis in Part Three we tried to make clear the magnitude and complexity of the tasks facing mankind. In every great division of human activity and interest formidable obstacles bar the way to human advance, difficulty vies with difficulty as problems press for solution, and both the good-will and the insight of men are overtaxed. The modern world demands effort on a higher level than men have reached. Undoubtedly a re-formed elementary education adjusted to the conditions of life as it is lived to-day, such as we have outlined in the preceding discussion, would go far towards narrowing the gulf that separates need from achievement. But the best possible elementary education could but narrow this gulf — it could never close it. Through an education that is intelligent the energies and idealism of adolescence must be released and harnessed. Those enthusiasms which are allowed to dissipate themselves in trifling activity and fruitless phantasy must through a wiser form of secondary education be yoked to the tasks of the world. If its problems are to be solved, society must fearlessly support that program which will enlist in the social service all the gifts of brain and heart which reside in its population. All men, even those of humble talents, must be made to interest themselves in the common weal. This is the promise that universal secondary education holds out to the community.

Has nature set definite limits to all forms of secondary education? One objection which is frequently raised to this expansion of secondary education deserves explicit attention. Nature, it is urged, has set definite limits to the extension of such opportunities. Since there are enormous differences in mental capacity, this argument seems to have some basis in fact. But in reality such an argument boldly begs the question. It assumes the finality of the content of the traditional secondary education, a content which was frankly developed to fit the capacities of a highly selected group of children. On analysis, this contention reduces itself to the pure tautology that an education which is adapted to a certain level of intelligence is only suited to that level. The advocates of universal secondary education need hold neither to the doctrine of native equality in mental endowment nor to the equally absurd doctrine that all secondary curricula must be alike. This discussion, however, raises two questions which merit careful and sympathetic consideration.

In the first place, does not the broadening of secondary education involve the lowering of standards of achievement and the consequent sacrifice of talent to mediocrity? Unless there is some provision made for different levels of ability, an affirmative answer must be given to this question. If the average student sets the standard for all, then, as a matter of course, the opening of the doors of the high school to all adolescents means the lowering of standards. But there is no good reason why the standards may not be as fully adjusted to the abilities of the individual as they ever were in the narrower secondary education of the past. In suggesting this solution no more is asked of the secondary school than a sound educational theory always demands of the elementary institution. The crime of neglecting differences in capacity is no greater in the one institution than in the other. Nevertheless in the process of shifting secondary education over to the broader base especial care must be taken lest that group of exceptionally talented adolescents be slighted which has been the primary concern of the secondary school of the past.

In the second place, there is an even more searching question. Is there not a point, reasonably high on the intelligence scale, below which it is socially unprofitable to extend the opportunities of secondary education? A direct answer to this question in terms of clearly demonstrable fact is impossible to-day. Moreover, since any answer must rest on certain assumptions regarding the worth of human personality as well as on scientifically determined conclusions, an objective answer that will compel agreement probably can never be given. If the entire range of mental ability from idiocy to genius is included in this discussion, unless education is made to cover custodial treatment, few would defend in terms of social welfare the extension of secondary education to the lowest mental levels. While the absolute limits of educability are probably never reached in even the most poorly endowed, for practical purposes such limits may be assumed to exist. But, since as yet there is no calculus with which to equate individual and social welfare and thus to show at what point the loss to the common good in educational expenditure overbalances the advantage to the individual, the precise determination of these limits is extraordinarily difficult. At present next to nothing is known of the social value of a year of secondary education extended to an individual of a given mental and moral endowment. At best the worth to society of the teaching of any secondary school subject can be measured only by the crudest sort of guessing. Perhaps the greatest need in secondary education to-day is for experimentation regarding the educational possibilities of various types of subject-matter at the different mental levels. But, unless this experimentation is forced by the pressure of a practical educational need growing out of the presence in the high school of an increasingly heterogeneous population, it is not likely to be undertaken. Moreover, owing to the great social demand for education, an answer to this question cannot wait. We shall therefore take the position, a position which circumstance is forcing upon us and which educators are probably helpless to influence, that to all children during the period of adolescence, except the clearly defective, should be extended the opportunities of education.

How does the extension of secondary education involve the abandoning of traditional notions? But if secondary education is to be education for adolescence, if the high school is to enroll practically all children of high-school age, if the activities of this institution are to be definitely related to the needs of life, those responsible for the administration of the enlarged program will have to discard academic prejudices, display an experimental temper, approach their task in a catholic spirit, and show an indefatigable industry. The old secondary education which was designed to meet the needs of the favored classes, and which was based on a static conception of the social order, presented relatively few and simple problems. Furthermore, its problems are not our problems; we work to-day from different premises. In their experimentation educators will have to cut completely loose from those traditions which are the obvious product of the old order, traditions which have no *a-priori* validity. Experience gained in such a different setting can provide but little guidance. What was good in an education designed to meet the needs of a narrow class may very well be bad in an education with broader purposes. The fact that a form rendered genuine service under the old régime affords no proof of its serviceability in the new order.   In many instances the presumption may well be the reverse. Without reference to past performance, old practices will have to reëstablish their worth in terms of changed standards of value.   If secondary education is to fit into the life of a modern democracy, its entire structure will have to be rebuilt.   Reorganization of secondary education is imperative; but effective reorganization can hardly proceed without correspondingly radical changes in other divisions of the educational system and especially in that part of the system which rests upon the high school.

What are the evils of college domination? As we have already observed, secondary education has always been dominated by the college. To a very large degree the activities which have constituted the secondary school curriculum have been dictated by the college. During recent years the high school, at least in some sections of the country, has gained a limited independence; but even here in many and subtle ways the influence of the college persists. If the high school is to render its largest service, if it is to become a school for adolescence, if it is to consider the needs of that great majority of its students who complete their formal education on leaving its halls, college domination must cease. This is especially necessary in the case of the small high school with its limited curriculum and restricted resources. Needless to say, the selected group of adolescents destined to go to college must not be neglected. But, without sacrificing to the degree which is now customary the broader interests of the secondary school, provision can be made for these students. College entrance requirements and methods of admission, derived from traditional rather than scientific sources, are excessively arbitrary and needlessly restrictive. Such questions of mutual interest to the secondary school and the college should be adjusted, not by the college acting alone, but by a body representative of both institutions.

How should the conflict between secondary school and college be resolved? The instrument with which the college has guarded its cloistered precincts and thereby regulated the practices of the secondary school is the entrance requirement. The college authorities have tacitly assumed that the only candidate fit to enter the higher institution is one who has completed an arbitrary number of units [1] of an arbitrary group of subjects. But, as to just what these subjects should be, there is little agreement. One is therefore faced by the anomalous situation of colleges enforcing the most diverse entrance requirements, yet each firmly believ-

[1] Unit is customarily defined in terms of "time spent" rather than in terms of achievement.

ing that the one road to educational salvation is that provided by the specific disciplines which it prescribes. Only in the realm of ecclesiastical bigotry is there such diversity of creed, coupled in each sect with such blind faith in the finality of its own peculiar revelation. Against such a narrow conception of entrance conditions evidence is accumulating that fitness to pursue the college course is less a matter of meeting formal requirements than one of possessing a high level of intelligence, superior facility in reading and in oral and written speech, good habits of study and thought, and earnestness of purpose. Given these qualities, which the rigid college conventions measure very indirectly and inaccurately, success in college is practically assured. If the college is to perform its special function, without needlessly restricting and hampering the work of the secondary school, the barriers which guard its doors should be both high and wide. Through the judicious use of carefully kept school records to determine moral and scholastic qualities and well-chosen mental tests to measure intellectual capacity and attainments in the native tongue, any college can select from the applicants for admission those young men and women who are best fitted by nature and training to undertake the higher education.

Under such a procedure the high school would be set free from the hampering and demoralizing paternalism of the college; its practices would be determined by those best qualified to determine them; and its philosophy would be developed in response to the needs of secondary education. This would mean the removal of one of the most serious obstacles which block the way to that fundamental reorganization of secondary education which its changed conception makes necessary. That we may allay the anxiety of those who cherish the notion that the college has been vouchsafed a special educational vision, it should be pointed out that, even after the abolition of the conventional entrance requirements, this institution would continue to exert a great influence over secondary education. So long as our high-school teachers secure a considerable portion of their training in the college, no one need fear lest the cutting of the leading strings whereby the college has held the secondary school in the narrow path of rectitude will be followed by an unseemly pursuit of false ideals. This powerful influence is the natural and legitimate force which should hold these two institutions together.

What forces have created the junior high school? One phase of reorganization, representative of the changed conception of secondary education, has already gained great impetus. This is the longitudinal extension of the secondary school to cover the period of adolescence. The old form of organization, made up of an eight-year elementary school and a four-year high school, was not the result of any careful study of the nature of either the child or social life. It was the fortuitous product of an effort to build into a single system educational institutions dominated by conflicting and incongruous purposes. As might have been expected, all educational critics agree that this plan has failed to justify itself in practice. The contradictions and inadequacies of the conventional form of organization are now apparent. As a consequence, the secondary school is being extended downwards to include the upper two years of the old elementary school, and the six years thus given to secondary education are divided into a junior and a senior division of three years each. This represents an effort to make secondary education cover the period of adolescence, the years from twelve to eighteen. It makes possible the bridging of that gap between the elementary school and the secondary school which was the legacy from the period when education followed class lines and society was organized on a class basis.   Although the closing of this gap is an important function of the junior high school, its purposes are as broad as the educational needs of children in the period of early adolescence.   Perhaps the greatest immediate service which this institution will render is that of providing an opportunity of organizing, free from the domination of college and convention, a modern secondary school.   In the junior high school experimentation can proceed with a boldness and a thoroughness which would not be permitted in an established institution.

What should be the criteria for the selection of the curriculum of the enlarged secondary school?   If we assume, therefore, that secondary education is to abandon the selective principle in both its social and psychological aspects, that it is to care for the educational needs of all adolescents, that it is to cover a six-year rather than a four-year period, that it is to view the question of preparation for college in proper perspective, and that it is to function in a society that is striving towards democracy, what are the activities that should be introduced into the public high school to make possible the realization of its purposes?   The first and most general answer is that the high school should continue on a higher level the work of the elementary school.   For the most part the same criteria, adjusted to a maturer age, should be applied here, that serve as guides in the lower school.   First, the activities of the high school should serve to induct the adolescent into the life of the group; second, they should be adjusted to his capacities and attainments; third, they should as far as possible appeal to his interests; fourth, they should not duplicate the work of the informal agencies; and, fifth, they should be drawn from the great common interests of men.

Which criteria merit special emphasis?   Certain of these general criteria must be given an emphasis in the secondary school which is somewhat different from that placed on them in elementary education. This is particularly true in the case of the third and fifth criteria. The interests of adolescents must be definitely recognized in the curriculum, but strong effort must be made to stimulate interest in the problems and tasks of social life. Youth must be taught to guide its behavior in the light of the more remote personal and more abiding social interests. More attention must be given in the secondary than in the elementary school to the development of far-reaching purposes. Also, in the high school there must be some measure of differentiation which recognizes not only differences in ability and aptitude but also differences in vocational expectation. Although such differentiation is not to be encouraged at this level, some specific vocational training, where opportunity permits, should be provided for those adolescents who early are forced by circumstance into wage earning. While the tradition should be stoutly maintained that the activities of the high school should be selected primarily because of their educational rather than their economic value, some concessions must be made to the immediately practical demands of a defective social order.

What can the secondary school expect of elementary education? In the difficult task of inducting the child into the great society of modern times the high school builds on and continues the work of the elementary school. This makes it necessary to summarize what we believe to be the desired outcomes of the first six years of education. By the time the child enters the period of adolescence, what are the more general powers which he should have gained through the processes of formal and informal education? In the first place, he should have a direct acquaintance with the immediate social and physical world. He should know something of the simpler activities in which men engage and the more obvious environmental factors which condition life. In the second place, he should possess a wide repertoire of habits, dispositions, and appreciations formed in the give and take of the social life provided in the school and in the community.   These acquired powers should provide the more elementary controls necessary to the promotion of health and to the furthering of the family, economic, civic, recreational, and religious life. In the third place, he should have such a mastery of the tools of knowledge as to enable him to meet the common demands of life. He should be able to speak, read, write, and use the essential processes of arithmetic. In the fourth place, through the medium of his own concrete experiences and the language arts, he should have entered vicariously into the heritage of the race and thus have been introduced to the world of men and things that lies beyond the world of immediate sensory experience. That achievement in all these directions, and especially in the last named, will vary greatly according to the capacity of the individual is of course obvious. In the first three fields certain minimum standards should be established. Although the attainment of these minimum standards will be expected of all, in many instances, after the individual has been exposed to adequate training and has failed to reach the standard, adjustments will have to be made. At least for children of inferior intellectual capacity, repetition of work is a dangerous solution of the problem. In the fourth, little can be done beyond guiding the initial steps of the learner as he enters those boundless realms which the accumulated experience of mankind has created. In this division there is a rapidly receding goal, a goal which even the most highly endowed cannot achieve in a lifetime.

What must be the basic function of the secondary school? In this last division of educational effort must the high school make its maximum contribution. Especially must

secondary education seek through the social heritage to
adjust the individual to the conditions of life in the modern
world and to give him insight into that world.   The degree
of insight, however, which an individual can acquire during
six years of education is as definitely limited on the high
school as on the elementary school level.   And in a secondary school which enrolls practically all adolescents, these
limitations will be especially pronounced in the less gifted
portion of its population.   The importance of the problem
of determining the educational possibilities of the lower
levels of intelligence has already been emphasized.   But in
each of the first three divisions, as well as in the last, must
the high school supplement the efforts of the elementary
school.   For all adolescents a wider first-hand acquaintance
with the world is necessary than can be provided in the
period of childhood.   Furthermore, as the individual gains
insight, he is able to make new observations and old observations take on new meaning.   The constant contact
with the local community, for example, should give significance to the principles which the student is expected to
grasp.   The development of habits, dispositions, and appreciations must also continue throughout the entire length
and breadth of education.   They become modified and are
given a wider range of application with the growth of insight.   Likewise, some attention must be given to the more
complete mastery of the elementary tools of knowledge.
Yet, if the work of the elementary school is well done, and
if the teachers in the high school are well-trained, further
achievement in the mastery of the tools of knowledge should
follow naturally as a by-product of the other activities in
which the student engages.   But the great function of the
high school will be to give insight into the social and natural
world and that general intellectual and moral equipment of
ideals and principles which may be expected to guide the

later conduct of the individual as he faces the difficult and critical situations of his life.

The foregoing discussion suggests that there must be great differentiation of activities to meet the varying capacities of adolescents and an increasing degree of differentiation to meet their diverse vocational expectations.   In recent years the need for differentiation has received much attention, but the emphasis has been at the wrong point. Differences in vocational expectation have been exaggerated, while differences in capacity have been relatively neglected. There has apparently been an underlying assumption that the immediate interests and the future vocational career of the student are the only factors to be considered.   That this tendency rests on no secure foundation, the analysis of social life presented in Part Three makes clear.   In each of the six great fields of human interest there is a large group of activities in which all, regardless of interest or vocational expectation, must participate to the limits of their capacity. Let us therefore consider those basic elements which should constitute the core of the high-school curriculum and serve as the fundamental education of all adolescents.   We shall then return to the question of the differentiation of the curriculum.

What are the universal needs in the field of health?   In order to discover those common activities which should constitute the core of the curriculum the demands made upon the school by each of the six great fields of human interest must be considered in turn — demands made by health, family, industry, citizenship, recreation, and religion.   What should the high school do in promoting physical efficiency? That there are but limited possibilities for differentiation here is obvious.   Since all adolescents maintain a corporeal existence and are subject to disease, lowered vitality, and death, every high-school student must participate in activities that will promote his own health and give him control over disease. Likewise, since success in furthering health and in combating disease is greatly dependent on collective enterprise, there are large questions of social policy about which all should be enlightened. Besides participating in activities which lead to the formation of desirable habits, every student should learn something about the present health situation and the prevalence of disease and physical defect; he should be given a colorful description of man's age-long struggle against disease; and he should be taught the elementary principles of both personal and social hygiene. He should be made intelligent about health and should be given a health conscience. If a student displays a special interest in health matters, he should be permitted to proceed further into this field. From such students may be recruited leaders in the conservation of human life. But the point to be stressed here is that within this field all must be given a certain minimum of experience.

What are the universal needs in the field of family life? In the promotion of family life the situation is very similar. Most secondary school students are members of families; the great majority of them will found families of their own and become parents; practically all of them possess sex impulses that insistently seek expression; and, since the future of society is so intimately bound up with family welfare, all should be aroused to interest themselves in the problems of family life. The position that adolescents, according to their own personal desires or passing whims, should be permitted to receive or renounce instruction pertaining to this important field of human activity is indefensible. The school has a distinct obligation to discharge. Every student in the high school must be made to recognize the great social significance of the family; he must be made to see clearly the functions of this institution; he must be enlightened regarding the problems of social adjustment in the realm of family relations; he must be given the best knowledge available regarding the hygiene of sex; he must be given some knowledge of the laws of heredity and their application to the problems of social life; he must be made to realize the responsibilities and difficulties involved in the founding of a family; he should be given some information about the care and growth of children; he should be equipped with those skills and knowledges and appreciations which make the home a pleasant place in which to live; and he should be made to regard conscious parenthood of a high order as a sacred function and as the highest type of social service. This should be the program for all. As in the field of health instruction, individuals should be permitted within limits to proceed further along profitable lines of interest.

What are the universal needs in the field of industry? In the realm of economic interests, there is a whole field of unspecialized activity that must be based on and made meaningful by a common experience furnished by the school. As pointed out in the discussion of Problem 14, the improvement of the economic life depends only in part on that narrow equipment ordinarily regarded as vocational. All students should realize the fundamental importance of economic life and economic forces; in imagination they should re-live the age-long struggle of the race in its efforts to gain food, clothing, and shelter from a somewhat niggardly and hostile environment; they should be given that general familiarity with the processes of production necessary to secure wise collective action; they should be brought face to face with those all but insoluble problems of distribution which are shaking western society to its very foundations; they should be taught to regard thoughtless and wasteful consumption as positively sinful; they should be acquainted with the criminal way in which our natural resources have been exploited and be taught to look upon these resources as a sacred heritage; they should be encouraged to respect all forms and levels of necessary work and to regard even the simplest types of labor as valuable social service; and, lastly, they should be inspired with a zeal to coöperate in the organization of an economic life that is calculated to develop rather than destroy human personality. This is the common program. In it to the limits of their capacities all should participate.

Within the narrower field of the vocational interest the school must make some provision for specialized training. To a degree it must impart those narrow skills and knowledges which constitute the equipment necessary to effective participation in specific callings. The extent of this program in the ordinary high school will receive consideration later in this section. But there are certain aspects of vocation which should be given a place in the common program. Many activities and studies, including both shop experiences and literary material, must be introduced into the school for the purpose of guiding the student to vocational decision. In a systematic way the adolescent should be made familiar with his own powers and with the more important vocational opportunities in the world. Also, quite apart from any special vocational purpose, subject-matter should be drawn from vocational sources because of their cultural and human content. No adequate insight into the behavior of men and the complexities of the social order can be gained without a sympathetic and enlightened study of vocational life.

What are the universal needs in the field of citizenship? In promoting the civic life, the need for an extensive common program is especially obvious. The student must not gain the impression, as he might and does in the present school, that the citizen may at his pleasure shirk the responsibilities of citizenship. Here, as in the elementary school, the social life provides an educational opportunity in which all should participate. But at this educational level particularly must instruction go far beyond these direct personal experiences. All students must be given some understanding of those basic human tendencies which shape and condition group existence; they must be given a wide view of coöperative life and human achievement in the past and thus be provided with perspective for the evaluation of problems and measures; they must be made familiar with the working of our political institutions and acquainted with their merits and defects; they must be made intelligent about the great civic and social problems of the present rather than be held to a tedious study of the problems of the distant past; they must be given a broad social consciousness and a feeling of membership in the larger groups; they must be given the most thorough training and guidance possible in the selection, following, and control of leaders; they must be inspired with those attitudes and ideals which, as we have shown in Problem 15, are essential to the conservation and improvement of life in the Great Society. At no point can this portion of the curriculum be determined by the desires of the individual student. The activities suggested, however, are of such a character that it should not be difficult to enlist the energies of the adolescent. As in other fields, to those of special interest and aptitude opportunity should be provided for special and more intensive study.

What are the universal needs in the field of recreation? In developing recreational interests much greater concessions must be made to the immediate desires of the individual. The educational objective is not that of equipping the individual to bring about predetermined changes in his material and social environment; it is rather that of promoting the growth of a liking for and of developing an interest in certain activities. This is one of the most delicate of educational tasks. Because of the very definition of play and its unique psychological status, formal procedures, enforced hours, prescribed curricula, and social regimentation are most dangerous. The school can give the opportunity, it can make the conditions most favorable, it can recognize individual differences, but, after it has done its utmost, it may fail; it cannot force the individual to like to play. Hence freedom must be the watchword of the recreational program. Provided the activity be one that does not place in jeopardy some other great objective, such as health or effective citizenship, the school should not oppose its inclusion in the curriculum. For a particular individual the recreational interest may be music, literature, art, biography, flowers, fishing, hiking, radio, or any one or combination of a thousand different activities.

Certain of these, because they either require prolonged training or possess potentialities for future growth, should receive the special attention of the educator. Others, because of the needs of American civilization, merit a favored position in the school. As was clearly shown in Problem 16, American life, to a peculiar degree, centers in the economic interest, in the creation of material wealth, in the exploitation of nature. The ordinary individual, caught in a ruthless struggle for material success and social position, leads a strangely intense and anxious existence. By engaging in some form of recreation which takes him away from the world of railroads, telephones, factories, and cities, he seeks compensation for the unnatural life he is compelled to live. America possesses no rich folk-life, no splendid artistic heritage which might serve to ease the strains and moderate the stresses of a highly competitive social order. This situation suggests the emphasis which should be given in the high-school curriculum. For the purpose of developing the æsthetic possibilities of our people, rich and varied offerings in music, literature, and art should be provided.   Beyond this perhaps the wisest suggestion is that the student be given some free time in the school day during which he is strongly encouraged to engage in some activity that has great recreational possibilities.

What are the universal needs in the field of religion? Finally, as we have contended in Problem 17, to omit from the school program any formal provision for the fostering of the religious life is to neglect the most important need of the individual and of society.   Socially such a negative policy is disastrous, and educationally it can be attacked on the grounds that it provides no adequate unifying principle for the varied activities of the school.   By the close of his high-school career every student must in one way or another have reached a working decision regarding the basic realities of life and the wider interpretations of the universe.   If our teachers are sincerely religious, much of this instruction will be incidental.   It will be provided through participation in the ordinary activities of the school and through intimate personal contacts between teacher and student.   But much more must be attempted in the secondary school.   Because of the interest that adolescents are known to manifest in religious matters, because of the idealism that can usually be called forth at this period of development, and because of the transcendent importance of religion in the life of man, religion must occupy an important place in the curriculum of the school.   If religious forms could be divorced from a narrow sectarian interpretation, opportunity to participate in religious devotionals should be provided.   All students should be introduced to the history of man's efforts to establish a more perfect relation with the underlying forces of the universe.   Under sympathetic guidance they should be made acquainted with the great religious figures in history.   All this must be provided in the formal curriculum. But it must never be forgotten that the religious consciousness is transmitted neither by signs nor by forms, but by spiritual contacts.

What types of experience will satisfy these six basic needs? The larger educational needs have now been considered. What should be the materials of instruction? From the foregoing analysis and exposition it is patent that the amount of curriculum differentiation dictated by differences in social expectation is limited, more limited certainly than the clear-cut divisions within the present high-school curriculum would suggest. From present practice one might draw the conclusion that students pursuing the different curricula were to live in different worlds. As a matter of fact, in spite of the inequalities and divergencies in social condition, they will all live in much the same world. There is a great body of interests, common to all men, from which should be derived a large part of the curriculum of the secondary school. In furthering health and in improving the family, economic, civic, recreational, and religious life, there is demand for much general instruction which cannot be imparted in the elementary school. General education, the basis for social integration and collective action, must continue throughout the entire period of adolescence. For the most part, the subject-matter of this general education, except that it is adjusted to a more mature intellectual and social experience, is not essentially different from that offered in the elementary school. The materials of instruction, therefore, which constitute the core of the secondary school curriculum, should include direct personal contacts, vicarious participation in the experience of the race, and training in the use of the tools of knowledge. The relative emphasis which should be placed on these three different types of subject-matter in the general education of secondary grade may now be considered.

What concrete experiences are necessary at the secondary level? The direct contacts should receive less emphasis at the secondary than at the elementary school level. Yet, for a very large proportion of the students in the public high school, because of their modest intellectual powers and interests, liberal provision for learning of this immediate and simple type must be made. By three different groups of activities, the social life of the school, contacts with the local community, and work in the shops and laboratories of the school, should these concrete and un-mediated experiences be provided. Perhaps the most important contribution can be made by the social life of the school, by that unofficial program of athletics, organizations, debates, parties, and gatherings which the students themselves have created. In these activities, refined and adapted to the achievement of educational ends, all should participate. Through contacts with the life and occupations of the local community, contacts which should be much freer and more numerous than are customary to-day, the work of the school can be placed in its natural setting. In the shops and laboratories the student can be brought into direct touch with certain of the more complex and remote activities of life. But the student should be allowed to pause over these concrete experiences only so long as they are educationally serviceable.

What provision must be made at the secondary level for vicarious participation in the racial experience? The work of the elementary school, combined with these concrete experiences provided at the secondary school level, should furnish a sound basis for those subjects of instruction in which the social heritage is more particularly conserved. Among these subjects the social studies are most important for inducting the adolescent into the life of the Great Society.

Hence, from the first to the last year of the secondary school, materials drawn from history, political science, economics, and sociology should occupy the center of the curriculum. These materials should be organized into two types of courses. In the first type, through a wide survey of human achievement and progress the student should be given social perspective and appreciation; in the second type, by a detailed presentation of pertinent material he should be informed about the great problems of contemporary life. Although the natural sciences do not merit as much attention in this general program as the social studies, they should probably be prescribed in each year of the junior high school. The modern world cannot be understood without constant reference to science and its applications. The subject-matter drawn from this division of the social heritage should therefore seek to acquaint the student with the more important applications of science to the lives of men and to give him an appreciation of the place and significance of science in the modern age. It should be designed to illumine man's condition: his place in nature, his hereditary equipment, and the principles of human hygiene. It should also aim at conserving and developing that interest in the natural world which every child brings to the school. But man has searched for the beautiful, as well as the true. The fine arts should form an essential part of general education at the secondary level. Primarily for the purpose of developing interest and taste literature, music, and art should be stressed in each of the six years of secondary education. While every student should not be compelled to engage in all of these activities, effort should be made to arouse in each individual a love for the fine arts.

What attention should be given to the tools of knowledge at the secondary level? The mastery of the tools of knowledge should receive explicit attention in the high school.

In gaining control over the fundamental processes of language and number, the work of the elementary school requires supplementation. In both divisions of the secondary school, classes in both oral and written composition may be held. In many individual cases, where bad habits have been formed, reading should be taught. And in the early part of the junior high school it may be necessary to require all students to pursue a course in general or composite mathematics. Care must be taken, however, lest standards of attainment be set up which are higher than either the needs of life require or the conditions of life will sustain. Sound pedagogy demands that most of the facility gained in the language arts at the secondary level should come incidentally from supervised participation in the other activities of the school.

What provision must be made for differences in interest and vocational expectation? Although this common program will require practically all of the time of the ordinary student in the first year of the junior high school, towards the end of the period of secondary education an increasing portion of his energies should be devoted to special interests. In our presentation of the needs in each of the six fields of human activity it was shown that only in the fields of economic and recreational interests are there large opportunities for differentiating the program. While in these two fields all students should have many experiences in common, nevertheless there are sound reasons for permitting education to follow special lines. After the more general demands of the economic life are met by the school, the narrower demands must be faced. One of the functions which the secondary school must perform is that of guiding the student to a decision regarding his future career. As the answer to this question begins to assume a definite form, the program of the individual should include subject-matter which would acquaint him more thoroughly with the nature of his prospective vocation and, at the same time, prepare him to meet its less specialized demands. At the level of secondary education, the introduction of systematic instruction in the narrow and highly specialized skills and knowledges of specific occupations should be scrutinized with great care. As we shall urge in our discussion of vocational education, the secondary school must be extremely slow to sacrifice its major function of continuing general education in favor of an education on the trade level. For the most part the more specialized skills and knowledges, where they cannot be acquired on the job, should be acquired later either in vocational and professional schools or through various forms of continuation education.

In developing his recreational interests, the student should also be provided with extensive opportunities for giving expression to his personal desires. But since vocation and recreation are thus linked together in this discussion of the differentiation of the educational program, a certain contrast between them should be indicated. In so far as the narrower vocational training is given, the student must of necessity follow a course that has been rather definitely prescribed by those who are familiar with vocational needs and conditions. Rigorous standards of achievement must be maintained. In the case of recreation the situation is very different. A long and detailed curriculum cannot be prescribed here by the authorities; the objective is an appreciation and not a mastery. The criterion is subjective change and not external product. Freedom is the essence of the recreational life; recreational interest can never be developed by strict regimentation and stereotyped curricula. However necessary at times may be these methods in other fields of instruction, in a recreational program they are incongruous. In placing this interest in the formal program of the school, this danger must always be in mind. Recreation touches life at too central a point to be left wholly to chance or personal responsibility, but, as the school seeks to foster this interest, caution must be exercised lest the spontaneity of the play activity be crushed. This difference between vocation and recreation, since sound education depends on its recognition, must not be forgotten or neglected.

What provision must be made for differences in capacity? While differences in vocational expectation should not be reflected in any large measure in the secondary school curriculum, the greatest possible provision should be made for differences in capacity. The extension of educational opportunities to an increasingly heterogeneous population necessitates such provision. Especially in that common program which should constitute the core of the high-school curriculum these differences must receive recognition. Wherever possible, students must be classified into relatively homogeneous groups, homogeneous, that is, with respect to the particular traits and abilities necessary for participation in the activity. There must, however, be some activities whose primary purpose is that of bringing together in normal social relations individuals of widely differing capacity. But where the outcome contemplated is some form of personal achievement or some form of intellectual insight, in which for the time the life of the group assumes a subordinate position, such classification is to be desired.

How should the program of classification be administered? The task of administering such a program would require radical re-adjustment and reorganization of conventional practice. In the first place, an extensive system of tests, records, and counsel should be instituted. Through this system, which should be especially active in the first and second years of the junior high school, but functioning throughout the period of secondary education, students would be classified and instruction would be constantly adapted to individual capacity and need.   In the second place, the content of the curriculum should be modified to suit the different levels.   The amount of material covered would be much greater in the faster than in the slower groups and the quality of the subject-matter would vary. At the lower levels concrete and illustrative material should abound, while at the higher levels the treatment should move forward to a much larger extent on the conceptual plane.   In the third place, not only content but methods of instruction should be adjusted to differences in capacity.   In the less gifted groups the recitation should move forward relatively slowly and emphasis should be placed on drill and repetition, while in the more gifted classes the recitation should proceed at a more rapid rate and drill should be reduced to narrow proportions.

Why must special provision be made for the gifted student?   This discussion of the adaptation of instruction to differences in capacity may well be closed by directing attention to the gifted student.   While no level of talent can be neglected, special provision must be made for children of superior gifts.   They constitute society's richest resource; potentially they are the greatest forces for both good and evil.   In order that their powers may be developed to the utmost, an enlightened society will give much thought and time to their education.   This attention to the superior individual, however, should be carefully tempered by large emphasis on social obligation.   The persistence in the high school of the American tradition of exaggerated individualism could only be disastrous.   Unless the gifted individual is made to feel a strong sense of obligation to turn his gifts to the promotion of social ends, his education may be an instrument turned against society.

What is the place of the languages and the abstract sciences?   The reader has observed that up to this point no direct reference has been made to those subjects which have constituted the major portion of the conventional curriculum. He must have feared that the discussion of what is commonly regarded as the essence of secondary education has been overlooked. Perhaps the best approach to a consideration of this subject is through the question: In the program of a secondary school which is to minister directly to the needs of all classes and of practically all levels of ability, what place should foreign language, advanced mathematics, and abstract science occupy? This question, like most other educational questions, can only be answered by reference to the educational needs and capacities of the particular individuals who compose the high-school population. Yet a general answer is not difficult.

Why must these subjects be restricted to a few students? Needless to say, there is an important place for these subjects in the general plan of the secondary-school curriculum which has been outlined. In the last analysis, they must be classed as subjects leading to specialized careers and be accorded the position in the curriculum which such specialized subjects should occupy. Modern civilization is based upon mathematics and science, and the intimate association of peoples makes necessary the translation of thought from language to language. There are thus created certain highly specialized functions which must be performed by specially trained persons. Society requires the engineer, the chemist, and the linguist; but the numerical representation of such callings in the general population is very restricted. Moreover, the educational value of any one of these subjects, unless a rather high degree of mastery is secured, cannot be great. Until these facts are recognized, instruction in language, mathematics, and abstract science will be ineffective, and the secondary school will be unable to achieve its wider objectives.

As illustrative of the position which these subjects should

occupy in the curriculum, consider the case of a modern foreign language. If the teaching of this subject is to be justified, a fair degree of mastery must certainly be achieved. Hence the emphasis should clearly be placed on quality rather than on quantity production. The folly of gathering into the language courses a multitude of students, regardless of their interest, aptitude, or future, is apparent. The mastery of a second language, unless the individual is placed in a practical situation where the ordinary affairs of life demand it and provide opportunity for its acquisition, unquestionably requires very unusual talent. The wisest course to follow with respect to such subjects would seem to be the reverse of current practice. Only students possessing special objectives, interests, and abilities should be allowed to study a foreign language; and in all language instruction in the high school serviceable standards of achievement should be rigorously maintained. In the smaller high schools, unless economic resources are abundant, probably no foreign language should be taught, while in the larger schools instruction should be provided in some languages which receive no attention to-day.

The thesis which is being defended here is conservative rather than radical. So long as secondary education was highly selective, there was some reason for expecting all students to pursue the subjects of the traditional curriculum. We are merely maintaining that these subjects should be given only to that type of mind for which they were originally intended. Linguistic, mathematical, and scientific talent possess greater social value to-day than they possessed in earlier generations. The population of the secondary school should be searched for such talents, and, wherever found, regardless of the social class in which they reside, provision should be made for their development. But it is educational folly to think in terms of great numbers. The growth of the

secondary school has rendered obsolescent for its wider population that curriculum which has served its narrow clientèle
in the past.

Why must the secondary school foster adult education?
According to the conception of education presented in this
volume, the more formal education of the masses of the population should cease at the close of the secondary school period.   If the ordinary citizen, however, is to meet effectively
the problems of life, if he is to live most fully, some provision
must be made for the continuation of education after the
termination of the formal instruction.   The modern world
is moving, new problems are constantly arising, new knowledge is being discovered, new hopes are being created, the
need for adjustment continues throughout the life-span of
the individual.   Opportunities for education must therefore
be provided for the old as well as the young, for those who
have assumed the burdens of maturity as well as for those
who enjoy the liberty of childhood.   To meet this situation
there are many agencies, such as the newspaper, the theater,
and the church, which perform large functions.   But if
knowledge is to be humanized, if experience is to be brought
into the service of the common life, the educational institutions must bear the major responsibility for the continuation
of education.   While both the elementary school and the
college should contribute to the achievement of this end, the
high school, because its facilities are greatly superior to those
of the elementary school, because it is much more accessible
than the college, and because its methods and purposes are
more in harmony with the need than those of either the elementary school or the college, should become the chief
agency and center for continued education in every community.

**What is the function of the secondary school in American
society?**   In these concluding paragraphs attention should

be directed to the wider educational faith. Earlier in the discussion the strategic position occupied by the secondary school was indicated. In the establishment of the public high school as an upward extension of the elementary school, the road to higher education was opened to the masses and a major contribution was made to the intellectual emancipation of men. That this extension of educational opportunity is coming none too soon the analysis in Part Three of life in the Great Society clearly reveals. While the educational tasks there outlined will require the combined efforts of all divisions of the system, the major part of the burden will have to be borne by the high school. Elementary education, though capable of being greatly improved in quality, is already extended to all; and the college enrolls many students to-day who hamper the achievement of its legitimate purposes. It is therefore at the secondary level that the expansion must come and that education must most profoundly affect social life. The high school, in which the masses will receive the final years of their formal education and to which they will return for continued education in hours of leisure, should become the people's university.

If the promise of American life is to be realized, a promise which for a century and a half has thrilled the peoples of all countries, it will be realized through the secondary school rather than through the instrumentality of any other educational institution. In a peculiar sense the free public high school is emblematic of the genius of America. On the material side this promise is well on the way to fulfillment; but on the side of the spirit, if it has not lost some of its vitality, it remains but a promise, an aspiration. America has achieved economic prosperity, material abundance, mastery over physical nature; but, unless this achievement promotes the more abundant life, unless it fosters simple kindliness, unless it increases the love of justice, unless it kindles a love for the beautiful, unless it stimulates the desire to know, unless it fashions a generous philosophy of life, unless it makes men happier, it is barren and unprofitable.   If she is not to disappoint the hopes of mankind, America must complete the work which she has begun.   Within the span of a single century she has risen from the humble position of a small and feeble state, lying on the outskirts of civilization and despised by the ruling classes of the old world, to a position of wealth and power unrivaled in the history of nations.   Will America, long the symbol of liberty, equality, and fraternity among the oppressed of all lands, now that she is able to put substance into these ideals, succumb to the temptations of material success and lose the vision of her youth?

Only through the generous support of an enlightened educational program, in which is brought to focus all the resources of the spirit, can the promise of American life be fully redeemed.   That which no other nation could do, even though the will to do it existed, America can attempt with confidence. The rest of the world is impoverished. Through the material destruction of the War the advance of civilization has been set back a generation and the extension of educational opportunities in other countries is necessarily halted.   Only in America can be found to-day that economic surplus which is essential to the support of the conception of secondary education which has been outlined in these pages.   The public high school may become a powerful instrument for bringing intelligence to bear on the solution of the great problems which the race faces in modern times. This institution, enrolling the entire youth of the nation and keeping in touch with the ever-changing needs of social life, may become the central agency through which the ideal America may be brought into the world of reality.

ADDITIONAL PROBLEMS FOR DISCUSSION

1. What underlying social philosophy, peculiar to America, has created the free public high school? What is the justification for the statement that the high school more than any other of our educational institutions is an American product?

2. List the more obvious changes in secondary education which may be traced to the growth of the four-year high school enrollment from approximately 200,000 in 1890, to over 2,000,000 in 1920? To what extent have these changes kept pace with this growth?

3. Why has so little direct attention been given in the ordinary high school to equipping the student to participate intelligently in the basic social activities outlined in Part Three?

4. Why is the small high school much more conservative than the large high school?

5. In view of the fact that but ten per cent of students entering high school go to college, explain the domination of the high school by the college? What are the dangers of this domination?

6. How is the educational welfare of the student sacrificed who ends his educational career at the secondary level after completing the college preparatory curriculum?

7. What are the forces which, in spite of official opposition, have been responsible for the very rapid expansion during the last half century of the extra-curriculum activities?

8. In view of the continued extension of secondary education, what place should those activities occupy which in the older academic school were regarded as extra-curriculum?

9. To what extent is the private secondary school a survival of the dual system of education in Europe which reflected class cleavage in society?

10. What would be the social consequences of attempting to give to the great majority of adolescents a secondary education consisting chiefly of foreign language and mathematics.

11. By what arguments would you justify the somewhat paradoxical statement that the traditional academic curriculum is essentially vocational?

12. To what extent is the attainment of the purposes of mathematical and linguistic instruction dependent on a rigorous selection of the students permitted to pursue these subjects?

13. What preparatory steps must be taken before an efficient system of vocational guidance can be established in the large city high school?

14. In what measure has the extension of the opportunities of secondary education lowered the intellectual temperature of the high school? Why is this question of such concern to the college?

15. In what respects should the content of instruction employed in the secondary schools of a democratic society differ from that used in the schools of an aristocratic society?

PROBLEM 21

WHAT IS THE FUNCTION OF THE COLLEGE?

Is the college a selective institution? — What responsibility has the college for the intellectually mediocre? — Can the college create intellectual interest in the ungifted? — How may the college raise its intellectual tone by selection and elimination? — What provision must be made for those eliminated? — What purpose will be served by this elimination? — What is the function of the college of liberal arts? — What is the responsibility of the college for training leaders? — How must the curriculum of the college reflect the six basic life activities? — What is the relation of the college to vocational specialization? — How is the elective system functioning? — How has the specialization of knowledge affected the college instructor? — What is the fundamental weakness of college education? — How may knowledge be integrated? — Why must the college stress social responsibility? — How must the student body be differentiated for instructional purposes? — Does the present college foster intellectual achievement? — How must the college redirect the extra-curriculum activities? — Why does the Great Society presuppose disinterested intellectual leadership? — How does the Great Society overtax the intellectual powers of the ordinary citizen? — What is the function of the college?

Is the college a selective institution? The elementary school is non-selective; slowly but surely the secondary school is drawing the total population. The elementary school but slightly and the secondary school in greater degree can only be selective through differentiated courses of study. As opposed to these two institutions the college must frankly restrict its opportunities to a portion of the population. Because of the nature of its task, its privileges must be available only to those who show evidence of possessing the properties of mind and heart which will enable them to benefit from its own peculiar activities and contribute to its wider social objectives. Before the aims of the college can be considered the selective function of this institution must receive attention.

What classes of students attend college? The college [1] as it exists to-day contains an extraordinarily heterogeneous student body. In spite of prerequisites and entrance requirements the stream of young men and women that are entering its gates shows a very wide diversity in training, mental equipment, intellectual interest, social ideals and future objective. This extreme diversity is at the same time both a challenge and a menace. For convenience, the students of our colleges may be divided into three classes:

(1) Those of high endowment whose main purpose is the perpetuation and advancement of the intellectual tradition and heritage;

(2) Those of equally high intellectual endowment who are training for important professional or administrative work; [2]

(3) Those who enter college primarily for its social life, or for the sake of the hall-mark of the diploma and who lack the native ability, the intellectual training, or the ambition necessary for the pursuit of any work of a high intellectual order. With this class may be included an increasing group of faithful students who, in spite of severe exertion, are unable, because of meager native endowment, to keep the pace to which the first two classes should be subject.

What responsibility has the college for the intellectually mediocre? This situation suggests the crucial question regarding the higher learning in America: Has the college, as a specialized institution, any responsibility to the growing number of students who obviously fall in the third class? Are the resources of the colleges, and indeed of the country,

---

[1] The Editor of *School and Society* kindly granted permission to use certain material from one of our articles, "The Failure of the College."

[2] In this group must be included many women preparing for homemaking in its most liberal interpretation.

sufficiently great to justify an attempt to give a college education to those whose intellectual capacities are but mediocre or to those who regard, and continue to regard, the intellectual activities as a necessary but evil concomitant of college life? Must the college assume educational responsibility for those of limited talent and interest who, under present conditions, are capable of satisfying the entrance requirements? That the college is able to render a distinct social service in the education of this class cannot be denied. But this is not the point at issue. The fundamental question is concerned with the degree to which this third class can be enrolled in the college without imperiling those larger interests of higher education which center in students of really superior intellectual gifts. Only in so far as full opportunity for entering college is being given to all members of the community who fall in the first two classes, can room be found for students of the third class. Furthermore, only as adequate and suitable disciplines and procedures are extended to the former, should society provide for the latter. The college must be primarily a selective institution. Only after it has met the demands of those who are nurtured by its intellectual life can it afford to divert its energies and resources to "holiday seekers" craving the diversions of a country club or students whose intellectual gifts are such that the academic life is a bondage hardly brooked.

Can the college create intellectual interest in the ungifted? The function of education is to produce changes. The rate at which these changes can be made at the higher levels of education is less a function of the teaching provided than of the intelligence of the pupil. The hope of educating in academic things those who lack the academic bent is conceived in folly. In intellectual matters many are called but few are chosen. Is it fair to expect the kindly and versatile professor, by some heaven-sent skill, to coax or dragoon the protesting many into the same fold? No country, even countries where the things of the mind are relatively more valued than in our own, has ever attempted to train in academic ways the intellectually mediocre. Can we with our different social values and incentives expect to achieve success? One can imagine the laughter of the gods as they see our colleges proceeding in all solemnity to their futile task. Some instructors, realizing the incongruity of college purpose and student material, drop all pretense at stimulating to high intellectual endeavor and fall back into " schoolmastering " the lower sections of the class. The fact is, to educate such heterogeneous groups together is impossible; either we serve the best and discourage the mediocre and poor, or else, as is commonly the case, serving the untalented we neglect the gifted. To neglect the latter, those alone who are capable of making a large social return, is nothing less than the folly of misguided democracy. Is it not high comedy to witness the colleges embarking seriously on a vain quest? To seek an impossible goal is the surest way to destroy morale; the lowering of the intellectual tone of the college, which is the serious factor to-day, is the inevitable result of this ill-conceived policy.

How may the college raise its intellectual tone by selection and elimination? In view of the limited facilities of the college, what must be done to meet the situation? The following are the main changes required: (1) much more generous but rigorous selection on the basis of intellectual endowment and interest; (2) more elimination from the college of liberal arts, particularly during the first and second years of the course. An active pursuance of the policy of more rigorous selection and of early elimination of students of low calibre would economize the effort of both faculty and students. The aims of the liberal arts college, as we shall show, are such that an appeal to a wide population is not to be expected. The differences in intellectual curiosity and desire to understand, which exist among men, are as marked as differences in other traits and, at the same time, are probably no more subject to educational influence. Even assuming the maximum influence which education can bring to bear on the individual in the attempt to kindle the desire to search out the ways of nature and of men, but few can be expected to embark on the whole-hearted quest for knowledge.

As a student, either because of limited intelligence or lack of effort, is found incapable of deriving great good from the college course, elimination should be the natural outcome. At the end of the second year, when presumably the foundations of culture have been laid, transference either to the occupational life or to the vocational schools should be the recognized course for many of the students. If the third and fourth years of college education are to be reasonably effective, the lower quarter or even half of the second-year class should be encouraged to withdraw. In view of the fact that this group has completed half of the course, some college certificate or diploma might be awarded. This diploma would indicate that the possessor had been subject to a general cultural course for two years and that he had enjoyed the social privileges of college life for a season. It would also indicate that his record or his objective at the end of the first two years did not justify the college authorities in recommending him to devote further time to a general liberal education.

What provision must be made for those eliminated? This elimination from the college of liberal arts, as we have previously suggested and as we shall further elaborate in our discussion of vocational education, will not mean that additional education is to be denied the student. Any further period of formal instruction, however, would be spent in studies leading directly to a specific vocation, studies so related to the future occupational career of the student as to arouse an interest and call forth an effort which is notably lacking in this type of student when subjected to the general studies of the college. The student who lacks the divine spark to kindle energy for the intellectual quest of the liberal arts course would not be dragged into the college to distort its aims and to overtax or falsify his own interests. He would be compelled to make a tentative vocational choice, and in the light of this choice would enter the professional department of his own institution or be transferred [1] to a professional school elsewhere. This does not mean that all general education must cease on entering the vocational school. Since nature makes no hard and fast lines between men, the measure of general education that will accompany these distinctly vocational courses will vary greatly; in every course there will be some cultural material, and for the better-endowed vocational student there will be an increasing amount. Thus, there will spring up, affiliated with our colleges, what eventually will be professional or semi-professional schools. These institutions will fit their members to engage in the various professional and semi-professional occupations which are evolving in modern life.

What purpose will be served by this elimination? For the few who have genuine intellectual interests the liberal arts college will be made more liberal; its methods, curriculum and spirit will be adjusted to the energies of the intellectually robust. For the remainder, which at the present time is by far the larger portion of our college population, an education which makes a much more obvious

[1] It cannot be made too clear that the superior student will take the full college course before entering the professional school, even though entrance to the school is permissible before the completion of the college term.

and direct contribution to the vocational life will be introduced. Through such a program three valuable aims will be achieved. Firstly, the stimulating social life of the campus will be enjoyed by a much larger group of the population than can possibly find a place in the liberal arts college; secondly, the liberal arts college will be freed from an incubus which threatens, if it has not already killed, the liberal tradition; thirdly, the passive resistance or passive assistance in learning, which marks such a large proportion of the behavior of the present college population, will be transformed into an aggressive pursuit of knowledge.

Why four years of college? One further point should be made. The conventional duration of the college course rests on no adequate analysis of the educational and sociological factors involved. No peculiar efficacy attaches to a four-year period of college education; certainly the incident of graduation does not deserve the dramatic place which it now occupies in American life. Some students can benefit from four, some from three, some from two, and some from one year of general education beyond the secondary school. In caring for this class of students, who are seeking the higher education in increasing numbers, the junior college may be expected to perform a valuable function. Each student should be encouraged to leave the college for the occupation or for specific vocational training as soon as the return from the general education received becomes socially unprofitable. Our colleges are full of so-called " students " who " just to graduate " are unwillingly bondsmen to the regime. Can work of a high order be done when the ranks of the student body retain so many of these time-servers?

What is the function of the college of liberal arts? With this smaller and more highly selected student body, the intellectual temperature of the college of liberal arts would be raised; instructors would be relieved from the onus which the presence of mediocre students imposes and could direct their attention to the consummation of the major aims of the college. These aims must now be discussed. Whatever may be the subsidiary objectives of the college course, one purpose is outstanding. While each of the separate courses may, in some direct or indirect way, contribute to vocational efficiency, the total college course of the student must be evaluated in terms of a wider purpose. We shall assume, as basic to the selection and evaluation of the activities of the college, that the larger outcome of a college education is to create in the student an understanding and appreciation of the principles upon which must be reared that society and that civilization for which the clear in mind and the pure in heart are continually striving. Stated in these terms, the main function of the college may appear to be so general as to be valueless, and so difficult to accomplish as to be discouraging. To combat this obvious criticism it will be necessary to state more explicitly this larger aim and then to examine the present practices of the college to see the reasons why such an inclusive social purpose is the necessary goal of this institution.

What is the meaning of the word "liberal"? Since the college is only incidentally a place of preparation for vocational efficiency, it must be judged mainly by the extent to which those who engage in its activities are being liberalized. For many reasons there is need at the present time to stress those values which are inherent in the very name of the institution — the college of *liberal* arts. The word "liberal" in its most obvious meaning, as applied to education, has a wide connotation. It signifies a generous and plentiful training, a training that frees from ignorance, superstition, dogmatism and narrowness in ideas, doctrines, or sympathies. To be liberal is to be free, to be liberated, to believe in the extension of freedom in educational, political, social, religious, and other institutions. It is something dependent upon knowledge, yet of a different order. Knowledge is but one element in the making of a " freeman." An individual is liberated not by information and by great learning, but rather by an attitude toward life. To be able to see two sides of a question, to realize ignorance, to appreciate expert service, to feel an abiding obligation to study and direct the course of social life, to be public spirited, to recognize the claims of national and international obligations, these are the hall-marks of the man whose education has made him free. Only as our colleges submit their students to broad, generous, and humane learning, calculated to foster these virtues, can they hope to send forth free citizens. Only as men and women of this temper take their places in the Great Society with a fixed determination to cleave to that which is good and to shun that which is evil, can any hope be held out for a more secure and humane world.

What is the responsibility of the college for training leaders? Put in another way, the aim of the college must be to train leaders who will be capable of viewing broadly and disinterestedly the problems of a coöperative society; leaders who will rise above class interests and class prejudices, who will be dominated by a spirit of service, who honestly and courageously will tread the paths which lead to progress. Into these chosen individuals must be inculcated, by a special type of education, those social ideals without which our material advance is mere emptiness. A new social consciousness and a new conception of the interrelations of the social order are imperatively demanded. Since the beginnings of formal education, the higher institutions may be said to have existed to train leaders; to-day care must be taken lest the college lose sight of this function which is peculiarly its own.

How must the curriculum of the college reflect the six basic life activities? Throughout the discussion of elementary and secondary education the importance of making instruction center around the fundamental activities of physical, family, economic, civic, recreational, and religious life, has been stressed. But the work of these lower schools, because of the necessary emphasis on tools of knowledge, and because of the immaturity and heterogeneity of their population, cannot be sufficient to give the more complete insight required by those who are to occupy positions of leadership. By the time the selected student is ready to pass into the college, having acquired the more fundamental tools and experiences, he is free to devote his energy to the important task of gaining a wider and more thorough understanding of these basic life interests. What the elementary and secondary schools have striven to do with reference to the six basic activities in a relatively simplified way, for the total population, that must the college continue to do at a higher level for its selected population. On account of the greater selection and greater maturity of its student body, it will be able to coördinate and correlate the various fields of human endeavor, in an attempt to show how each makes its essential contribution to the progress of mankind and the satisfaction of worthy human aspirations. Unless the college activities are selected, arranged, and weighted to give this wider vision of human activities, the student will enter the specialized training of the professional school or the specialized training of the vocation without the perspective or world outlook which is to give significance and value to the occupational life. In other words, the college must make the individual capable of being something more than a specialist in his particular chosen field; it must liberate him from the narrow confines of his specific occupation and show him the wider obligations and fields of service which are open to him who is socially minded, as well as professionally minded.

What is the relation of the college to vocational specialization? Though much may be done to furnish useful professional background, the liberal college must never adopt as its main function that of providing vocational training. The professional schools or the vocations themselves must be held largely responsible for the specific information and skills which the specialized vocations demand. If the college abandons its own peculiar function, that of imparting to its students the larger viewpoint of society, it abdicates its high calling. Other institutions, with other aims, can never take the place of the college in this liberalizing work. Unless the social interpretations of life are stressed by the college, however successful may be the later professional training, the members of the profession, because of their limited vision, will be incapable of rendering their maximum contribution to the body politic. To adopt the wider objective will not lessen effectiveness in the specialized occupation, but will rather add a richness to it and give it a range of application which is lacking and must always be lacking if the pressure for vocational training has been permitted to oust the humanistic disciplines.

How is the elective system functioning? Before examining critically the various activities of the college, it will be well to state again what we believe to be its chief aim. This is, to create in the student an understanding and appreciation of the principles upon which must be reared that society and that civilization for which the clear in mind and pure in heart are continually striving. The significance of this statement will become clearer as we evaluate present practices in terms of their contribution to this larger purpose of social realization and world unification.

The activities of the college are sufficiently uniform to

admit of general examination. Throughout the four-year period a number of courses in a varying number of subjects are taken by the student. Although, as a general rule, the courses are independent, prerequisites and sequences are often demanded. Some of the courses, particularly in the first and second years, are compulsory; the remainder are optional. Within limits, diverse schemes of major and minor studies control the range of free electives. Since the elective system was instituted at Harvard the general tendency has been to increase the freedom of choice. Not only has this practice been extended on account of the ever-growing number of studies, but it has also been favored by that changed attitude toward mental discipline which has already been discussed. Since no particular subject or group of subjects could be justified because it possessed some peculiar power of disciplining the mind, since the range of subjects offered was constantly enlarging with each new department, the path of least resistance was to adopt the *laissez faire* method of procedure. With certain minor restrictions, this was to present the vast menu and allow the student to choose at will his intellectual banquet. Provided a certain number of good plain dishes were chosen at the beginning, provided the rest of the meal presented a semblance of balance, the student was left to select according to the dictates of his mind, heart, convenience, and inclination the remaining constituents from which his intellectual sustenance was to be derived. Such is a fair account of the elective system as it is working in the majority of our larger colleges.

How may the elective system be criticized? Since it replaced a traditional course of study which was practically uniform for the whole student body, the free elective system inevitably has been subject to the most stringent criticism. What is to ensure that the student choose from pure motives? What is to guarantee that his course of study does not reflect an ignorance of the true purpose of a college education? May not even the serious student exhibit a lack of aim, a scattered aim, or an aim so narrow that he misses the unity of knowledge? Is he not inclined to select courses because of a specific and limited vocational appeal? All these questions and many more have faced the administrators of our colleges since this system was introduced. To offset these dangers, numerous and sundry regulations are in vogue, designed to insure suitable sequences and balanced courses. These regulations, seeking to prevent the student from undue specialization, are good, but they will never of themselves accomplish the purpose for which they are set up. Better selection of isolated courses is not so much demanded, as is a different philosophy of college education, and a different spirit manifested in the teaching of each division of knowledge.

How has the specialization of knowledge obstructed the fulfillment of the aim of college education? Without considering the twofold question as to the general viewpoint of the teacher, and the specific aim which directs his teaching of the subject, it is idle to discuss the manner in which any particular course or subject contributes to the liberalizing of the mind of the student. Even philosophy and history, taught by well-informed specialists with the aim of producing academic specialists, may fail to give the student the wider view of his relationships to life for which we believe the college to exist. If this criticism applies to these noble subjects with their ample domains, how much more applicable must it be to the narrower fields of knowledge which find a proper place in the college curriculum. Isolated courses, in isolated subjects, taught by isolated specialists, are ill adapted to accomplish the end that has been laid down for the college. But, in repeating the word "isolated," we may rightly be accused of assuming that which we set out to establish.

How has the specialization of knowledge affected the college instructor? Let us examine the typical college instructor to see the preparation and bias which he brings with him into his teaching relationships. In the better institutions he is an individual who has been trained for many years in the field that he is teaching. In all probability during his college course he majored in his present specialty; during his graduate course he spent the larger part of his time within this field and made at least one intensive investigation into some more or less recondite issue. Since entering teaching, in order to become acquainted in the most detailed manner with some specialized aspects of his subject, he has increasingly narrowed his interests. His reputation in his subject and his rapid promotion have been largely dependent on his success as a scholar and investigator. It is not to be marveled at that an individual with academic leanings before such a training, becomes increasingly academic in his interests, until eventually, from the ways of men cut off, he shows all the narrowness and pedantry of the academic mind. Is it any wonder that, "seeing through a class darkly," he values above all else academic precision, and regards his own subject as occupying some specially favored position in the eyes of Athena? Is such a man, with his intense parochial loyalty, likely to be interested in the broader interpretation of his field? Is he not precluded, by his worship of the academic fetish and by his meticulous regard for a formal exactitude in knowledge, from integrating his own work with other fields of knowledge in which he knows himself to be a relative tyro? The cobbler must stick to his last, and the college professor, though education languish and his students perish, must not stray from his own specialty. Even if his long intensive training has not made him averse to such apparent digressions, by the fear of encroaching on his colleagues and by the fear, apparently a most terrifying fear, of revealing an absence of the most recent knowledge in the allied field, he will be prevented from taking the students on these illuminating excursions. Such is, admittedly, an extreme picture, but it is sufficiently true to disclose one of the perils of college instruction.

What are the limitations of his teaching? As a man feels in his heart, so will he teach. Unless in his teaching a college instructor is willing to forget the research bias of his training and of his study, the breadth of his influence will be limited. If his teaching is merely an adjunct to his research, he will impart his subject as an isolated intellectual discipline, he will select his subject-matter and choose his procedures with the conscious aim of training individuals to become specialists and investigators within his field. The fact that ninety-nine per cent of his class are certain not to pursue the academic path is disconcerting; but, through the conscientious and continuous repression of this disheartening thought, he can still bring himself to believe that the instruction must be dominated by the academic motive. All the leading men in his field, whom he has become accustomed to admire, were trained with this subject-matter and with these methods; therefore, it follows without question, that these same means must be employed in his own teaching. Every hour is harnessed and every step taken to produce that acquaintance with the subject which is of maximum value for further investigatory advance in the same line. Here is the most obvious weakness of college teaching. It is thorough, it is logical, it is accurate, above all, it is academically respectable, but it fails signally to produce that for which it is presented to the student body of the college. Instead of revealing the manner in which the particular field of endeavor integrates with other fields in the attack on the problems of human existence, instead of exhibiting the reasons for the patient study of such problems by showing their human applications, it rather tends to confine the mind within a narrow compass, full of academic interest, but empty of human interest for all except the specialist. It may serve a narrow vocational purpose, it may acquaint the student with certain specific or even general procedures, but it fails, because its aim is wrongly conceived, in giving that wider vision which is the peculiar obligation of college education.

What is the fundamental weakness of college education? The isolation of one subject from another, and the isolation of each subject from a social content is the greatest obstacle which the college faces in its task of providing that world point of view which the German word *Weltanschauung* so admirably connotes. Such division of subject matter, largely for the convenience of investigation, is apt to destroy the unity of knowledge, or at least make it exceedingly difficult to give the student a clear realization of the unified attack which by their specialized work scholars in various fields are furthering. Instead of seeing languages and literature, the natural sciences and mathematics, the social sciences and philosophy as tools, forged by man to attack the insistent problems of living, instead of seeing these as an ordered and integrated scheme for furthering human knowledge and satisfaction, he is apt, under present conditions, to engage in each as a separate and isolated discipline. On this account, he fails to derive from the study its most significant meaning. Instead of a unified and integrated educational experience with a single purpose to which all other aims are subsidiary, each experience remains an isolated unit and the subsidiary aims occupy the focus of attention. This unfortunate state of affairs is the result of the increase in the bulk of knowledge which has brought in its train an increasing degree of narrow specialization. Just as the worker in industry, engaged in his task, never sees the bearing of his work on the larger aims of the industry, so the student in his various specialized studies never realizes the larger aims of knowledge.

What type of instructor is demanded? To correct this obvious defect of our present methods of instruction several proposals have been made. The ideal manner in which to meet the situation would be to create a corps of instructors more broadly trained and more humane in their interests. In the place of the research objective,[1] or at least on an equality with it, the training of the college teacher should aim to give such a knowledge of the significance of the particular subject and of its various relationships to other fields and to the wider problems of human existence, that the teacher, when imparting the limited facts and methods of his particular subject, could not refrain from showing the wider implications of his discipline. This is difficult to accomplish, it implies a different emphasis in our graduate schools; but it must be planned for with an assiduity which at the present time is given almost wholly to research activities. The research point of view is necessary to give vitality to the teacher's intellectual life, but it must be supplemented by a broadness of outlook, for which at the present moment our graduate schools, the source of college teachers, feel little responsibility. The older professor of general philosophy or of natural science who regarded the divisions of human knowledge, which are now so religiously followed, as largely accidental and of little importance for elementary

[1] It may be desirable for certain graduate schools to offer a teaching Ph.D. as well as a research Ph.D. For the teaching degree a small amount of research would be demanded, and the time saved would be devoted to inculcating an interest in and a technical knowledge of the educational and teaching problems of the college.

teaching, had many merits. He had a vantage point as a teacher of the liberal mind, which our present specialists lack. But this is a difficult solution and is at best delayed. Under existing conditions, what must be done to further the liberalizing influence of the college?

How may knowledge be integrated? At least one significant experiment is being tried. As we pin our faith naïvely to courses in the separate fields, it is but natural that the first step should be to establish another course, wide in its conception and inclusive in its subject-matter, the chief function of which is to exhibit to the student that unity of knowledge which the separate courses lack. In this course, the primary aim is to acquaint the student with the larger problems of our civilization and to show how the various fields of intellectual endeavor are making their contribution to the total body of knowledge. For this course, and for this course alone, in the solution of the problems of contemporary life, the various divisions of knowledge, which have become artificially separated for specialized investigation, are drawn upon as though such hard and fast lines had never been laid down. Anthropology, biology, chemistry, history, literature, physics, psychology, sociology, and the other sciences are all harnessed together in the attempt to show the student that each has its specific contribution to make to the satisfaction of human needs and the realization of human ideals. Such a course presents great difficulty in organization; it implies a wide range of interest in the instructor or instructors responsible; it necessitates the overthrow of the professional prejudice that prohibits an instructor from giving any information except in that field in which he is a specialist; particularly it means the breaking down of narrow academic barriers. In the selection and statement of the problems, and in the collection of materials for such a course, whole-hearted coöperation among the departments is demanded. The peculiar objective of this enterprise makes it desirable that the various fields of knowledge shall not be taught by separate individuals; the course must have a unity which can only be obtained by making a single instructor, of wide and humane training, responsible for its entire conduct. Introduce a series of specialists into the teaching corps, and the unity for which the course is working automatically disappears. That such a proposal is not a dream, but a feasible plan capable of much good, is proved by the experiment which Columbia and other institutions have already made. Growing out of an emergency course in " War Aims " a course for freshmen in "Contemporary Civilization," occupying five hours throughout the week during the whole year, has been jointly organized by the various departments. Initiated by the department of philosophy in coöperation with other departments and taught by a group of instructors, each one of whom is responsible for its whole range, this course and its general management have been found to be practicable. While the outcome of such an ambitious program cannot as yet be evaluated, and while its academic lineage is all too apparent, this initial experiment indicates that a permanent contribution has been made to the curriculum of the college. In spite of initial early opposition the course has won its way and is now welcomed by most of the departments. Experience shows that it makes more significant and more rapid the later instruction in the relatively specialized fields.

Is a synthetic course desirable at the close of the college period? Whether a course of this kind should be given only as an introduction is a point of debate. There is a considerable amount of evidence in favor of introducing in the senior year another unifying course which would correlate the common fields of knowledge traversed during the college training. In the college of liberal arts, as we have projected it, relieved from the burden of narrow professional training, these common fields will be of considerable area. With an initial course introducing the student to the problems of civilization, and with a more comprehensive final course which once more makes evident the unity of knowledge, the college will have freed itself from much of the criticism to which it is now rightly subject.

Why must the college stress social responsibility? Our position being clear as to the main function of college education, we may now turn to discuss, briefly, some further changes which are necessary if the college is to render a fuller service to its students and to society. Attention has already been directed to the necessity of more rigorous selection of the student body; the college has no room for those who lack the capacity or the inclination for its strenuous discipline. College education should be a reward of past promise and an earnest of future usefulness. At every turn the social obligation which the advantages of a college education impose must be stressed: too often have we preached the monetary value of a college education; too widely have we bred the conviction that the training is advantageous because it enables the individual to get ahead; too insidiously have we spread the doctrine that the college opens up avenues to the exploitation of less capable men. Higher education involves higher responsibility and nobler cares; this cardinal truth must be impressed upon every recipient of its advantages. In season and out of season, social service, and not individual advancement, must be made the motif of college training. High standing in pre-college work, seriousness of purpose, and feeling of social responsibility must be the requirements [1] for entrance

[1] Since any entrance requirement or retention requirement stressing social purpose will be extremely difficult to define, the necessity of making the social appeal during the college course is the more urgent.

to the higher institution. For the want of a certain arbitrary number of units in certain arbitrary academic subjects, the college cannot afford to debar individuals of first-rate capacity. In view of the changing conceptions of education, the gates that guard the college must be high and, at the same time wide; high in that they must demand sterling qualities of mind and heart, wide, lest they shut the gates of service on youth of talent.

How must the student body be differentiated for instructional purposes? But, even if we assume that higher and broader standards of entrance are established, the student body will still be sufficiently heterogeneous to demand considerable differentiation of teaching procedure. In the interest of high achievement, especially of the better students, a "pass and honors system" of student classification must be established. Of the pass student, work of a thorough order will be required; but to the few who early in their school and college course show great superiority of intellectual reach and interest, greater stimulation and wider facilities must be given. This small group must be favored above the rest of the student body by being given more instructional care. This instruction must be adapted to the interests of the group and to the rapid rate at which learning can proceed. Furthermore, the better students must increasingly be relieved from the obligation of class attendance; they must be allowed to form early in their academic life the habits of independent study. With this in view, examinations must be given in definite fields in which no courses are given. The abler students must learn to master extensive bodies of information without continual routine and ridiculous motivation by minor tests and quizzes. While this freedom from lectures, recitations and quizzes will particularly mark the work of the honor students, the pass students must be given more lib-

erty than the present college student enjoys.   The tragi-
comic course system, with its elaborate book-keeping, with
its mysterious credits, with its emphasis on minimum rather
than maximum attainments, needs radical modification.   As
a system it is not conducive to high thinking.   Students
must graduate, not because as docile hearers and learners
they have amassed a certain number of credits, but because
they have learned certain procedures and exhibited mastery
in certain fields of knowledge.

Does the present college foster intellectual achievement?
The college must not schoolmaster its pupils, for in so doing
it fails to create the habits of self-education upon which
the individual must rely after the college period.   All
students, whether pass or honors, must be given more
searching examinations; the course system with its minor
tests, which are mere licenses to forget, must be replaced
by more comprehensive schemes of study and examination.
At the end of the college course each student must be
responsible not only for the correlating course which is
given in the last year, but also for an examination which
covers the major portion of the work of the last two years.
Only the student that is capable of passing such a formal
examination should be awarded a four-year college degree.
This comprehensive examination would create an incentive
for more thorough and more permanent learning.   The
college must employ all the measures that are available for
stimulating the student to greater intellectual effort.   The
American college can rightly be criticized because of its
failure to produce within its own precincts a meet and
proper respect for high intellectual achievement.   A reasonable leaven which regards intellectual pursuits and intellectual attainments as of great worth is a mark of an advanced civilization.   Can we expect such a leaven to exist
in society when in the very seats of learning no adequate

leavening force is at work? This point can be made clearer by contrasting the intellectual with other phases of college activity.

On the athletic side the college has set up certain objectives which by social pressure have been made to appear of great worth. Men will strive for years previous to their entrance into college, will train strenuously for long periods during their college course, to attain distinctions of this kind — often empty baubles. Is it not possible to set up equally respected and equally difficult academic objectives, which for their attainment would demand exceptional native ability, long training, and intellectual stamina? Surely an institution primarily created to impart learning and to foster the intellectual life can by its general atmosphere make these objectives so individually and socially desirable that competition in their attainment might be at least a faint shadow of the competition for the prizes in athletics. The very fact that such a large bulk of the thinking population considers the qualities developed by athletics and extra-curricula activities to be of such great worth as compared with those derived from learning, gives further proof of how low the intellectual fires are burning. Intellectual leadership of the right kind must work strenuously among the alumni and in the student body to bring about these necessary changes in emphasis.

What can the college do to foster intellectual achievement? What is needed are intellectual objectives which shall be as definite and as tangible as those erected in the athletic and financial realms of college activity. This is the machinery for the solution of the present problem. The supreme task of the college and university will, however, be in breathing into these objectives the breath of life. In an academic community, strange though it may seem, academic attainment must be a goal which naturally chal-

lenges the greatest effort.   For it, the intellectually minded
must scorn other delights and live laborious days.   If the
teaching body of a college cannot set up these standards and
at the same time create the spirit which will make them
coveted, is not this a sure proof that this body, whatever
its other merits, is not fit to assume leadership in an institution whose primary aim is intellectual?

Some may urge that intellectual attainment is its own
reward, and that the external incentives of social commendation are pernicious.   The same argument may be applied
to athletics.   Bodily exercise, in even greater degree, carries its own reward; yet, great achievement in sport is
only produced by close competition and by continuous
external incentives.   It would be academic in the last degree to argue that intellectual and moral work of the most
refined order will not always be motivated by the commendation and plaudits of the group.   Not that the higher
motive must be lost, but rather that it must be supplemented by the powerful social motive.

**How must the college redirect the extra-curriculum ac-
tivities?**   In considering the total work done by the college,
we must study the activities outside of the classroom proper
to see the nature and the extent of the contribution which
they are capable of making to the student life.   As a cynic
has pointed out, " student activities " of the college never
refer to the activities of studying!   The assumption would
imply that the student is merely passive in his intellectual
experiences.   The extra-curriculum interests of the college
student have rapidly come to be regarded as of first-rate
educational importance; by many they are considered
of higher value than the intellectual discipline of the library
and the classroom.   The reason for this anomalous state
is not far to seek.   They call forth in the student a greater
degree of effort, and demand the exercise of certain social

traits of immense importance in the wider relations of life. The solution of the problem, raised by the undue prominence which parents and students give to these activities, is not to be found in their elimination but rather in their skillful redirection and also their application to the intellectual activities of the institution.   With a more intellectually minded student body, with a common outlook furnished by the interrelating courses at the beginning and end of the college course, with the freedom from lectures and courses afforded an increasing proportion of the students, place must be found for more work of an informal discussional order.   Since intellectual interest is " caught rather than taught," students in small groups, with and without their tutors, must be encouraged to discuss intellectual matters. The Oxford and Cambridge tutorial system,[1] with its emphasis upon the social aspect of learning, might well be incorporated in a modified form into our own college procedure. If this were done, there is every reason to suppose that a good deal of the energy which is now directed into relatively unprofitable channels might be used for the purpose of socializing the student and advancing the intellectual aims of the institution.

Why does the Great Society presuppose disinterested intellectual leadership? In closing this discussion we must once more call attention to the peculiar service of the college in the educational economy.   Since it furnishes the pre-professional training of the best minds of each generation, the major function of the college is to equip for leadership. In our own day this service becomes of paramount importance. If in the other sections of our discussion our enthusi-

[1] Such a system does not seem to harmonize with the mass-production methods which the college has borrowed from industry. But this only raises the more fundamental question as to whether the mass-production method does not defeat its own purpose — namely, the encouragement of thinking in society.

asm and faith in education have led us to overestimate the extent to which knowledge of personal, community, and public affairs can be imparted to the ordinary citizen, here is the opportunity of correcting our reading. As the issues of life become more complex, as the body of social doctrine expands, the competence of the ordinary citizen to pass upon the problems of his life in society correspondingly diminishes. Even a superficial examination of man's present condition reveals a fact which is most disconcerting to the naïve theory of democratic control. Only the simple problem can be solved by the simple mind. All the other problems of our group life can be grasped only by superior minds and then only by superior minds placed in an advantageous position where they can command an unprejudiced and comprehensive view of the facts involved.

How does the Great Society overtax the intellectual powers of the ordinary citizen? Our closely knit coöperative society is not so simple that the man of mediocre intelligence, by turning his attention momentarily to great issues, can by a God-given intuition make great decisions. The solution of the more complex problems must perforce be delegated to the more complex minds of each generation; and it is the training of these superior minds which furnishes the most important opportunity for the college. Here must be assiduously cultivated those intellectual and moral virtues which as Plato so clearly argued should be the necessary concomitants of concern with the major issues. The college group contains within itself that small portion of the population to which the people must with confidence be able to turn for help in problems which their own ability and information are impotent to solve. The activity of the ordinary citizen can only be helpful in the major issues as education furnishes him with sufficient knowledge and warnings so that he can recognize able and disinterested leadership and give it the support without which it is power-less to achieve.

The easy belief that the growth in effectiveness of our educational agencies can equip the ordinary well-meaning citizen to discharge with insight and knowledge the intricate tasks of coöperative living, is a false reading of human nature and involves a failure to appreciate the intricacy of modern society. As an educational and social philosophy it can only lead to disastrous consequences. All but the simplest type of society must rely on leaders, and an edu-cational system that does not make the maximum provision for their training is guilty of a criminal shallowness.

What is the function of the college? Only as the liberal arts college devotes the major part of its energies to the training of superior minds can it expect to send out into society men and women, who through later specialization can be relied upon to meet the crises of social existence. By giving a limited amount of specialized training which has a vocational bearing, by providing the student with the social experiences which foster coöperative living, and above all and in all by furnishing the student with the larger understanding of and the deeper sympathy with his fellow-men, the college can perform an unique service to the individual, and, through his leadership, to the com-munity and the Great Society which comprises the world. In this way, and in this way alone, can the gifted individual make return to the common citizen through whose labors and deprivations he has been afforded the leisure and secu-rity necessary for advanced education. "For unto whomso-ever much is given, of him shall be much required; and to whom men have committed much, of him they will ask the more."

ADDITIONAL PROBLEMS FOR DISCUSSION

1. What may be said for and against the present proposal that admission to college be dependent almost exclusively upon a high level of intelligence and facility in the vernacular?

2. What is the social justification of freeing an individual from the burdens of economic production during the four years covering the college period?

3. What influence has the growth of secondary education in the last half century, coupled with an uncritical attitude toward the function of the college, had upon the modification of the college of liberal arts?

4. In an extremely wealthy society, what educational devices should be set up in order to justify the extension of formal education to twenty-one years of age for the whole population?

5. What present conditions suggest the advisability of allowing a considerable number of our present college students to leave the liberal college at the end of the first, second, or third year, to enter a vocation or to receive training specifically vocational in its aim? What relation has this necessity to the growth of the junior college?

6. How does co-education facilitate and hamper the realization of the purpose of the liberal college?

7. How has the absorbing interest in research, on the part of the more gifted members of the faculty, led to the neglect of the educational function of the college?

8. How do you explain the fact that a college student can take half a dozen science courses without gaining any adequate knowledge of scientific method, or an appreciation of the place of science in the modern world?

9. In view of the relatively large amount of time that has to be devoted to an adequate mastery of foreign tongues under present conditions, and in view of the accessibility of translations, the increase of culture content, and the short period of formal instruction, criticize the contention that for the ordinary student the aims of a college course can be most economically achieved through an acquaintance with the English language alone?

10. In view of the aim of the college advocated in this discussion, what attitude would you take up toward the marked decline in the study of philosophy in the college?

11. To what extent is the cost of higher education in America inflated by the tendencies toward wasteful and extravagant expenditures in its social life?

12. Discuss the following motives for going to college: (1) vocational success, (2) intellectual interest, (3) social prestige, (4) interest in athletics, (5) interest in social life of the college, (6) desire to render a larger public service, (7) an unwillingness to make a vocational choice,

(8) a desire to loaf, (9) compulsion of parents, (10) a desire to enter remunerative but easy callings.

13. In an industrialized society, what are the difficulties of developing, even in a highly selected proportion of the population, an interest in intellectual pursuits?

14. What are the dangers in the current tendency of operating the college on the principle of mass production and in accordance with stereotypes evolved in the industrial field?

15. Show how an uncritical pan-sophism, or the tendency toward an encyclopedic type of education, still dominates the philosophy which lies back of the elective system?

16. In accordance with the liberalizing function of the college, if you had your period of college training to take over again, what subjects (courses) would you eliminate and what would you substitute?

17. How do you account for the relative absence of intellectual interests in the social life outside the classroom on the part of both students and faculty in the American college?

18. What forces resident in society, faculty, and the student body would hamper the realization of the aims of the college as set forth in these pages?

19. In what respects should the content of instruction employed in the colleges of a democratic society differ from that used in the colleges of an aristocratic social order?

20. How can society insure that all intellectual talent, in whatever stratum of society it appears, will be developed and made available for the common good? What advantages will accrue to a particular college from appropriations which will enable it to provide scholarships, covering all expenses and tuition, to the best intellectual talent discoverable in the secondary schools of the country? Compare in social value and significance such a use of the resources of the state or of wealthy donors with the common practice, to-day, of erecting monumental and ornamental buildings.

PROBLEM 22

WHAT IS THE RESPONSIBILITY OF THE SCHOOL FOR VOCATIONAL EDUCATION?

What is the contribution of occupational life to general education? — Is there any question concerning the necessity of vocational training? — What are the various types of vocational training? — How has occupational differentiation complicated the problem of vocational education? — What are the conventional divisions of formal vocational education? — Why is a classification on occupational levels more useful? — In what divisions of the school system do the various levels of training fall? — Why has the scope of professional training increased in modern society? — What general education is prerequisite to professional specialization? — What are the issues involved in pre-professional and professional education? — What is the responsibility of the school for training at the lower occupational levels? — What contribution can the elementary school make to industrial training? — How has specialization in industry affected the problem of vocational training? — How has this specialization affected the higher and lower levels of training? — Should the school undertake training at the lower levels? — What are the administrative difficulties of introducing industrial training? — To what extent should vocational training be provided through part-time education? — What warnings must be given in the field of industrial education? — How has the changed economic status of woman affected her vocational training? — Why must vocational education disregard the traditional concept of woman's sphere? — What determines the nature of a vocational curriculum? — Why is occupational analysis so difficult? — How can the spirit of service be injected into the occupational life?

What is the contribution of occupational life to general education? The richness in social content of the wider industrial and economic activities has been emphasized in Part Three. To evaluate or understand the meaning of modern life, acquaintance with the means whereby men gain their livelihood and an understanding of the interrelationships of the economic order are essential. General education, if it is to be significant to the pupil in the later adolescent years, must make the maximum use of this material.

Especially is this true for those pupils whose intellectual equipment is meager and who will therefore find their place in the intellectually less exacting levels of the industrial and commercial system. To enable the individual to understand a little more clearly the principles upon which the production and exchange of goods depend, to show the tyrannies of capital and the shortcomings of labor, to show the conflict of interest between the entrepreneur, the worker, and the consumer, to show the supreme importance of the conservation of natural resources, to show extravagance here and niggardliness there, to establish a better conception of the interdependence of groups, to create a bond of sympathy among all who render service and to foster higher social ideals for workers and consumers of all levels — these for every boy and girl must be among the important aims of general education. To realize these aims, the social and economic facts of our industrial and commercial life must be marshaled, and given the high place which as culture material they deserve. Not to use the occupational life of the community as a background for much of cultural education is shortsighted in the last degree, and must be traced to the divorce of work and culture in the older and aristocratic societies.

What is meant by vocation? While centering around the vocational life, this aspect of general education must not be confounded with vocational education proper. For clearness of thinking, rather than for separation in practice, general or liberal education must be differentiated from education for specific callings. General education is concerned with the bodies of knowledge, the special skills and attitudes which, irrespective of the particular occupation followed, are requisite for successful living: whereas vocational education is concerned with those special bodies of knowledge, those special skills and attitudes which are requisite for successful participation in specific occupations. In spite of the rhetorical appeal of the argument that the largest vocation of any human is to live, to use "vocation" in this sense in an educational treatise is an abuse of terms. The word vocation must be restricted to that integrated body of particular activities which an individual follows when engaged in his major, economically productive, specialty. With this limitation of the term, vocational education must be regarded as a specific training for the specialized activities of a particular calling.

Is there any question concerning the necessity of vocational training? The acquisition of vocational skill and information is the necessary concomitant of the life process however primitive; the performance of the necessary tasks in the simplest order of existence leaves behind it specific skills and it precipitates more or less organized bodies of information. Without the results of such experience, the basis could never have been laid for the development of vocational life. As through the efforts of these primitive tradesmen, especially the more gifted, there evolved a vocational culture, the need for its transmission became urgent. Other things being equal, so basic is the vocational economy, those groups which made provision for the economical transmission, to the younger generation, of vocational dexterity must have been favored in the struggle for survival. Only in this way was it possible for all members of the group to benefit directly from the accumulated inheritance of the past. The skill and knowledge derived by the more gifted and experienced of the group were thus made available for individuals whose capacity and experience never would have permitted them to make the discoveries for themselves. Even for the gifted, the process economized their energies and enabled them to turn their powers to the advancement of culture. Thus in the field of vocation, as in other fields, each generation could build on the labors of the past. That for every member of society vocational training is absolutely essential is patent, but there remains the fundamental educational problem: To what extent shall the formal agency assume, for any particular occupation, responsibility for the training? The ease with which this question can be answered varies greatly with the level of the vocation. With an unskilled occupation, such as road sweeping, the school need have no concern; but, for a calling such as medicine, the formal agency must give prolonged and intensive training.

What are the various types of vocational training? Vocational training may be provided in various ways. Of these methods the following may be noted:

(1) *Incidental training.* All skills and knowledges acquired incidentally by following the occupation. (Teamster.)

(2) *Apprenticeship.* All skills and knowledges acquired through more or less supervised contacts with skilled workmen in which theoretical training is not stressed. (Locomotive engineer.)

(3) *Part-time education.* Special skills and knowledges acquired within the occupation but supplemented by simultaneous theoretical training provided either by the industry or by the public school. (Tool-maker.)

(4) *Continuation education.* Special skills and knowledges acquired within the occupation but supplemented by later theoretical training. (Agriculturist.)

(5) *Academic vocational training.* Basic theoretical training given in the school but the special occupational skills and knowledges acquired later in the occupation. (Lawyer.)

(6) *Complete formal training.* Basic theoretical and specific practical training given in the school so organized as to afford both. (Physician.)

What sociological conditions determine the type of training provided? The point for the reader to observe is that regardless of the method employed vocational training proceeds. The education may be purely of the informal order acquired by the fisher-boy who, by going out with the boats, "picks up" the numerous skills of the job, and the detailed information of seasons, tides, places and weather indications; or, at the other extreme, it may be of the most formal order such as that provided within a professional school. Only as the third, fourth, fifth, or sixth method, listed above, is employed does the school — the formal agency — undertake vocational education. The point of dispute is not with reference to the necessity of vocational training; rather it centers around the conditions under which such training shall be acquired. How can society distribute the burden of vocational education so that the interests of the individual and the group are given the maximum consideration? The problems of vocational education, especially industrial education, cannot be solved merely by a study of vocational activities; this entire question is linked up with a theory of values, and a wide philosophy of life. It must be considered from various angles and at different levels of occupational complexity. Obviously the mode of vocational education depends greatly on the nature of the occupation, the demand for workers, the training facilities of the occupation, and the procedures, equipment and objectives of the formal school.

How has occupational differentiation complicated the problem of vocational education? Before discussing these basic questions, we shall do well to enquire into the forces which have brought into existence a world of intense occupational specialization. Even in primitive society there are well-marked subdivisions of labor. Differences in sex, age, and environmental setting all tend to make advantageous some apportionment of the necessary work of the group. As society has evolved, as the demands of men have multiplied, as the body of lore, knowledge and skills has constantly grown, as intercommunication and interdependence have increased, as machinery has brought in its train a revolution in the methods of industrial production, the occupational life has become differentiated to an extreme degree. So rapidly has this development proceeded in the last century and a half that a degree of occupational complexity has been attained of which the early settlers were totally unaware and of which our grandparents hardly dreamed. To gain an adequate conception of the almost unbelievable variety of occupations that are now followed by the American people one has only to glance at the Occupational Classification compiled in the United States Census. Here will be found a list of thousands of occupations in which is distributed the total population gainfully employed. Through either formal or informal education the individual members of the oncoming generation must be guided into this vast array of callings and be furnished with the training adequate for their different tasks. Only as the reader grasps the astounding number of these differentiated occupations can he realize the scope of the undertaking or appreciate the problems which have to be faced in inaugurating and maintaining a program of vocational training.

What are the conventional divisions of formal vocational education? In educational writings the following divisions of vocational training are commonly recognized: (1) professional and higher technical education; (2) commercial education; (3) industrial education; (4) agricultural education; (5) home-making education. Such a classification merely follows the lines of the unanalyzed growth of our educational agencies; however convenient it may be for purposes of educational administration a division along these lines is not the most helpful for gaining the wider view of the problem which is necessary in grasping the principles of vocational training. It calls attention to the various fields of vocational endeavor and not to the various levels of vocational activity. Within each of these divisions, in modern society, all grades of occupational training are demanded. To separate professional and higher technical education from commercial and industrial education is to do violence to the ordinary meaning of the terms industry and commerce. This will be made clear by reference to the work of any large industry. Here the following occupational divisions or levels may, at once, be recognized: (a) managerial; (b) technical and professional; (c) commercial; (d) clerical; (e) skilled artisan; (f) machine operative; (g) unskilled laborer. Thus within a single industry are found all the occupational levels from that of the highly trained engineer to the unskilled hand. Similarly within the agricultural field, the whole gamut is covered from the research chemist to the farm laborer.

Why is a classification on occupational levels more useful? On this account a classification based on the different training levels will be much more significant for the purpose of this discussion than the one given above which directs attention to the various departments of occupational life. Taussig's well-known classification recognizes five such training levels: (1) professional occupations; (2) semi-professional occupations; (3) skilled occupations; (4) semi-skilled occupations; (5) unskilled occupations. These divisions are, of course, not clearly defined. There are imperceptible gradings within the professional group. As knowledge increases occupations evolve from a semi-professional to a professional level and as mechanical invention replaces the need for knowledge and skill, an occupation may regress to a lower level. Consequently the precise nature of the difference between the lower forms of semi-professional work and the higher forms of skilled labor is always uncertain and difficult to define. The distinction between skilled and semi-skilled is equally vague, and the difference between the lower form of semi-skilled work and the less simple of the so-called unskilled occupations is impossible to make definite. However, in spite of these practical objections, the fivefold classification is useful in that it calls attention to the gradual increase in occupational complexity. At one extreme are the many occupations which require almost no specialized abilities not possessed by any individual who has had the ordinary experiences of life or qualifications which the occupation is powerless to produce. At a slightly higher level are occupations requiring elementary and isolated skills which can be learned in comparatively short periods of training on the job itself. At an intermediate level are occupations which may demand long periods of manual training and some acquaintance with science, mathematics and technical subjects. At a higher level are occupations where the intellectual elements are more pronounced; here the transition to the semi-professional and professional occupations takes place. In these callings, especially the latter, the content of the training is predominantly intellectual and the procedure scientific.

In what divisions of the school system do the various levels of training fall? The changing conditions of our vocational life preclude the possibility of giving any definite and final denotation to the terms professional, semi-professional, skilled, semi-skilled and unskilled. But assuming reasonable agreement and taking our point of departure from the existing social order we may note that professional training of the higher type is the function, to a small degree, of the senior college, but primarily of the university in which are congregated the various higher professional schools. Professional training of a lower order and semi-professional training are part of the function of the junior college, but the major portion of such training must be provided in the lower professional schools such as those for nursing, dentistry, home economics, journalism, business administration, salesmanship, etc. The distinction between these higher and lower professional schools, between, for example, the school for nurses and the first-rate medical school, is to be found in the prerequisites for admission, and the duration and rigor of the instruction. Training for skilled and semi-skilled occupations, in so far as it is undertaken by the formal agency, will fall at the secondary school level.

What are the more urgent problems of vocational education? Following this general introduction, we shall now content ourselves with a few comments on some of the educational issues involved in professional and semi-professional training. We shall, however, reserve most of our time for a consideration of the point of maximum dispute in vocational education, the dispute that centers around the wisdom and feasibility of giving within the school direct training for the skilled manual occupations of industry. Having examined these aspects of vocational training, we shall, in closing, consider the following problems: (a) the vocational training of women; (b) curriculum construction through occupational analysis; (c) social orientation of the worker.

Why has the scope of professional training increased in modern society? Professional training is but one form of vocational training. In many circles, by restricting the last term "vocational" to those employments which do not demand prolonged theoretical training and which, consequently, under ordinary conditions, are not given the social recognition accorded to the professions, professional has often been contrasted with vocational education. But no useful purpose is served by such differentiation; vocational education is all-inclusive, professional training is but one branch of the total field. Owing to the growth of modern science and the development of our involved social and economic life, there have appeared a wide variety of callings requiring long and sustained training which fall outside the older liberal professions of the ministry, teaching, medicine and law. On this account, the conventional limits of the term "profession" cannot be maintained, for any social activity which demands prolonged educational preparation of a theoretical nature must be regarded as professional. Training for these callings, as rapidly as they develop in the social order, must be given in the so-called graduate and professional schools. Law, medicine, engineering, theology, agriculture, dentistry, journalism, forestry, teaching, diplomacy, military science, already have their own disciplines sufficiently specialized to justify separate institutions.

What general education is prerequisite to professional specialization? The general tendency of the professional school is to base its special training on a rigid course of general education, provided in the non-vocational school. The better schools of law and medicine are calling for the completion of the four-year college training as a condition of entrance. With this general education as a background, the professional school can direct its energies almost exclusively to the task of specific occupational training. Where, however, the professional school, as is often the case in engineering, demands for entrance no training beyond that of the secondary school, the usual procedure is to give simultaneously the general and the specialized vocational training. Where graduation from college is required for entrance into a professional school, the student, as a rule, will have received some prevocational training through the college. Through the selection of certain studies from the academic college course he is usually enabled to shorten his later professional training. As we have pointed out in our discussion of college education, such selection upon the basis of future occupation may become so narrow as to imperil the liberalizing function of the college; in fact, at the present time, a distinct tendency exists to make the college more and more a prevocational, if not a directly vocational, school. While there is no doubt that the college can make a substantial contribution towards preparation for the more exacting professions, this work should be incidental to its main task of providing a sound general education. When the subjects demanded by the profession are of such limited significance as to narrow the general education, the proper place for such subjects is in the professional school itself. To shorten the general college course for many students and thereby to keep its aim separate from the limited vocational objective is better than to convert the college, for the majority of its clientele, into a place of vocational training. This question has already been discussed at length in our consideration of the function of the college. The extent of the general and pre-professional education required before professional specialization raises a problem which demands careful investigation.

What are the issues involved in pre-professional and professional education? This study must take into account all the educational and sociological factors involved. While superficial analysis would tend to show the desirability of insisting on a maximum period of general and professional education, further analysis reveals many difficulties. In studying this problem three questions arise: — If very prolonged academic training is required for entrance to the professional school, will persons enter in sufficient numbers, and, when trained, will they render their service to society at a cost which is not prohibitive? Is it feasible to expect the ordinary pre-professional student to pursue a four-year college course of which the aim is avowedly liberal and not vocational? Can the college hold the interest and enlist the effort of such individuals over this long period?

In addition to these questions regarding entrance a further question of great professional and sociological importance is suggested: Should there be professional courses of varying periods of duration rather than a single stereotyped course for all desiring to enter the profession?

How may the wider social interests be guarded in professional training? A frank recognition and discussion of these problems would result in marked changes in the junior college, senior college, professional and semi-professional schools. If the semi-professional and professional occupations are to be adequately manned, and if the professional service is to be procurable at a reasonable rate, the general educational prerequisites of some of the professional schools must be lowered. Many who desire to enter these occupations and who are capable of rendering valuable service within them, have not sufficient intellectual curiosity to motivate the close application which two, three, or four years of effective work in the general college course demand. Furthermore, the use of the college degree as a method of ensuring a highly selected student body for the professional school is archaic. By school records, personal ratings, psychological and educational tests, intellectual ability can be gauged much better than by the completion of the arbitrary requirements of a stipulated number of years at college. Three facts which bear upon this question must be recognized: firstly, many of our present college students, since they need a type of education in the lower professional schools which is distinctly related to future occupation, benefit but little from a general education; secondly, admission to our higher professional schools should be provided for those individuals who are capable of rendering certain distinct services in the occupation but who are not adapted to the protracted pursuit of general education; thirdly, the graded demands of life situations on the professions would suggest that in the professional schools courses of different lengths be given, depending on the ability and future objective of the student. For example, the assumption that all nurses should be submitted to a training course of just four years is, on the surface, absurd. The needs of society demand the services of nurses having one year, two years, three years, four years or more of training. If a certain level of attainment is the objective, then individuals of different capacity need different periods of training. It is not too much to say that in some instances professional and semi-professional education reflect a narrowness of conception of function and a limitation of social vision that would be out of place in the organization of a trade union. The motive back of the prolonged training is often that of monopolizing the service and artificially raising the remuneration of the members of the profession. Tradition and pious aspiration must be left behind and the whole question be subjected to analysis in the light of individual needs and social demands.

What is the responsibility of the school for training at the lower occupational levels? Leaving professional and semi-professional training, we may now pass on to consider the problems which arise at the lower levels of vocational education. Since, as we have already suggested, the school can be expected to make no direct contribution to the acquisition of those simple skills and knowledges required in the semi-skilled and unskilled occupations, the sole remaining problem has to do with the skilled trades and the various callings of this level. In the fields of commerce, industry, agriculture and home-making there are numerous occupations of this degree of complexity. In an adequate discussion each of these divisions should be given separate treatment, but in the short space at our disposal we shall be compelled to restrict our attention to the problem of training for the skilled occupations in the field of the manufacturing and mechanical industries. In this field the problem presents the greatest difficulty. By common usage, industrial training has come to be applied exclusively to that vocational education which aims to train the manual worker in the manufacturing and mechanical industries.[1] Its object is to prepare for the skilled trades. Training for the semi-skilled occupations, which are legion in modern society, can be given more effectively and more directly in the factories than in the school. Industrial education, as the term is used here, falls in the secondary field, beyond the elementary school and below the college.

What contribution can the elementary school make to industrial training? The only contribution which elementary education may make in this field falls under the somewhat general and vague category of manual training. The aim of this subject-matter is not the acquisition of commercial skills and knowledges, but rather an appreciation and understanding of the nature and significance of the manual occupations. Industrial training, in our belief, has no proper place in the elementary school. As the Cleveland Survey points out: "The most important contribution to vocational education the elementary schools can make consists in getting the children through the course fast enough so that two or three years before the end of the compulsory attendance period they *may, if desirable,*[2] enter a vocational school where some kind of industrial training is possible."

---

[1] This is, in one sense, a mistaken usage, for industry in modern society calls for all levels of occupational training.

[2] These words inserted in place of "will" in the survey report.

How has specialization in industry affected the problem of vocational training? The need for such industrial training can be traced to at least two major causes: (a) the breakdown in the new industrial order of the old apprenticeship system; (b) the increase in the theoretical and technical knowledge required to guide industrial practice. Under the first cause may be noted the specialization of work, the loss of contact between employer and employee, and the absence in the workman of the motive to learn anything but the essentials of the immediate job. All these factors tend to reduce to a minimum the training which the industry itself affords. The increase in the technical knowledge required for successful pursuit of the calling has made the training incidental to the old form of apprenticeship participation inadequate. These and other causes have led to an increasing demand that the school take over the task of training the skilled manual workers or at least supplement the training provided by the industries. As there is direct vocational training for the professions, so, it is claimed, in the interests of the equalization of opportunity, there must be direct vocational training for the lower occupations. While this simple justification of school training for industrial occupations makes a great appeal in a democratic society, it behooves education to analyze very carefully the vocational demands of the new industrial order before capitulating, in any wholesale manner, to the slogan "Vocational training for all." Consideration will first be given to the changed condition of industry; and, afterwards, in the light of these changes, the administrative difficulties of the school will be studied.

The coming of the factory system with its minute specialization of labor and the opening of wider markets with its consequent demands for increased and cheaper production have banished in many trades the old order in which all men possessed more or less the same skills, had the same degree of training, and consequently were expected to be capable of performing any operation of the trade. In the place of this homogeneity of personnel in the industry has arisen a degree of differentiation which in its extremes can be well contrasted. At one end is the designing engineer whose position in industry must be understood if one is to see clearly the changed relation of education to the ordinary industrial worker. In the interests of greater production, this technician has directed his knowledge to the construction of machines capable of performing with great rapidity and with the minimum of skilled attention work which a generation or so ago would have required skilled artisans. The concentration of the higher knowledge and skill in the hands of the designing engineer has enabled the producer to dispense with trade skill in the operative. In many instances, a few hours or a few days are sufficient to "break in" or give the maximum usefulness to a "green worker." The rank and file of the workers have ceased to be skilled artisans and have become mere "hands." Under these conditions, and there is every sign that these conditions will continue to multiply, there is a vast army of industrial workers, who, though running marvelously intricate machines, are unskilled in any trade. In fact they possess no skill except that which is demanded by a mechanical obedience to the routine of the machine being operated.

How has this specialization affected the higher and lower levels of training? As far as vocational education is concerned these two trends are working in opposite directions. The "mind" of the organization, the professional man, the technical engineer, becomes increasingly dependent on specialized education for the pursuit of his vocation; informal education of the apprenticeship type is totally incapable of giving him the necessary scientific information or

advanced skills.   The burden of his education necessarily
is thrown back upon the formal agencies.   On the other
hand, the mere operative, the "brawn" of the organization,
following slavishly the movements of his machine, needs
only the shortest period of time "on the work" to reach a
satisfactory degree of efficiency.   The regular receipt of a
pay envelope demands regularity and reliability of a mechanical sort but it calls for no trade proficiency and makes
no demand that the worker understand the manner in which
"his job" integrates with the work of others.   To deplore
this state of modern industry, with its consequent narrowing
of the life of its participants, is easy; but unless the present
social order is to be fundamentally changed, the reduced
status of the worker has to be faced as one of the conditions
of the problem.

Should the school undertake training at the lower levels?
In view of this minute specialization, it is obvious that a
considerable portion of the secondary school population
will require none of the narrow specific vocational training
of which we are writing.   Even in the case of the less simple
or routine occupations very strong evidence can be presented
in favor of the proposal that vocational training be given by
the industry and at the immediate expense of the industry.
The industry has the latest machinery, it can work on a
production basis, it will train only those who are to engage
in the occupation.   Why is it not the logical place in which
to provide the training?   Several objections are raised to
this solution of the problem.   First, there is the wastefulness
of time and effort in the more or less haphazard training of
the shop.   Second, the mobility of labor prevents the employer from training in any elaborate manner individuals
who may leave his employ at any moment.   Third, the individual may be sacrificed because of the narrowness of the
training in industry.   Where every procedure has to be

justified by relatively immediate economic returns, that training will be provided which is most profitable to industry and the interests of the individual may be ignored altogether. In spite of these and other difficulties which could be named, in the opinion of the authors, the school must be extremely slow to accept responsibility for any type of vocational training which industry is in a position to give, or can be adapted to give. The mere fact that to give this training interferes with the production of the plant is beside the point and should be of no great concern to the educator. The reply is obvious, let industry accept this loss of time; it is better for the workman to lack effectiveness for a few months of his long working life, than to reduce the already too short period of general education.

What is the justification for the introduction of this training? It should be noted that wherever vocational education is provided, whether in the school or in the industry, its ultimate support must be borne by society and must be derived from the social income. Only when the occupation demands a knowledge of elementary science or mathematics, or a specific skill such as typewriting or shorthand which, under present conditions, cannot be advantageously or economically given within the vocation itself is there sound reason for the introduction of vocational training into the school. This, as we have already seen, is the justification for the higher vocational schools which lead to the professions. Not to relieve industry of the responsibility of training, not merely to increase initial pay in a competitive world, but, rather to give certain types of information and a facility which the individual, under present conditions, and with reasonable economy to society, would be unable to secure in industry, must be the major criterion for placing the burden of providing narrow vocational training upon the school.

What are the administrative difficulties of introducing industrial training? But, before the school can provide the desired training in these occupations where industrial facilities for adequate training are lacking, great administrative difficulties have still to be faced. Theoretically, for every occupation, some form of direct training could be given within the school. But, as an administrative practicability, vocational education of any level within the formal agency demands:

(a) an occupation socially serviceable;

(b) an occupation of a certain degree of complexity;

(c) a detailed analysis of the occupational requirements;

(d) an effective form of vocational guidance;

(e) a sufficient number of students congregated in one place to justify the cost of equipment and instruction;

(f) a high probability that those taking the training will enter the occupation;

(g) an assurance that the training cannot be given, with greater social economy, by agencies outside the school.

Why must occupational frequency and size of school be considered? These conditions must be carefully weighed by those who imagine, because professional education is so well established and at the same time comparatively simple in its operation, that the training of skilled workers can readily be put on the same footing at a correspondingly lower level. To show one of the more formidable obstacles, we may quote from the Cleveland Education Survey report on "Wage Earning and Education." Commenting on vocational education in the junior high school of ordinary size this report says: "the greatest difficulty in the way of trade training for specific occupations lies in the small number of pupils who can be expected, within the bounds of reasonable probability, to enter a single trade. Hand and machine composition, the largest of the printing trades, will serve as an example. In a junior high school of one thousand pupils, boys and girls, the number of boys who are likely to become compositors is about five. However, to teach this trade, printing equipment occupying considerable space is necessary, together with a teacher who has had some experience or training as a printer. The expense per pupil for equipment, for the space it occupies, and for instruction, renders special training for such small classes impracticable. All the skilled occupations, with the exception perhaps of the machinist's trade, are in the same case. An attempt to form separate classes for each of the eight largest trades in the city would result in two classes of not over five pupils, three classes of not over ten pupils, and only one of over thirteen pupils.

"Number of boys who will probably become:

Machinists	36	Carpenters	13
Steam engineers	11	Painters	10
Electricians	9	Plumbers	7
Compositors	5	Molders	5

"The table shows the number of boys, in a school of this size, who are likely to enter each of these trades." According to this report, within the junior high school intensive trade training for any large proportion of the pupils is impractical. The best that can be done is to introduce for boys a general industrial course in which is stressed the applications of mathematics, drawing, physics, and chemistry to the more common industrial processes. Upon this general foundation later trade proficiency can be built. For girls this course would be paralleled by one stressing certain aspects of the household arts and home-making.

In order to congregate a sufficient number of students to justify giving direct preparation, at the secondary level, for even a few of the typical callings, central vocational schools will be necessary. Here for a limited number of occupations, selected with reference to the demands of the community, as a result of data accumulated by a Department of Sociological Research within the school system, it will be possible to assemble the requisite equipment and teaching force. But it will always be true that the wide variety of skilled occupations which the pupils are destined to enter will preclude the possibility of giving specialized vocational training to all prospective artisans enrolled in the secondary school.

To what extent must we depend on part-time education? For some of these occupations for which the secondary school, on account of numbers or equipment, cannot give formal training and for which the industry unaided cannot furnish the total training, a system of part-time or continuation education, given during the working hours and supplementing the practical work in the industry, will have to be established. While some large corporations, by establishing apprentice schools within their own plants, may take upon themselves the complete responsibility of training their own employees, these isolated agencies can never train more than a small portion of those entering the skilled trades. Only large plants can institute such training methods, and then only when there is a reasonable ground for believing that the plant will be enabled to retain, for some considerable period, the services of those receiving the training. For this reason the problem of coöperation between industry and the formal continuation school is of great importance.

What warnings must be given in the field of industrial education? The general situation with regard to the training of skilled workers in the manufacturing and mechanical industries may now be summarized. Any attempt to give specific vocational training to pupils before fourteen years of age should be discouraged; after this period, for those who are intending to enter some of the wider fields which demand certain common informational elements and specific skills, such as machine work or the building trades, it is administratively possible to provide specific training. Owing to the large number of occupations into which the rest of the school population is going, only in exceptional cases can specific occupational training be given within the school. Such courses must only be provided by the school when careful inquiry reveals a definite demand in the industrial life of the community. Furthermore, these courses must not be given merely to relieve the industry from the burden of the training, nor in the interests of larger initial wages for those entering the industry; they must only be established when the nature of the occupation is such that the training which the job affords is inadequate and uneconomical. Even under these conditions the possibility of a combined school and industry course through part-time or continuation education must be examined before the school shoulders the complete responsibility. It may be urged once more that only as vocational training can be provided with less cost by the school than by the industry should the formal agency assume the responsibility for such training. It must never be forgotten that whether vocational training is to be supported through public taxation or through the increase in the price of the commodity, the burden cannot be escaped. But the evidence which has been presented shows most clearly how enormous will be the expense to society if the formal school, unaided by the industry, attempts to give vocational training to all artisans. In view of the fact that the most strenuous task of present-day education is the control of industrialism in the interests of a democratic humanism, educators must be everlastingly watchful lest an unanalyzed theory of values, erected by our economically obsessed society, be accepted as the basis of a philosophy of education.

How has the changed economic status of woman affected her vocational training? We may now turn to a problem of vocational education which has become particularly acute within our own generation. Any discussion of occupational training, however brief, is compelled to recognize the existence of marked differences in the demands of the two sexes. The rapidly changing conception of the place of woman in the modern world makes difficult any formulation of the means and ends of her vocational preparation. In spite of the fact that usually women have not been recognized as wage-earners, women as a class have always been self-supporting. It is interesting to note that in certain States, by legislating to women half the earned income of the husband, the law has recently come to recognize their economic contribution within the home. Whether such official recognition is given or not, the fact is clear that except in rare instances the woman has naturally contributed to the economic life of the household. While this statement is in the main true of the modern mother, only the most casual observation is needed to reveal great changes in the conditions of family life — changes which are working, on the one hand, to simplify and reduce the labor of the house, and on the other hand, to complicate and increase the demands made on woman in the home. Owing to the division of labor in modern industrial society, most of the products, which but a generation or so ago were manufactured within the home, are now delivered ready-made at the householder's door. Owing to the growth of modern invention and its successful application within recent years to the domestic labor problems, the mechanics of the home have been much simplified. Because of the decrease in the number of children within the average family, and the extension of universal education, covering from eight to ten years of the child's life, the tasks and responsibilities of the mother have been materially lessened. As against these factors, which reduce domestic labor, we may note the increasing demands for comfort of the ordinary household, the increasing technical knowledge called for by its methods and procedures, and the increasing conviction that home should be more than a place for which to toil, and in which to sleep, to eat, and to procreate. All of these factors, both positive and negative, are working to modify the objectives and change the emphasis in the vocational education of women.

What is the dual rôle of woman within the home? Two aspects of woman's work within the home need to be differentiated. In the first place, there is the housekeeping which is concerned with the basic problems of clothing, food and shelter. Here certain skills are demanded, but more particularly sound judgment and accurate knowledge in the field of household economy. In the second place, there is home-making. While all members of the family are responsible for creating that peculiar atmosphere which makes a home, the mistress who presides over the household, and whose life concerns center around it, is in the best position to give direction to those activities and interests which are the mark of a congenial home. The contrast between housekeeping and home-making is clear: the first is concerned with carrying out effectively certain more or less definite activities which can be catalogued and objectively evaluated; whereas home-making is concerned with the less tangible but equally important factors through which a happy household is created. In so far as man rises above the animal he needs a home, for his happiness is bounded by considerations other than those of shelter, raiment and food. As will readily be seen, the question of vocational education for housekeeping is comparatively simple; with full allowance for differences in vocational expectations, every girl must be given an opportunity to learn something concerning foods and their preparation, home nursing and the problems of infant care, expenditure of income, sewing, household furnishing and home management.

What provision should be made for home-making? The problem of training for home-making is much more intricate; here the different theories of values, the different capacities, the different interests and the different tastes of various individuals and groups make formal instruction for this aspect of family life most indefinite. In so far as the basic human qualities which are the foundation for a happy home are required of men and women alike, this training in home-making will constitute a part of general education for both sexes; but since woman has a peculiar responsibility, it would seem that somewhere in the course of her education the girl should be given the opportunity to study the human problems of the home. The increasing leisure of all members of the household, due to the advent of coöperative industry, places a great responsibility on the parents. Especially must the mother be trained to make the home a pleasant and stimulating place in which to live, and an advantageous environment in which to develop the various personalities of the family.

Why has woman been forced into an adventitious position? The peculiar economic position in which woman has been placed by the development of the closely knit coöperative society of our own generation remains to be considered. In primitive society man, it may be noted, started out to earn his living by fishing, hunting and other occupations remote from the family hearth. But as population increased and pressed upon the food supply, as the advantages of specialization of labor became apparent and as the worth of the more civilized occupations was appreciated, man proceeded to take out of the home, one after another, the occupations which, at one time, were followed almost exclusively by woman. In so far as this has taken place, woman is left occupying a somewhat adventitious position: this is especially apparent in the homes of the wealthy where the women tend to lead an idle and aimless existence. As a result of this movement, if the married woman is to confine her energies within the home, she must find an outlet for her energies in the broader activities of home-making. If, for one reason or another, due to absence or departure of children, or to service facilities, the home does not give sufficient outlet for this energy, unless she is to be parasitic, two courses lie open to her. Either she may enter the economic world and compete on an equal footing with man or, better, she may initiate, administer, and "man" the large number of social and civic organizations and enterprises which are working within the community for human betterment. There is urgent need for directing the attention of women to the second alternative, and for giving them the necessary training which will stimulate interest, and provide the skill and judgment necessary for the effective rendering of these various forms of social service. But the chief result of man's entering the home and taking the occupations of the woman into the industrial world has been that woman, either willingly or under compulsion, has followed her occupations and has entered into the wider industrial and economic world, outside the household.

Why must vocational education disregard the traditional concept of woman's sphere? Since such a large number of women regard their sojourn within the economic world as bridging a gap between leaving the home of their childhood and entering the home of their choice, woman's position in this sphere of service obviously differs from that of man. The transitory stay of woman in industry and her consequent reluctance to undertake work that requires prolonged training with little economic return complicates the problem of her vocational education. To the extent that she enters this realm and remains, the problem of the vocational training of women does not differ materially from that of the vocational training of men. The idea that on a wide scale certain occupations are more suited to the capacities of women than they are to those of men and vice versa is to a large degree in error. The differentiation of occupation between the sexes is much more a result of environmental forces than of innate psychological differences. Woman is hampered in her fight for personal and economic independence by stupid notions of this kind, which are but rationalizations to cover the true motive — the desire of man to keep woman in the position of subservience. If the "stronger sex" can specialize in pediatrics and earn its living by selling women's stockings, corsets, and baby food, even a man-made world must recognize the right of women to plead at the bar and to gain her independence by selling bonds, real estate, and razors. It is a fond delusion that women can return to the status that was hers in an older civilization.

From early times, sentimental writing has encircled the home with a halo of idealism; there is on this account a constant tendency to urge the return of woman to the sphere where, according to legend, she led a life so "wondrous, sweet and fair." A little knowledge of the real facts of family life in past generations is sufficient to shatter this comfortable notion. Education, particularly, cannot seek refuge from the facts of life in this antiquated conception of the sphere of woman. Woman alone can determine her true place in society. Through radical experimentation education must enable her to demonstrate her capacities and limitations; capacities and limitations which, in the opinion of the authors, will prove to be remarkably like those of men. Students of comparative civilization are revealing the striking interchangeability of rôles played by the two sexes, rôles which in our civilization where man is dominant, we regard as distinctive of one or the other sex. It is safe to assume that the emancipation of woman, and her increasing independence of marriage as a means of establishing her social status, will necessitate a program of vocational education equal in scope to that provided for man and not so different in direction as many believe. This program must fit her for the manifold positions which in our economic life she is coming to occupy, naturally and gracefully. In addition to these vocational courses for the extra household activities, either in the regular school course or through a widened continuation education, she must be enabled, when the need arises, to acquire under formal supervision some of the more basic skills and knowledges required in housekeeping and child rearing. Also she must be provided with the opportunity to become better acquainted with the means, in so far as they are communicable, whereby a house expresses the personalities of its inmates and reflects the cordial spirit of a home.

What determines the nature of a vocational curriculum? Having considered the professional and industrial education, we may in closing direct attention to the general question of vocational curricula and vocational perspective.

The principles which control the nature of the curriculum in vocational education are, *mutatis mutandis*, the same for the vocations at all levels. If an accurate and well-understood occupational terminology may be assumed, the first prerequisite is an intensive study of the actual situations and problems which are met by workers in the occupation under consideration. Occupational analysis, or, at its lower levels, job analysis, furnishes the intimate knowledge of the requirements of vocational proficiency. To be valuable this analysis must be carried out in great detail, and must be the result of the examination of the actual work of typical mem-

bers of the occupation.   Those habits and skills, those facts
and ideas, those procedures and techniques which are being
constantly employed by the most proficient workers must be
made the definite objectives of the instruction.   The effectiveness of the school must be judged by the manner in
which the learner attains these specific objectives.   If the
training is to be of an economical and modern order, constant introduction of new material in the light of the newer
phase of the calling, constant experimentation with new
arrangements of studies, constant trial of new methods of
teaching will be necessary.   Because of the growth of knowledge, vigilance must be exercised, especially in our professional schools, to prevent the course of study from becoming
overloaded: there is constant danger lest, even to the willing
and superior student, the curriculum may become a weari-
ness to the flesh.   In many of our medical schools the ordinary student can be likened to Bunyan's pilgrim — "a book
in his hand and a great burden on his back." [1]   Traditional
elements in the curriculum, having lost their relative usefulness, must be abandoned, and the time saved must be devoted to more thorough mastery of the more essential elements of the course or to the inculcation of new practices
and theories.

Why is occupational analysis so difficult?   While occupational analysis of the simpler callings is comparatively easy,
the analysis of the wider professions such as law, medicine,
engineering, the ministry, teaching and diplomacy is most
difficult.   The fact that the professional man is responsible
for meeting the unexpected issues and crises of individual
and group life makes a definite analysis most intricate.
For the ordinary demands of the profession, theoretical
background is important and, for the advancement of the

[1] It cannot be too clearly recognized that the "difficulty" of a course
of study is a function of the speed of instruction.

profession and the improvement of its practice, becomes essential. This necessity for theoretical background makes the problem of deciding just what shall be included in and excluded from the professional course unusually complicated. Analysis of activities may easily stress the more practical and more limited parts of the course at the expense of the wider and more theoretical training. So extensive are the ramifications of these callings, so specialized within themselves, as to render almost impossible the discovery of the essential elements.

How can the spirit of service be injected into the occupational life? As this brief discussion of some of the problems of vocational education is brought to a close, misunderstanding may be avoided by calling attention once more to the peculiar and narrow connotation of the term *vocation*. It has been used to signify the teaching of the direct skills, informational elements and procedures demanded by the occupation. But the mere skills and information are only one part of the vocational equipment; provision must also be made, somewhere in the training of the student, for the creation of the larger occupational viewpoint, and the inculcation of a direct social responsibility with respect to the particular calling. That those embarking on the higher callings must have high professional standards and large perspective has always been taken for granted; but the necessity for definite standards of conduct, for greater realization of responsibility, for greater understanding of the significance of human toil is necessary for all engaged in the work of the world. In the main, general education will have to create these standards, but the industrial school, the agricultural school, the commercial school, the normal school, the graduate school, and the higher professional school must insure that the individual, both prior to and during his specialized training, gets some understanding of the larger rôle which he is to play. Through definite and systematic instruction he must acquire those attitudes and adopt those ideals which lead to the pursuit of the specialized calling in a spirit of social service. Certain of these attitudes and ideals will have to be taught with direct relation to the specific vocation, but the vast majority can be made the subject of instruction in the more general courses which precede or accompany the vocational training. Vocational training for individual advancement and social exploitation must give place to an education for individual ministration and social service.

ADDITIONAL PROBLEMS FOR DISCUSSION

1. To what influence may be traced the enormous increase in professional and semi-professional occupations during the last century?
2. How has the extension of the age of compulsory education focused attention on the problems of vocational education?
3. What educational and social advantages and disadvantages would accompany placing complete responsibility for industrial training on industry?
4. In view of the trend of modern industry, what are the probabilities that the proportion of workers in industry requiring extensive training will decrease?
5. Show how the prerequisites for admission to a professional school are dependent on the elaborate interplay of educational, sociological and economic forces?
6. What are the educational shortcomings of a system of professional training which thrusts upon the community a large number of individuals who use their special knowledge for exploitation?
7. List the major reasons favoring the general educational position that the school should be very slow to undertake the burden of providing the narrower vocational training.
8. To what extent is the enthusiasm for industrial training to be traced to the desire to use public funds to enable certain individuals and certain industrial groups to attain a privileged economic position in a competitive industrial system?
9. Show how the differentiation of industry and the increase in the number of occupations have made ridiculous the proposal for the extension of formal vocational training to all.
10. From the standpoint of educational values and the expenditure of public funds, criticize the common practice of giving narrow voca-

tional training to an individual who subsequently enters a totally different type of vocation. How can this evil be remedied through vocational guidance?

11. From the standpoint of training, what are the advantages of the part-time method in which the student divides his time between formal instruction in the school and work in the industry? What are the dangers inherent in such a scheme?

12. Give specific illustrations justifying the statement that the occupational life of the community forms an essential background for much of the cultural education. Show how this form of education, though possessing vocational bearings, is not vocational.

13. Show how vocational education proper must accept the present industrial order, whereas general education with a vocational background must be extremely critical of the industrial order and work for its progressive modification.

14. How should the philosophy of vocational education for a democratic society differ from that adapted to a stratified society under autocratic rule?

15. What do you consider will be the main changes in the economic position of woman during the coming century?

PROBLEM 23

WHAT METHODS SHOULD CONTROL THE CONDUCT OF INSTRUCTION?

What is the nature of method? — Can method be considered apart from content? — What is the need for a study of methodology in instruction? — How can the products of instruction be classified? — What methods should control the acquirement of narrow skills? — What methods should control the acquirement of organized knowledge? — In presenting organized knowledge, what are the more general aspects of instruction? — What aspect of instruction does preparation stress? — What aspect of instruction does presentation stress? — What aspect of instruction does association stress? — What aspect of instruction does generalization stress? — What aspect of instruction does application stress? — What methods should control the acquirement of intellectual habits? — Why must the problem be the vehicle for training in thinking? — What methods should control the acquirement of attitudes and appreciations? — What are the major procedures of teaching? — What are the merits and demerits of the lecture method? — What are the merits of the discussional method? — What are the dangers of the discussional method? — What is the function of the demonstration and laboratory method? — What is the place of the dramatic method? — How does the task-master conception of instruction misread the aim of education? — What are the larger aims of education? — What are the more tangible results of instruction? — How may these products be more effectively measured? — What has been the major contribution of the measurement movement?

What is the nature of method? Speaking before a group of educators, an eminent university professor opened his address with the statement that he thanked the gods he had never studied " methods of teaching." Strange to say, this same individual would have been among the first to bear grateful testimony to the benefit he derived from a painstaking study of the methods of research. Yet " method " in instruction does not differ in its essential nature from " method " in any other activity. When the cook proceeds to make an omelette, when the carpenter proceeds to make a cabinet, when the physicist proceeds to investigate the properties of matter, or when the teacher proceeds to make clear the meaning of democracy, each in his respective activity employs a particular method. By an analysis of these various activities the nature of method becomes apparent. Method is nothing more than a form of procedure; it is the manner in which the individual uses the material at his disposal to produce or attain some end.

Can method be considered apart from content? Whether the cook, the carpenter, the scientist or the teacher is considered, the method of each is judged good or bad as the activity is carried out in a way which produces the desired result. If there is no method, there will be no product; if there is a poor method, there will be a poor product; if there is a good method, there will be a good product. Excellence of method exhibits itself in that selection of material and that ordering of the activity calculated to yield, in the most economical manner, the highest quality of product. That method cannot exist apart from an activity which is in progress is platitudinous. Method always has a particular setting and always deals with particular material. But for convenience of thought, method may be abstracted from content and given separate consideration. If general methodology is to be studied, method must be isolated and freed from the particular elements to which in practice it is always joined.

What is the need for a study of methodology in instruction? Methodology in education does not differ in its essential nature from methodology in any other field. It is only to be distinguished from methodology in other realms by the fact that it operates in different media and has correspondingly different ends. From the standpoint of the scholar, method is a guide to the employment of various means; it is an instrument for dealing effectively with the materials of his problem.   From the standpoint of the teacher, our chief concern in this section, method signifies such selection and arrangement of the teacher's activities and through these of the activities of his pupils as will yield, with the maximum economy, the results for which the activities are initiated.   It would be passing strange if a close study of methods of procedure in education, a procedure which of necessity involves the most complex activities on the part of both teacher and pupil, did not yield a body of most valuable information.   For the teacher, a knowledge of the skill or subject-matter to be taught is but the beginning of wisdom.   This knowledge is the *sine qua non* of the activity, but to its insufficiency as an assurance of good teaching, the classrooms of our schools, and more particularly the lecture halls of our universities, bear constant and pathetic witness.   The supercilious attitude of many teachers, especially in our higher institutions, towards the study of methods of teaching would be justified only on the assumption that the art of teaching cannot be learned, or else that it is such a simple procedure that any individual of reasonable intelligence could, in a short period of trial and error, learn all that is to be known concerning its conduct. " Teachers are born not made " is a comfortable doctrine, but, like so many other doctrines of a similar nature that confirm us in evil practice, it suffers from the great demerit of being in error!   Previous statements in this paragraph show the absurdity of the second assumption.   " Methods of teaching " can no more be economically learned without the skillful guidance of a teacher than the "methods of research " can be acquired without the skillful guidance of an investigator.

What are the reasons for this need?   Three factors make essential a careful study of methodology.   Firstly the time of the pupil is limited; secondly, the raw material of the process is human time and human energy; thirdly, the methods of the school and the methods of the teacher become the methods of the pupil. But while stressing the importance of methods we must at the same time warn the reader that formal procedures in instruction, like procedures in any other field, may easily become a fetish; they may corrupt good teaching; they may confine the activity rather than give it freedom. These are the abuses and not the uses of method. Methods must be flexible, they must serve as general guides, they must not be worshiped as idols, they must be used as instruments.

How can the products of instruction be classified? The field is now clear for a closer analysis of the problem. In achieving the main purposes of education the teacher must so direct his own activities and through these the activities of his pupil as to give the wisest aid to the latter in the acquirement of:

(1) Narrow skills and habits, and the association of relatively isolated symbols with meanings.

(2) Organized knowledge.

(3) Habits of study, habits of thinking and habits of investigation.

Appreciations, aspirations, and ideals.

discussion will therefore concern itself with the methodology which should control the activities of the teacher and the pupils, as they co-operate to attain these various ends of instruction.

What methods should control the acquirement of narrow skills? In activities which have for their aim the acquisition of certain narrow motor skills or the acquirement of certain isolated facts, such as the multiplication or addition combinations, spelling, or the meaning of symbols, the basic function of the teacher is to present, with suitable explanation, a copy or model, and then allow the pupil to practice under supervision. In the simpler instances, economical learning demands a careful copying of the model. On account of the simplicity and directness of the response there is but little need for analysis. But as the activity becomes more complex, the need for analysis increases. The teacher must strive to ascertain the relative importance of each component of the activity by noting its effect on later efficiency; he must determine the order in which these components are to be introduced, and he must give adequate exercise to each. The trial-and-error phase of the learning may usually be reduced by emphasizing certain aspects of the activity, and by calling attention to the places where mistakes are liable to occur. While the pupil must be allowed the opportunity to make those mistakes which are essential to effective learning, it is to squander the experience of the past and to defeat the very purpose for which formal education exists, if the pupil is permitted undirected experimentation. The pupil cannot be allowed to fritter away his time in trying out a series of wrong responses. There is room for considerable judgment on the part of the teacher in allowing sufficient error in practice to insure security in the skill. Sound judgment is required at this point lest the errors merely consume time, energy, and material without giving power.

The general rules which control habit formation have already been discussed at some length in Problem 6 and the reader is referred to the general principles there outlined. But in this inquiry into the modes of acquirement of skills, these general principles may be made more definite by calling attention to the following aids:

(1) Analyze the components of the skill, and call attention to those of greater difficulty.

(2) Give adequate exercise under close supervision to each component.

(3) Provide a good model.

(4) Let the pupil know the precise nature of the objective.

(5) Arrange, wherever possible, that the pupil himself know whether the skill is being successfully acquired or not.

(6) Motivate the practice in every way possible.

Can the tools of knowledge be acquired incidentally? Before we leave the question of the acquirement of the elementary tools, one further point demands specific mention. In the acquirement of these tools to what extent is it wise to rely on incidental rather than formal instruction? Restricting ourselves to the matter of routine skills, we may note that there is no simple answer to this question. It will suffice to mention the two opposing positions. One is that the tools of knowledge can be acquired incidentally in the carrying out of other activities which are undertaken for their own sake. Thus, it is contended, the child can learn the combinations of arithmetic, or learn to read, in order to accomplish some wider purpose. He may be trusted "to pick up" the material, to acquire the skill as part of a larger enterprise. On the other hand, the opponents of this incidental method of learning point out that the very reason for which the school came into existence was that the child failed to gain this efficiency incidentally in his other activities. Furthermore, they urge with great effect that every scientific investigation into the learning of the more complex skills and use of tools shows how wasteful may be the forms of incidental learning. If the bonds are to be formed in the right order, if they are to be formed correctly, if they are to be exercised adequately, if they are to be tested properly; if, in other words, there is to be economy of learning, the training must be formal rather than informal. Education is sadly in need of studies investigating detailed rates of learning of diverse mental levels under different methods of instruction. Until such studies are available, to dogmatize is foolish. But it is perhaps not too much to say that every analytical study of the process of learning of such skills as reading, spelling, arithmetic, algebra, etc., makes the educator feel less inclined to rely on incidental methods.

Perhaps the two positions may be somewhat reconciled. Admitting the fact that there are great dangers in pure formal training, the wise educator will take care that wherever possible the tools and basic skills are made to show their contribution to a wider purpose. Motive will thus be introduced. The tools and skills will be not final aims but transitional means; in this sense instruction will be incidental rather than formal. But whenever the tool or skill is being taught, the teacher must insure, that the pupils without necessarily being conscious of his direction, are given the full benefits of practice under the conditions which modern psychological analysis is showing are essential to effective learning.

What methods should control the acquirement of organized knowledge? After the first fundamental skills in the various fields of instruction have been acquired by the pupil, the imparting of isolated facts should become increasingly rare. The problem of the teacher is that of introducing the pupil to certain organized and closely related bodies of knowledge. This brings us to the second division of our objective. The aim ceases to be the acquiring of a skill or the memorizing of separate elements, and becomes that of understanding and retaining a body of facts which is logically integrated. To say that the body of facts is logically integrated would seem to imply that the task of the teacher is exceedingly simple. He has merely to follow in order these logical sequences and hold his pupils to this task. Unfortunately, the problem is more complicated. The material of education — history, science, literature, etc. — exists in a form which is organized to appeal to the mature and trained mind. Its arrangement makes for conciseness, easy reference, and further investigation. It reflects an order which has existed in the mind of one who is interested in the subject itself, quite apart from its relation to life's activities. But this order which makes such an appeal to the trained and interested specialist is a stumbling-block to the untrained and uninterested child. The teaching process culminates in bringing the pupils to see the reason for its organization and to appreciate its usefulness. But to present to the immature mind subject-matter in the form in which it may be most readily employed by experts is obviously absurd. In order that the pupil may be brought to see the significance of the material it is necessary to consider his point of departure, his contacts, his interests, and his capabilities. The logical method of presentation must give way to the psychological mode of approach. In the initial stages, one is not so much a teacher of organized bodies of knowledge as a teacher of immature minds. There is no desire to make any ultimate distinction between the psychological and the logical: this is not the point at issue. The contrast is rather between a procedure which is dictated by the interests, needs, and capacities of the child (psychological), and a procedure which is wholly controlled by the interests, needs, and capacities of a trained student (logical). The psychological will lead to the logical or it is worthless; but the manner of approach and the general organization of the material of instruction, using the first method, will differ considerably from that employed in the strict logical presentation.

How must methods be adjusted to different levels of instruction? In the interests of making the learner independent of the teacher — the final goal of all good instruction — we must insist, as time proceeds, that the pupil be freed from the necessity of the psychological mode of presentation in which, for reasons of immaturity, great sacrifice is made to conciseness, ease of reference, and application. In so far as the psychological approach is wasteful, the pupil must be so trained that the logical mode of presentation, because of its economies, becomes more helpful to him than the psychological. While instruction must begin with the infant mind as the focus of the problem, care must be taken that the weaning process is consummated. Otherwise the same infantile methods of teaching will have to be employed in the higher institutions of learning. Spoon feeding of pre-digested material must cease in our colleges and universities, and even in our high schools for children of superior minds. The individual must be taught to make independent use of the treatises in which human learning and experience are stored. These repositories of human learning, these means of intellectual salvation, must be made accessible to the better minds without the mediating ministrations of a pedagogical priesthood. These treatises are, and always will be, organized not for the understanding of infants but for the logically trained thinker. To enable the student to take a logically organized presentation of a certain field of knowledge and, without assistance, to gain an understanding and mastery of its elements and connections, to bring him to welcome this logical mode of presentation rather than a less concise and logical mode, must be one of the major objectives of higher education. If, as some educators seem to advocate, the methods of teaching in the elementary school should be applied throughout the whole range of education, this aim can never be accomplished.

In presenting organized knowledge, what are the more general aspects of instruction? The method of procedure is intimately dependent upon the particular subject-matter of the field in question, and as the preceding paragraph shows, it is also intimately related to the degree of intellectual maturity of the student. This fact makes it dangerous to formulate a general method which should be followed in imparting a body of information. But with suitable changes to meet the specific conditions under which they may be employed, attention may well be directed to the so-called " Five Formal Steps " of the Herbartian system. Although Herbart expounded his system in terms of a psychology of isolated ideas which is now discredited, his analysis can easily be restated in the terms of modern psychology. Abandoning his idea of steps to be traversed in favor of the conception of processes to which attention must be directed, and following later writers as regards terminology, we may consider the five aspects of instruction which were stressed by Herbart. These are: (1) preparation; (2) presentation; (3) association; (4) generalization; (5) application. These five divisions of the total activity, if followed too rigidly, may easily hamper instruction; but, if used with discretion and freedom, they afford helpful guidance by calling attention to important aspects of the instructor's problem in presenting any well-defined unit of instruction.

What aspect of instruction does preparation stress? In the process of preparation, the teacher consciously attempts to prepare the mind of the pupil for the information which is to follow. Varying with the intellectual maturity of the learner, this may be achieved in a multitude of ways. With young children, by means of question and answer, instruction will begin with the summoning of any relevant knowledge pertaining to the new topic. This serves to direct the general flow of thought into the channels desired, and should end in a clear statement of the aim of the discussion. In the interests of kindling the thought process, whenever possible, this aim should be stated in the definite form of a problem. With the statement of the problem, the responsibility of the teacher does not end; particularly with younger children, it is essential that the problem be made to appear worthy of the effort required in its solution. This may be accomplished by showing its relation to various elements of past experience and the larger social life. This important phase of the teacher's problem properly belongs under presentation.

What aspect of instruction does presentation stress? In the process of presentation, the teacher becomes the focus of attention. At this point the new material is presented. In so far as it is new, to extract the information from the pupil is of course impossible. Here, the teacher should proceed to acquaint the pupils with the new material and refuse to be daunted by the fact that he, rather than the pupil, must do the talking. Much time may easily be lost, at this stage, by a teacher obsessed with the notion that every new idea must be teased out of the experience of the pupils even though there is every assurance that these ideas are lacking; at this point the attempt to extract the new information, rather than to give it directly to the pupil, is wasteful of time and effort. Through direct statement, illustration, explanation, and interrogation, the new problem is solved, or the new field developed.

What aspect of instruction does association stress? The process of association can hardly be separated from the process of preparation just discussed. If the new material is to be understood, it must, of necessity, be associated with past experiences; and, if the new material is also to be retained effectively, it not only must be associated in as wide a manner as possible with past experiences, but also it must be articulated with future activities. While presentation stresses the mere understanding of the material presented, association calls attention to the obligation of the teacher to interweave the new material, by as many strands as possible, with the old pattern. In this process discussion should be freely employed.

What aspect of instruction does generalization stress? In the process of generalization, under the guidance of the teacher, the pupils attempt to summarize the information which has been given, or to state the solution of the problem in a helpful and concise manner. In its most adequate form, this process culminates in a general proposition, a definition, a rule, or a law. But, in those cases where there is no possibility of reduction to a simple formula, a well-worded and brief summary of the material presented should be made. At this point, in ordinary class room procedure, the burden is upon the pupils. The teacher acts as a selective agent and is responsible for the form of the final summary.

What aspect of instruction does application stress? In the process of application, following the statement of a general proposition, whether a law in physics, a rule in grammar, or a principle in human conduct, the attempt is made to ascertain whether the formula is a series of empty words, or whether it summarizes a body of significant experience. The best method of testing this crucial point is to investigate the extent to which the new information can be directed to the solution of new problems, or the understanding of new phases of the work. In order to free the principle from its immediate setting, to show that it is applicable in other directions than the specific one in which it originated, the teacher must develop its wider application. Here is the teacher's strategic opportunity to give conscious attention to the problem of transfer of training; responsibility always rests upon the teacher to see that the body of information developed has the maximum range of usefulness. Only as these new ideas are applied in other settings

than those in which they were acquired will they assume
that richness of significance which assures transfer.   At
no point is the distinction between good and poor teaching
greater than in this process of application.   The poor
teacher leaves the new information with a narrow range of
application, while the good teacher is careful, by comments
and questions, to show its broader availability.

From the description of the five processes which has been
given, the reader will see that the last four are intimately
related. Any attempt to make a unit of instruction follow
in a rigid and slavish fashion a sequence of five steps would
be disastrous.   Regarded, however, as different aspects of
instruction, no one of which should be overlooked when the
teacher and pupil engage in the coöperative enterprise of
learning, Herbart's divisions have distinct value.   The
degree of emphasis given to these different divisions will
vary greatly with the age of the pupil and the precise aim of
instruction.   With the intellectually mature, the process of
presentation and generalization will preponderate, the
individual himself being responsible for the detailed work
which the other processes demand.   Obviously, when the
lecture system is employed, great assumptions with reference to the abilities, coöperation, and self-discipline of the
hearers are made.   But whether the discussional method
or the lecture system is followed, these five aspects of the
total process of instruction serve to remind the teacher of
his various obligations; only as these are recognized is the
maximum service rendered to the learner in acquiring new
and fertile points of view.

**What methods should control the acquirement of intel-
lectual habits?**   The analysis of the methods whereby organized knowledge is presented to the learner indicates how
arbitrary was our classification of the ends of teaching.
Habits of study and thinking — the third division of our

analysis — are so inextricably interwoven with the procedures employed in presenting information that their separation seems artificial. The justification for such separation must be found in the degree to which it directs specific attention to the opportunities which exist for helping the pupil to acquire the best methods of study and gain the maximum facility in thinking permitted by his endowment. The teacher must instruct the student in those methods of study which are employed by all capable thinkers. Restricting our attention, more specifically, to aids in acquiring and retaining the information upon which effective problem solving is dependent, we may note that the student must be made to acquire the following powers:

(1) The habit of getting a clear insight into the meaning of the material to be learned.

(2) The habit of assigning relative values within the material.

(3) The habit of concentrating on the important elements.

(4) The habit of attempting to recall, from paragraph to paragraph, page to page, topic to topic, the salient points covered.

(5) The habit of reviewing the material, at increasing intervals.

(6) The habit of reviewing in spare moments material which has been learned.

(7) The habit of concentrating on forgotten elements.

(8) The habit of learning almost verbatim key phrases, definitions, rules, laws.

(9) The habit of making outlines and marking texts.

(10) The habit of effective reference to authoritative sources.

(11) The habit of note-taking which will insure ready availability of material, or ready reference to sources.

(12) The habit of applying newly acquired principles in wider fields.

If we add to this list the important procedures catalogued in our discussion of transfer of training on page 389, a wide group of intellectual and study habits is assembled. These should form the conscious objectives of school training.

Why must the problem be the vehicle for training in thinking? In the earlier discussion of the psychological foundations of education, attention was repeatedly focussed on the fact that learning is essentially an activity, the most exacting activity in which man engages. All that the teacher can do is to insure the economical direction of the activity. In the section on reflection, the importance of the problem and the extreme value of the problem solving attitude have been stressed. Only by cultivating this attitude can we hope to train the individual to think. To teach the individual to think to the maximum extent of his capacity may be said to be the major goal of the educative process. Information should be presented, methodology should be controlled to accomplish this end. Dewey lists as the marks of the effective thinker: (a) flexibility; (b) directness; (c) openmindedness; (d) whole-heartedness. These character- istics can be favored only by continuous exercise in thinking itself. The importance of having much of the instruction center definitely around problems akin to those in which the individual will need facility in his adult life cannot be over- stressed. Problems, problems, and again problems should be the basis of instruction. All the orthodox subject-matter of the school should be examined to see the manner in which its essential elements can be taught around problems which grow wider and wider in their scope and demands. At first the problems will be simple and the guidance in their solution detailed; as time progresses, not only will the problems become more involved but the degree of guidance in their solution will diminish. Eventually the mature student must be responsible for:

(1) Realizing and stating his own problem.

(2) Collecting information to solve the problem.

(3) Self-criticism in the various steps of solution.

Education must finally make the pupil independent of the teacher and independent of extremely simplified texts. It is this fact that makes the reliance on elementary methods in our colleges, and still more in our universities, so harmful. Methods which are to be highly favored at one level of instruction may be condemned at another. To gain a more adequate conception of the place of the problem in instruction the reader is referred to the discussion of reflection in Part Two. With the statement that the derivation and solution of problems should be the keynote of the intellectual activities of our educational institutions and with the warning not to permit too much squandering of valuable time in unguided effort in the process, this phase of the teacher's obligation may be left.

What methods should control the acquirement of attitudes and appreciations? We now come to the consideration of the fourth division of pupil objectives of instruction. This division concerns itself with the development of appreciations, aspirations, and ideals. With reference to the method to be employed in gaining these objectives, formal guidance of a definite order is most difficult. Appreciations and ideals, to be effectively acquired, must make an emotional appeal; they can never be reduced to a mere formula of words; routine teaching, unless ably given, encourages humbug and priggishness in the pupil. In spite of this danger, the educator is responsible for the acquisition on the part of the pupil of a multitude of graduated and varied feelings with reference to certain ideas, objects, and social practices. Plato, in considering this difficulty, could give no better advice than to surround the children, from their earliest years, with that which is good, beautiful, and estimable.

In attaining this objective the maximum use must be made of the tendency to cling to that to which the individual has been accustomed; he must be kept from contact with that which is evil, ugly and unworthy. The enthusiasm of the teacher must be caught by the pupil. The prestige suggestion of great minds and great souls must be brought to play upon him. In many cases, without knowing why, he should come to share the ideals and appreciations of mankind. The intellectual appeal is, at best, one-sided and limited in its scope. The immature individual is immensely suggestible on the feeling side, so suggestible as to make him a menace; but this very suggestibility, which has its dangerous aspect, may be harnessed for the useful purpose of imparting to him the aspirations and ideals which are the mark of the civilized and cultured man. The ideals and the appreciations which the student is to share must be set up as definite objectives of instruction; they must not be left to assume form by themselves, but must be worked for with the same zeal and with greater subtlety than are the more tangible goals of teaching.

What are the major procedures of teaching? Up to this point, only the more general aspects of method in teaching have received consideration; only the more general guides for instruction have been laid down. The various instructional methods which are used in educational institutions must now be catalogued. There are five large modes of directing the experiences of the learner, which may be found separately but more usually in combination. These are: (1) the discussional method; (2) the laboratory method; (3) the demonstration method; (4) the dramatic method; (5) the lecture method. In an instructional system, each of these modes of teaching has its proper place. It is not a matter of deciding the superiority of one but of attempting to show the true place of each. In view of what has been said with reference to the extreme importance of making teaching consist essentially in the solution of problems by the pupils, and remembering that learning is self-activity, the teacher will be compelled to rely chiefly on the discussional, dramatic, and laboratory methods, to a less degree on demonstration and to a still less degree on the exclusive lecture method. If we examine some of the weaknesses of the lecture method, we shall be better oriented to discuss the other four procedures.

What are the merits and demerits of the lecture method? The lecture system has been condemned for the following reasons:

(a) It admits of almost complete passivity on the part of the student.

(b) It does not *of necessity* give the student any exercise in the thought process; for there is no friction of minds, no stimulation of the group.

(c) It separates the teacher and the student, consequently it affords but little guidance as to rate or success of presentation; it divorces the teaching from the learning process.

(d) It deadens interest and is less liable to make the deeper impression which discussion produces.

(e) It assumes a high level of intelligence on the part of pupil and a considerable facility in note-taking.

In a pure form the lecture method, when the aim is to convey information rather than appreciation, is only justifiable when eager and trained students desire to get in the shortest time a body of information which is not available, or not readily available, in written form. For advanced students, who have already had considerable training and who bring to the lecture a problem attitude of mind, the lecture of an eclectic order performs a unique function. But it can readily be seen that the lecture has no place in the instruction of the immature whose interest and capacity for thinking need rigorous training; consequently with younger pupils combinations of the discussional, laboratory, demonstration, and dramatic methods must be employed.

What are the merits of the discussional method? If the discussional method be examined, it will be found to obviate the demerits of the lecture system. In a lesson conducted by a skillful and spirited teacher, the pupil shares in, and indeed is, the activity; he cannot assume a passive attitude; he is responsible for more than absorbing in memoriter fashion; he is called upon to exercise his ability in thinking by helping in the solution of problems which are continually arising. The teacher and the pupil are in close contact, the stimulation of the group kindles the mind of each member; every opportunity is given to observe the extent to which the point is being understood, the pupil is allowed to ask for further explanations at the points of special difficulty and the rate of instruction synchronizes with the speed of learning. Interest is maintained by the give and take of discussion, a give and take which has always made appeal to the human mind. The student is in a position to challenge the interpretation of the instructor and is able to free himself from dogmatic presentation.

What are the dangers of the discussional method? But the very informality and looseness inherent in this discussional or, unfortunately styled, socialized recitation [1] introduce attendant dangers. Perhaps the greatest of these dangers is evident in the teaching of the recent convert to the Socratic method of instruction; hastening from the "method

[1] The term "recitation" as used in education in the United States is most unhappy. Literally, to recite means to re-cite, "to repeat as something prepared, written down, or committed to memory." (Webster.) This activity is just the one that should be discouraged. A "socialized recitation" comes very near to a contradiction of terms; it does not convey the meaning of those who use the phrase.

courses " where he has been told that the successes of the discussion may be measured by the extent to which the teacher is silent and the pupil is vocal, the young convert proceeds to efface himself; this, forsooth, when he is the only member of the group who has the necessary informa- tion or exact knowledge concerning the goal of the activity. To attempt to extract information from uninformed pupils is the height of folly. Even in the discussional mode of instruction, the teacher must not hesitate to " lecture," but he must not lecture long. The eliciting of pupil infor- mation may easily be reduced to the absurdity of the situa- tion where a teacher having given lessons on the dog and cat, opened the next lesson by the question — " What do you think we are going to talk about to-day? " After sev- eral minutes of asinine guessing, presumably, "to kindle interest," it appeared that the answer for which the class was waiting with trembling eagerness was "The Cow"! The pupils are in the group to learn, and only when they have something definite to contribute or can learn something definite through talking, should they be allowed to talk. Again discussion may easily become irrelevant; idle com- ments which contribute nothing to the main issue may be allowed. The teacher must always remember that those who are coöperating with him in the discussion are immature and are engaging in the activity for purposes of training; if great care is not exercised, the thirty or forty untrained debaters will carry off his feet the one individual who knows whither the activity is tending. Furthermore, these thirty or forty participants represent wide levels of mental acuity. If some of the stupid and loquacious are allowed to occupy more than their fair time on the floor, the discussion readily becomes extremely tedious, and demands no effort on the part of the majority.

In the case of adult students, particularly, the discussional method must be used not because it is interesting, nor yet because it is easy for the student, but because it makes exacting demands on attention and mental capacity. All too often it is given its high rank because it calls for less mental exertion than does a straight lecture when rigorously followed by a wide-awake student. To lecture is difficult enough, but to conduct a good discussional group, where every individual is a contributor and working to the limit of his capacity, is infinitely more arduous. Many think the reverse. This is often because their standards of relevance and intellectual effort in the discussion are much lower than they would be in a formal lecture. Let him who finds that discussion is easy, examine himself to see whether he is not in many cases discussing the obvious, or proceeding at a rate which demands no intellectual vigor. With these necessary warnings, we may conclude that except in the rare cases to which attention has been drawn, the discussional developmental method will be the common procedure of teaching.

What is the function of the demonstration and laboratory method? With younger pupils, the demonstration and laboratory modes of instruction will usually form parts of the discussional lesson. Demonstration, whether in block building, handwriting, or a science lesson, is employed to enable the pupil, in an economical and effective manner, to understand and master some new procedure. In most cases this method should be accompanied by a repetition of the same or a similar activity by the pupil. Demonstration has the great merit of being rapid, of permitting the teacher to exhibit a technique and to call attention while the process is unfolding before the pupil to its salient aspects. This often saves much of the time which is consumed in the unguided process ordinarily accompanying laboratory work. Because teacher demonstration without pupil performance often fails to give sufficient acquaintance with the procedure for effective execution or an adequate understanding of the activity, education must not be led to the other extreme of expecting the pupil to discover everything for himself. No better occupation for filling the void of eternity can be conceived than that of setting the pupils to " rediscover " the procedures and truths which have been laboriously accumulated by the best minds of each generation. In the first place, they can never do it; and, in the second place, if they could, it would be an enormously wasteful process of learning. While every attempt, under simplified and well controlled conditions, should be made to have the pupils get some understanding and appreciation of the discoverer's point of view, this method of rediscovery squanders the experience of the past, and violates the fundamental principle for which the school was brought into being. Laboratory work, under this "heuristic system," is extremely time-consuming. Teaching by project, which is but one phase of the laboratory method, in so far as it fritters away time and energy in routine activity, exhibits the same fault. The planning of a good project is excellent training, the execution of the project up to the point where it requires adaptation of means to end and the acquisition of new skills and appreciations is also valuable; when routine begins to settle on the activity, and this may be very early for the brightest pupils, its educational worth diminishes. In teaching by the laboratory and project methods, constant vigilance must be exercised to short circuit those phases of the activity which are mechanical in their nature and not productive of educational growth. The school life of the pupil is too short to justify mere " busy work." While the teacher must insure that the pupil gains confidence in his own powers by carrying out a plan to a successful conclusion, a little imagination or a little symbolism at various parts of the activity will often prevent a useless expenditure of energy.

What is the place of the dramatic method? So important a place does learning through the dramatic method occupy that it well deserves its position among the more commonly accepted and dignified methods which have been listed. At a time in educational thinking when learning through action is so much stressed there should be little danger of neglecting this useful mode of inducting the child into the emotional and the intellectual group life. We have already called attention to the intimate and persistent manner in which social pressure is brought to play upon every individual to imitate those about him. Life for the child is endless imitation; in a single day he plays many parts. The appeal of the dramatic is impelling. The school has been slow to see what a powerful instrument for good, particularly in the early years of formal instruction, is this desire to dramatize. Through its agency, reality could be given to the otherwise remote, interest to the otherwise dull, insight to the otherwise incomprehensible. It requires no strict adherence to any doctrine of psychology to realize how well the acted part, because it compels the actor to assume certain bodily postures and certain facial expressions, introduces the child to the emotional experiences of others. Through the agency of the drama, however simple, and the story, however crude, and the picture, however bizarre, mankind has derived attitudes, appreciations, and understandings that could hardly have been conveyed in any other way. Dramatization will always occupy a strategic position in the methodology of education, for while in its beginning it is narrow imitation, in its end it is unfettered creation.

How may petty school procedures be unduly exalted? Whatever may be the larger methods or the smaller devices of instruction, their success must in the last analysis be judged by the extent to which the pupil acquires the skills, knowledges, procedures, aspirations and ideals which are the objectives of the activity. This, the ultimate criterion, is, as we shall presently see, difficult enough to apply when the measurement of a skill or the acquisition of knowledge is involved. But when the demand is for the direct measurement of the degree to which the pupil is the master of certain procedures of a wider order, and for the measurement of the extent to which he has adopted interests and associated himself wholeheartedly with certain ideals, the task becomes so subtle, the objectives so intangible, the values so imponderable, the chance for hypocrisy so great, that one grows more and more distrustful of any simple measuring rods set up to measure these, the most important and far-reaching products of education. Skill and knowledge may be imparted; the routine of the school may force these upon the pupil; but the very methods which produce these changes may defeat the wider aims of education. Though mechanical facility flourish, though knowledge flourish, interest in intellectual growth or desire to improve the condition of life may languish. To this point we shall return when we evaluate the movement for the measurement of the objectives of education. It has been mentioned here in order to show the need, in estimating the success of instruction, for instruments of precision other than those which are at present available in the field of educational measurements.

How does the taskmaster conception of instruction misread the aim of education? From the very beginning of human intercourse, the need has been felt for some measure to determine the relative effectiveness of different individuals in changing the minds and hearts of their associates. Group life and concerted action have been intimately dependent on the ability of leaders to instruct and inspire others. The abilities required in the teacher are not different in their essential nature from those found in the **reformers** and the inspirers of all ages. The teacher's mission is to reform, his vocation is to inspire. Such a statement would seem platitudinous were not the time-honored picture of the schoolman that of a taskmaster, driving his pupils to unwelcome toil. The taskmaster may succeed well in teaching skills, he may instill a modicum of information, but he will leave no desire for further learning nor will he give his pupils a body of social ideals. Attention has already been directed to the extremely short time that the teacher has at his disposal; even during school life the hours of instruction are relatively limited and the school life of most pupils is but eight or ten years. The taskmaster conception is at fault, not only because of its inhumanity, but, because of its failure to do that for which the school primarily exists.

What are the larger aims of education? The procedures of the school, even in the early years of instruction, and increasingly in the later years, must be ordered and controlled with the specific purpose in mind of making the pupil more and more independent of the inspiration, guidance, and stimulation of the teacher. When the eye of the taskmaster is turned, or the stimulus of the teacher is absent, further work is not forthcoming. For the pupil engaging in work under these conditions the last school bell of his school life is the signal for the abandonment of further effort to study and enjoy the things of the mind. If the school fails, during the limited period at its disposal, to give to the pupil a wide range of interests, to give him motives for further observation and reading, to give him desires to understand a little more clearly the intricacies of living, to give him longings to seek and to find the beautiful in nature and in man; if the school, immersed in its petty routine, fails to do these things, whatever may be the mechanical ability, or erudition of its product, it has failed indeed. However great may be the evidence that the children have been fully occupied, that they can read, spell, write, figure and translate to satisfy the most exacting pedant, unless the student leaves with the desire to be a student for the rest of his life, the final verdict must be " Failure." The teacher may have been busy, the pupils may have been busy, they may have busied themselves about many things, but they have chosen the poorer part. On this account the process of instruction in the later years of school life must be judged, not in terms of the mechanics of learning, but by the extent to which it is fostering initiative and inculcating motives in its pupils. Only as these two objectives are consciously formulated as the ends of education, only as methods and procedures are painstakingly adjusted to further these ends, can the school hope to fulfill its true function. This function is that of sending out interested citizens who at their various levels are eager to continue their education in life's great continuation school, where the last bell will never sound, where the doors will never close, where the activities will never cease.

How can teaching further these larger aims? If instruction is judged more by these larger ends, and less by the mechanics of teaching which are still the bane of the normal school, the attitude of the pupils, both towards their formal school training and towards the wider training that life affords, will be effectively changed. The standards for judging instruction which McMurray has formulated follow these general lines and, with certain changes and additions, may be applied here. At all levels of instruction the procedure must be judged by its success in:

(a) Supplying motives to the pupils for further activity.

(b) Exercising the pupils in discriminating the values inherent in the elements of an activity.

(c) Giving the pupils exercise in the organization of the contributory elements of an intellectual or social activity.

(d) Encouraging initiative on the part of the pupils.

(e) Freeing, from the necessarily limited setting in which they originate, the skills, information, procedures, and ideals imparted in the school, so that they may be most generally applicable to the appreciation and interpretation of life.

Each of these larger criteria of instruction focusses attention upon changes made in the pupils. While these somewhat intangible and imponderable objectives do not, and probably never will, admit of exact measurement, they must always serve as the guiding philosophy of instruction.

What are the more tangible results of instruction? But contributory to these more fundamental changes made in the pupils, are a number of more specific modifications. It is in terms of these changes that we commonly think when reviewing the aims of the school. The child must learn to talk without serious grammatical error, he must learn to read, figure, and write; at higher stages, he must become acquainted with other civilizations, he must acquire facility in handling apparatus, he must learn to speak and read foreign languages. Because these powers are so essential to the achievement of the wider purposes of education, they tend to become its exclusive aims. The ends are lost in the means, the forest is obscured by the trees. These definite powers must be acquired, they are essential to the larger enterprise; but the educator must be constantly watchful lest transitional aims become the final aims of instruction. But, while these narrow abilities do not constitute the larger values of education, their very narrowness and definiteness permit the educator to investigate, with considerable exactitude, the degree of their attainment. The limited nature of the objective makes easy the direct measurement of its attainment.

How may these products be more effectively measured? By tests and examinations the schoolmaster from early times has attempted to measure the success of his instruction. He may have been in doubt as to whether his instruction was influencing the wider behavior and character of his pupil, but he was in no doubt as to the ability of the scholar to decline *amo*, or to re-cite the factual elements of the subject taught. It is extremely fortunate for accurate thinking that, in certain well-defined directions, the abilities of groups and of individuals may be accurately measured. Owing largely to the work of Thorndike a movement has been well launched to make more analytical, more accurate, and more complete the methods of testing the capabilities and acquirements of pupils. No schoolmaster has ever been so foolish as to attempt to teach without, in one way or another, testing his pupils. But the tests applied have usually been crude in conception, difficult in application, and limited in interpretation. Adopting the methods of other quantitative sciences, the measurement movement in education has striven to improve examinational devices so that they will have a wider range of usefulness.

Whether the native or acquired efficiency of pupils is to be measured is not the point at issue. The question is rather one of procedure. Shall the judgment be the opinion, necessarily subjective, frequently offhand or prejudiced, of some one individual, or shall the rating be made by the use of tests devised by specialists and standardized by a series of careful measurements? If pupil efficiency is to be measured with any degree of exactness, clearly defined units and carefully constructed scales for measurement are required. These objective scales which are relatively independent of individual opinion must as far as possible replace the subjective scales now in use. In the measurement of classroom products educators must construct large numbers of these objective or universal scales. Every such instrument, before being employed for the testing of a pupil, must fulfill at least three essential requirements:

   (a) It must yield a consistent objective measure of a desirable educational product in the individual tested.

   (b) It must lend itself to economical administration and scoring.

   (c) It must be so simple in its interpretation as to render it suitable for ordinary use.

Furthermore, if comparisons outside the group tested are to be made, records of other individuals must be accessible. From these records norms or standards for various groups, grades, and mental levels can be established.

What is the range of measurement? Tests and scales have been constructed to measure the acquirement of skill and information in most of the elementary school subjects. Objective standards in the secondary school subjects are being rapidly constructed and, already, the movement is spreading to the college and professional school. So fruitful have been the results obtained from the application of these methods, and so numerous are the measuring devices, that one is encouraged to believe that the same methods will be employed in wider fields than those of skill and information. Where the procedures, appreciations, and ideals are defined with a reasonable amount of clarity, it is only a matter of ingenuity to invent instruments for objective measurement. It is safe to assume that further experimentation will provide educators with means of accurate measurement in at least some phases of the larger objectives of education to which reference has already been made.

What has been the major contribution of the measurement movement? So productive has this movement been in its initial years that claims may be made that standardized mental and school tests, wisely employed, are capable of accomplishing the following ends:

   (a) Making definite the aims of education and determining the possibility, for individuals of varying mental levels, of attaining these aims.

   (b) Furthering the detailed analysis of the processes of learning.

   (c) Aiding individual diagnosis and group analysis.

   (d) Improving classification and promotion, and educational and vocational guidance.

   (e) Improving school records and methods of reporting.

   (f) Establishing definite standards of achievement for various individuals and groups.

   (g) Enabling comparisons to be made external to the group tested.

These are the more obvious uses of the tests. Under controlled conditions, with more adequate scientific checks, the principles underlying the testing movement can be used for the more elaborate purposes of evaluating teachers, textbooks, and modes of instruction. They can also be employed to investigate questions of curriculum procedure, such as the distribution of time and the influence of age on learning.

What are the dangers of the educational measurement movement? The extravagant claims which have been made by enthusiasts in this field must not imperil the forward advance of the movement. The methodology is sound, the point of view is essential, and the merits of both are independent of stupid errors in their application. This point must be made clear before we proceed to consider some of the more obvious hazards which attend the creation of the new instruments. Because certain of the narrower aims can be measured with such precision, there is grave risk that attention will be concentrated on these aims with a consequent neglect of the broader issues. If certain narrow limited objectives are set up and instruments of precision devised to measure their attainment, then the activities which lead to these objectives may be unduly stressed at the expense of other more important activities. This danger the extension of the movement to the measurement of wider phases of behavior will of itself correct; but as long as all the aims of education cannot be measured this peril of emphasis must be watched. To measure the product and present practices of a wrongly conceived educational system, and thereby to derive certain objectives and standards of achievement, is obviously a vicious circle and a procedure which leads to false aims and false standards. Uniformity of procedure and uniformity of product, quite apart from any careful consideration as to the desirability of such uniformity, may easily be an unfortunate outcome of the present standardized tests. A consensus of practice is no criterion of excellence. With its bias toward uniformity the movement for the educational measurement of school products must be continually scrutinized. Standardized instruments, unless they are rapidly changed to keep pace with more enlightened educational aims and practices, may easily have a reactionary influence on the activities of the schools of the country. But these abuses in application of the methodology must not prejudice opinion concerning the value of the methods themselves. No prophetic ability is needed to forecast that on account of the more adequate knowledge and increasing control which the scientific movement in education is furnishing to teachers and educational philosophers, the next twenty-five years will witness great changes in educational procedures, and, what is more significant, great changes in educational aim.

ADDITIONAL PROBLEMS FOR DISCUSSION

1. Why have college instructors been inclined to regard courses in methodology as superfluous and unimportant, and suited only to the needs of elementary-school teachers? What can be said for and against this attitude?

2. Why have those occupations which are allied with teaching, in that they seek to enlighten, persuade, and teach others, such as acting, salesmanship, journalism, and public speaking, given such an important place to methodology?

3. How do you account for the fact that occasionally a football coach, who is only moderately skillful himself, has signal success in producing excellent players and teams? How do you explain the reverse situation?

4. What is the justification for the accusation that in many normal schools methodology has been regarded as an end rather than a means?

5. In the ordinary instruction of the classroom, which two principles of the Herbartian system are most often neglected? Justify and explain your decision.

6. How, with slight modifications, may the principles of the Herbartian system be applied to the acquisition of some of the narrower skills?

7. What is the justification for the point emphasized in the text that the five Herbartian principles must be regarded as aspects of the teaching process rather than five formal steps in a lesson plan?

8. In associating symbols with meanings in the learning of a foreign language, how is the direct method superior to the translation method?

9. In telling a story to young children, how does the teacher make use of the lecture and dramatic methods of instruction?

10. What is the place of the lecture at various levels of instruction?

11. In order to insure, on the part of the student, an appreciation of the wider applications of a general principle, what procedures must the teacher employ? How would the methods of the teacher vary with the level of intelligence of the student?

12. Justify the statement that the clear recognition of the place of the problem in instruction is the most significant contribution to the methodology of teaching made during the last century.

13. What are the criteria by which the educational worth of a problem for presentation to the group is determined?

14. In view of the fact that problems always evolve out of the experience of the individual, why is it difficult and even impossible for the teacher to thrust problems on the pupil? To what extent have the problems of the school been teacher problems rather than pupil problems? What is the psychological difference between the so-called teacher problem and the so-called pupil problem?

15. How is the problem method in complete accord with the changed attitude towards the child which is commonly ascribed to Rousseau?

16. From the standpoint of the psychological processes involved, distinguish between the learning of facts and the development of appreciations.

17. What are the weaknesses of formal education which give some justification for the accusation that the individual submitted to it loses that curiosity which is so evident in the young child?

18. Why has the school given so little attention to the inculcation of purposes and motives for further educational growth in the post-school life of the individual?

19. What psychological principles operate to make dangerous the rigorous application of any general method of instruction to all individuals?

20. What contribution can the measurement movement make to the formulation and realization of the purposes of education? Why can measurement, from its very nature, never determine an educational value?

21. Why in a philosophy of education does the measurement movement occupy such a subsidiary position?

22. Why has the growth of the measurement movement with its added control over the processes of learning increased the necessity for study of the philosophy of education?

23. In what respects should the methods of instruction employed in the schools of a democratic society differ from those used in tne schools of an autocratic social order?

PROBLEM 24

TO WHOM SHOULD SOCIETY DELEGATE THE EDUCATIONAL FUNCTION?

What position would the teacher occupy in an ideal society? — What position does the teacher occupy in American society? — What is the professional status of teaching to-day? — How is the present status of teaching to be explained? — Why must the status of teaching be raised? — How can the status of teaching be raised? — How are the ranks of the teaching profession recruited? — What constitute the attractions of a profession? — How is the status of teaching dependent on financial remuneration? — How is the status of teaching dependent on opportunity for doing creative work? — How is the status of teaching dependent on freedom of thought and action? — How is the status of teaching dependent on social recognition? — How is the status of teaching dependent on a high professional sense? — How is the teaching profession in a strategic position for elevating its own status? — How should compensation be adjusted to different levels of the educational system? — How should compensation be adjusted to the sexes? — By what methods should candidates for professional training be selected? — What should be the training of teachers? — What provision should be made for growth in service? — Why does the teacher occupy a unique position in controlling the evolution of society?

What position would the teacher occupy in an ideal society? Writing in the year 1619, Johann Valentin Andreae gives the following description of those to whom was delegated the responsibility of teaching the youth in the ideal state of Christianopolis:

Their instructors are not men from the dregs of human society nor such as are useless for other occupations, but the choice of all the citizens, persons whose standing in the republic is known and who very often have access to the highest positions in the state. For surely, no one can properly take care of the youth, unless he is also able to discharge the duties of state; and he who succeeds with the youth, has thereby already established his right to serve in governmental affairs. The teachers are well advanced in years, and they are especially remarkable for their pursuit of four virtues:

dignity, integrity, activity, and generosity. For if they are not successful with their scholars and disciples and are not highly valued by the public; if they do not excel others in reverence toward God, uprightness toward their neighbor, and in firmness and moderation in their own lives, and are not an example in virtue; if they do not give evidence of skill, wisdom, and the highest power of judgment for instruction and education, as well as a recognition of crises in the natures of their pupils; if they do not prefer to spur their charges on as free agents with kindness, courteous treatment, and a liberal discipline rather than with threats, blows, and like sternness; if these are not their ideals as instructors, then the citizens of Christianapolis do not deem them worthy of organizing this miniature republic, the successor of the greater, nor of being intrusted with the very substance of their future safety.[1]

This is the ideal picture; but is it a picture of the current social estimate of the teacher?

What position does the teacher occupy in American society? Writing almost three centuries later in the year 1911 Coffman, in summarizing a nation-wide study of the public school teacher, thus describes those who are actually engaged in teaching the youth of the world's greatest republic, a state that surpasses all others in its material prosperity and its faith in the efficacy of education:

The typical American male public school teacher . . . is twenty-nine years of age, having begun teaching when he was almost twenty years of age after he had received but three or four years of training beyond the elementary school. In the nine years elapsing between the age he began teaching and his present age, he has had seven years of experience and his salary at the present time is $489 [2] a year. Both of his parents were living when he entered teaching and both spoke the English language. They had an annual income from their farm of $700 which they were compelled to use to support themselves and their four or five children. . . . His first ex-

---

[1] Andreae, Johann Valentin, *Christianapolis*. Tr. by F. E. Held, p. 207.

[2] It should be noted that this study was completed before 1911. The salary figures here presented must, therefore, be interpreted in terms of the value of the dollar at that time.

perience as a teacher was secured in the rural schools, where he remained for two years at a salary of $390 per year. He found it customary for rural school teachers to have only three years of training beyond the elementary school, but in order for him to advance to a town school position he had to get an additional year of training. He also found that in case he wished to become a city school teacher two more years of training, or six in all beyond the elementary school, were needed. . . . His salary increased rather regularly during the first six years of his experience, or until he was about twenty-six years of age. After that he found that age and experience played a rather insignificant part in determining his salary, but that training still afforded him a powerful leverage.

The typical American female teacher is twenty-four years of age, having entered teaching in the early part of her nineteenth year when she had received but four years' training beyond the elementary schools. Her salary at her present age is $485 a year. She is native born of native born parents, both of whom speak the English language. When she entered teaching both of her parents were living and had an annual income of approximately $800 which they were compelled to use to support themselves and their four or five children. The young woman early found the pressure both real and heavy, and anticipated to earn her own way. As teaching was regarded as a highly respectable calling and as the transfer from the school room as a student to it as a teacher was but a step, she decided upon teaching. . . . Her first experience as a teacher was gotten in the rural school where she remained but two years. If she went from there to a town school promotion was based almost solely upon her experience as no additional training was required by the officials of the town. If she desired to teach in a city school, she was compelled to secure at least one more year of training in all, but each additional year of training she found increased her salary. . . . So far she has profited each year of her brief experience by having her salary increased and this will probably be true for the next two years should she find it necessary to remain in teaching that long.[1]

How must this picture be interpreted? That Coffman is speaking in this passage of the public school teacher should

[1] Coffman, L. D., *The Social Composition of the Teaching Population,* pp. 79–81.

be explicitly stated. Although an investigation of the teachers found in non-public schools would in all probability reveal a situation resembling very closely that which he describes, his generalizations, derived from a random selection of those teaching in the public schools, do not apply to private schools. Moreover, since about six out of every seven teachers in the public schools are working in the elementary field, the picture which he draws is that of the elementary school teacher. Furthermore, owing to the great number of rural schools, the very poorly equipped rural teacher is the basic ingredient in determining the character of the teaching population in the United States. In a very real sense he who has charge of the rural school is the typical American school teacher. Yet, because of the wide range in capacity, training, and compensation represented within the profession, it is somewhat misleading to speak of the typical American school teacher. In the city the condition of the profession is much better than in the country; and on the higher levels of the educational system its status is much more favored than in the lower schools. As a rule, the college or university instructor is highly selected and relatively well-trained. But in this discussion attention must be focused primarily on that great body of teachers on whose shoulders rests the responsibility of providing the educational opportunities for the great masses of the people during the earlier years of life.

What is the professional status of teaching to-day? In spite of the description of the public school teacher presented in Coffman's study, no one could bring the charge to-day that the ranks of the teaching profession are recruited from "the dregs of human society." The status of the teacher has improved in no small measure since the days of Andreae. Nevertheless, we have traversed but a short distance on the road to the ideal set forth by this early humanist. While it is true that our teachers "are not men from the dregs of human society nor such as are useless for other occupations," it is equally true that they are not "the choicest of all the citizens, persons whose standing in the republic is known and who very often have access to the highest positions in the community." Those who are intrusted with the discharge of this basic social function are simply not carefully selected from the standpoint of either native gifts or acquired powers. Their most ardent champion could only claim that they reflect somewhat favorably the varied qualities and conditions of the population. For the most part, they are of limited background, of mediocre capacity, of narrow cultural attainments, and without professional training. In many instances they are immature boys and girls whose sole motivation is financial necessity and whose chief qualification is the buoyancy and eagerness of youth. They possess no grasp of the meaning of education, no technique for the realization of educational purposes, no genuine interest in the work of the teacher, and no serious expectation of finding a career in the profession. An indifferent society has permitted the function of teaching to become a temporary means of livelihood for those who are in a state of vocational indecision; it has allowed teaching to become a source of revenue for impecunious young men and women contemplating law, medicine, politics, business, or matrimony.

How is the present status of teaching to be explained? The explanation of this anomalous status of teaching is not difficult to discover. Whatever advance the present shows over the past, education remains to-day a most primitive and unappreciated calling. Neither the teacher nor the citizen has adequate regard for the service actually rendered by the school, much less an adequate conception of its possibilities in bringing relief to man's estate. In spite of the ease and regularity with which a hypocritical public kneels at its shrine, education is not regarded by the controlling powers of an industrial society as a charge of first-rate importance. If the needs of education come into conflict with the demands of military armament or the narrower interests of commercial enterprise, education seldom emerges triumphant. In case of a fuel shortage the schools are among the first establishments to be closed down by official order, and when there is a demand for economy in public expenditure education is not the last to have its budget pruned. Notwithstanding the extraordinary growth of the school, education is still looked upon as a marginal instead of a focal concern of life. In their more amiable moments, with their heads in the clouds, "practical" men are fond of saying that the teacher renders to the state a service of infinite worth, but at other times, with their hands in their pockets, they refuse that material support which would give substance to their avowed faith. When it comes to the test the actual confidence which the public places in education is sadly limited. One important reason for this neglect of education is that the returns on the educational investment are deferred. Man is proverbially improvident. He places an excessive valuation on the present and trusts that the future will care for itself. The demands of to-day are insistent and real, while those of to-morrow are remote and unsubstantial. Mankind seeks some less laborious and less tedious path to salvation than that which education can either promise or afford.

Another cause of the low repute attaching to formal education is that the ordinary citizen has never been made to realize its wider functions. He regards education merely as a means of abolishing illiteracy, he considers literacy an end in itself, and he never senses the larger purposes for which a population must be literate. He has never been brought to see the absolute dependence of social life on the language arts and the essential contribution which these arts make to effective and happy participation in the great human activities of health, family, industry, citizenship, recreation, and religion. He has failed to see how the teaching of the tools of knowledge has helped to bring into existence a world demanding an education which will guarantee more than literacy. Obviously, if education means nothing more than the mastery of the language arts, important as such an achievement is, the enlistment of the services of "the choice of all the citizens" in the performance of this task would be a seriously wasteful dissipation of a people's energy. The teaching of the tools of knowledge, though a complicated process, may be reduced to a routine which can be followed by a person of decidedly mediocre gifts. If this alone is the teacher's work, the type of individual who serves society in this capacity to-day, provided he be somewhat better trained, probably represents the wisest and most economical utilization of the man-power of the state. Really superior talent must be reserved for the most important and difficult tasks of the nation.

Why must the status of teaching be raised? But, if what has been suggested in this volume, or any important part of it, is sound educational and social doctrine, the present situation is deplorable. We have insisted throughout that public education must break the bonds that have bound it to the narrow program of abolishing illiteracy. We have maintained that the scope of education should be commensurate with the needs of man in his effort to adjust himself to his environment. The program which we have outlined aims to conserve the social heritage by embodying in the lives of children those values which have been sifted from the experience of the race; it aims to bring a more abundant life to the great masses of mankind that march in the ranks of the Great Society; it aims to give to the individual and to the group the power of continuous growth and the ability to reconstruct experience. But, in the absence of those teachers who alone are able to give it reality, this program must remain a figment of the imagination. The burden is altogether too heavy to be borne by those who preside over the schools to-day. This task, which is the most difficult and fundamental of all social tasks, cannot be performed by individuals who are merely capable of following a routine. Those to whom the educational function is delegated should be carefully selected and thoroughly trained; they should be the equal of any professional group found within the state. The ideal of Andreae is none too high for an enlightened society to set up for the body of citizens to whom it entrusts the training of its youth.

How can the status of teaching be raised? If the status of the profession of teaching is to be raised, adequate provision will have to be made for both selection and training. This suggests the two major problems about which the rest of this discussion will revolve. How should those who are qualified by nature to carry the heavy burdens of teaching be selected from the younger generation? And after selection, how should they be trained? Although some have been inclined to minimize either the one problem or the other, both are of great importance. In certain quarters one is sure of winning applause by saying that teachers are born and not made, while in others one secures approbation by reversing the statement. In teaching, as in any other complex calling, talent is indispensable, but talent alone is sterile. This whole controversy suggests confusion of thought and a condition of primitive ignorance regarding the process of teaching. Although selection must take place prior to training, no attempt will be made here to discuss the comparative merits of these two questions. They are merely two aspects of a single problem. But since the need for selection is peculiarly insistent at present, and since a minimum of training is always certain to be provided either before or during service, chief attention will be given to the problem of recruiting a higher level of capacity for the profession.

How are the ranks of the teaching profession recruited? The selective process which operates to-day in determining the character of the teaching profession is unanalyzed and unintelligent. For the most part, the only selection provided is that which occurs automatically as individuals without guidance pass through the educational system. The barriers which guard the occupation at the lower levels are formidable only to the mentally defective or the criminally minded. Students who do not reach the low standard of intellectual attainment required by those who employ teachers are of course excluded from the profession. Likewise those of doubtful moral character are eliminated. But, as a general rule, young men and women who offer themselves for teaching, if they are able to meet certain formal requirements which make very limited demands on either capacity or training, are gladly accepted. The explanation of this fact is simple. The profession of teaching holds but little attraction for the youth of this generation. Few are called; so most of them must be chosen. Only from the ranks of those who desire to teach can selection be made. This suggests the fundamental question upon which the fortune of the profession and the future of education rest: How can a larger number of young persons of exceptional gifts be induced to look with favor on teaching as an attractive vocational choice? This is the supreme question in the field of education to-day. Until it is clearly answered in theory and until this answer is expressed in social and educational practice, the regeneration of the work of the teacher will be quite impossible and the problem of training will be of secondary importance. The educational fields are white unto harvest, but acceptable laborers are few.

What constitute the attractions of a profession? Teaching must be made so attractive that it will rival those other callings which are drawing more than their share of talent to-day. But what are the particular features which make a calling attractive to youth of the type needed in the enterprise of education? What does teaching lack which other callings possess? Some, and they are vocal to-day, reflecting the bias of a commercial age, would answer at once that the complete solution to the problem is to be found in increased pecuniary rewards. While this is undoubtedly an important factor in the situation, the question is by no means entirely a financial one. No such simple answer is possible. In fact, the problem is so complex that a complete solution is not available. But in order to make clear the major issues involved, we may well direct attention to the following five factors which contribute to the attractiveness of any calling: (1) adequate financial remuneration, (2) opportunity for doing creative work, (3) freedom of thought and action, (4) social recognition, (5) high professional sense. Each of these will now be considered as it relates to the occupation of teaching.

How is the status of teaching dependent on financial remuneration? In the first place, the financial rewards of teaching should be sufficient to facilitate the proper and efficient discharge of the duties of the calling. It must not be forgotten that life, even the life of a teacher, has its material basis. To function in the classroom even the most refined spirit must maintain a corporeal existence! Compensation must be sufficient to provide the necessities of life. It should be adequate to encourage that long and expensive training necessary for thorough preparation; it should be generous enough to insure a modicum of leisure for continued growth in study and travel; it should be sufficient to provide insurance against unemployment, sickness, and old age. In the name of justice such modest remuneration should be guaranteed all workers, but in the interests of efficiency it must be furnished the teacher. Only as these material needs are met will the teacher be relieved from worry over extraneous matters and be wholly set free for the performance of his task. All of these are legitimate demands that the teacher, in the social as well as in his own interest, must make on the community. The penurious treatment accorded the profession in so many quarters greatly retards the development of education and does serious injury to the common good.

The function of pecuniary rewards, however, in elevating the profession of teaching has very definite limitations. This fact must be clearly recognized. The rise to power of the commercial classes has tended to foster the delusion in the minds of many that the dollar is the master key which unlocks every door. The view is commonly accepted that, if high ability is not lavishly remunerated, it will betake itself to quarters where such remuneration is forthcoming. While this notion perhaps makes a nearer approach to truth to-day and in America than ever before, because of the fashion to associate success with money making, it contains serious error. Through the current distortion of values many within the teaching profession, particularly at the higher levels, seek money not for the immediate reward of its possession, but because of the social approval and general community prestige attaching to financial success. The complex question of human motivation cannot be answered by a simple economic formula. By nobler motives and by diverse summons are the energies of men called forth. To make material compensation a primary rather than a secondary consideration in the profession of teaching would be a grave mistake. The teacher should neither be paid so niggardly that his economic condition will be a source of constant anxiety, nor yet with such munificence that he will be tempted to transfer his allegiance from his work to the accumulation of worldly goods. He should be so remunerated that the question of remuneration may always remain a marginal interest. The school is not run for private profit, and such a motive is not congruous with its purposes. To amass wealth is not and never should be the great object of teaching: no one with such an interest should be encouraged or even permitted to engage in the professional work of education, for however well equipped he may be to promote some commercial enterprise, he is totally unfitted for the task of the teacher. Human, and not material, interests must be dominant in the school.

How is the status of teaching dependent on opportunity for doing creative work? In the second place, if superior talent is to be drawn into the work of teaching, education must come to be recognized as a source of power in society. The school must be rescued from the tradition of playing a passive rôle in the social order and must be dedicated to the tradition of positive service. This institution has the unenviable reputation of always being acted upon and of never initiating action, of following respectfully and humbly, and at a safe distance, those forces which are perpetually refashioning the world. It has conserved, but seldom created; it has obeyed, but seldom commanded. There is consequently a persuasion abroad that the work of education is not sufficiently difficult to engage the energies of a really virile mind. The aims of the school have been too restricted and colorless to challenge the attention of the more gifted and vigorous members of the coming generation. By raising the standards of financial compensation a certain type of individual can be attracted to the calling, but unless opportunity is provided to engage in great creative work the highest forms of ability will seek opportunity elsewhere. The truly ambitious man wants to accomplish, to bring about some change in the world in which he lives, and he chooses those occupations in which this is possible. Education must therefore be defined in terms of its unlimited potentialities in directing the course and rate of social advance. Young men and women must be brought to realize that the school occupies a strategic position in society and that it provides the fullest opportunities for the expression of their own powers. They must envisage the school as a powerful instrument forged by society to grapple with the great problems of mankind; they must see that through this instrument placed in their hands they can create the better world of to-morrow. They must recognize that in education there is always an element of adventure, an element of difficulty, an element of hardship. To follow the vision of education, to grasp its purposes, to sense its values, to perform its labors, requires the rarest insight, the most delicate appreciation, and the highest fortitude.

How is the status of teaching dependent on freedom of thought and action? In the third place, if education is to become a positive force, the teacher must be accorded greater liberty of thought and action. Society must see to it that this liberty is securely guaranteed. At present the teacher is hampered at every turn by restrictions, prohibitions, and directions. Narrow and petty bounds are often set to both personal and professional conduct. His tenure of position is insecure and he is often dismissed in arbitrary fashion. The primary sources of these restraints and tyrannies are the community and the administration. The former has usually reserved to itself the right, by interfering at any point in the process of education, to enforce its will in arbitrary fashion. Oftentimes, to be sure, this disturbing factor is not the entire community, or even a major part of it, but rather some powerful and active minority which presumes to speak for the whole. That the community should give the teacher a free rein to work his own will on the school is, of course, not to be expected. Such a practice would be impossible of realization and certainly undesirable from many standpoints. The contention is rather that there is a certain field of activity upon which the educational layman should never trespass. Through its representatives society should register its opinion on broad educational policies and purposes, but the teaching staff should be given wide liberties in realizing these purposes and in putting these policies into operation. Peculiarly pernicious in undermining the morale of the teaching profession is the tendency in many communities for aimless busybodies to pass upon the private life and opinions of teachers. These self-appointed custodians of good taste and public morals are so numerous and so divergent in their demands that the teacher in order to avoid their censure is constrained to lead a vapid, spiritless, and spineless existence. Teachers are ordinarily denied the most elementary rights of citizenship. Freedom from these stifling influences will come only as members of the profession, by rendering exceptional service, make clear their title to public confidence and, through organization into powerful societies, guard the broader public as well as the narrower professional interests. Only through their own efforts will teachers emancipate themselves from the arrogant domination of narrow and unscrupulous forces and attain that security of tenure which is the sole foundation of freedom.

In recent years, because of the development of our great systems of education, this question of freedom has manifested new aspects and has grown particularly acute. This development may be traced to the growth of cities and the tendency towards centralization within the various states. Wherever a large system of schools comes into existence the problem of preserving the freedom of the individual teacher becomes urgent. The administration of such a system, through which many may work together in the attainment of educational ends, requires minute specialization and differentiation of function. In meeting the demands of this situation educational administrators have borrowed heavily from the experience and practice of large scale industry. Much authority in the determination and execution of policy has been placed in the hands of the administrative and supervisory staff. To the members of this staff the chief opportunities for creative work have been given and their status has been exalted over that of the teacher. Under this form of organization the rank and file of teachers are often expected to display the passive virtues and slavishly follow the directions of their superiors. In many instances training institutions, by emphasizing narrow devices and procedures, have fostered this conception of the teacher's work.

Fairness demands the observation, however, that at this point cause and effect are rather inextricably interwoven. This limitation of freedom has in some measure been the necessary product of the character of the teaching force. The schools are manned largely by immature and untrained teachers who have no great interest in teaching and who plan to leave the profession when opportunity offers. To individuals of this type little authority and few responsibilities can be delegated. But, if gifted young men and women are to be drawn into the educational service, this situation must be changed. By elevating their own qualifications and by demanding greater freedom in the control of special educational procedure teachers alone can break the vicious circle. Under ideal conditions the teachers of a school or of a school system would through conference, visitation, and discussion formulate the wider policies of their own institution. Each would then be expected to choose and adapt ways and means for the execution of these policies. Only in the degree that this condition is achieved will teaching assume the characteristics of a profession.

How is the status of teaching dependent on social recognition? In the fourth place, the teacher must be accorded a higher social status than he is given to-day. The public must be taught to feel a keener appreciation of the importance of the work of the educator. This enhancement of social prestige is not to be distinguished rigidly from the three conditions already discussed. In the social mind it is the product which flows from the establishment of these conditions. As the latter are fulfilled, as the financial compensation, power, and freedom of the teacher are increased, the social status of teaching will be raised. This social appraisal of the community, however, is so important a factor in our problem that it deserves separate attention. Any consideration of the compensations of a vocation cannot neglect the intangible rewards of public esteem. Compensation is by no means entirely pecuniary. In fact one might very cogently maintain the position that, given the minimum financial compensation necessary to provide the physical necessities and simpler comforts of life, the nonmaterial rewards of a calling are more alluring than the material. Man is a social creature, and there are few things which he prizes more highly than the favor of his fellows. In the study of the growth of personality the point has been stressed repeatedly that much of human behavior can be understood only in terms of effort to secure approval and avoid disapproval. The high competition for wealth to-day is due largely to the social prestige attaching to its accumulation. As every page of human history shows, youth will make the greatest sacrifices, it will endure the severest hardships, it will even "dice with death," to secure the plaudits of the multitude or to gain the commendation of the elect.

Social approval can glorify any task, and its force must be brought into the service of education.[1]

How is the status of teaching dependent on a high professional sense? In the fifth and last place, the schoolmaster must place a high value on his own calling. Unless the teacher himself is convinced of the worth of his service, society is not likely to value it highly. Here perhaps is the key to the solution of the problem. At least, this is the point at which initial effort should be concentrated in bringing the profession to that level of excellence which the achievement of educational purposes requires. Teachers must cease to show embarrassment when caught in the act of teaching, they must discontinue the practice of apologizing for the work in which they are engaged, they must no longer feel flattered when mistaken for bankers, lawyers, merchants, or politicians, they must resolutely refuse to be a party to the disparagement of their own profession. They must display something of the courage and faith which, during the darkest hours of the struggle for public education in Massachusetts, moved Horace Mann to write:

Neglected, lightly esteemed among men, cast out, as it were, from the regards of society, I seem to myself to know that the time will come when education will be reverenced as the highest of earthly employments. That time I am never to see, except with the eye of faith; but I am to do something that others may see it, and realize it sooner than they otherwise would.[2]

---

[1] Not only must the teaching profession as a whole be accorded a high social status, but within the calling opportunity must be provided for rendering really distinguished service and such service must be commensurately rewarded. At present teaching suffers because recognition and advancement are too intimately dependent on years of service rather than on meritorious achievement. In education a limited number of prizes must be offered which will compare favorably with the finest prizes provided in the other occupations. Unless teaching can give overt recognition of a high order to exceptional achievement, the competitive feature which is a strong factor in the vocational appeal will not operate to call into the ranks of the profession individuals of extraordinary gifts.

[2] Mann, Mary; *Life of Horace Mann*, p. 121.

That teachers do not place a high estimate on their calling is suggested by the casual way in which they enter it, by the aspersions which they cast upon it, and by the readiness with which they leave it. They have had so little faith in their own work that they have made no consistent effort to acquaint their pupils with the place and function of education in American society. In the teaching of history and civics, for example, although the growth and nature of the various social institutions constitute the basic subject-matter of these courses, the attention given to the development and function of education has been most unenlightened and perfunctory. In a country that has made such significant contributions to the evolution of educational institutions as has the United States, this neglect is most culpable. When those engaged in the work of education are blind to its social meaning and its unrivaled opportunities for service, young men and women who have been under the influence of these persons through childhood and adolescence can hardly be expected to view education itself in proper perspective or look with favor on teaching.

How is the teaching profession in a strategic position for elevating its own status? This last point requires some elaboration. The members of any other calling, finding themselves caught in the meshes of a complex industrial society and driven by the unseen forces of tradition and circumstance, might with reason feel helpless to improve their condition and feel forced to accept as inevitable the existing social evaluation of their occupation. But in the task of determining the character and destiny of their own profession teachers occupy a uniquely strategic position. Through their hands the entire population moves to occupational decisions. Their values may become the values of their pupils. If they do not impress their charges with the importance of education, they have only themselves to reproach. A systematic attempt should be made to give to the members of the younger generation an elementary knowledge of the evolution of our educational system, a sympathetic account of the struggles and ideals of our educational leaders, an appreciation of the benefits which are received from the school, and a realization of the great social function of education. Through these means teachers must definitely encourage gifted students to enter the profession and as definitely discourage the recruiting for education of the untalented and incompetent.

What two special issues arise regarding financial compensation? Having now examined the five major factors which determine the attractiveness of teaching, we may turn our attention to two questions bearing more directly on the problem of financial compensation. These must be considered in any discussion of the means to be employed in attracting talent into the profession. First, how should the more tangible rewards of teaching be adjusted to the different divisions of the educational system? Should those who teach children be less highly compensated than college instructors? Second, how should these rewards be adjusted to the sexes? Should women receive the same compensation as men? To an examination of these two questions the attention of the reader will now be directed.

How should compensation be adjusted to the different levels of the educational system? Consider first the question of adjusting rewards to the several divisions of the educational system. Customarily secondary school teaching is remunerated more highly than elementary, and college teaching most highly of all. Since the compensation even in the higher schools is meager, since nowhere is the remuneration more than sufficient to satisfy the simpler economic wants, the consequences of this practice are obvious. The more talented and the better trained teachers are at the higher levels of the system; they are engaged in teaching the more mature and the more highly selected portion of the school population. Also the tradition is fostered that promotion means advancement from a lower to a higher division of the system, from the teaching of children to the teaching of adolescents, and from the teaching of adolescents to the teaching of youth. Hence the teacher who is fitted to work with one age level is frequently stimulated to undertake a less congenial task in the teaching of older children. This discrimination in favor of those teaching in the higher schools is due in part to certain educational misconceptions resident in the popular mind and in part to the superior demands made on both capacity and training at the upper educational levels.

According to a common belief, which is rooted in American educational tradition, a young and inexperienced girl, though confessedly unqualified to train the more mature mind, is adequately equipped to guide the process of learning in its more elementary phases. This notion is apparently based upon the assumption that education is largely a matter of school keeping, that it is more physical than intellectual. To the uncritical observer, who merely reflects the influence of bad educational practice, the teacher requires but two qualifications. First, he must be able to keep order, to administer punishment, to enforce discipline as a physical achievement. A very young and feeble person may discharge these duties with the pupils of the primary grades. Second, the schoolmaster must know more than the pupil of the subject-matter to be taught, or be more facile than he in the skill to be learned. Obviously, for very young children, a quite stupid and ignorant person may meet this requirement. In so far as intellectual attainments have received consideration, knowledge of subject-matter has been the chief criterion for the selection of teachers; and, since the child's knowledge in any field is highly circumscribed, it has been assumed that the knowledge of the teacher need be only less meager. But this conception of the nature of education is in error. Discipline is not essentially a physical achievement, and knowledge of subject-matter is but a part of the teacher's equipment. The distinctive work of the teacher, especially of the teacher on the lower educational levels, is concerned with the learning process, and not with the mastery of some body of specialized knowledge. As the child advances from level to level in the educational system, he should gradually acquire the power to direct his own learning and become independent of the guidance of the teacher. Thus, if the work of the lower schools is effective, the instructor in the higher schools can give less attention to the learning process and can specialize more fully on subject-matter. The equipment of the elementary school teacher, though different from that of the college instructor, should under ideal conditions be equally thorough. To guide the child of six in his first steps of formal education is probably no less difficult than to instruct the university student in the more abstruse portions of the higher curriculum. Moreover, the quality of this early education is of great importance in determining the direction of intellectual and moral growth. The thesis should not be difficult to maintain that the current severe discrimination against the teachers on the lower educational levels is without final justification.

At the present time, however, superior demands on talent and training are necessarily made in the higher schools. That it is as difficult to provide the ideal environment for the early education of the child as to teach differential equations to the college student is undoubtedly true, but to-day much less is known about the child than about differential equations. The development of mathematics is well advanced, whereas our knowledge of the nature of the child and the conditions that promote its growth is in a primitive state. Moreover, there are probably certain types of work, usually required of university teachers, such as research and the direction of research, that will always demand the best talent in the profession. But, as there accumulates a body of professional knowledge that requires for its mastery and application greater talent and more thorough training, the rewards which accompany teaching in the lower grades should approach those attached to secondary and college instruction. This principle, and this principle alone, is the sound basis for equality of compensation.

How should compensation be adjusted to the sexes? The second, and closely related, question of sex discrimination may now be considered. In the salary schedule of the school, men are commonly favored above women. Many, thinking in terms of certain abstract conceptions of social justice and disregarding the needs of education, maintain that this discrimination should cease immediately. They demand "equal pay for equal work." The ideal back of this agitation commands the sympathy of all, but before it is adopted as a practical program in our present economic system, its probable effects on education should be considered.

One of the outstanding characteristics of the teaching population in the United States is its large percentage of women. The process of feminization has gone so far that men have practically disappeared from the elementary schools and constitute but one third of the teaching force in the secondary institutions. Because the teaching profession was one of the first occupations of reasonable respectability outside the field of household interests to be opened to women, they have crowded the field of education. With the growth of a highly complex civilization and the evolution of many new callings of professional grade, there has been greatly increased competition for men possessing the talents and attainments required in teaching. At the same time the intellectual emancipation of women has proceeded somewhat more rapidly than new occupational opportunities have been won by them. The inevitable consequence of these two tendencies has been the feminization of teaching.

Let us now return to the question of equal compensation. In recent generations teaching has become progressively less attractive for men and progressively more attractive for women. If the popular slogan of the feminist movement quoted above were now enforced, the tendency would be to drive men yet more completely from the profession. But, if there were no fallacy in this slogan when applied in the realm of education, the passing of the male teacher would be no cause for serious concern. However sound may be the doctrine that the work of a female clerk is equal to that of a male clerk, it is very misleading to make the corresponding statement in the field of teaching. While, owing to lack of experimental evidence and differences in educational philosophies, no one can speak with absolute certainty on this point, there is some reason for assuming that in achieving certain of the more subtle aims of education the contribution of a woman, though equal in value, is unlike that of a man. In the teaching of arithmetic or grammar the one sex may be just as effective as the other, but in the development of attitudes, ideals, and appreciations the situation may be quite different. In all probability there are certain educational values which require the efforts of either the one sex or the other, or possibly of both working together in certain proportions. Until the contrary is clearly proved, effort should be made, particularly at the secondary-school level, to attract and hold gifted men in the profession.

If the one sex cannot do the work of the other, if the contribution of each is in a measure unique, it is folly to talk of "equal pay for equal work." In the economic sense, the sense in which the slogan is here used, there is no equality of work. If men are needed, women cannot be substituted. The converse of this statement is equally true, and would be stressed if the representation of the sexes were reversed. The principle of equality of compensation, at any rate in our present order of society, can hardly promote the achievement of the purposes of education. Equality of compensation in teaching will gradually come as other fields of economic opportunity which are closed to-day are opened to women, but the premature application of this principle would merely increase the representation of women within the calling. Where men are required, compensation must be raised to the level that will permit them to enter the profession. This is not discrimination in favor of or against either sex, but rather the shaping of policy in the light of educational needs and the existing economic order.

By what methods should candidates for professional training be selected? If the conditions which have been outlined in the foregoing pages have been so far achieved that men and women of superior gifts are attracted to the field of education, there remains the problem of selecting those most capable of discharging the duties of the teacher. Schemes which are designed to select primarily on the basis of acquaintance with certain fields of subject-matter must be discarded in favor of tests of capacity. Acquaintance with subject-matter is necessary, but provision for this should be made after the individual is selected for teaching and not before. Through the use of intelligence tests and early school records, and through the study of personality traits, individuals must be rigorously selected for the training school. The student population of the high school should be diligently searched for teaching talent.   When this talent is found, if the economic condition of the prospective student makes financial assistance necessary, the state should subsidize his training.   Only by some such positive program can we hope for the advancement of the profession of teaching.

What should be the training of teachers? After their selection these individuals must be given that training which is the necessary equipment of teachers.   Since this is a problem of professional education, and since this form of education has been already discussed at length, the question of teacher training will not be given detailed consideration here.   There are four guiding principles, however, which should be followed.   First, the prospective teacher should be given as broad a general education as possible.   Preferably this education should be of the type outlined in the discussion of the college of liberal arts.   Primary emphasis would be placed on giving the student broad human interests and sympathies and a thorough understanding of the nature of man and of society.   The subject-matter would be drawn largely from biology, psychology, and the social sciences, from literature, art, and philosophy.   Second, following the general course he should be required to concentrate his efforts on the special subject or group of subjects to be taught.   The extent and thoroughness of this training should depend on the character of the teaching position for which the student is preparing.   Third, he should be made familiar with that special body of knowledge which centers about the learning and teaching processes.   The extent and worth of this field of science, while sadly limited to-day, is being gradually increased.   Through the efforts of those engaged in educational research and experimentation this body of professional knowledge may ultimately rival in both amount and precision that employed in the training of the physican or the industrial engineer.   To its development and refinement the energies of a measure of the finest talent of the profession must be dedicated. Fourth, under supervision and guidance he should acquire the more elementary skills of the art of teaching. Only through actual participation in the activities of the school can this practical technique be mastered.

What provision should be made for growth in service? Through the fourfold training here outlined the student may be prepared to begin the work of teaching, but as yet he is only a novice in the art. After the young teacher has entered upon his career the process of training must continue. Through summer school, sabbatical year, educational meeting, professional reading, school visiting and travel, professional growth must be insured. But the major burden must fall upon the supervisory staff. The members of this staff, chosen primarily because of their knowledge of education and their capacity for leadership rather than because of their ability to police and inspect, should be the source of educational guidance and counsel within the school. Through them the teacher should be stimulated to search out and grapple with his problems and to gain increased mastery over the technique of his profession. Only by teaching under such stimulation can he gain that mastery of self and procedure which is characteristic of genuine professional service. Only through his own continuous growth will he retain the power of stimulating boys and girls to an ever deeper appreciation of the life of man and nature and of guiding them into an intelligent participation in the ways of society.

Why does the teacher occupy a unique position in controlling the evolution of society? In concluding this discussion we should observe again the breadth of the potential dominion of the teacher. All thoughtful men agree that the possibilities of education are without practicable limit. These possibilities are co-extensive with man's capacity to progress. The teacher, and he alone of all the workers within the state, could make the world over within a single generation. But the achievements of education are directly dependent on the creative energies, the training, the discipline, and the ideals of the teaching profession. The position which this profession may ultimately assume in society can be limited only by the powers of its own members. Never was America in greater need of that regenerating influence which can flow only from a purified intellectual leadership. If a fair measure of our people's talent can be directed into teaching, a calling which in its very nature is dedicated to the promotion of the intellectual and moral interests, from this profession might come the necessary leadership. The frontier has played an important rôle in the history of America and has attracted many of her boldest and most original spirits. The physical frontier has gone, but in another sphere the frontier remains. There is a cultural frontier which will never disappear, a frontier which widens as it is pushed forward. On this frontier are found the outposts of man's endless struggle against ignorance and superstition, the advance guard of the quest after truth and power over nature and self. On this frontier a highly selected and adequately trained teaching force must take its stand and lead each succeeding generation to a more advanced position.

ADDITIONAL PROBLEMS FOR DISCUSSION

1. Show how the status accorded the teacher to-day is but a measure of the misconception of the strategic place which education occupies as a social force in the community.
2. To what extent does the status of the teacher reflect the lowly origin of the calling?
3. What social and economic forces have been responsible for the feminization of the teaching profession in America to a degree quite unknown in other parts of the world?
4. From the standpoint of the education of adolescent boys and girls,

what are the weaknesses of the accepted slogan of the feminist movement, "equal pay for equal work"?

5. What effect may the extension of wider economic opportunities to women have upon the composition and remuneration of the teaching profession?

6. Criticize the statement that a serious concomitant of the feminization of the teaching profession in America has resulted in the delegation of the teaching function into the hands of individuals who lack the humanizing experience of normal family life.

7. How may the realization on the part of society that the primary function of education is not the perpetuation of literacy but rather the reconstruction of social life, be expected to alter the composition of the teaching force?

8. To what extent is the method of administration of the American public school system calculated to destroy that initiative and freedom in the teaching force which are essential to good teaching and the elevation of the profession?

9. Why has society made no systematic effort to give to its youthful members an adequate comprehension of the great social function rendered through education? What effect would definite instruction in the secondary schools and colleges on this subject have upon the general attitude towards education?

10. What may be said for and against the organization of teachers for the purpose of collective bargaining and general protection of what they regard as their own interests?

11. What arguments can be used for and against the affiliation of teacher organizations with labor unions?

12. What would be the effect on the composition of the teaching profession if the colleges of the country embarked on the definite program of clearly presenting to their better students the unrivaled opportunities for self-expression and social service which the career of the teacher affords?

PROBLEM 25

HOW SHOULD SOCIETY SUPPORT AND CONTROL EDUCATION?

Why is the educational enterprise a basic social responsibility? — What are the two aspects of this responsibility? — What two policies has society followed in the support of education? — Why cannot society rely wholly on private enterprise for the support of education? — Upon what theory is the public support of education to be justified? — How may public support of universal education be justified? — What is the defensible theory for the public support of selective education? — To what extent is public education free? — What should be the unit of support? — How should the burden of taxation be distributed? — What should be the guiding principle in the control of education? — How has education been controlled in the past? — Is the day of private enterprise over? — What are the dangers of public control of education? — How may the interests of public education be endangered by "politics"? — How may the interests of public education be endangered by powerful minorities? — How may the interests of public education be endangered by the limitations of the ordinary citizen? — How may the interests of public education be endangered by the weaknesses of the political state? — What restraints should be placed on the public control of education by the state? — How should educators regard private enterprise? — How should educators regard the centralization of control? — How should educators regard the freedom of the teacher? — What attitude should society take towards academic freedom in colleges and universities? — What is the social purpose of education?

Why is the educational enterprise a basic social responsibility? To shape educational policy is to guard the path that leads from the present to the future. Whether men fearful of the unknown and satisfied in their enjoyment of privilege have opposed change, or whether men restless in bondage and suffering under tyranny have craved change, they have, irrespective of their different conditions and needs, recognized the power of education and have sought to enlist this force under their conflicting banners. Through education diverse peoples have been knit together into a single nation, through it powerful governments have been overthrown, and through it religions and philosophies have been spread among men. Throughout the centuries since special educational agencies were first established, the strategic position of the school has been appreciated by kings, emperors, and popes, by rebels, reformers, and prophets. Hence, among those opposing forces found in all complex societies, a struggle for the control of the school is always evident. Every group or sect endeavors to pass on to its own children and to the children of others that culture which it happens to esteem; and every privileged class seeks to perpetuate its favored position in society by means of education. By withholding, as well as by extending, the opportunities of education the ruling classes have paid tribute to its power. In a democracy an institution that contributes so much to the formation of public opinion is clearly of fundamental importance. Under a despotic form of government it occupies an equally strategic position. Indeed the enlightened and discerning autocrat has found it more economical and more effective to subsidize schools than to maintain police. In varied fashion has education been manipulated to serve ulterior ends. The history of the school and the present-day situation both reveal the importance of the problem which concerns itself with the social responsibility for education.

What are the two aspects of this responsibility? There are two aspects of this social responsibility which must be clearly recognized and separately considered. There is, on the one hand, the question of support, and, on the other, that of control. Although control may seem to be the natural concomitant of support, comparative education clearly proves that this relationship is by no means inevitable. Under despotisms peoples are forced to maintain educational systems in determining the policies of which they have no voice; and under free governments, because of faith in the virtues of an unfettered education, an enlightened citizenship may voluntarily surrender a measure of control. Only an education operating under a minimum of external control can reflect the dynamic nature of social life, and make the school an effective agency in modifying and ameliorating the old social order. Furthermore, as the process of education becomes more complex and more dependent on expert guidance, authority must be increasingly delegated to selected individuals with special training. Moreover, support is regarded as a burden to be tolerated, whereas control is esteemed as an instrument to be prized.

What two policies has society followed in the support of education? In the support of education, society has in varying measure followed two policies. Education has been supported either through private or public enterprise. By leaving the maintenance of schools to the initiative of individuals, families, philanthropic societies, religious sects, lay associations, commercial interests, and social classes society has always to a certain degree pursued a *laissez faire* course. Under this policy the necessary funds are secured from voluntary contributions, collections, assessments, endowments, and fees. At other times, the support of education has been regarded, at least in certain of its phases, as a matter of public concern. This practice is particularly common in western society to-day. By bringing compulsion to bear on the recalcitrant members when necessary a levy is placed on the resources of the entire community through taxation. A brief consideration of the first of these policies will be sufficient, while, because of its wide adoption in the modern world, a more detailed examination of the second is necessary.

Why cannot society rely wholly on private enterprise for the support of education? Private initiative has played a large rôle in the development of educational institutions. For centuries the extension of educational opportunities was almost completely in the hands of the church. Whether the motive was that of equipping the individual to read the Bible or that of spreading particular religious doctrines, the responsibility was borne by the ecclesiastical authorities. Even after the appearance of state interest in education the work of private agencies continued. Because under free governments the rate of advance in public enterprise can never exceed the rate of popular enlightenment, even democratic societies have been constrained to rely on private initiative. Having demonstrated the efficacy of formal education in the rearing of their own children, particular favored individuals and groups, possessing an uncommon measure of understanding, idealism, and courage, have sought to extend corresponding privileges to the masses. The need and worth of education were first proved on a small scale by sects and classes, and the earliest steps toward the extension of educational opportunity to the masses of the people were taken by individuals and societies of philan-thropic purpose. Governments probably would never have concerned themselves with the establishment of great systems of schools, if their value had not been clearly proved by far-sighted and altruistic men and women who dared to experiment and who possessed the resources for experimen-tation. A large proportion of the new ventures in education have been financed by private means; and there is no good reason why this form of support, at least for the promotion of certain types of educational endeavor, should not be utilized to the full. All channels for the support of educa-tion should be kept open. But private initiative and volun-tary effort are restricted in their purpose and are inadequate to meet the vast need for education in the complex life of to-day. In the absence of collective support there would necessarily be great gaps in the extension of educational opportunities to the masses.   The scale on which the work must be done and the social spirit which must animate it transcend the limits of private enterprise.

Upon what theory is the public support of education to be justified?   In the whole field of social economy there is probably no principle that is more generally accepted than that of the public support of schools.   In all modern nations education is thought so important that the extension of some kind of formal instruction to all classes of the population is insured by the use of funds drawn from the public treasury.   What is the explanation of this public concern? On what grounds may the public be called upon to provide educational opportunities for the children of all the citizens? In recognition of what principle may the rich be taxed for the education of the poor, the Jew for the education of the Gentile, or the Catholic for the education of the Protestant? Finally, in accordance with what law of equity may the citizen without children be required to share the burden of educating the children of others?   As governments and social philosophies change, the answers to these questions vary. The reasons given for the public support of schools in an autocracy are radically different from those offered in a democracy.   Further, among any people or under any government the theory that would justify public expenditures for education must vary with the type of school.   Thus the theory that would serve as a basis for the support of elementary education through taxation might be quite inapplicable to secondary, college, or professional education.   Let us therefore pass to an examination of the theory that lies back of the public support of the various forms of education in a democratic society or a society that is striving towards democracy.

Can the same theory of support be applied to both universal and selective education? Although the different forms and levels of education are many, for the purposes of this discussion they may all be brought under two categories. In this way the analysis will be both clarified and shortened. Education may be either universal or selective in its incidence. Up to a certain point in the educational system, or up to a certain age in the life of the child, by the passage of compulsory legislation the community aims to secure complete attendance at school. Beyond this point, due to the operation of various forces, education becomes increasingly selective. This continues until, in the higher years of the university, there is enrolled but the merest fraction of the young men and women of suitable age. For the most part, universal education covers but the first eight years of formal schooling. Elsewhere in this volume we have maintained that education should be made practically universal and that all children should remain in school from six to eighteen. But the scope of this form of education is not the question for consideration here. The significant fact is merely that in the more highly developed countries to-day there is a longer or shorter period of education which is provided for all, and that following this period the selective principle operates in increasing measure at the successive levels. Obviously theories of public support which may be suited to the one form of education are not applicable to the other.

How may public support of universal education be justified? The use of public moneys for the extension of some measure of education to all the children in a democracy is not difficult to justify. This problem therefore will receive but limited consideration. Such a practice may be defended in terms of either an individualistic or a collectivistic philosophy, in terms of either individual or social welfare. In a democratic society the ideal of providing for all children equality of opportunity, regardless of conditions of birth, is rightly cherished.   Since education is in itself one of the greatest opportunities and is at the same time a force that levels artificial inequalities due to other causes, it logically follows that the community which holds to egalitarian social doctrines is under obligation to provide a degree of education for all.   At least, to the extent that it is not provided by private means it should be furnished by society.   In adjusting himself to the complexities of the modern social order, the individual finds that the assistance of some formal educational agency is indispensable.   In fact this order, as it exists to-day, is the direct product of an ever-widening extension of educational advantages during the past few centuries.

This suggests the social basis of the public support of universal education.   If society is to survive, even in the imperfect state in which we know it in this generation, the work of the school must continue.   In a political democracy, since the ultimate source of sovereignty resides in the ordinary citizen, the necessity for education is perhaps most obvious in the performance of the narrower civic functions.   Free governments, recognizing this source of sovereignty, have usually sought to educate the masses of the population. But it is rapidly becoming clear that individual happiness and the social welfare in its economic and recreational, as well as in its civic aspects, is directly dependent on the appreciations, intelligence, and good will possessed by the rank and file of the members of society.   These needs, essentially educational in their nature, constitute the social justification of providing a measure of universal education at public expense.

What is the popular justification for the public support of selective education?   In the case of selective education, however, the argument for public support is much less obvious.   Up to the point that education is universal, up to the point that it is provided for and adapted to all, there is no discrimination for or against any individual or class. All receive equal favors from the public treasury. The case for the taxation of all for the support of this form of education seems clear. But beyond the limits of universal education the problem assumes a different aspect. The number of students progressively diminishes in the higher levels of the system, and, because of the operation of various geographical, sociological, and psychological factors, education becomes increasingly selective. At present the higher educational opportunities are extended primarily to those young people living near our high schools and colleges, to those belonging to the more favored social classes, and to those possessing superior native gifts. Since the burden of taxation is not always borne by those who pay the taxes, but to a degree by the ultimate consumer of goods and services, this means that the fortunate are enjoying educational privileges which the unfortunate are helping to provide. While many of the injustices of the present social order may be expected to disappear, and while the extension of higher educational opportunities may become less contingent on the influence of fortuitous circumstance, it nevertheless remains true that there will always be some measure of selective education and that its recipients must be provided with the necessary leisure and security. Under what conditions may the general public be called upon to bear this burden? Since the public support of selective education is to-day taken for granted and is commonly justified on the same grounds as the public support of universal education, this question requires the most explicit and unequivocal answer.

The doctrine of equality of opportunity cannot be brought into service in answering this question. Beyond the point of universal attendance, education necessarily involves the unequal treatment of individuals by society. In no way can an ego-centric philosophy justify the practice of providing at public expense sixteen to twenty years of education for some and only eight to twelve for others. It is, to be sure, speciously argued to-day that equality of opportunity really means extending to the individual as many years of education as will be profitable to him. Apparently there is an assumption that the ordinary individual is educable during but a comparatively few years of his life; but this assumption begs the question. The available evidence suggests that there is no absolute limit set by nature to educability. This argument further assumes that society, composed for the most part of ungifted persons, is under some obligation, for reasons not mentioned, to provide superior educational advantages for the gifted. The ancient dictum, "To him that hath shall be given," is accepted as adequate justification for favoring the favored. Education will have to probe much deeper to discover a defensible theory for the public support of selective education.

What is the defensible theory for the public support of selective education? In a system of schools maintained through public taxation the only justification for unusual attention to any group is to be found in the return that society may expect from such an investment. This principle must be applied to the higher education. The community is in need of various services that demand special talent and training; it must have leaders in its social, political, and economic life; it must have lawyers, doctors, teachers, chemists, and engineers, artists, poets, prophets, and seekers of truth. Provision for the training of these leaders and specialists is necessary, not only for the achievement of further social advance, but even for the conservation and utilization of our present human heritage. Not that particular classes or individuals may be raised to positions of privilege and opportunity, but rather that it may secure needed services, does society tax itself for the maintenance of various forms of selective education. The community feels that through this selective expenditure on particular individuals the common good will be advanced. Through the higher schools society is not seeking to bestow gifts on superior individuals; it is making an investment through which its more permanent interests are guarded and upon which its very existence hangs.

What emphasis in higher education does this theory involve? If this social investment is to be most productive, two conditions must be met. In the first place, a continual search must be conducted on the lower educational levels for individuals possessing those special and superior qualities of mind and heart which will respond most easily and completely to the advanced opportunities which society provides. Interest in the gifted child is not justified on the grounds that he has any natural right to special privileges, but rather in the conviction that by providing for his continued education the community makes the best possible disposition of its resources.[1] An enlightened and humane society will not continue to repeat the greatest of all social blunders. It will not continue to neglect its richest resource, the abilities of all its members; it will not draw on talent

[1] The above statement should be supplemented by directing the attention of the reader to the fact that the satisfaction of intellectual curiosity for its own sake, quite apart from any return which it may make to society, is in the last analysis a recreational activity. It should be noted, however, that intellectual curiosity can hardly exist without making a social return. Only as an individual possessing this trait is completely insolated from his fellows, can it be entirely barren of social value. In the artist, in the seeker after truth, provided his influence is felt, provided he participates in the common life, there is the ideal and complete reconciliation of the individual and social interest. Manifestly, such a creative spirit, regardless of his attitude towards the community, is of great social worth. Said Frederick the Great on recalling Wolff from banishment: "A man that seeks truth, and loves it, must be reckoned precious in any human society."

only as talent appears in certain respectable quarters; it will not tolerate barriers which make it difficult for the gifted individual to force his way to recognition. In the second place, these individuals of superior gifts to whom exceptional privileges are extended must be imbued with a deep feeling of social obligation. As society puts into their hands the technique and insight provided by the higher education, it relinquishes control over its destiny and gives itself in bondage to its own children. We have been prone to consider an educated man, a man who has enjoyed special educational advantages, as necessarily an asset to his community. We have assumed that, regardless of the manner in which he directs his energy, he will be a social benefactor. This view is obviously in error. Every time an individual is graduated from high school, college, or university deficient in the feeling of social obligation, a dangerous person is turned loose to prey upon his fellows. Only too often to-day the higher educational institutions, whose support is ultimately derived from the sacrifices and savings of the masses, produce the anti-social or at least the narrowly social mind. Many who have been favored with superior educational advantages, without feeling of shame, seek sheltered callings and positions of ease. Clearly the use of public moneys for the support of a selective education that is regarded by its recipient as a right to which he is entitled, as an opportunity for self-aggrandizement quite shorn of its social significance, is wholly indefensible and immoral. Those who attend the higher schools are the trustees of society. They should consequently be taught to recognize the serious nature of the obligations which they assume on entering these institutions. Only as a feeling of social responsibility is inculcated, only as special service is rendered the common man, can the public support of this form of education be justified.

To what extent is public education free? In the foregoing discussion the term support has been used as if it always carried a definite and constant connotation and as if it always existed in a single measure. This is an over-simplification to which a correction must now be applied. Public support may be provided in varying degrees; it may be either partial or complete. Wherever communities have seen fit to carry educational burdens, the provision for the total maintenance of the individual under instruction has never been made. In the United States what is known as *free* education is probably extended to the people on a larger scale than in any other great country; yet there are many who, especially at the higher levels, because of financial limitations, do not attend the schools. This condition suggests that where public schools exist the entire cost of education is not borne by the community. Public support of education usually means merely public provision of school buildings and teachers. Education means leisure; and since leisure is an expensive luxury for the individual who has reached the age of possible economic productivity, this constitutes but a part of the cost of education. Hence, in no small measure advanced educational opportunity is contingent on the financial circumstances of the family. How far society should go in providing maintenance allowances for the children of the poor in order to free them from the handicaps of birth is to-day an unsettled point. But, if we have sufficient intelligence and courage to make the most of the biological resources of our people, steps in this direction will have to be taken until the present economic inequalities are removed. It must suffice, however, to raise the problem and to point out that in recent generations the scope of public interest in this field has been continually widened and that the limits to community action in this direction are by no means set.

What should be the unit of support? If the contention be granted that some measure of both universal and selective education should be provided at public expense, there remains the fundamental and practical question of the equitable distribution of the burden of taxation. This question naturally divides itself into two parts. First, how large should be the political unit from which a particular school derives its support? And second, how should this burden of support be distributed within this unit? The uncritical answer to the former question is that the support of a school should obviously come from the area which it serves. This seems nothing more nor less than simple justice; yet, because of the great inequalities in the distribution of wealth from community to community, and because of the difficulty of determining in our highly integrated society the precise limits of the service rendered, this does not constitute a wholly satisfactory solution. Within every state may be found relatively rich and poverty-stricken neighborhoods, side by side. According to a federal report for 1918, the amount of taxable wealth for each pupil in school varied greatly among the states, ranging from but slightly more than $2500 in Mississippi to almost $40,000 in Nevada. In the interest therefore of equalizing educational opportunity it has been suggested that the unit for support should be as large as possible, perhaps embracing the entire nation. This again seems inadvisable. Relieving the local community, as it undoubtedly would, of all direct responsibility for the maintenance of education, it would at the same time undermine popular interest in the schools. Perhaps the wisest policy is to follow a middle course and distribute the burden of support over the local community, the state, and the nation. Without destroying local interest and initiative this would insure some measure of equalization of educational burdens and opportunities.

How should the burden of taxation be distributed? The second part of the question, which pertains to the distribution of the burden of support within the unit or units taxed for school purposes, is the center of much attention to-day. In the past the major source of revenue has been real property. Because of great changes during the last century, the old forms of taxation have become ill-adapted to existing conditions. A hundred years ago the ownership of real estate was a fairly reliable index of "ability to pay" and was therefore an equitable basis for the levying of taxes. But, with the rise of the present complex economic order with its far-reaching associations and subtle relationships, property has assumed many novel and intangible forms which fall quite outside the incidence of the tax on real estate. Moreover, income, from which all revenue must be derived, is less clearly dependent than formerly on property ownership. The only solid basis for the support of schools is the social income, regardless of the type of property or service from which it is derived; and, if the educational program is to undergo the expansion which has been suggested in these pages and which is so plainly required by the needs of modern life, our methods of taxation will have to be radically altered. The social income must be taxed wherever it may be found.

What should be the guiding principle in the control of education? Having examined the question of support, we come now to a consideration of the closely related problem of control. Of all the problems that crowd the field of education there is probably none that is of greater importance and more difficult of solution. Upon the nature of those forces that control the schools the character of educational policy depends. Upon these forces rests the ultimate responsibility for the kind of education provided and for the results that flow from the efforts of teachers. The aims of education, however clearly conceived, are impossible of realization, unless they can be translated into practice in the schools, and the key to the door of the school is always in the possession of some constituted authority. This question of control demands the closest attention; and the answer offered must be formulated, not in the light of any *a-priori* principle regarding the relation that a community should sustain towards its schools, but rather with a view to achieving the fundamental purpose for which schools are maintained. This fundamental purpose is to render the largest possible service to the individual and society. Since the school can have no ulterior aim, the great object of control should be that of promoting education. The form which control takes should be determined with the single purpose of achieving this object.

How has education been controlled in the past? As in the case of support, the primary agencies for the control of education have been private. For centuries practically all the schools of the western world were under the control of the church. In more recent times social classes and great philanthropic societies have determined the course of education. For the most part the object of these efforts has been that of either preserving and spreading some particular set of doctrines or perpetuating special privilege and the ascendance of a favored class. In other instances, however, private enterprise has been broadly humanitarian in its outlook and has led the way in promoting both educational and social progress. As we have suggested in an earlier paragraph, if the worth of the school had not been clearly demonstrated through this courageous experimentation, it is doubtful if, on its own initiative, the state would have undertaken the task of organizing a system of education. Moreover, since the public established its first schools, the improvement of materials and methods has depended in no small measure on private effort.

Is the day of private enterprise over? At present American society is apparently so thoroughly convinced of the importance of education that it has developed a great system of public schools which reaches into every community. The state is also maintaining in many places special agencies for experimentation in which current theory and practice are being carefully tested in the light of the findings of educational science. Certain critics are therefore contending that, however valuable private enterprise has been in the past, its contribution in this field has been achieved. They would urge that all private schools be closed. This raises the question: Should all educational effort in a democracy be brought completely under the control of the state? Before attempting an answer to this question, the nature and defects of public control as it has functioned in actual practice may well be considered.

What are the dangers of public control of education? Throughout the western world the principle is commonly accepted to-day that the control of education is essentially a function of the state. Whether the form of political organization is autocratic or democratic, the government is ultimately responsible for determining educational policy. Of course, the state may, as it often does, delegate a portion of its authority to non-public agencies. The concern of this discussion, however, is primarily with the fortunes of the school as it is directly administered by the community, and as its policy and program are formulated and modified by the representatives of the state. In the United States the public control of education is customarily secured through different types of boards — local, town, county, and state. These boards are composed of members chosen in various ways and responsible either directly or indirectly to the people. While this method has genuine merits in giving to the masses of the people some control over their education, merits which we should be the last to discount, there are, notwithstanding, certain shortcomings which should be passed in brief review.

How may the interests of public education be endangered by "politics"? In the first place, there is constant danger that the educational interests will be subordinated to politics and the fortunes of politicians. Whoever is honestly and deeply concerned about the welfare of the school, whether his path leads him into the country, the village, the city, or the state capital, is certain to have the heart-breaking experience of seeing some promising educational program sacrificed to the personal ambitions of an office-seeker. Again and again the very machinery which society has created for the purpose of guarding and promoting the educational interests becomes an instrument for hampering the work of the schools.

How may the interests of public education be endangered by powerful minorities? In the second place, powerful minorities, while presuming to speak for the common good, may by gaining control of boards of education advance their own selfish interests. Thus the schools become centers of propaganda through which some class or sect pleads a special case or willfully distorts the picture of the world that is passed on to the coming generation. Charges are made to-day, and probably with a fair measure of truth, that, because of the extraordinary power exercised by vested interests over those directly responsible for the administration of the schools, our educational institutions serve to perpetuate with all of its injustices the existing economic order. That this will always take place to some extent in any social order may reasonably be expected. The management of the affairs of society will usually be delegated to those who have been successful in the world as it is and who are consequently prejudiced in its favor. This fundamental bias in the control of education is revealed by a study of the social composition of boards of education in our states and cities and the boards of trustees of our colleges and universities. These bodies are made up almost exclusively of representatives of the more fortunate classes; and, although many individuals will strive earnestly to formulate educational policy in the light of the needs of all classes, the great majority will quite uncritically identify the whole of society with their own particular group.

How may the interests of public education be endangered by the limitations of the ordinary citizen? In the third place, from the nature of the case, the ordinary individual suffers from such limitations in his knowledge of education that he is very inadequately equipped to participate in the shaping of educational policy. It is largely for this reason that forces of corruption and powerful minorities, driven by self-interest and consciously aggressive for their own ends, are able to secure control of the schools and violate a great social trust. Students of politics are becoming increasingly and painfully aware that good will, unaccompanied by knowledge and insight, is not equal to the task of bearing the heavier burdens of government. Students of education are also coming to realize that education is an exceedingly intricate enterprise which must be left in large part to those who are especially selected and trained for the task. The ordinary citizen in a democracy must be taught that, while it is his duty to become informed about and to contribute to the evolution of the wider educational policies, the detailed prescription and execution of programs must be left to specialists. Efforts which are being made to-day in legislative halls and through oratorical display to determine the content of courses in biology, hygiene, and social science are tragic, as well as ludicrous. In the field of education, as in other realms of collective activity, there must be developed a wholesome respect for the man with specialized knowledge.

How may the interests of public education be endangered by the weaknesses of the political state? In the fourth place, the political state, whatever the source of its power, is subject to all the ills which fall to the lot of men. Any institution which is created by men exhibits human weaknesses. For the non-conformer, liberty may be as difficult to secure under free governments as under despotisms; and new ideas may be as unwelcome in a democracy as in an autocracy. The tyranny of the majority is notorious. It is the blind and unreasoning, the compelling and oppressive tyranny of the herd. Furthermore, the interests that center in the national state are not the only interests of mankind. Indeed, the thesis might be vigorously defended that these political ends are of far less importance than others which, because they are the common possession of mankind, transcend the boundaries of states. The point to be emphasized is that, however valuable an instrumentality the existing political state may be in promoting the life of man, however serviceable it may be at a particular juncture in the evolution of human culture, it is only a means to an end; it is a tool to be used and not a divinity to be worshiped. In the control of education the state, even though completely representative of a nation, is certain to commit the grossest stupidities. The most for which men may legitimately hope is that its errors will be only less costly than those of any other available agency.

In order to show how in extreme instances the state may force education to support unintelligently the existing order, to inculcate social superstition, and to bar the way of human advance, an extract may be quoted from an address of King Frederick William IV of Prussia. Speaking before a national convention of normal school teachers in 1849, the year following the attempt at revolution, he reviewed the existing social situation, accused education of fomenting political unrest, and castigated the members of the teaching profession. He then proceeded to dictate the manner in which he would alter the educational system and supervise educational methods in order to prevent social change and further the interests of the monarchy.

All the misery which has come to Prussia during the past year is to be credited to you and only you. You deserve the blame for that godless pseudo-education of the common people which you have been propagating as the only true wisdom and by means of which you have destroyed faith and loyalty in the minds of my subjects and turned their hearts away from me. Even while I was yet Crown Prince I hated in my innermost soul this tricked-out, false education strutting about like a peacock, and while I was Regent I made every effort in my power to overthrow it. I will go ahead on this beaten path without allowing myself to deviate from it. First of all, these seminaries, every one, must be removed from the large cities to small villages, in order that they may be kept away from the unholy influence which is poisoning our times. And then everything that goes on in them must be subjected to the closest supervision. I am not afraid of the populace, but my bureaucratic government in which up to now I have had proud confidence, is being undermined and poisoned by these unholy doctrines of a modern, frivolous, worldly wisdom. But as long as I hold the sword hilt in my hands, I shall know how to deal with such a nuisance.[1]

While nothing so crude as this attempt at military coercion may be expected in democratic states, only a rash man would assert, in the light of our own experiences during the period of the Great War,[2] that the popular majority, carried away in some moment of great excitement, might not follow as unenlightened a course as that taken by this feudal king

---

[1] Reisner, E. H.: *Nationalism and Education since 1789*, p. 162.

[2] Compare the banishment during the war period of German language, music, and culture from the schools of some of our largest cities in our most advanced states.

of Prussia. The following statement, quoted from a letter issued by the School Board of Lancaster, Ohio, in 1828, shows the limited vision of public officials:

You are welcome to the use of the school house to debate all proper questions in, but such things as railroads and telegraphs are impossibilities and rank infidelity. There is nothing in the Word of God about them. If God had designed that His intelligent creatures should travel at the frightful speed of fifteen miles an hour by steam, He would clearly have foretold it through His holy prophets. It is a device of Satan to lead immortal souls down to hell.

What restraints should be placed on the control of education by the state? Admitting that there are certain serious objections to the absolute and complete control of education by the state, we are faced with the practical question: Are there any restraints which may be placed on the political authority in this realm? To the writers there seem to be three ways in which the educational interest must be safeguarded against the undue interference of the state. First, practically complete freedom should be given to private initiative in the promotion of different forms of educational enterprise; second, the centralization of educational control in the hands of federal authorities should be extremely carefully watched and, in our opinion, vigorously opposed; and third, wide liberty of action, especially on the upper levels of the educational system, should be guaranteed the teacher in the discharge of his task. Let us now consider each of these proposals in some detail.

How should educators regard private enterprise? Private schools may be divided into three large classes. First, there are those which are frankly experimental in their purpose and are being maintained largely for the purpose of testing educational theory and advancing educational science. The worth of this type of school is so generally recognized that it needs no defense. A wiser disposition of wealth which has accumulated in private hands would be difficult to imagine.

Second, there are many private schools, often of college grade, which are animated by a broad social spirit and which aim to provide superior educational opportunities of the conventional type. Such institutions, although usually drawing their students from the favored classes, relieve the public of certain educational burdens. Few would argue that these schools should be abolished.

Third, there are schools, usually supported and controlled by sects and classes, whose primary object is the perpetuation of some philosophy of life or attitude towards the world which is not taught in the public schools. In this group would fall all denominational and parochial schools, most of the great private preparatory schools for children of wealthy parentage, and finally such institutions as the labor colleges which receive their support from labor organizations and aim to develop leadership for the working class. From many quarters to-day come sharp criticisms of these institutions and bills are being presented before state legislatures, sometimes with success, providing for their abolition. The sectarian schools are attacked in some instances on the grounds of promoting a foreign culture; the schools for the wealthy are said to be undemocratic in their sympathies; and the labor colleges are accused of spreading radical social and economic doctrine. With the purposes of some of these institutions we are not in accord, but we feel it would be a grave mistake to attempt to legislate them out of existence. Our attitude is much like that expressed by Voltaire in writing to his adversary Helvetius: "I wholly disapprove of what you say — and will defend to the death your right to say it." The most pernicious of the existing educational agencies merely reflect the class organization of an undemocratic society and are but symptoms of conditions that can be altered only by striking at those forces which lead to social stratification. We would further contend that liberty of thought and of conscience requires the granting of practically complete freedom to any group of citizens to establish schools for the perpetuation of any set of doctrines sincerely held. That the teachings in such institutions are not anti-social in their character and are in accord with the spirit of the fundamental law of the land is of course assumed. Except to make certain minimum requirements regarding the teaching of those basic subjects which are necessary to life in a complex society, the state should not proceed in regulating the conduct of these schools. The passing of private enterprise from the field of educational effort should not be forced by legislative enactment but should be the natural outcome of the improvement of the public school and the unification of the social order.

How should educators regard the centralization of control? The second safeguard against the exercise of arbitrary and short-sighted authority on the part of the state is the decentralization of control. If each of the forty-eight states is allowed that complete freedom of action in educational matters which is provided by the federal constitution, ideas of promise which are given a hostile reception in one state may be granted a favorable hearing in another. From the standpoint of the development of a democratic system of education this is without doubt the great merit of our federal system. Somewhere, sooner or later, advanced educational and social theories are almost certain of a trial. In this limited setting before they are given a wide adoption their worth may be proved. A richer field for educational experimentation than exists in the American commonwealth would be difficult to find. Much freedom should also be allowed the local authorities, the cities, the counties, the towns, and the villages, in the control of education. The work of the state organization should be confined very largely to that of stimulating and harmonizing the growth of education within the state. At certain points, where the essence of the educative process is not at stake, standardization is desirable, but that bureaucracy which is the curse of many governments must be rigorously avoided.

How should educators regard the freedom of the teacher? Finally, within the field of his specialty, the teacher must be given a large measure of freedom. This is even more necessary to the promotion of the basic educational interests than the fostering of private initiative and the decentralization of control. Some have suggested that the formulation and development of educational policy should be placed by society entirely in the hands of teachers. Only in this way, so they contend, can the larger spiritual values be conserved in a society which at the moment is so completely dominated by the mechanisms of the economic and political life. Certain it is that the present social order takes its standards of value from industry and the national state. But fairness demands that we recognize explicitly that the teaching profession has given little evidence in the course of its history of possessing the capacity to bear responsibilities of such magnitude. Too frequently it has lived in a past age and, desiring only to be let alone and jealously guarding its vested rights, it has resolutely barred the way to educational advance. The give and take between teachers and society is greatly to be desired. In the adoption of general policies, although the profession should always be in a strong position to make its voice heard on all educational questions, the public must cast the deciding vote. But the execution of these policies, once adopted, must be recognized as the peculiar province of the teacher into which the layman must not venture.

The great problem in this connection is that of persuading the state to relinquish a portion of its control. In order to prevail upon it to do this the people must be convinced that the largest educational returns can be secured only as a wide measure of freedom is extended to those engaged in teaching. While the thorough organization of the profession is necessary for the proper protection of its members, it must not be forgotten that in the last analysis the liberty which teachers enjoy will depend on the will of the community. Hence, the first task is that of convincing the citizen that the more permanent interests of society will be guarded by placing large responsibilities on the teacher. The work of education is of such a nature that it can be carried on successfully only under a minimum of external control. But the degree of freedom which we have advocated here can be extended to the profession only as the level of the ability and training of its members is raised. The point to be emphasized, as we have urged in the previous section, is that the teacher should be carefully selected and thoroughly trained, and then entrusted with the work of education. Since in a very real sense the teacher represents to a greater degree than the members of the school board the interests of the inarticulate members of society and of future generations, the training which he receives should emphasize the nature of the far-reaching obligations assumed.

What attitude should society take toward academic freedom in college and university? In the colleges and universities especially must society grant to the teacher and the investigator the very largest degree of freedom. The case for academic freedom has perhaps never been stated more forcefully than in the bill on the general organization of public instruction which Condorcet presented to the Legislative Assembly of the French Republic in April of 1792. According to the provisions of this bill the educational system of the new republic was to be crowned by a National Society of Arts and Sciences which was to provide the highest grade of education and exercise large powers of control over the rest of the system. The degree of freedom which Condorcet proposed for the members of this institution is thus described in the report:

Freedom of teaching constitutes, in a way, one of the rights of the human race. . . . Since truth alone is useful and since every error is an evil, by what right would any power, no matter what it might be, dare to determine what is truth and what is error? A power which would forbid the teaching of an opinion contrary to that which has served as the basis for enacted laws, would attack directly the freedom of thought, would contradict the purpose of every social institution, namely, the improvement of the laws, which necessarily follows from conflicts of opinion and the spread of enlightenment. For that matter, the French Constitution makes such independence our rigorous duty. It has recognized that the nation has the inalienable and indefeasible right of reforming all its laws. . . . The intention of the Constitution is that all the laws should be discussed, that all political theories should be allowed to be taught and opposed, that no system of social organization should be offered to enthusiasm or to prejudice as the object of superstitious worship, but that all political beliefs and systems should be presented to reason as different possibilities among which she has the right to choose. . . . Should we have in reality respected the inalienable independence of the people if we had permitted the government to fortify any particular system of belief with all the weight which universal instruction would give it; and would not the power which would arrogate to itself the right to choose our opinions have veritably usurped a portion of the national sovereignty?" [1]

What is the social purpose of education? In concluding this discussion of the relation of society to the school we can do no better than to quote yet further from this remarkable document. In the following words Condorcet painted an impressive picture of the function and character of education

[1] Reisner, E. H.: *Nationalism and Education since 1789*, p. 22.

in a democratic society, a picture which, if slightly retouched in the light of the advance made in educational science, would stand to-day as a compelling social ideal.

To offer to every individual of the human race the means of providing for his wants, of insuring his well-being, of knowing and exercising his rights, of knowing and fulfilling his duties. . . . To insure to each the means of improving in his daily task, of making himself better fitted for the social function to which he may rightly be called, to develop the entire array of gifts which he has received at the hand of nature, and thereby to establish among the citizens an equality in fact, making real the political equality recognized by the law. . . . Such should be the predominant purpose of a national system of instruction, and, from that point of view, it is a fit function for the state to undertake. . . .

To direct education in such a way that the perfection of the arts will increase the happiness of the people at large and the prosperity of those who labor; in such a way that an ever-increasing number of persons will become better fitted to perform the work necessary to our social existence; in such a way that progress, keeping step with enlightenment, shall open an inexhaustible source of supply for our wants, of remedies for our ills, and of the means of individual happiness and common welfare. . . . To cultivate, finally, in each succeeding generation all the powers of body, mind, and conscience, thereby contributing to the comprehensive and gradual improvement of the human race — the final objective toward which every social institution should be directed. . . . Such should be . . . the purpose of education; and it is a duty imposed upon the state by the common interest of society and of mankind.[1]

ADDITIONAL PROBLEMS FOR DISCUSSION

1. To what extent has the growth of the experimental spirit in public education reduced the need for the private support of educational experimentation through foundations, societies, and individuals?
2. How do the differences in per capita wealth, the shifting of population, and the interrelationships of modern society, bear upon the problems of support?
3. To what extent does control automatically follow support in education?

---

[1] Reisner, E. H.: *Nationalism and Education since 1789*, pp. 117–18.

4. How do you explain the fact that the ordinary citizen, though unacquainted with the larger educational issues, is, nevertheless, ever ready to issue final pronouncements on the most difficult questions of educational policy?

5. At what point should the line be drawn between the function of the ordinary citizen and the trained educational specialist in the formulation and achievement of educational purposes?

6. Do the social ideals which govern the ordinary college graduate in his occupational life justify expenditure of public funds for his education?

7. How far does the principle of equalization of educational opportunity demand that society should go in providing maintenance grants to students at the higher levels of education? Can the practice of "working one's way" through college be regarded as a satisfactory and permanent solution of this problem?

8. To what extent is the support of private schools derived from the desire for ostentation and social differentiation on the part of individuals and families?

9. Is it possible for the educational institution to identify its program with the wider social interests, rather than with the interests of narrow but powerful financial groups?

10. How does the relatively complete reliance in America on the public school, by stereotyping the ideas and ideals possessed by the whole population, tend to promote a monotonous uniformity?

11. In what respects does the source of support, whether public or private, place limitations on academic freedom in our colleges and universities? In what subjects would this restriction of academic freedom manifest itself?

12. In the private college and university, what is the nature of the interests dominating the alumni with respect to their *alma mater*, and what effect have these interests in determining the atmosphere and working ideals of the institution?

13. In the determination of educational policy in the United States, what is the degree and nature of the influence exerted by each of the following interests — the farmer, industrial labor unions, financial interests, the American Legion, the Army and Navy, the religious denominations, the women of the country, the teaching force?

14. If we assume that a degree of universal education is provided in both democratic and autocratic societies, what are the differences in motive and social philosophy underlying such apparently similar action?

APPENDIX

SUGGESTIONS FOR THE USE OF THIS TEXT IN INSTRUCTION

SINCE an effort has been made in the construction of this book to follow a procedure which will expedite instruction, there need be no apology for directing the attention of the teacher to certain points of methodology.

In the first place, Part One gives the wider view of education, and establishes the place of the formal agency in society. Moreover the second, third, and fourth problems of this part cover in a general manner the fields elaborated in Parts Two, Three, and Four. Thus the entire volume is given in epitome in Part One. The aim of this division is to orient the student. On this account he may have some difficulty with it and may feel it to be somewhat abstract. The teacher should therefore not demand too rigorous understanding of this part at the first reading. The authors have found it serviceable to encourage the student to re-read this first division of the book at the close of the course.

In the second place, the book is written around twenty-five major problems of education. Each of these larger problems is subdivided into a number of subsidiary problems. The object of this procedure is to stimulate thought on the part of the student. With this fact in mind the teacher will not be too harsh in his criticism of certain questions which are so wide in their scope that only incomplete answers can be offered. The authors have found that these minor problems not only add zest to the discussion, but also constitute the framework of their teaching notes.

In the third place, a number of additional problems close each section. These questions are not mere echoes of the text, but are problems that we should like to have treated had space permitted. Many of these have actually arisen in classes where the materials of this volume have been presented. Through these questions the teacher may expand the volume without limit.

In the fourth place, at the discretion of the teacher, the technical material in Problem 7, which relates to language habits and the implications of the strictly mechanistic theory of behavior may be omitted. This can be done without impairing the integrity of the treatment, and for the immature student will undoubtedly be a wise procedure. Also the book may be shortened at certain places. Particularly, if time presses, the treatment of the more theoretical or more specialized major problems in Part Four may be curtailed in the light of the student objective.

SUGGESTIONS FOR FURTHER READING

IN the pursuit of his reading in the wide field of education as depicted in this text, the student has an almost unlimited choice. Before proceeding to more specialized fields he will do well to acquaint himself with the educational classics and with the ideas contained in the following bibliography. These more modern books will often present views at variance with those contained in the text; but such conflict is to be welcomed.

Bagley, W. C.   *The Educative Process.*
Bobbitt, F.   *The Curriculum.*
*Bode, B. H.   *Fundamentals of Education.*
Cubberley, E. P.   *Public School Administration.*
Cubberley, E. P.   *Public Education in the United States.*
*Dewey, J.   *Democracy and Education.*
Gesell, A. L.   *The Pre-School Child.*
*Henderson, E. N.   *Principles of Education.*
Hudson, J. W.   *The College and New America.*
Inglis, A.   *Principles of Secondary Education.*
Kilpatrick, W. H.   *Source Book in the Philosophy of Education.*
*MacVannel, J. A.   *Outline of a Course in the Philosophy of Education.*
McDougall, W.   *Social Psychology.*
Monroe, P.   *History of Education.*
Paulsen, F.   *Introduction to Philosophy.*
Snedden, D.   *Vocational Education.*
*Spencer, H.   *Education.*
Thorndike, E. L.   *Educational Psychology.*
Wallas, G.   *The Great Society.*
Ward, L. F.   *Dynamic Sociology.*
Watson, J. B.   *Psychology from the Standpoint of a Behaviorist.*

For further readings and for more detailed guidance with reference to specific topics in education the student is directed to the excellent bibliographies contained in the texts of Henderson or MacVannel.

*These texts give the more systematic treatment of Principles of Education.

INDEX

Ability, recognition of differences in elementary school, 432.

Abnormal behavior, 142.

Abstract principles, how they derive force to modify behavior, 135.

Activities, basic human, why they should be reflected in the elementary school curriculum, 411; of present elementary school, 403; two sets constituting high-school program, 440; recreational, 298; values, 299; school, evaluation of, 368; relationship to basic life interests, 381.

Adaptation, involves not only change in the individual, but attempts to change conditions, 4; mental and physical, 9; motivated by social impulses, 19.

Adjustment, the relation of education to, 3–12; not merely adaptation to environment, 3; education as a method, 3; true meaning, 4; biological and educational, 4, 9; not produced by environment, 8; as a function of an organism seeking its own ends, 8; range of, 9; necessary factors, 10; rôle played by reflection, 20; how furthered by inborn tendencies, 57; relation of religion to, 331; educational, how necessitated by reproduction, 13; man's equipment for, 14.

Agriculture, evolution of methods, 237.

Americanization, 306.

Analysis, occupational, 536.

Andreæ, Johann Valentin, *Christianapolis*, quoted, 573.

Anticipation of approval, of actual society, as force in modifying behavior, 128; of ideal society, 129; a present satisfaction, 130.

Application, aspect of instruction stressed by, 551.

Approval of society, as a force modifying behavior, 128, 129.

Artificiality, of school environment, 170.

Arts, America's contribution to, 316; reasons for limited achievement, 317; significance of absence of artistic creation, 318; possibilities for enriching the recreational life, 321.

Association, aspect of instruction stressed by, 550; social, advantages of, 25.

Attainment, standards in elementary school, 429.

Attitudes and appreciations, the acquirement of, 555.

Behavior, how modified by experience, 16; how complicated by integration of habits, 19; how it reflects inner drives, 55; errors in interpreting, 59; the instinctive element in, 64; complicating factors, 66; difference between that of civilized man and that of savage, 71; how refined by language habits, 84; objective physiological theory, 87; rôle played by language, 89; how affected by conscious processes, 94; instinctive origin of, 125; how modified by material and social forces, 127; how motivated by belief in supernatural sanctions, 133; how modified by force of abstract principles, 135; to what extent rational, 138; abnormal, 142; value of concepts in studying, 152. *See* Conduct.

Behaviorism as a methodology, 94; limitations as an educational philosophy, 97.

Behaviorism and interactionism, determination of choice between, 96.

Behaviorist, theory upon language and education, 91.

RIVERSIDE TEXTBOOKS
IN EDUCATION

Edited by ELLWOOD P. CUBBERLEY
Dean of the School of Education, Leland Stanford Junior University

History of Education

CUBBERLEY: The History of Education
CUBBERLEY: Readings in the History of Education
CUBBERLEY: A Brief History of Education
CUBBERLEY: Public Education in the United States

General Educational Theory

ALMACK AND LANG: The Beginning Teacher
ALMACK AND LANG: Problems of the Teaching Profession
CHAPMAN AND COUNTS: Principles of Education
CUBBERLEY: An Introduction to the Study of Education
CUBBERLEY: Rural Life and Education
DOUGLASS: Secondary Education
GESELL: The Pre-School Child
INGLIS: Principles of Secondary Education
MCCRACKEN AND LAMB: Occupational Information in the Elementary
    School
MOSSMAN: Principles of Teaching and Learning in the Elementary School
PROCTOR: Educational and Vocational Guidance
SMITH: An Introduction to Educational Sociology
SMITH: Principles of Educational Sociology — Revised and Enlarged
SNEDDEN: Problems of Secondary Education
THOMAS: Principles and Technique of Teaching
WALLIN: The Education of Handicapped Children

Methods

ALMACK: Education for Citizenship
BOLENIUS: Teaching Literature in the Grammar Grades and High School
CRAWFORD AND MCDONALD: Modern Methods in Teaching Geography
DOUGLASS: Modern Methods in High School Teaching
FREELAND, ADAMS, HALL: Teaching in the Intermediate Grades
KENDALL AND MIRICK: How to Teach the Fundamental Subjects
KENDALL AND MIRICK: How to Teach the Special Subjects
KIMBALL: Current-Events Instruction
MARTZ AND KINNEMAN: Social Science for Teachers

HOUGHTON MIFFLIN COMPANY
BOSTON   NEW YORK   CHICAGO   DALLAS   SAN FRANCISCO
2602a

RIVERSIDE TEXTBOOKS
IN EDUCATION

Edited by Ellwood P. Cubberley
Dean of the School of Education, Leland Stanford Junior University

Methods (continued)

Minor: Principles of Teaching Practically Applied
Newcomb: Modern Methods of Teaching Arithmetic
Stone: Silent and Oral Reading — Revised and Enlarged
Stormzand: Progressive Methods of Teaching
Stormzand, McKee: The Progressive Primary Teacher
Thomas: The Teaching of English in the Secondary School — Revised and Enlarged
Thomas: Training for Effective Study
Trafton: The Teaching of Science in the Elementary School
Woofter: Teaching in Rural Schools

Healthful Teaching and Healthful Schools

Averill: Educational Hygiene
Averill: The Hygiene of Instruction
Ayres, Williams, Wood: Healthful Schools. How to Build, Equip, and Maintain Them
Hoag and Terman: Health Work in the Schools
Keene: The Physical Welfare of the School Child
Terman and Almack: The Hygiene of the School Child

Administration and Supervision

Almack and Bursch: Administration of Consolidated and Village Schools
Briggs: The Junior High School
Cubberley: The Principal and His School
Cubberley: Public School Administration — Revised and Enlarged
Cubberley: State School Administration
Nutt: The Supervision of Instruction
Pittenger: An Introduction to Public School Finance
Rugg: A Primer of Graphics and Statistics for Teachers
Sears: Classroom Organization and Control — Revised and Enlarged
Sears: The School Survey

HOUGHTON MIFFLIN COMPANY

BOSTON NEW YORK CHICAGO DALLAS SAN FRANCISCO

2602b

RIVERSIDE TEXTBOOKS
IN EDUCATION

Edited by ELLWOOD P. CUBBERLEY
Dean of the School of Education, Leland Stanford Junior University

Administration and Supervision (continued)

SHOWALTER: A Handbook for Rural School Officers
STONE: Supervision of the Elementary School
WILLIAMS: Graphic Methods in Education

Psychology and Child Study

AVERILL: Elements of Educational Psychology
AVERILL: Psychology for Normal Schools
BROOKS: The Psychology of Adolescence
EDWARDS: The Psychology of Elementary Education
FREEMAN: Experimental Education
FREEMAN: How Children Learn
FREEMAN: The Psychology of the Common Branches
PECHSTEIN AND McGREGOR: Psychology of the Junior High School Pupil
PECHSTEIN AND JENKINS: Psychology of the Kindergarten-Primary Child
WADDELL: An Introduction to Child Psychology
WALLIN: Clinical and Abnormal Psychology

Educational Tests nd Measurements

FREEMAN: Mental Tests. Their History, Principles, and Applications
HINES: A Guide to Educational Measurements
MONROE: An Introduction to the Theory of Educational Measurements
MONROE: Measuring the Results of Teaching
MONROE, DE VOSS AND KELLY: Educational Tests and Measurements.
    Revised and Enlarged Edition.
RUGG: Statistical Methods Applied to Education
TERMAN: The Intelligence of School Children
TERMAN: The Measurement of Intelligence
    Test Material for use with The Measurement of Intelligence
    Record Booklets. Sold only in packages of 25
    Condensed Guide for the Binet-Simon Intelligence Tests
    Abbreviated Filing Record Cards. 25 in package

HOUGHTON MIFFLIN COMPANY
BOSTON   NEW YORK   CHICAGO   DALLAS   SAN FRANCISCO
2602c

Dr. Benson N. Y. U.
Room 502 (Main Bldg.
4$\frac{15}{}$ P. M. - Fridays.